PSYCHOLOGY

CORE CONCEPTS AND SPECIAL TOPICS

Accompanying the text

READINGS IN PSYCHOLOGY: CORE CONCEPTS AND SPECIAL
TOPICS
edited by Frank H. Sjursen, Jr., and Lee Roy Beach

STUDY GUIDE for Beach, PSYCHOLOGY: CORE CONCEPTS AND
SPECIAL TOPICS
by Frank H. Sjursen, Jr.

INSTRUCTOR'S MANUAL for PSYCHOLOGY: CORE CONCEPTS
AND SPECIAL TOPICS and for READINGS IN PSYCHOLOGY
by Barbara H. Beach

PSYCHOLOGY

CORE CONCEPTS AND SPECIAL TOPICS

Lee Roy Beach

University of Washington

HOLT, RINEHART AND WINSTON, INC.

New York Chicago San Francisco Atlanta Dallas Montreal Toronto London Sydney

To Barbara

The knowledge of the world is only to be acquired in the world,
and not in a closet. Books alone will never teach it you;
but they will suggest many things to your observation,
which might otherwise escape you; and your own observations upon mankind,
when compared with those which you will find in books,
will help you to fix the true point.

From Lord Chesterfield's letter to his son
dated October 4, 1746

PREFACE

This book is in response to my students' protests against the encyclopedic textbooks that are generally used in introductory psychology courses. I grew tired of hollowly defending my choice of text against the students' yawns and their annoyed complaints that somehow psychology ought to be more interesting than the text allowed it to be. After I realized that even I avoided reading these texts because they bored me, I decided that something had to be done. So I began this book, which I hope (and that the students who have used it in draft form seem to think) is solid enough to be respectable yet is interesting enough to be palatable.

It seems to me that there are two basic approaches that can be taken in teaching people about psychology. One approach is to focus on *the science* of psychology and to teach about what psychologists do; that is, what things psychologists study, how they study them, and how their view of man is influenced by what they find. The other approach keeps the science in the background, and focuses upon *the subject matter* of psychology; it emphasizes the "whats," "hows," and "whys" of human and animal behavior. While I've elected to take the second approach (the subject matter, after all, *is* the point of the whole endeavor), I have also attempted to keep a solid scientific base and a decidedly scientific flavor to the book.

My philosophy about what psychology is, and what it should become, is outlined briefly in Section One. The point of this first section is to make my biases clear to the reader and to state the assumptions that underlie the rest of the book. This section and Appendix 1 on scientific psychological research are kept brief so that the instructor may control how much or how little he or she wants to emphasize the scientific aspects of psychology.

Section Two actually is the beginning of the book. Sensation and perception are viewed primarily in terms of information-gathering mechanisms. The viewpoint is heavily influenced by J. J. Gibson's idea that sensation and perception, rather than being merely passive processes, are in fact very active.

Section Three is my version of the "learning" chapter that usually is found in most introductory psychology texts. Recent work in memory, growing general dissatisfaction with strict stimulus-response interpretations of learning, as well as the reality that learning isn't the whole story make a traditional presentation out of the question. The first part of this section (memory) is based on the recent work of Dr. Richard Atkinson and his co-workers at Stanford and is somewhat simplified to facilitate presentation. The second part of this section (rules) is an amalgam of many sources of information, including some notions from zoology that I acquired in an ethology class taught by Dr. Gordon Orians at the University of Washington and the views of the late Dr. Edward C. Tolman. The language in this part of the section may seem a bit foreign to many psychologists, but I chose it in order to make the section consistent with the rest of the book.

Section Four is a fairly straightforward discussion of social psychology. The first part of this section has a strong ethological emphasis that reflects rather recent and exciting ideas about territoriality, dominance hierarchies, and social development. Examples of the social behavior of some animals are included in order to emphasize our continuity with the rest of the animal kingdom rather than to draw any precise parallels. The remainder of this section focuses on the groups we belong to and on how they influence our behavior and our attitudes, a discussion that sets the stage for Section Five.

Section Five is my version of the usual "personality" or "mental health" chapter. I do not think that a recitation of theories, from Freud to Perls, would fit comfortably in this book. Therefore, I have tried to record what I think is a coming trend in personality theory and clinical psychology. The impact of Gestalt therapy and the humanistic views of such eminent psychologists as Carl Rogers or Abraham Maslow previously have had little impact on academic psychology, but the time is at hand. I have tried to reflect this coming wave in the "know thyself" theme that dominates this section. As far as I know, the three strategies that serve as summarizing concepts in this section are my own invention, but they are not far removed from how many other psychologists currently conceptualize the problems of human adjustment.

Section Six contains topics that I have found to be interesting to my own students. Because these topics are of limited scope, and because they are both important and interesting to students, it seemed best to cover them in some detail. For these reasons, I decided not to try to cover these topics in the earlier sections. Instead, the plan is for the student to read the appropriate special topics after he has completely read the related general discussion in the core of the book. Thus, for example, the special topics of language and decision making (Section Six, Parts 1 and 2) should be read after completion of the core section on memory and rules (Section Three). Of course, the instructor is free to assign the special topics in whatever order he or she pleases, but this is how it was planned, and I think, the logical progression of study is enhanced if the plan is followed.

There are two appendices. The first is a discussion of research methodology and the basic concepts of statistics. The second is a very brief, very elementary outline of neurophysiology. These are designated as appendices because the rest of the book does not depend upon the students' understanding of their content; the instructor may delete them without worry.

The shaded boxes that appear throughout each of the sections contain supplementary information. In order not to interrupt the flow of the text, the students should wait until they complete the text of a section before reading the material in the boxes.

This book is fairly short because I want it to be suitable for either a semester or a quarter course. Most books are designed to so fully fill a semester that only limited use can be made of other sources. To use these large books in a quarter course necessitates asking the students to read an excessive amount of very concisely written material or requires deletion of parts of the text with consequent disruption of continuity. The alternative is to use this short book and to augment it with outside readings, thereby tailoring the material to fit both the students and the semester or quarter time span. Students like this plan because it combines the continuity provided by the text with the variety provided by the readings. Instructors like it because by proper selection of the readings they can control the level of the rigorousness of the course and cover the topics that they deem most important in as much detail as they think best.

To provide augmenting material, a book of readings has been prepared to accompany this book. In addition, at the end of each section there is a rather long annotated list of suggested readings. Almost all of the books in these lists are recent, inexpensive, topical, highly readable paperback editions that are readily available through a bookstore. These lists should be of particular value when students wish to look further into issues raised in the text, either because of personal interest or for material for term papers. Finally, a list of references at the end of the book contains material specifically alluded to in the text. Together, these three sources of augmentative material should permit the instructor to control both the breadth and level of the course, while at the same time providing the more adventurous students with the sources they will need to pursue things on their own.

In addition, an accompanying Study Guide consists of programmed units and self-administered objective tests. For each section of the text, the guide has a pretest that helps the student to evaluate how well he has understood the material he has read. Following the pretest is a programmed study unit. Finally there is a posttest which permits the student to evaluate his progress.

There is also an Instructor's Manual containing supplementary sources, multiple choice and short essay test questions, term paper topics, and recommended films for each section of the text. It also includes multiple choice and short essay test questions, and discussion questions for each article in the book of readings.

No matter how much an author likes to think of a book as his own work, many people are involved in the final product. It therefore is my pleasure to acknowledge the aid of many friends and to thank them, while absolving them of any blame for whatever shortcomings this book may have. Direct help has been received from my wife, Dr. Barbara Beach, who reviewed every word (and changed a good many of them). Professor Frank Sjursen has been a critic and friend both while editing a book of readings to accompany this book and while using the manuscript of this book in his classes in an effort to find the snags and straighten them out before publication. Professor Robert Bolles was an early partner in the venture and has continued to be helpful to me. Three secretaries, Ms. Lana Leckman, Ms. Terese Meyer, and Ms. Dorothy Kulwin, have worked on the manuscript and have served as critics of both style and content.

Indirect aid has come from the following colleagues with whom I have had long discussions or whose classes I have attended: Dr. Helen Bee, Dr. Samuel Bobrow, Dr. Philip Dale, Dr. Robert Douglas, Dr. Walter Makous, Dr. Gordon Orians, and Dr. Nathaniel Wagner. I particularly want to thank Drs. Bee, Dale, and Wagner for their invaluable aid in my efforts to find reliable information on poverty, language, and human sexuality and Dr. Earl Hunt for his editorial aid.

L. R. B.
Seattle, Washington
January 1973

CONTENTS

xi

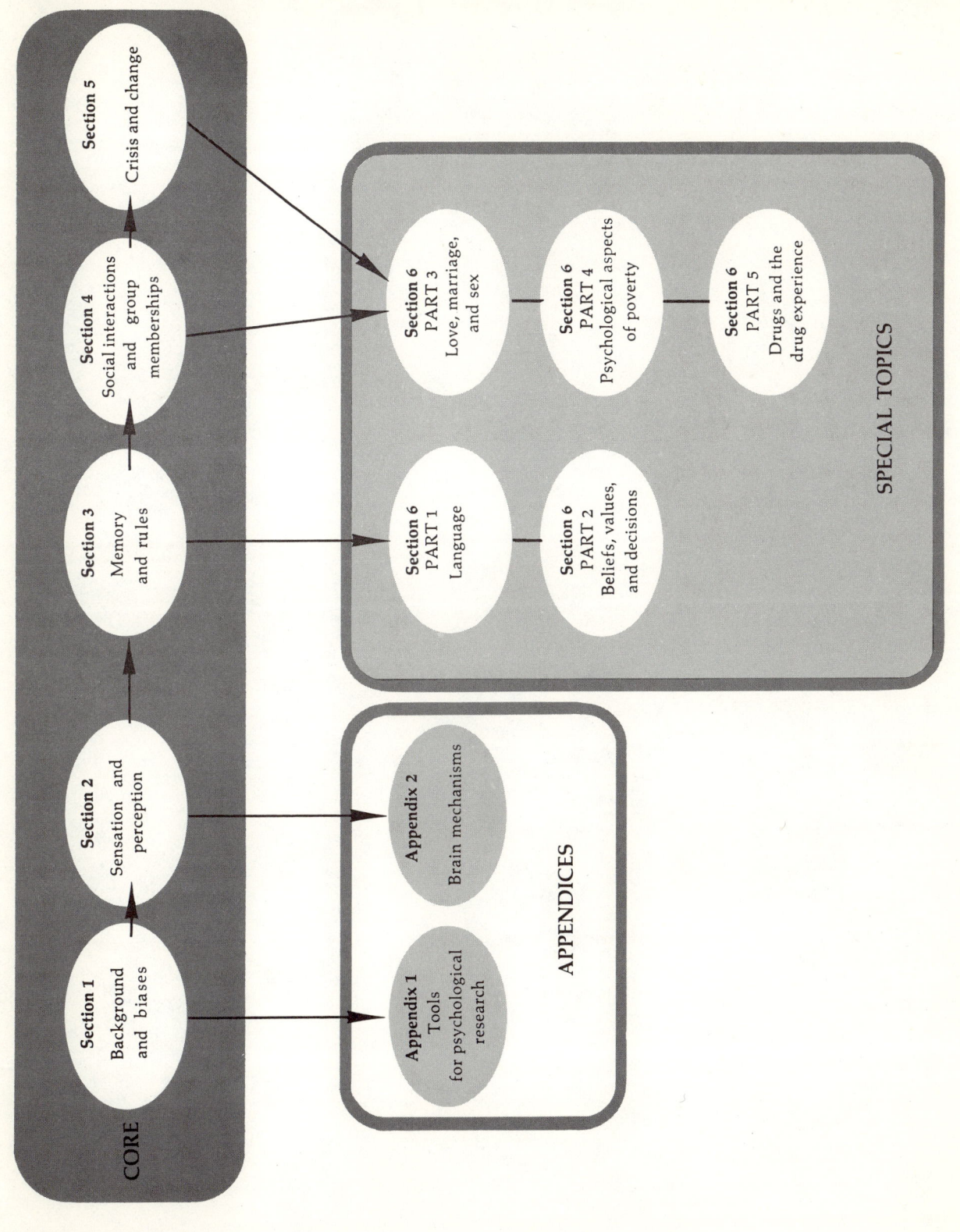

CORE

Section 1 Background and biases

Section 2 Sensation and perception

Section 3 Memory and rules

Section 4 Social interactions and group memberships

Section 5 Crisis and change

SPECIAL TOPICS

Section 6 PART 1 Language

Section 6 PART 2 Beliefs, values, and decisions

Section 6 PART 3 Love, marriage, and sex

Section 6 PART 4 Psychological aspects of poverty

Section 6 PART 5 Drugs and the drug experience

APPENDICES

Appendix 1 Tools for psychological research

Appendix 2 Brain mechanisms

PSYCHOLOGY

CORE CONCEPTS AND SPECIAL TOPICS

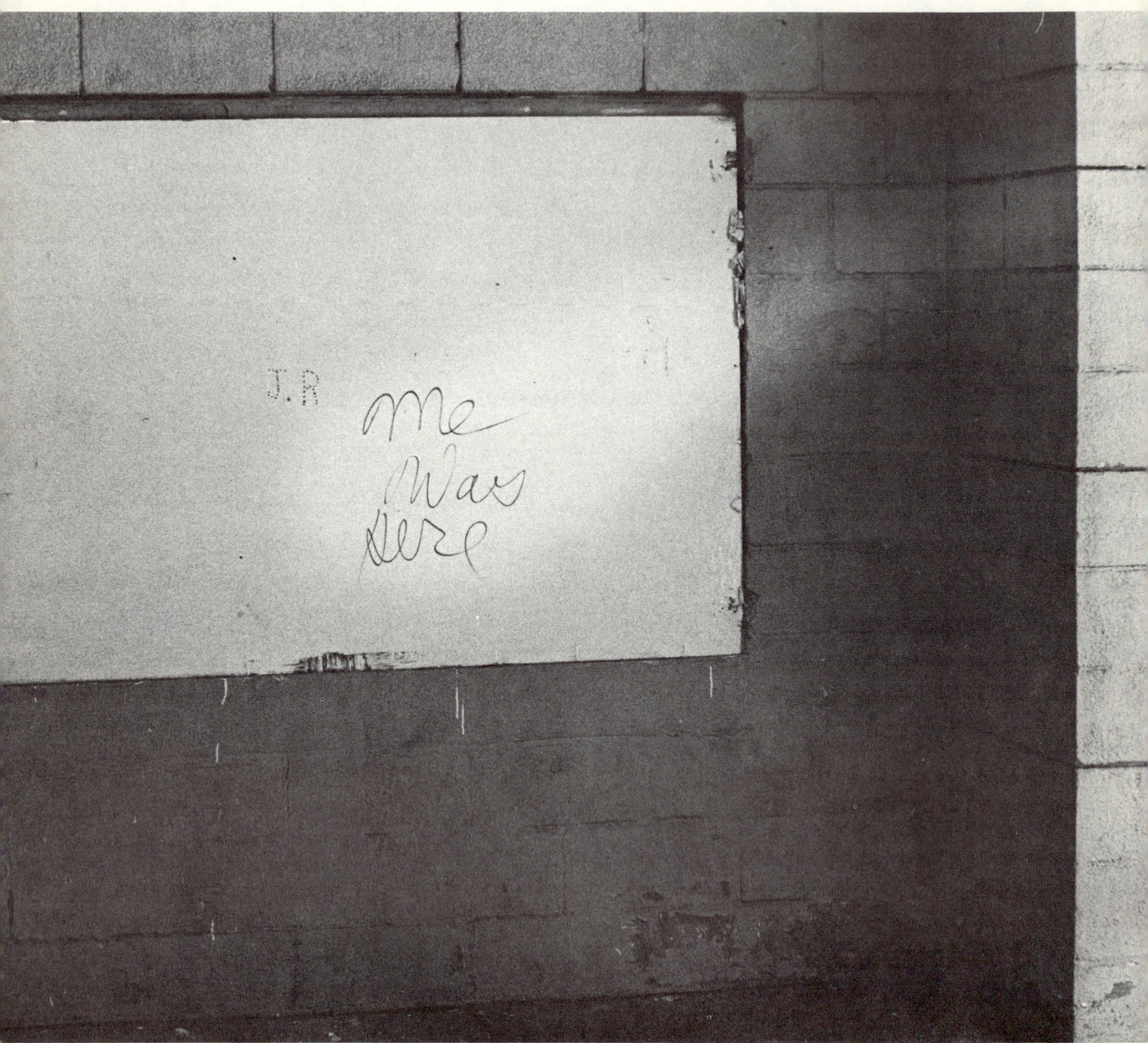

Courtesy of Fred Weiss

Introduction: Background and Biases

ONE

Compared to physics or chemistry, psychology as a recognized science has a relatively short history. It started as a branch of philosophy, and, in fact, in many European universities it is still part of the philosophy curriculum. Philosophers have always been interested in the intricacies of people's behavior and the subtleties of their mental experiences, and it was from those interests that psychology grew. By about one hundred years ago, the field had developed to such an extent that, like many other sciences before it, it became independent of philosophy and began to determine its own course in the scientific world. This course was heavily influenced by the then revolutionary idea that the methods of science could be as reasonably and as profitably applied to the study of biological and social phenomena as they were already being applied in the investigation of physical phenomena. So, the fledgling science of psychology emerged as a mixture of new scientific techniques and old philosophical questions, with its goal being the application of the new techniques to answer the old questions.

Fields, Speciality Areas, and Levels of Analysis

You might think that the path would have been clear for the young science. After all, scientific techniques have proved so powerful that it sometimes seems that any topic must quickly yield its secrets to them. This did happen in psychology to some degree, but in the process an unforeseen problem arose.

The problem is that the secrets yielded to scientific psychology have never fit together into the nice, orderly, unified picture that we've come to expect from science. We tend to think of science as being a bit like an archeological excavation project; each scientist works at his part of the excavation until, through the combined efforts of all the scientists, the object of

1

their search is fully uncovered. Then the scientists can walk around it, look at it, and generally agree about its structure, size, shape, and so on. Unfortunately, while this analogy is only partially valid for any science, it is not even vaguely valid for psychology. Indeed, to the casual observer each psychologist appears to be working on his own excavation, and there appears to be virtually no agreement about the object of these various searches or about how to interpret the findings that emerge.

Yet the situation is not as chaotic as it seems. It doesn't result from the perversity of psychologists nor from the lack of solid objects for which to search. Rather, it results from the fact that there are actually a number of different sciences of psychology; that is, psychology can be divided into a number of narrower *fields*. Of course, these divisions are not clear-cut because the fields overlap a great deal, but for convenience I have divided the science into the four fields illustrated in Table 1.1.[1]

TABLE 1.1   The Four Major Fields of Psychology, with Some Examples of Speciality Areas within Each Field Arranged According to the Level of Analysis That Is Used to Study Them[a]

Levels of Analysis	Fields			
	Sensation and Perception	*Behavior Acquisition*	*Social Behavior*	*Counseling and Psychotherapy*
Molar (General)	Music and art appreciation	Creativity	Leadership	Mental health programs
	Perceptual errors (illusions)	Decision-making	Social interactions	Effectiveness of psychotherapeutic techniques
	Recognition of objects, people, events, etc.	Learning	Conformity to group pressure	Effects of drug use and overuse
	Perception of distance, color, sound, taste, smell, etc.	Instinctive behavior	Human and animal territoriality	Formation and change of attitudes
Molecular (Specific)	Physiological bases of sensation and perception	Physiological bases of memory, thinking, learning, etc.	Physiological bases of social behavior	Physiological bases of mental illness

[a] Of course, there are many other speciality areas, each of which could be placed at an appropriate location in a larger version of this table; a complete table would be a "portrait" of psychology.

[1] A fifth field, child psychology, is essentially all the other fields combined and focuses exclusively on children. For example, a child psychologist might study the same things as a social psychologist except that the former would be concerned with the development of children's social behavior while the latter would be concerned with the same behavior in adults.

We can go a step further and subdivide each field into *speciality areas.* Thus, within the field of social psychology one psychologist might work in the speciality area of leadership style (Section 4, Part 3) and another might study the ways in which people and other animals establish and maintain the boundaries of territories that they regard as their own (Section 4, Parts 1 and 2). Finally, we can arrange the speciality areas within a field along a continuum of *levels of analysis* that extends from *molecular analysis* at one extreme to *molar analysis* at the other. Molecular analysis means that the speciality area studies very narrowly defined basic processes, for example, the psychological experiences that result from physiological activities in specific parts of the brain. Molar analysis means that the speciality area studies very broadly defined global processes, for example, what cultural and perceptual factors influence one's opinions about art and music. Between these two analytical extremes in each field there are speciality areas that represent different degrees of molecularity-molarity, and a full "portrait" of the science of psychology would be an elaborate version of Table 1.1.

When psychology is divided according to fields, speciality areas, and levels of analysis, the seeming disarray and apparent contradictions decrease considerably and the whole picture begins to take on a semblance of order. The former appearance of chaos results from the fact that each subpart of the elaborated version of Table 1.1 is pretty much self-contained, having little in common with any but its closest neighbors. Indeed, a counseling psychologist and a psychologist who studies the physiology of the brain have as little to say to each other professionally as a political scientist and a surgeon. While they might find it worthwhile to talk to one another, their different approaches to their different speciality areas make it unlikely that the conversation would have much impact on their work.

Biases

All of this does not mean that a person in one speciality area is naive about areas other than his own. On the contrary, most psychologists have a fairly broad knowledge of the science as a whole. But the partial isolation that results from working in one particular speciality area gives a psychologist a rather biased view of the rest of psychology. He tends to see the rest of psychology as an extended version of his own speciality. It is as though each psychologist unknowingly wears colored glasses—with each speciality area having its own color and neighboring areas having similar, but not identical, colors. When the psychologist looks out across the science, he sees that, lo and behold, it all bears the same general hue as his own speciality area. To verify his interpretation he describes what he sees to the person in a nearby area; the latter concedes that the description is almost correct, but that actually the whole thing tends to be a bit more like the hue of his own speciality area. And, of course, the further two psychologists' areas are from one another, the less similar will be their descriptions. To make matters worse, it is unlikely that anyone in psychology wears plain, uncolored glasses; almost by definition, to be a psychologist (or any other kind of scientist, for that matter) is to be biased in one's description of psychology (or the other science).

It might seem that the only hope for an objective description of psychology is for someone from outside the science to come in and tell us how things look when one is not biased. The problem is that such a person would start with his own personal biases (if you'll think about it, you have your own preconceptions about what psychology is—or, at least, what it *ought* to be). Then he would have to study psychology in order to know what he was talking about. In the course of his study, his bias would begin to be molded by the books he read (written by biased psychologists) and by the instructor who taught him (another biased psychologist), if only because the psychologists' biases would lead them to emphasize this and de-emphasize that, to include this and exclude that. Indeed, your instructor and I, as biased psychologists, are going to end up biasing you.

Actually, it's not so bad being biased as long as you realize what your biases are and as long as you don't mistake them for Truth. And that is why I've brought you through this rather long discussion—I want you to know the biases that underlie this book and to realize that if you were to read another introductory psychology text, you probably would find different biases. By knowing my biases I think you'll better understand the rest of this book; why I have included the things I have and why I have either excluded or only briefly covered some things that might play a central role in a book written by someone with different biases.

The Author's Biases

First Bias: The Decision-making Theme

My speciality area is in the upper portion of the second column from the left in Table 1.1. I study people's decision-making processes and try to devise ways of helping them make better and more satisfying decisions. Because I tend to think in terms of decision-making, you will find that this is an underlying theme throughout the book. My view is that almost everything that a person (or animal) does is part of an effort to achieve some desired goal or goals. A decision is merely an evaluation of, and a choice among, the alternative available courses of action that might attain the goals.

Evaluation of alternative possible actions requires that you be informed about what is going on around you and inside of you. Some of this information is provided by sensory and perceptual mechanisms such as your eyes and ears. Other information comes from within you in the form of desires and needs. Still other information is in the form of memories about past encounters with the current perceptual and need information. The remembered information aids in the interpretation of the perceptual and need information and permits you to formulate behavior appropriate to the circumstances. Sometimes this behavior consists of merely doing what you've done in the past in similar situations. Sometimes you have to examine the situation closely and try to come up with some new course of action that will be better suited to the circumstances and that will more adequately lead you to your goals.

Choices about what to do in various situations are heavily influenced by the people around you. Your parents taught you how to behave in certain situations and your friends encourage some kinds of behavior and discourage others. Indeed, many of the goals you try to achieve involve other people's approval and friendship.

Sometimes you find yourself in situations for which no course of action seems adequate; it may be that there is no clear way to deal with the situations, or it may be that no matter what you do things are bound to get worse. In these "crises" you sometimes find yourself behaving in ways that appear rather strange to other people. This strange behavior often consists of futile efforts to deal with the situation by hiding your discomfort, frustrations, and fear from yourself and others. For some people this evasive behavior complicates the already difficult situation, and they require outside help in the form of a friend or counselor in order to extract themselves from the dilemma.

Second Bias: Admiration of Mankind

In addition to my decision-making bias, you will notice throughout the book that I have a fairly strong bias about mankind. In general, I think that people are admirable. Aside from a lamentable tendency to kill each other, we seem to me to be fairly reasonable beings who merely are trying to do the best we can given the circumstances. In part, I suppose this bias is a reflection of my own persistently optimistic approach to life, and in part it reflects the fact that the majority of people I have known have been at least moderately congenial most of the time. But mostly this bias about people results from my continual surprise that we are as capable as we are. From our amazingly sensitive and cleverly designed sensory-perceptual systems on up to our ability to formulate rules to guide our behavior, we are indeed impressive creatures. Unfortunately, this impressiveness is somewhat tarnished by the fact that we're not too good at understanding the far-reaching implications of what we do (consider such man-made problems as overpopulation, pollution, war, and racism) and by our tendency to let other people do our thinking for us. However, these faults are problems to be worked on; for me at least, they fail to dim the impressiveness too much.

Third Bias:
Goals of Psychology

There are as many opinions about what the goal of the science of psychology should be as there are psychologists. My bias is that the main goal should be to help people better understand why and how people do the things they do and to help them choose courses of action that are best for themselves, as long as these actions do not seriously infringe on other people. As a part of this, I think psychologists have the duty to help people broaden their horizons in regard to understanding and tolerating their own and others' behavior and in regard to considering alternative ways of behaving for themselves. The primary long-term goal of psychology, I believe, ought to be to help people grow toward freedom, the freedom that comes when you cease to behave in stereotyped, automatic ways and begin to search for alternative behaviors that are as personally satisfying as possible.

The only way this goal is going to be reached is by expanding our knowledge about how and why we do what we do—that is, by the growth of the science of psychology. The key to this growth is research at all levels of analysis in all fields. For the most part, things are progressing well on the research front; psychology has developed an impressive arsenal of research tools and continues to explore new areas. Appendix 1 provides a broad picture of these tools, and you'll see the products of their application throughout the book. Even more highly sophisticated and versatile tools currently are in the process of being developed, and as this happens there will be important changes in the kinds of questions psychologists will be able to tackle. We already have begun to study areas of extreme social importance that twenty years ago were unassailable—for example, the psychological aspects of poverty. With the development and application of new research tools to areas of intense human concern—human sexuality and drugs, to name but two—psychology will be in an even better position to aid people in choosing courses of action that will best suit their own needs. For a science that is only one hundred years old, psychology is doing pretty well.

Fourth Bias:
Psychological Laws

It is common to expect a science to produce statements that are adequate descriptions of its subject matter and that permit predictions about what will occur in specific situations. When these statements are accurate and when they permit extremely precise predictions, they are called *laws*. The question is whether psychology has discovered any such laws, or is likely to. I think that the answer to the question has to be both yes and no. As I see it, there are statements that approach the status of laws at molecular levels of analysis, but there are none that I know of at molar levels. For one reason, molecular phenomena tend to involve physiological processes to some degree or other, and because people are similar physiologically and because physiological processes tend to be fairly automatic and predictable, there is a high degree of orderliness in the results of the research at this level. Descriptive statements about these orderly results are accurate, and they permit precise prediction of what would happen if the research were performed again. Therefore, these statements might qualify as laws.

When we move from molecular levels of analysis toward molar levels, however, the orderliness of the research results decreases sharply. With this decrease in orderliness there is a decrease in the accuracy and predictive capabilities of the descriptive statements about the results; I hesitate to call these statements laws. When speaking about these kinds of research results, one must resort to such phrases as "people tend to," "are prone to," "are inclined to," "have a propensity to," "are likely to," and so on. That is, while many people's behavior coincides with the descriptive statement, some people's behavior never does and it is seldom that anybody's behavior always does.

The fact that a descriptive statement has to imply some uncertainty does not mean that it is wrong—it is just not sufficiently detailed to cover the multitude of different circumstances that influenced the people's behaviors at the time they were observed. Different people's behaviors are never based on the same factors in even the most simple situations; each person interprets the situation and its demands slightly differently, each has a different degree of motivation to deal with the situation, and each has a different history of success, failure, frustration, or indifference in encountering situations like the one in question. So, when observing the behavior of a number of different people in some situation, the psychologist tries to extract the core of commonality from the diversity of behavior exhibited by the whole group. This common core becomes his descriptive statement of what people tend to do in that kind of situation. But because the statement seldom fully accounts for all of the things that the various

people did, unlike statements produced at more molecular levels of analysis, it cannot be thought of in terms of a law. I think that the search for
precise laws about molar phenomena is a futile undertaking and that we
will have to be satisfied with our imprecise statements. The implication of
this for you is that when in the course of reading this book you come
across sentences that imply that such and such is a psychological fact, you
will have to remember to take such statements with a grain of salt; there
are many exceptions to every rule that is described.

The following is a good example of what can happen if you fail to recognize that psychological "facts" usually are only a core of commonality in
the midst of diversity. Social psychologists have found that eldest children
tend to strive to achieve, and actually do succeed, more than their younger
brothers and sisters. This tendency is not universal, but it exists to some
degree or other in quite a few eldest children. Inevitably, whenever I men-
tion this finding in my classes, at least one student concludes that the
statement is wrong because, for example, his older brother dropped out of
school to become a laborer while he, the younger brother, is getting
straight A's and hopes to become a medical researcher. What the student
fails to understand is that the description is not an immutable law but simply a statement about how eldest children *tend* to be. There are lots of exceptions, and citing one of them is not presenting very strong evidence that
the statement is inaccurate in general.

Fifth Bias:
Determinism
versus Free Will

A major assumption in science is that the course of all events is determined by preceding events. This notion of cause and effect, called *deter-*
minism, is familiar to most of us and we take it for granted. Indeed, it is so
familiar that the fact that it underlies virtually all of science arouses no discomfort in most of us—until we begin to think about its implications for
the science of psychology.

Determinism in physics, chemistry, or geology is easy to accept, but
most of us get a bit resentful when the possibility is suggested that our
own behavior is merely cause and effect; that if someone knew all about
our past, the causes, he could predict *everything* we will do in the future. I
don't know about you, but statements like this always make me feel like
an automaton, and I do not like it. Indeed, I enjoy the feeling—be it illusion or not—that my behavior is under my own control and that it is not
some automatic, mechanical consequence of my past experience and the
circumstances in which I find myself. In short, I insist that I have the *free*
will to decide my own course of action.

My own thinking leaves me in a quandary, however. I believe that a science of psychology is a necessity if we are to help people help themselves live reasonably satisfying lives. And, the determinism assumption is an article of faith in science. Moreover, I know from my own experience that much of what I do each day, how I react to various situations and the goals for which I strive, can be easily traced to the way in which I was raised and to the various adventures I have had along the way to becoming the person I am today. On the other hand, I also know that in my better moments I am capable of a fairly reasonable and logical analysis of the events that comprise my life, and I think that I make choices that are not merely blind reactions based on past experience. So, as a psychologist I seem bound to accept the assumption of determinism, yet as a private person I am quite unable to accept *or* reject it.

I have spent long hours with a beer in my hand and a pained look upon my face (a look that I took to be properly philosophical) contemplating the question of determinism versus free will. I suspect that the most valuable component of these sessions was the beer. This is because it has gradually dawned on me over the years that my own behavior, either as a psychologist or a private person, probably would not change very much no matter how I decided the issue. Now it seems to me that if the answer to a question is inconsequential, the question itself may be inconsequential. Moreover, the fact that strict scientific laws do not seem to be forthcoming in psychology means that the deterministic nature of behavior cannot be proved or disproved, at least in the near future. If it is possible that the question is both inconsequential and unlikely to be settled in the foreseeable future, my bias is to refuse to make up my mind about it. Therefore, I have stored it away as one of those imponderables that I only ponder from time to time without solution.

You may regard my biased nonsolution of the determinism versus free will question a bit cavalier, and indeed it is. I assure you that it leaves me unsettled, but I frankly don't know how to solve it. I have elected to tell you about this bias not to confess my indecisiveness but so that you'll understand the apparent contradiction that on the one hand this book emphasizes that a scientific approach is the only sound way for psychology to attain the goals just outlined, while on the other it rests on the belief that human beings are capable of guiding their own behavior. However, I hope my "cop-out" solution displeases you enough to make you try a beer, a pained expression, and a little contemplation of the question on your own.

A Parting Shot

The study of psychology is rather disconcerting to many people because much of it is plain common sense. Yet the fact that psychology often does not appear to have moved too much beyond common sense ought not be regarded as an indictment of the science. Rather, this characteristic attests to the high quality of common sense—most people are fairly competent intuitive psychologists even though they often don't realize that they know as much as they actually do. This unrecognized competence is one key to why a course in psychology is valuable; the course can help you become aware of the breadth of your intuitive knowledge and it can give you a *framework* in which to place this knowledge. Of course, I hope that your increased awareness will be accompanied by an expansion of your knowledge; psychology actually *has* progressed beyond common sense even if this is not always obvious. Too, there is always the problem that common sense isn't always right, and we don't all share the same "common sense." Even when common sense is right, we can't be sure it is until we have subjected it to verification by research. Psychologists are doing much of this kind of research, and it will be described throughout the book.

In an effort to provide you with an appropriate framework, this book is arranged along the lines of the decision-making bias outlined earlier. We begin with an examination of sensation and perception as sources of information about the world around us (Section 2). We then move on to the ways in which that information is tempered by information that is stored in memory and how all of this is used to attain various goals (Section 3). Next, we explore how other people influence our behavior—both by teaching us how to behave in certain situations and by exerting pressure on us to do or not to do certain things (Section 4). Finally, we examine what happens when we find ourselves in situations for which no behavior appears appropriate—the conflicts and stresses that result from this dilemma and what these may lead to (Section 5). The last section (Section 6) is a set of special topics. These topics actually are subparts of the previous sections, but I believe that they deserve more lengthy presentation than would be feasible if they were to be included in those sections. At the end of each section the heading "Special Topic" indicates which part or parts of Section 6 (or Appendices) are appropriate extensions of the discussion just completed. Your instructor may want to assign these parts in some other order (and I suspect that nearly everyone will read the part about love, marriage, and sex without delay), but I believe the order I've suggested is a reasonable one.

Special Topic   Appendix 1: *Tools for Psychological Research*

Further Reading   BORING, E. G.   *A History of Experimental Psychology*
New York: Appleton, 1950, 777 pages.
This book is generally regarded as *the* authority on the history of psychology. It traces the major issues and themes from their first recorded origins in Greek philosophical thought up to modern times. There is a good deal of interesting detail about the lives and thinking of the men who have shaped psychology, and these accounts make the book more interesting than its title might lead you to expect. It is, however, fairly steep in places (but then, who says you can't skip those places?).

BRUNO, F. J.   *The Story of Psychology*
New York: Holt, Rinehart and Winston, 1972, 209 pages (paperback).
A brief history of the men, from ancient times to the present, who have influenced the development of psychology. The book is not only full of interesting anecdotes about these men but also contains ten multiple choice questions at the end of each chapter so the reader can evaluate his understanding of the material covered.

WATSON, R. I.   *The Great Psychologists*
Philadelphia: Lippincott, 1968, 613 pages (paperback).
Aristotle, Locke, Wundt, Binet, Watson, and Freud are just a few of the philosophers and psychologists whose views are discussed in this book, which tells the story of psychology through discussions of the men who made psychology what it is today.

WERTHEIMER, M.   *A Brief History of Psychology*
New York: Holt, Rinehart and Winston, 1970, 163 pages (paperback).
Wertheimer was a student of E. G. Boring (author of the history of psychology listed above) at Harvard University. Therefore, it is not surprising that this book has much in common with Boring's book except that it is briefer and more up to date. Because Wertheimer himself is both the son of one of the men who heavily influenced the development of psychology as well as a distinguished psychologist in his own right, he has a particularly interesting and insightful view of the history of psychology, a view that is well presented in this concise book.

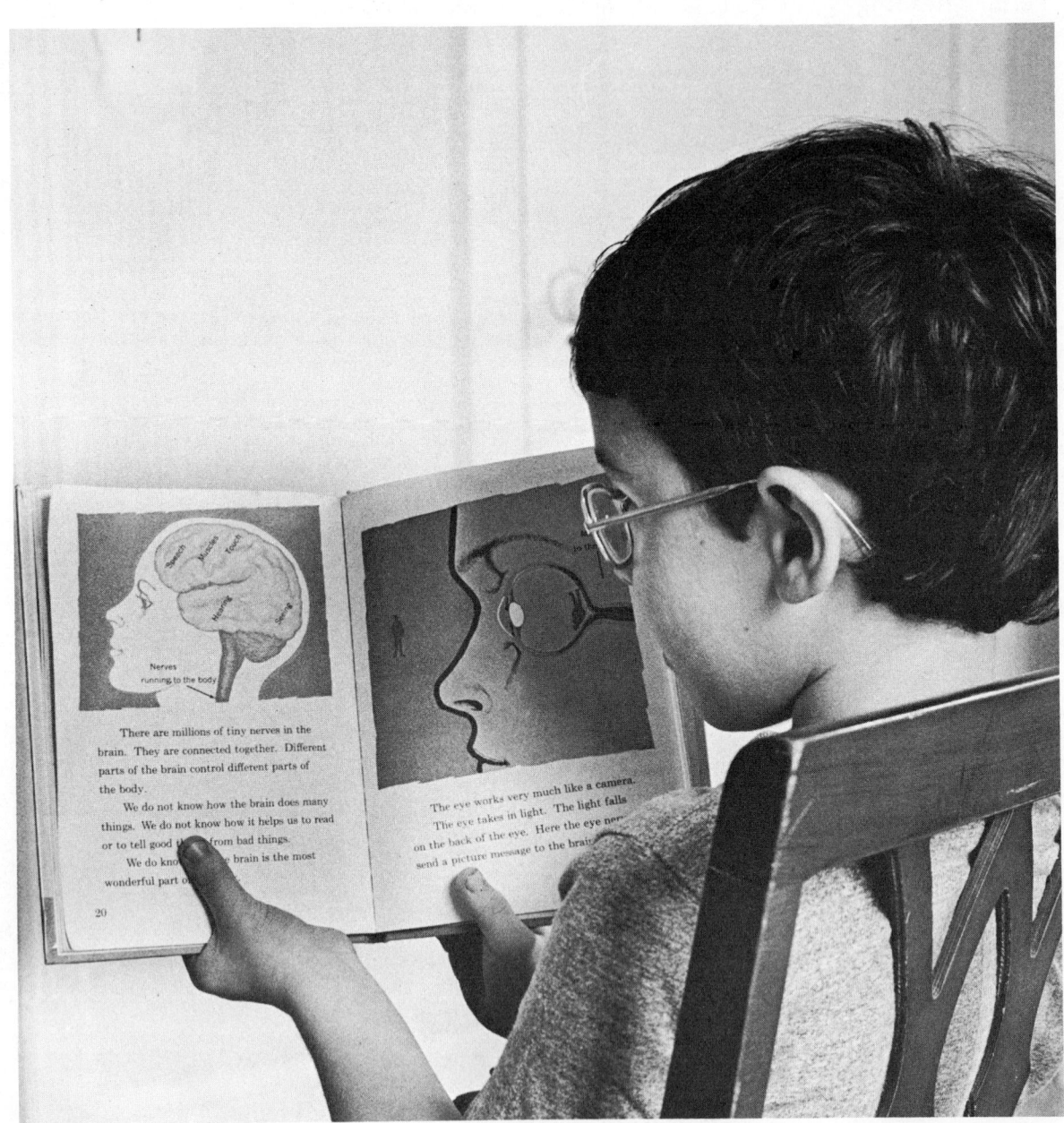

There are millions of tiny nerves in the brain. They are connected together. Different parts of the brain control different parts of the body.

We do not know how the brain does many things. We do not know how it helps us to read or to tell good things from bad things.

We do know that the brain is the most wonderful part o

20

The eye works very much like a camera. The eye takes in light. The light falls on the back of the eye. Here the eye ner send a picture message to the brain

Sensation
and Perception
TWO

We live in a busy and complicated world. This world, our *environment*, contains the things we need and want in order to survive and be comfortable, *our goals*, and it also provides *the means* for obtaining them. In order to know about these means, and the goals to which they lead, we must have information about the structure of the environment, that is, about the persons, objects, and events that surround us. This information is not so easily obtained as you might at first think. Indeed, the sensory and perceptual processes by which we acquire such information are among the most complex and fascinating aspects of living beings. This section, which deals with these processes, will, I hope, convey to you an appreciation of their beauty and importance.

The biggest barrier to understanding sensory and perceptual processes is that it is difficult to stand back and be objective about them. The experiences of seeing, hearing, touching, and the rest are so continuous and so important to us that we tend to take them for granted. We fail to realize, for example, that the world appears to us as it does *both* because of the way the human body is constructed *and* because of the way the world itself is constructed. For example, if through some accident you had been born with one normal human eye and one eye like a fly has, you would find that your two eyes would produce vastly different visual experiences since each eye would be constructed differently. It seems reasonable to assume, therefore, because of the differences in eye structure, that the visual world of flies is quite different from that of human beings. The fly's world is not necessarily any more or less "the true world" than ours; it merely is different.

Or, to take another example, when you look at another person you experience him as a solid, real thing that exists independent of your own existence. And yet, in a way, that person is a product of your mind; your experience is built on all the bits and pieces of information that come through your

13

separate senses. No one sense provides a full description of your friend—his looks, voice, touch, odor, and so on—yet when you encounter him you end up with an integrated, unified experience. It is as though a central computer receives messages from a number of different information centers and, on the basis of these messages, infers the nature of the object in front of you. You are never aware, however, of the complex processes that the "computer" must go through to make this inference.

To obtain a fresh perspective on sensation and perception, let us pursue the analogy of messages going from different information sources to a central computer. Try to think of a person or an animal as some sort of roving information gatherer that an engineer might design to explore an exotic environment like Mars or Jupiter. The body of this information gatherer is a vehicle with a variety of very selective sensing devices hooked to it. Some of these devices are sensitive to electromagnetic energy (light), some to vibrations of the air (sound), some to chemicals (smells and tastes), some to pressure (touch), and so on. As the vehicle wanders around, each of these sensory devices collects information about that part of the environment to which it is sensitive. This information is relayed to a central computer (the brain) that analyzes and integrates messages from all of the senses. From these integrated messages the computer makes inferences (perception) about the layout of the environment in which the vehicle finds itself and about the objects, persons, and events that populate that environment.

If this analogy is to be usefully applied to human beings, we must make a very strong assumption about our vehicle and its sensory devices: they are not solely *passive* recipients of information; rather, they are capable of *actively* seeking information. That is, the entire system can actively interact with any particular aspect of the environment—just as you strain to hear footsteps on the stairs, go to the window to investigate a noise in the street, or reach out to touch an iron to see if it is hot. The active and passive states of each sensing device can be studied both in terms of the information they contribute to the central computer and in terms of the computer's use of this information to form theories about the environment.

Part 1   THE FIRST SENSORY SYSTEM, KINESTHESIS

The most constant feature of the environment is gravity. The human body is systematically organized around a central axis, extending from the top of the head to the heels of the feet, that is defined by gravity. Balance and posture are in reference to this axis and to gravity; if you move an arm or a leg, you must compensate by moving other parts of your body or you will lose your balance and tumble to the ground. To make this delicate balancing act possible, we must have an accurate and dependable source of information both about our orientation with respect to gravity and about our own movements.

The term "kinesthesis" means "sensitivity to movement" and generally refers to sensitivity to posture, to location of the body and its parts in space, and to their orientation with respect to gravity. It is the sense that tells us where we are and what the various parts of our bodies are doing. In some ways, kinesthesis is the most fundamental of all senses, the one we depend upon most, even though we are not even aware of it most of the time.

In human beings there are two kinesthetic systems that provide information about gravity and movement. The first is the *vestibular system*, which is sensitive to movement of the head. The second is that part of the *touch system* which is sensitive to the movement and location of body parts.

Vestibular Kinesthesis: Movement of the Head

As Figure 2.1 shows, you have two vestibular organs, just as you have two eyes and two ears. These organs are located in the bone of the skull on each side of the head near the apparatus for hearing. Each vestibular organ consists of two parts, the *utricle* and *saccule*, which are sensitive to gravity, acceleration, and deceleration, and the *semicircular canals*, which are sensitive to rotary motion.

Structure of the Utricle and Saccule

The utricle is sensitive to gravity while the saccule is sensitive to acceleration and deceleration. The utricle is oriented so that it is level when your head is level; the saccule is oriented at a right angle to the utricle. Both are hollow chambers in the bone and are filled with fluid. The floor of each chamber is covered with a multitude of small cells that are like tiny hairs. These hair-cells are embedded in a gelatinous membrane, and near their tips are small pieces of calcium. At the base of each hair-cell is a *neural element*[1] that is sensitive to the degree to which the cell is bent. The pieces of calcium make the top of the gelatin heavy, so that when you move your head the top of the gelatin is more influenced by inertia—that is, is slower to move—than the bottom, causing the top to lag slightly behind the bottom. This differential movement of the top and bottom of the gelatin causes the hair-cells embedded in it to be bent, causing, in turn, stimulation of the neural elements. These elements then send a message about the movement to the brain.

---

[1] For the sake of simplicity the term "neural element" will be used to mean receptor cells, neurons, nerves, and all manner of components of the nervous system. For a more specific description, see Appendix 2.

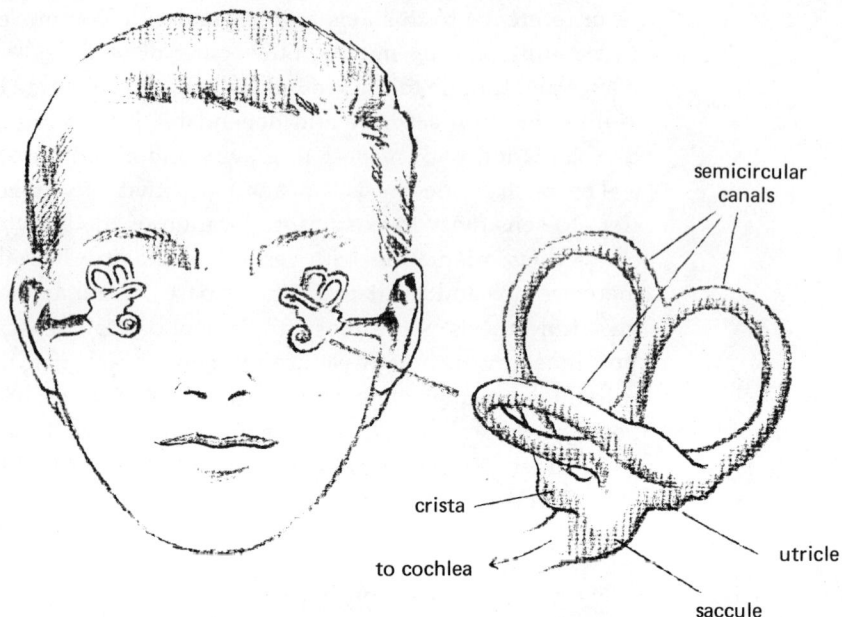

FIG. 2.1 *The locations of the semicircular canals, utricles, and saccules.*

*Structure
of the Semicircular
Canals*

The second part of the vestibular organ consists of the semicircular canals. As illustrated in Figure 2.1, these are three fluid-filled tubes in each ear, each having a small chamber at one end. The chamber in each canal contains the *crista*, a brushlike group of hair-cells that, like the hair-cells in the utricle and saccule, are embedded in gelatinous membrane. The hair-cells in the crista are connected at their bases to neural elements that are sensitive both to the direction and to the degree to which the hair-cells are bent.

The canals are sensitive to movement of the head in any of the three primary directions—turning from side to side, raising or lowering (as when you bow your head), and tipping from one side to the other. The position of each canal enables it to be particularly sensitive to one of these three kinds of movements.

To understand how these canals work, perform the following simple experiment which affects your horizontal canals; the other two canals work in the same way but for different directions of movement. Stand in an open area, turn around quickly for as long as you can, and then stop suddenly. When you began to turn, the inertia of the fluid and the cristas in the canals caused the movement of the cristas to lag a tiny bit behind the movement of your skull. Because the bases of the cristas are fixed to the skull, they cannot lag. Thus inertia influenced only the tops of the cristas, causing the hair-cells to bend, which then stimulated the neural elements at the bases of these hair cells, resulting in the brain being told that you had begun to turn.

As the turning continued and the inertia of the cristas was overcome, they quickly returned to a normal position and the acceleration messages to the brain ceased. Then you stopped. This time the inertia of the fluid and the cristas caused them to continue moving after the head stopped. Again the hair-cells were bent and a message went to the brain, telling it that you had stopped turning.

Touch Kinesthesis: Movement and Location of Body Parts

Having information about the orientation and movement of your head is not enough to make you keep your balance. Other information is needed if you are going to move around effectively. You must know about the posture of your body and about the relation between your head and the rest of your body. Are your feet underneath, supporting your weight? If your head is moving forward, are your feet moving forward too so that your whole body is moving ahead? This kind of information is obtained very rapidly and very accurately, so that you rarely fall over, even when you engage in intricate and energetic movements. All of these adjustments are based upon information furnished by the kinesthetic part of the touch system—by neural elements in your joints, in your skin, and in your muscles.

Joints

Information about the location of your limbs and about posture is provided by neural elements located in the joints between the bones. These neural elements are extremely sensitive to the precise angle at which the joints are bent, and they constantly send this information to the brain, where it is integrated with other information in order to determine the exact location of the limbs.

Skin

When you stand up your feet press against the floor. When you sit, your back, your rear end, and the backs of your legs press against the chair. Within your skin are neural elements which are sensitive to these pressures. This pressure sensitivity supplements the vestibular system by providing information about your orientation relative to the surfaces that surround you.

Muscles

When you carry an object, neural elements in your muscles provide information about the resulting increase in muscle tension. This information, along with information about the increase in the pressure of your body against the floor or chair and the degree to which your joints are bent, is integrated and then used for maintenance of balance.

Touch Kinesthesis: Passive and Active Stimulation

When you move your arm, which is active stimulation, you are aware of where it is going. When someone else picks up your arm and moves it, which is passive stimulation, you also know where it is even though your muscles didn't do the work to get it there. That you know where it is is due to the neural elements that tell you how much your joints are being bent and secondarily to the elements that sense the pressure of your arm against the hand of the person who is moving it and the surface upon which it is placed. Even when you are asleep you know enough about your body's location to keep from falling out of bed or from taking more than your share of the bed.

While it is difficult to do so for the other two components of touch kinesthesis, you can actively vary your awareness of your body's pressure against objects. If you think about it, you can feel the chair you are sitting on or the elbow and hand with which you are propping your head. Notice that you are able to do this without having to move to produce a detectable change in pressure. Now, close your eyes and casually hold something rather heavy out in front of you. Try to become aware of your joint angles and the muscle strain. You will find that what you actually are doing is falling back on pressure again; you feel the pressure of the object against your hand and perhaps some ill-defined strain in your arm, but no very specific joint or muscle experience. Pressure against the skin probably plays a larger role in our conscious awareness of body position, but joint angles and muscle strain are also very important in the automatic kinesthetic processes that govern balance and body positioning.

Part 2   *THE SECOND SENSORY SYSTEM, TOUCH SENSITIVITY*

The general touch system is vitally important because it provides not only kinesthetic information about body orientation and support but also crucial information about the nature of the environment. Our skin tells us if we are in danger of being burned, cut, pinched, and so on. It also tells us if the surface we are stepping on is firm or if the thing we are touching is hot, soft, smooth, or whatever. Our interest in the environment most often lies in the *objects* that surround us, and while we can tell a good deal about objects by smelling them, listening to them, and particularly by looking at them, it is also useful to be able to feel them.

The Touch System: Structure

Touch has no unitary sense organ similar to the vestibular organs. Instead, the system consists of many different neural elements embedded in the tissues of the skin. There still are many questions concerning which of these elements are sensitive to what aspects of objects, but we can speak of three general classes of elements without doing too much damage to the truth.

Class 1

The first class consists of neural elements embedded in the skin and the muscles that are sensitive to temperature, pain, and to some form of deformation of the skin and to the pressure of an object against it.

Class 2

The second class consists of elements that are in the joints and that react to movement of the joints.

Class 3

The third class of neural elements are associated with the hair that covers virtually all of the human body. Although the hair on human beings is less obvious than on most furry animals, close inspection of almost any external part of your body will reveal small light-colored hairs, the only exceptions being the palms of your hands, the soles of your feet, and the areas immediately surrounding the body openings. The root of each of these hairs has a neural element wrapped around it. Movement of the hair causes the element to react and send a message to the brain about the disturbance. Integration of these messages with messages from other hairs permits the brain to determine the size and location of an object that is touching the skin.

Detection of Objects

A major function of touch is to detect the location, size, texture, and temperature of objects that contact your skin. As you might expect, not all parts of your body are equally equipped to do this. The body parts that you use in manipulation of objects, such as the palms of your hands, your fingers, or your tongue, are very sensitive to being touched. However, nonmanipulatory parts such as your back, belly, or the soft underside of your forearm are not so sensitive.

You can demonstrate to yourself the differential sensitivity of the various parts of your skin by performing a simple experiment. Get two nylon-tipped pens, one red and one black; the tips must be sharp and the ink should be washable. Cajole a friend into helping you. Close your eyes, and while they are closed have your friend touch you gently—just enough to bend the skin slightly—for a brief moment with the point of the black pen. Immediately after he has touched you he should say, "Now," whereupon, with your eyes still closed, you must try to touch the same place with the point of the red pen. Do this first for five or six different places on the palm and fingers of your hand; then do it the same number of times on the underside of your forearm or on the upper part of your belly. Open your eyes and compare the degree to which the red spots correspond to the black ones. You will find that on your hand you were very accurate in locating the place where you were touched. On your arm or belly, however, you were a good deal less accurate.

Results similar to these can be obtained both for temperature detection and for your ability to discriminate the size, and in some cases the shapes, of objects that touch the skin. However, these experiments require more complex apparatus than just nylon pens, so you can't do a simple experiment to demonstrate the results to yourself.

Active Interaction with Objects

The parts of your body most clearly involved in active touch are your hands. We tend to think of the hands on the arms as similar to hooks at the end of the boom on a crane; as though they are carried to the appropriate location by the arms and their sole role is to pick things up and move them about. Actually, picking things up is but one role for the hands. The active procuring of information is probably more important.

While orderly information arises from active handling of objects, an outstanding feature of the process itself is that it appears to be very disorderly. When handed a strange object, you do not proceed to explore it in some prescribed order, like a pilot going through a preflight checklist. Instead, you may scratch it with your fingernail, heft it, hold it in your hand in various positions, and explore it by wrapping your fingers around it in different ways. You may also run your fingertips over the surface and use them to explore the edges, the holes, and the bumps. If you were a baby, you would let your tongue and lips have a go at it. Were you to receive another strange object you would go through many of the same activities again, but not necessarily in the same order nor in exactly the same way. What with all of this confusion in your investigation of objects, it would be easy to conclude that you must glean precious little information from active touch. Of course, this conclusion would be totally wrong.

Suppose I had you close your eyes and asked you to feel Object A in Figure 2.2. Then I gave you one of the other objects and asked you to feel it and tell me if it is the same as or different from Object A. With a little practice with these strange shapes you would become quite accurate in your judgments even though you used the disorderly, exploratory touch methods that seemingly should lead you to be inaccurate. In short, this active, apparently disorderly, process yields very accurate information about the objects.

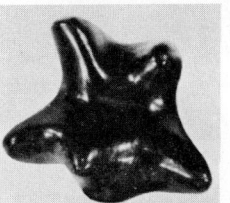

Object A

Comparison Objects

FIG. 2.2   Sculptured objects for the study of touch. The person is blindfolded, given Object A to feel with his hands, and then attempts to select the identically shaped object from among the comparison objects. (Reprinted by permission of Houghton Mifflin from The Senses Considered as Perceptual Systems *by J. J. Gibson, p. 124.)*

Temperature Sensitivity

It is not really very clear how you detect the temperature either of objects or of the air around you. Most likely you use your own body temperature as a reference point. When an object comes in contact with your skin there is a heat exchange; whichever is cooler, you or the object, absorbs heat from the one that is warmer. People are very sensitive to the rate at which heat is exchanged and can use this information to detect the temperature of objects. Some people can even close their eyes and tell whether their fingertips are

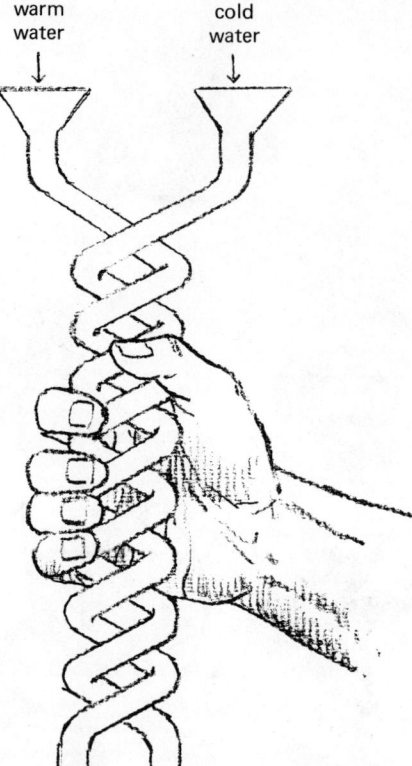

warm
water

cold
water

FIG. 2.3 There is warm water in one tube, cold water in the other; together the tubes feel hot.

over a dark surface or over a light surface. Because the dark surface absorbs radiated body heat more quickly than the light surface, the person can use this information to make highly accurate judgments about whether the surface is light or dark.

Apparently we have two kinds of neural elements that are sensitive to temperature. One is sensitive to cold and the other is sensitive to warmth. Surprisingly, the experience of hot is a result of the stimulation of both of these elements at the same time. If you make an apparatus like the one in Figure 2.3 and run cold water through both A and B, the tubes will feel cold when you grasp the coil. Warm water in both tubes will feel warm. However, the combination of cold water in A and warm water in B will feel hot, implying that the interaction of cool and warm neural elements is responsible for the experience of hot.

Of course, what is warm and what is cold is relative to what you have recently experienced, as this simple experiment will demonstrate. Fill two containers, one with warm water and one with cool water. Put your right hand in the warm water and your left hand in the cool water and leave them there for about a minute. Then reverse your hands; the warm water will feel hot to the (cool) left hand and the cool water will feel cold to the (warm) right hand.

Pain Sensitivity

Pain is an important, usually unpleasant, sensation that ordinarily is regarded as a signal of imminent danger or injury to some part of the body. However, it is an imperfect signal. Often injury occurs without pain being felt at the time—for example, sunburn or tooth decay. Sometimes there is pain when no real injury has occurred—for example, tension headaches. Moreover, the pain experience is not always very precise; sometimes it is difficult to locate where pains are, and they often seem to come and go in a very capricious manner. For example, it is not uncommon for people to have a painful toothache disappear as soon as they enter the dentist's office. Similarly, a headache or the pain of a sore muscle may disappear during an interesting TV program only to reappear during the commercial.

In general, not much is known about the mechanisms or the experience of pain—partly because most researchers are unwilling to inflict pain on themselves or others in order to gain scientific understanding. Too, researchers are constantly tempted to assume that pain is a "pure" sensation that is uninfluenced by anything other than bodily damage. However, recent psychological findings indicate that this assumption is unrealistic. Pain begins with stimulation of rather nonspecific neural elements in the skin (called *free nerve endings*), and the information goes to numerous parts of the brain where the resulting experience is elaborated upon in light of one's motives, emotions, and interpretations of the situation at hand. In short, pain is a complex experience that is influenced by many other psychological events rather than the simple sharp sensation it sometimes appears to be.

This conclusion about the complexity of pain is supported by many studies. For example, there is evidence that some people are less sensitive to pain than are others, but it is difficult to know whether this means that those who are less sensitive don't feel pain as easily or that they tolerate it better. Moreover, if people know what kind and amount of pain to expect, say after surgery, they subsequently are less uncomfortable and require less painkiller than if they had not been told what to expect. Again, it is difficult to know exactly what this means; do they feel less pain or do they tolerate it better?

BOX 2.1

Adaptation: When the Senses Disagree

No doubt you are familiar with the fact that your senses are able to *adapt* to prolonged, unchanging stimulation so that you no longer notice it. For example, if you work in an office, you soon become unaware of the sound of typewriters; if you put on sunglasses, you quickly cease to see the greenish hue; if you accidently put on too much cologne, you soon become unaware of its odor, even though it may be very strong. Each of these is an example of adaptation within a single sensory system. There is, however, another kind of adaptation that is less familiar to us and, therefore, more curious than single-sense adaptation. This adaptation occurs when there are conflicting messages from two or more sensory systems; the curious part is that the adaptation sometimes persists a short while after the sensory disagreement has ceased to exist.

Ordinarily, the messages you receive from your various senses agree with one another; when you rise from your chair, the changes in what you see are compatible with the messages from your skin, muscles, vestibular system, and so on. Sometimes, however, something happens to alter this familiar agreement between the senses, and then it takes time for you to adjust to the new state of affairs. For example, when you get new glasses, it may take a day or so for you to approach curbs and stairs with complete confidence. This is because you must learn to coordinate your new visual world with your habitual ways of moving around in your old visual world.

When they occur in real life, discrepancies in sensory agreement are seldom very large; new glasses aren't all that much of a change, and adaptation to the new state of affairs is relatively rapid. However, it is possible to radically alter sensory agreement in psychological experiments and to examine how quickly and how well adaptation takes place and also to see how long the adaptation persists after the sensory disagreement ceases to exist, that is, the *after-effects* of adaptation.

Quite a few studies have been done in which a person wears goggles with lenses that are designed to alter his visual field so that it no longer agrees with the vestibular and kinesthetic messages he gets while moving around in his environment. These alterations consist of shifting the visual field a few degrees to one side or the other, turning it upside down, completely reversing it left to right, or any combination of these. The person usually wears a pair of lenses for some specified period of time during which his ability to perform various tasks is studied and his descriptions of what he is experiencing are obtained. The earliest of these studies (1896) was carried out in England by G. M. Stratton. For eight consecutive days, Stratton wore lenses that inverted everything he saw. At the end of the eight days, he reported that he could get around in his new visual world quite well and that, as long as he did not think about it, he was not particularly aware that things were upside down. But if he paused to concentrate on his visual experience, things immediately looked inverted. When the experiment was over and he took the lenses off, the world did not now look upside down, as it might have had his visual system been completely retrained. However, he did experience several hours of what he described as "bewilderment."

Complete adaptation to the new visual world never occurred for Stratton—but then, he wore the lenses for only eight days. Later, in the late 1950s, Dr. Ivo Kohler and Dr. Theodor Erismann in Austria had people wear lenses for periods of weeks.* In one of their experiments, the lenses caused strange expansions and contractions of the visual field as the person's eyes moved (rather like the distortions you see when you move in front of a fun house mirror). After a time, adaptation reportedly occurred and the person was no longer disturbed by the distortions. However, a strange thing happened when the lenses were removed; the visual field was still distorted when the eyes moved, but the new distortions were *exactly the opposite* of the ones induced by the lenses. These after-effects diminished in a much shorter time, a matter of days, than had been necessary to induce adaptation in the first place.

Similar adaptation and after-effects to sensory disagreement have been observed in a very different kind of experimental setting. At Pensacola, Florida, the U.S. Navy performed a number of studies on how well people can adapt to living in a rotating environment.† The studies were done in order to predict what might happen to people who lived in rotating space stations. Volunteers in these studies lived for twelve days in a self-contained room that was mounted on a turntable, the speed of which could be varied. The room had a kitchen, a toilet, beds, TV, and so on, so life could go on reasonably normally. The peculiar thing about the room, from our point of view, is that the extra force resulting from its rotation made it necessary for the occupants to alter the way in which they walked and moved their bodies in order to move around successfully in the room. Because the room had no windows, its movement relative to the outside world was difficult for the occupants to judge, and, as a result, the room appeared perfectly normal and stationary to them. But the moment the occupants tried to move or perform any simple task, kinesthetic muscular messages were severely at variance with visual messages.

After a few days aboard the room (after they got over being motion sick), the volunteers learned to adjust their movements, and, as long as they moved fairly slowly, they could walk about with little difficulty. With practice they could also perform a variety of simple and complex tasks fairly well. Then came the

---

*I. Kohler, Experiments with goggles. *Scientific American*, 1962, **206**, 63–72.

†A. Graybiel, R. S. Kennedy, E. C. Knoblock, F. E. Guedry, W. Mertz, M. E. McLeod, J. K. Colehour, E. F. Miller, and A. R. Fregly, Effects of exposure to a rotating environment (10 RPM) on four aviators for a period of twelve days. *Aerospace Medicine,* 1965, **36**, 733–754.

end of the experiment: The room stopped rotating, the volunteers stepped out into the stationary world, and none of them could walk in a straight line or even stand up very well. In short, they had adapted so well to the strange forces produced by the rotation and to the resulting discrepancy between their visual and vestibular-kinesthetic systems that they were no longer able to walk or stand in a stationary world. But, as was found in the Kohler and Erismann experiments, these after-effects disappeared in a matter of hours, a much shorter time than was needed for initial adaptation to the rotating room.

Just what is necessary to promote adaptation to sensory disagreement? One possible answer is that one needs merely to know that there is such disagreement; we'll call this the *passive* hypothesis. Another possible answer is that one must have experience in the environment that is causing the discrepancy so that a sort of "recalibration" of the two sensory systems can take place. We'll call this the *active* hypothesis.

A series of experiments by Dr. Richard Held and his associates at the Massachusetts Institute of Technology has shown that the active hypothesis is the correct answer.‡ One example of their experiments will give you an idea of their general findings. The experiment began in a dark room which had a dim slit of light at one end and a swivel chair at the other. Each volunteer sat in the swivel chair and turned until he felt he was exactly facing the dim light at the other end of the room. The experimenter then measured the accuracy of his alignment. Next, the volunteer put on a pair of lenses that moved his visual field either to the right or to the left of normal and then, while wearing these lenses, he either walked (active) for an hour along an outdoor path or was wheeled in a wheelchair (passive) along the same path. Finally, he returned to the dark room, removed the lenses, and again realigned himself with the dim light while the experimenter measured his accuracy. If adaptation to the lenses had taken place and an after-effect existed, it should have been in the form of a greater alignment error after wearing the lenses than before. Also, if the active hypothesis about adaptation is correct and the passive hypothesis incorrect, only those volunteers who walked the path should have adapted, and therefore only they should have shown the after-effect in the form of alignment errors. And, indeed, the results favored the active hypothesis—the active (walking) volunteers showed after-effect errors that were from two to nine times larger than those of the passive (wheeled) volunteers, who showed nearly no errors at all. Moreover, the size of the after-effects for the active volunteers depended upon how long they wore the lenses; the longer they wore the lenses, the greater the realignment errors.

In summary, these studies, and others like them, show that at least for some

‡R. HELD, Plasticity in sensory motor systems. In R. C. Atkinson (Ed.), *Contemporary Psychology: Readings from Scientific American.* San Francisco: Freeman, 1971.

human senses, adaptation can take place when sensory messages disagree. More-over, when the disagreement ceases, a short period of readaptation often appears to be necessary before the person can function normally again.

Studies have demonstrated that chronic pain, which is usually related to long-term illness, is dramatically influenced by social context—for example, people suffer more pain in hospitals where it is expected and tolerated than when they are elsewhere; by attention from family and friends—especially when pain gets concerned sympathy; by habit—one's life-style can come to revolve around pain, in which case the pain may continue even after the illness is cured; and by suggestion—pain often can be "cured" by giving the patient a *placebo,* that is, a sugar pill that he thinks is a medicine. Indeed, pain plays many roles: it signals bodily damage, it obtains love and attention, it can dictate a life-style, it provides a topic of conversation, it relieves boredom, and, under the proper circumstances, it might even serve to win money in a lawsuit. What is more, we sometimes go so far as to seek virtue in pain, through hard work, strenuous exercise, or a strict diet. And many people find mild pain sexually arousing. From all of this you can see that pain is not a simple experience. Like our other sensations, it is elaborated upon and used in conjunction with other aspects of our ongoing psychological experience in order to inform us of what is happening to us and/or to influence the events that are occurring around us.

BOX 2.2

To Live without Pain: A Case History

When you are suffering from a sunburn, a stomach ache, a scraped knee, a sore back, and all the other discomforts that flesh is heir to, it may seem that pain sensitivity is one of the most troublesome of human endowments. However, calm examination of the matter will show you that however unpleasant it is, pain serves a useful purpose when it warns us that something is wrong.

Medical records contain a few case histories of people who have been born without pain sensitivity. In most cases it has not been clear why they felt no pain; the nervous system did not appear to be abnormal. Some of these people, as in the case reported below, lived fairly normal lives and their lack of pain appears to have caused them little difficulty. Indeed, one such person made his living for a time by appearing on the vaudeville stage and letting people stick sterilized pins deep into his skin and muscles. Once he even went so far as to have himself crucified on stage, but a woman fainted when the spike was driven through his hand so he dropped this feature from his act.

Other people who lack pain sensitivity have been less fortunate. They have severely injured themselves or acquired serious diseases, but lacking the pain that would force most of us to seek medical treatment, they neglected their maladies until, in some cases, it was too late to avoid permanent bodily damage or even death.

The following case history, written by Dr. Kenneth R. Magee, is a description of a 56-year-old insurance man who was first examined for an altogether different complaint at the University of Michigan Medical Center in 1957.

During the [examination] . . . it became apparent that he was indifferent to various types of painful stimuli on all parts of his body. The patient stated that this indifference had been present as long as he could remember. There had been no tendency to develop greater appreciation of pain as he grew older. He did not perceive itching and was not ticklish. As a child he could be lifted and pulled by the hair without crying or feeling upset. He could pull hair out of any part of his body without discomfort. On several occasions, after injuring a fingernail, he had peeled off the whole nail without anesthetic and did not experience discomfort. He had noted, for example, that other people who struck their finger with a hammer would cry out with pain; however, he thought they were "sissies" and did not consider it abnormal when he did not react in the same manner. He had received many burns and foreign particles had lodged in his eyes, but he had not felt pain. . . . He had broken his wrist and leg without discomfort. Despite his indifference to pain, the patient stated that he was quite aware of the intensity of painful or thermal stimuli. Therefore, early in life he had learned to a fairly satisfactory degree to avoid situations that would harm him. Consequently, although he had received many injuries, none was mutilating. After injuries were incurred, they healed normally.

Despite the indifference to superficial pain, the patient did complain of headaches. He also noted that a full bladder produced an "uncomfortable" sensation, as did hunger. It was difficult to assess the degree of visceral pain that he experienced for there was always a question as to whether the patient fully understood what was meant by the term "pain." However, headaches, a full bladder, and hunger did produce some sensations of discomfort when no cutaneous* stimuli could be given that were interpreted as unpleasant in any way.

Formal sensory examination disclosed that, at all times, the patient could perceive the difference in intensity of stimuli produced by slight variations in pinprick. It was impossible, however, to give a stimulus that produced dis-

---

*"Cutaneous" means "skin."

comfort. There was no action on the part of the patient (or reaction of his autonomic nervous system) to cutaneous stimuli intense enough to draw blood. Testing of deep pain by squeezing the Achilles tendons or testicles produced no evidence of discomfort. Discrimination of degrees of temperature was also accurate; however, when sufficient heat was applied to burn the patient's skin, he made no movement to withdraw, nor did he show objective or subjective signs of pain. . . .

. . . electrical stimuli [were applied] to the teeth. During a maximum electrical stimulus (50 to 60 microamperes at a frequency of 5,000 cycles per second) applied to several vital teeth, there was no subjective or objective evidence of discomfort to the patient. A skin and a muscle biopsy† were performed without anesthetic. The skin was removed without any sign of discomfort. When the muscle was cut, the patient stated that he experienced a sensation that was "disagreeable," and therefore the surgeon injected local anesthetic. The patient did not think this necessary, stating that the disagreeable sensation was very mild. It was evident, however, that the skin incision produced no discomfort but that cutting the muscle produced some type of unpleasant sensation. Preparations of skin from the biopsy . . . demonstrated normal nerve endings.

The patient's behavioral responses and galvanic skin resistance to sudden electrical shocks were studied. The patient showed no subjective or objective evidence of discomfort to shocks which were very painful to normal subjects.

Psychologic evaluations disclosed that the patient was intelligent (IQ of 111). Extensive psychiatric and psychologic examinations revealed no evidence of psychopathology.

The patient was examined at frequent intervals until he died unexpectedly, apparently of heart failure, at the age of 58.‡

† A biopsy is a microscopic examination of pieces of tissue that are cut from the body.
‡ K. R. MAGEE, Congenital indifference to pain. *The Archives of Neurology*, 1963, **9**, 635–640.

Part 3   *THE THIRD SENSORY SYSTEM, VISION*

All animals, even the most primitive one-celled organisms, are sensitive to light. All animals have some biochemical means of detecting bright light and darkness so that they can avoid one or the other. Higher animals have not only this basic ability but they have *eyes* which form images of distant objects on special light-sensitive cells so that information about the shape, size, and sometimes the color of these objects can be obtained before coming into physical contact with them. This remarkable ability is called vision. In human beings it is, after kinesthesis, the most important sensory system, and vision provides the information about the world that we are most aware of and that we pay the most attention to.

Vision: Structure of the Eye

A great deal is known about the human eye. Its structure is shown in Figure 2.4. Constructed something like a round camera, its shape is maintained by a rather firm membrane around the outside and by a liquid on the inside. Light is kept from coming in the wrong places by a dark outer coat and is admitted through a series of transparent coverings over the hole in the front of the eye. The first of these transparent coverings, the *cornea*, is a clear membrane that serves to protect the inner parts of the eye. If you ask a tolerant friend who wears contact lenses to let you look closely at his eye, you will see that his lens floats on the surface of his cornea.

Light entering through the cornea passes next through the *pupil*, the hole surrounded by the colored *iris*. The iris is a muscle that opens or closes to regulate the amount of light that enters the eye. In fact, you can watch the

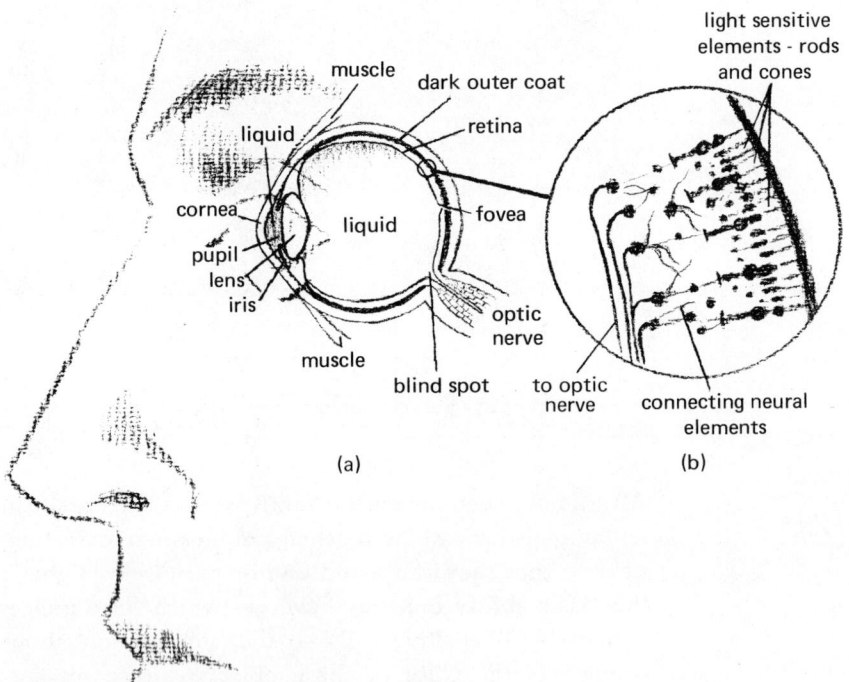

FIG. 2.4   *The structure of the eye.*

iris work by having a friend close his eye for a minute and then open it in the presence of fairly bright light; you will be able to see the iris quickly close as it cuts down the amount of light entering your friend's eye.

Immediately behind the iris is the *lens*, which operates much like the lens in a camera in that it serves to focus the light that goes through it. The lens is composed of transparent cells and is surrounded by muscles. When these muscles relax or contract they compress or stretch the lens, thereby making it thicker or thinner at its center. These changes in the shape of the lens, called *accommodation*, permit light from sources that are both near or far to be focused—that is, to produce a clear image—on the back of the eyeball. If you have ever experimented with glass lenses, you know that if you focus the image of, say, a candle, on a piece of paper with a lens and then move the candle closer to the lens you have to either alter the distance of the paper from the lens or you have to leave the paper where it is and use a different lens in order to get a clear image. The eye is designed to use the second solution. Because the back of the eye is a fixed distance from the lens, the eye adjusts to changes in the distance of the light source by changing the thickness, and hence the focusing properties, of the lens.

The visual apparatus we have been discussing thus far exists solely to put clear, well-focused images of the light source on the *retina*. The retina consists of a sheet of light-sensitive neural elements that lines the back of the eyeball. The retina in each of your eyes contains about one hundred and thirty million small neural elements that are most densely packed near the center (the *fovea*) where the image is focused; vision is most sensitive in this center area of the retina. Each element reacts to various components of the image. Information about the image is then transmitted from these elements through a series of connecting elements to the brain.

One surprising and inexplicable characteristic of the construction of the retina is that instead of having its light-sensitive elements facing the incoming light, they face the back of the eyeball (see Fig. 2.4). Moreover, the neural elements to which the light-sensitive elements connect form a mat that lies between the sensory elements and the entering light. This means that light must go through all these neural elements in order to reach the light-sensitive elements that face the other way. At first it seems that this cumbersome procedure should make the eye very inefficient, yet quite the opposite is true. Under the proper circumstances, the eye can detect exceedingly low levels of light. Some scientists have estimated that, were the night sufficiently dark, you could see a lighted match seventeen miles away.

Information received by the light-sensitive elements is conveyed through

FIG. 2.5 *Demonstration of your blind spot. Close your left eye and stare directly at the round spot with your right eye. Then move the book slowly toward and away from you. When the rabbit disappears, its image is falling on your blind spot.*

the connective elements to the *optic nerve* and thence to the brain. The optic nerve is a cable of neural elements, the components of which connect to the cells throughout the retina, and then all come together at one spot where they go out through the back of the eyeball and on back to the brain. This spot has no light-sensitive elements and, consequently, you are blind there. If you follow the instructions in Figure 2.5, you can demonstrate the existence of your *blind spot.*

Our eyes are constantly moving—not so much as in the novelist's phrase, "His eyes darted about the room!" but in very small side-to-side movements. Such movement is called *physiological nystagmus,* and it is of fundamental importance to vision. Nystagmus causes the image coming through the lens to move rapidly back and forth across the retina. As was the case with the backward construction of the retina, one might think that the efforts of the lens to produce a focused image would be thwarted by nystagmus and that vision would be impaired. Again one would be wrong. It is possible, using some rather sophisticated scientific machinery, to compensate for the eye's nystagmus and thereby to project an image that moves along with the eye as it moves. This means that the image is stabilized. That is, it no longer sweeps back and forth across the retina but remains in one place. Under these circumstances the image fades and the owner of the eye can no longer see it. Thus nystagmus, far from interfering with vision, plays a vital role in our ability to see. One hypothesis about the function of nystagmus is that movements of an image on the retina permit the retina's neural elements to "share the work," so to speak, and thereby maintain a higher level of efficiency and sensitivity. Curiously enough, physiological measures show that even when a person no longer reports seeing a stabilized image, the neural elements are still reacting to its presence.

The Retina's Neural Elements

The light-sensitive elements of the retina have two functions: first, to detect the movement and shapes of images, and second, to detect the color of images.

The research on the role of retinal elements in movement and shape detection is new and incomplete and has been done on animals rather than people, but I will try to give you some idea of the general findings thus far on the assumption that they also hold for human beings. First, the retinal elements are highly interconnected with one another, which permits them to act together in what I will call *units,* for want of a better term. Some of these units transmit information to the brain about the straight edges of images, some about curved edges, and some about dark portions of images rather than about light portions. Some units detect only movement, some are sensitive to movement only in a specific direction, and some react only to a decrease or an increase in the general amount of light coming into the eye.

What is more, readings of the amount of electrical activity in various parts of the brain show that certain parts of the brain are associated with vision and that subparts of these larger parts receive the information from specific types of retinal units. Thus, a specified part of the brain will show activity when a light on the retina dims, but not when the edge of an image passes across the retina. Conversely, some other part of the brain will register information about edges but not about dimming.

There are two kinds of retinal elements that react to the composition of the light that makes up images. The first, called *rods,* are sensitive to the brightness of the light but not its color. If these were the only elements you had, the world would always appear as it does in a black and white movie.

The second kind of elements, called *cones,* are sensitive to the wavelength of light, which we experience as color (provided the wavelength falls between approximately 400 and 700 nanometers, the only range of electromagnetic energy that the human eye can see). There are three kinds of cones. The first, primarily sensitive to wavelengths in the 430 nm range, yield the sensation of blue. The second, primarily sensitive around 540 nm, yield the sensation of green. And the third, primarily sensitive around 575 nm, yield the sensation

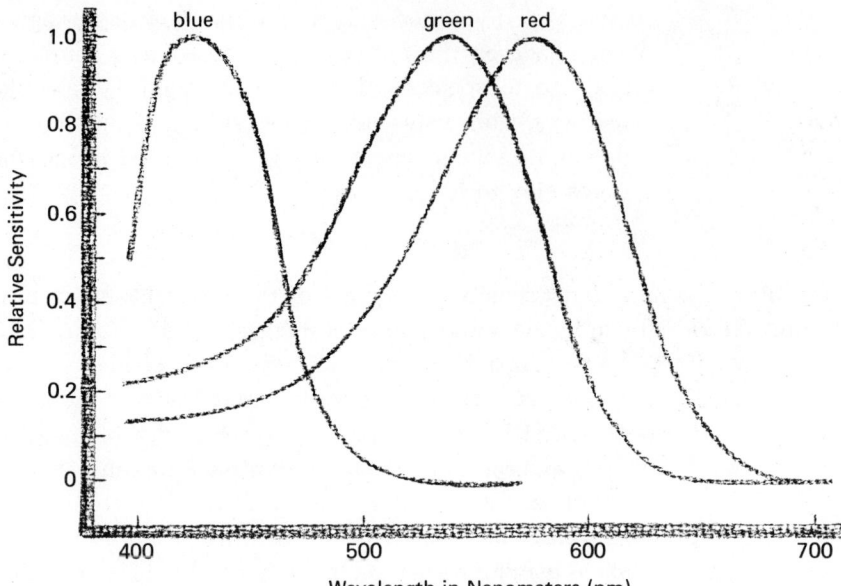

FIG. 2.6   *Relative sensitivity of each of the three kinds of cones to various wavelengths of light.*

of red. As you can see in Figure 2.6, there is a good deal of overlap in the ranges of sensitivity of these three kinds of cones. Therefore, whatever the color of an image, it usually stimulates more than one kind of cone. For example, if the image is a fairly pure red, it will primarily stimulate the third kind of cone, but it also stimulates the other kinds to some degree. If the image color is a less pure red, for example, if it contains some green and therefore is located somewhere in the middle of the range, it will stimulate the red cones less and the green more. Apparently it is the degree to which each kind of cone is stimulated by the color of an image that tells the brain what color the image is.

There is also evidence to indicate that the three kinds of cones and their higher neural connections somehow are interrelated so that they are associated with the perception of certain pairs of colors. Each pair of colors red-green, blue-yellow, and black-white, are known as *complementary colors,* that is, pairs of colors which when mixed together produce grey. You can convince yourself of this possible neurological linking of complementary colors by observing *after-images,* experiences with which you probably are quite familiar. Stare straight at the back cover of this book for about a minute and then look at a light-colored wall. This particular after-image is called a *negative after-image* because each color is the complement of the original color in the picture.

This suggests that prolonged staring at each color in the picture has in some way created a fatigue or imbalance of the pair of neural elements that are sensitive to that particular color. Thus, when you look at a neutral surface, the antagonistic, or opposite, member of the pair is free to function without the interference of the fatigued element. The result is that the neutral surface of the wall now is capable of stimulating a *subjective color*, a color that is not real but that is a product of the way in which your color-sensitive visual system works.

Cones require quite a bit of light in order to function; as illumination decreases they cease to work. Rods, however, are sensitive to very low levels of illumination. This is why things look black and grey when you walk around the house at night with all the lights out; the cones are not functioning and the rods are insensitive to color.

The degree of sensitivity of the rods and cones depends on how much light they have been exposed to just previously. For example, if you have been reading late at night and you turn out the light and immediately try to walk through the darkened room, you are likely to bump into something. If you wait in the dark for a few minutes, however, your rods will begin to adjust to the decreased light level, a process known as *dark adaptation*, and you'll become better able to see and proceed safely to bed. Similarly, going from a lighted lobby into a dark theater may result in your accidently sitting on someone's lap unless you pause shortly in the dark before searching for a seat. You may also notice that upon coming out of a dark theater into bright sunlight you have some difficulty seeing until your eyes adapt to the increased light level, a process known as *light adaptation*. While complete dark adaptation takes as long as thirty minutes, light adaptation is usually much more rapid, being complete after approximately fifteen minutes.

Seeing: An Active Process

Having spent so much time on the mechanical details of the eye, let us turn to the psychological aspects. Seeing is an active process that involves integration of multiple kinds of information into a unified experience. This information comes from the current visual image, from past memories, from assumptions about the structure of the visual world, and so forth. For the most part the integration appears to occur in the brain rather than in the eye itself; the brain merely uses the retinal information as one important source among many.

Seeing: Objects

In the abstract, a physical object can be described as a space that has edges and surfaces. These contours can be either ill defined, like a jet of steam from a tea kettle, or well defined, like the edge of a table. In either case they are

Symphony No. 40 In G Minor

FIG. 2.7   *When you focus your attention on the sheet of music, the spot becomes a hole through which you see the page in the background. When you focus on the spot, the music becomes the background.*

sufficient to delineate the object and to set it off as a separate thing that stands out as a *figure* against a *background*. A figure is defined as being in front of the background, but this is merely a way of signifying what part of the environment is being attended to. For example, in Figure 2.7, if you think of the white spot as a ball, it is a figure and the surrounding sheet of music is background. But if you think of the spot as a hole, the sheet of music becomes the figure and the spot is background. In short, as we move the focus of our visual attention, different aspects of the visual field become salient and others cease to be so. The salient object is called figure and the rest is background.

Some images are more readily perceived as unitary and objectlike than others. The sets of lines in Figure 2.8 provide examples. In (a) similar elements are seen as being a unit, particularly if they are near one another (that is, units of ‖). But making the elements approximate the shape of a common geometric figure, as in (b), changes which elements seem to be related to each other (that is, units of ⌐⌐). If alternate elements in (b), that is, elements 1, 3, and 5, were to suddenly start vibrating in unison, these elements would be seen as one unit; the unified movement would dominate the geometrical configuration and

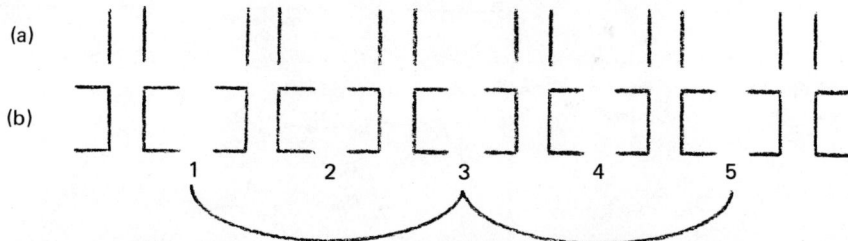

FIG. 2.8   *Some conditions that promote perception of unitary form: (a) similarity and proximity to one another, (b) approximation to geometric shapes.*

make the forms appear as a related unit of rectangles. We see then that there is a hierarchy of determinants of "objectness" for simple patterns:

Elements that *move in unison* are considered a unit.

Elements whose configurations *approximate a simple geometrical shape* are seen as a unit if the subparts do not move.

Elements that are *close together* (are in proximity) are seen as units if the movement or geometrical considerations are not operative.

Elements that are *similar* are seen as related in lieu of the other considerations.

It is reasonable to think that these rules for simple patterns also operate on more complex visual images and that they are the basic rules by which an image on the retina begins to be perceived as an object.

Seeing:
Simple Events

Objects are not the only things we perceive. Interactions among objects are also important and these we shall call *events*. Of course, complex events like an election or a war are not examples of perception in the sense that we are using the term. However, there are simple events that we perceive quite readily and that we apparently do not have to think about to understand. Primary among these is cause and effect. For research purposes cause and effect can be studied by using the machine illustrated in Figure 2.9. It is called a "Michotte machine" after Professor A. Michotte, who performed the experiments that I am going to describe. When the disc rotates behind a screen, you see only two colored rectangles in the slot. Depending upon how the lines are drawn on the disc, the rectangles can be made to appear to move back and forth in the slot in a variety of patterns and speeds. Professor Michotte found that if rectangle A appeared to rush across and touch rectangle B and then both of them moved on to the end of the slot, people reported that A had *pushed* B. If A rushed and touched B and then A slowed down while B rushed to the end of the slot, people reported that A had *hit* B. If A touched B and stopped and then there was a pause before B moved on, people reported

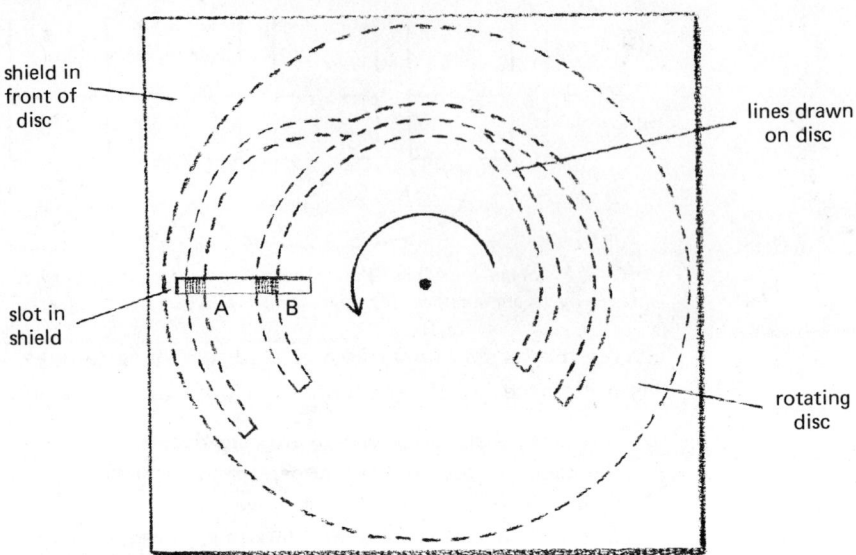

FIG. 2.9   The "Michotte machine." When the hidden disc rotates, the rectangles in the slot appear to move back and forth from one side to the other.

that A had *launched* B. Note that in all cases the energy from A seems to the observer to have been transmitted in some manner to B. This, of course, is the usual common sense notion of cause and effect.

Most people who see these events on the Michotte machine report that their interpretations of what happened are immediate and compelling. These and related experiments suggest that when simple interactions between objects can be interpreted as transfer of energy from one to the other, the interactions are ordinarily perceived as cause and effect.

Seeing:
Object Constancy

Sometimes the most important psychological phenomena are the most easily overlooked because they are taken for granted. One of these is the fact that objects can undergo very pronounced perceptual transformations and still be recognized as the same stable objects. This phenomenon, called *object constancy,* has three aspects: color constancy, size constancy, and shape constancy.

Color constancy   If someone sneaked into your bedroom and illuminated it entirely with green light, you would still know it was your bedroom when you walked in, even though the colors of the image on your retina would be quite abnormal. After a few moments in the room yellow objects might look orange, white things purple, blue things violet, and green things pale purple, grayish, or green; yet you would be quite sure it was your bedroom.

Color constancy is a common phenomenon. Every time you go into different illuminations, say from outdoors into a house or from one room to another, the lighting is different. This means that the colors reflected by, say, your clothes change with each change in illumination. Nonetheless, you do not perceive the changes as constituting a change in the color of your clothes; rather, you perceive an overall change in illumination.

Size constancy   The second kind of transformation that objects frequently undergo is that their distances from you change as you and they move around. This means that the sizes of their images on your retina change a good deal. Perform the simple experiment illustrated in Figure 2.10. Use your thumb and index finger like a pair of calipers and, closing one eye, "measure" the height of someone who is standing at the other end of the room. Then, keeping your arm, fingers, and eye just as they are, ask the person to walk toward you. As he does so, his image on your retina will rapidly exceed your earlier "measure" of his height.

As this experiment demonstrates, every increase or decrease in the distance between you and some rigid object changes the size of its image on your retina. However, you do not perceive these changes as changes in the size of the object. Rather, you interpret the changes for what they are, changes in distance. Usually, however, you are unaware of any kind of change in your visual experience; you merely see the object moving around in a three-dimensional world.

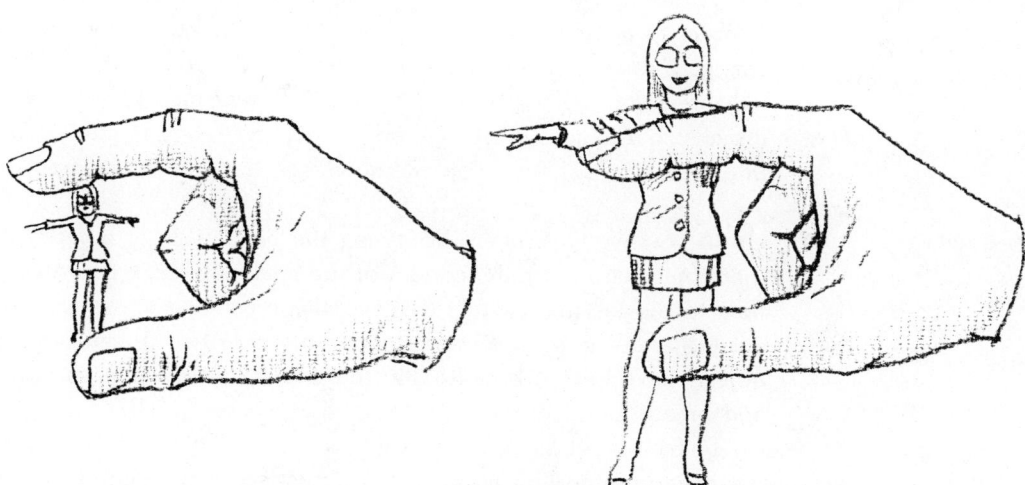

FIG. 2.10   *How to use your fingers to demonstrate changes in retinal image size as a person walks toward you.*

FIG. 2.11 The image of a rectangular table top actually is a trapezoid on the retina, and yet we see it as a rectangle.

Shape constancy The third transformation that objects undergo is change in orientation. For example, if you walk around the room while looking at the top of a table, the image on your retina changes greatly. Even so, you do not perceive each change in shape as a differently shaped table. This phenomenon is called shape constancy. However, if I merely presented a line drawing of the top of the table in Figure 2.11, you would call the shape a trapezoid and never even entertain the notion that it is the representation of a rectangular table top viewed from one end. To comprehend the profundity of this seemingly trivial ability of yours, hold a pencil in front of your eyes, rotate it end to end, and imagine the changing shape of the pencil's two-dimensional image on your retina.

Note that in all three of these examples of object constancy, your ability to maintain constancy is dependent upon your knowing about the situation. You had to know about the green light to correct for it in color constancy; you had to know that the person couldn't shrink or grow as he moved around in order to maintain size constancy; and you had to know how an object was changing in its orientation to your eye in order to maintain shape constancy. All three of these phenomena go beyond mere passive reception of the two-dimensional images of objects on your retina. They require active perceptual interpretation in light of other knowledge that you have about the situation.

Seeing:
Space Perception

Up to now we have been discussing the perception of objects, but it is clear that objects are not independent of the space in which they exist. Let us turn now to the fascinating fact that we all perceive space as three-dimensional, even though the images on our retina are only two-dimensional. That is, real objects have height, breadth, and depth, but retinal images have only height and breadth.

To facilitate this discussion let us first clarify the fact that there are two particularly important points for you in space. One point is you and the other is the place at which your gaze is *fixated*, that is, the object or place at which you are looking. These two points essentially define the framework against which all objects, distances, and spatial locations are judged. Of course, you don't have to use both eyes to see three-dimensionality. The cues used when you look with only one eye (*monocular*) are supplemented by those that depend on both eyes (*binocular*); we will discuss the two classes of cues separately.

Monocular cues for depth   Imagine that you are a movie camera sitting on the floor. You have only one eye and you record all you see as a two-dimensional image on your movie film. Now, imagine that I roll a golf ball toward you and that you photograph this situation, changing your lens to keep the ball in focus at all times. Figure 2.12 shows frames from your film that show what happens to the image of the ball.

FIG. 2.12   *How a camera would record a ball rolling toward it across a carpet. Note how the textures become better defined as the ball approaches. (Courtesy Paul Kopelman.)*

The image of the ball gets larger as the ball approaches the camera.

The image moves from near the top of the picture to the bottom.

The image covers part of the texture of the floor as it expands and as it descends from the top to the bottom of the picture.

The texture of the surface of the ball becomes clearer.

You know how much you had to change the lens in order to keep the ball in focus.

Because you keep the ball in focus, the foreground comes into focus as the ball moves toward you and the background goes out of focus.

In short, there is a variety of changes in the two-dimensional image; each change aids in making inferences about the nature of the three-dimensional space in which the ball moved.

Artists have perfected the use of monocular cues for depth in order to give their two-dimensional paintings a three-dimensional realism. Some of these cues are illustrated in Figure 2.13, a reproduction of the painting "Scene in Venice: The Piazzetta" by Antonio Canaletto. If you look at the diagram of the painting, you can identify where the artist used some of the depth cues to produce the illusion of three-dimensional space on a two-dimensional surface.

(A) The nun and the shack in the foreground illustrate the cue of *partial overlap;* nearer objects partially conceal those further away from the viewer.

(B) *Linear perspective* is illustrated by the diminished size of the further portions of the building.

(C) *Highlights* and . . .

(D) *Shadows* combine to indicate the source of the light, probably a late afternoon sun, low on the left. There are two kinds of shadows, the first, *attached* shadow (D_1), is on that part of the object that does not receive direct light from the light source. The second kind of shadow, *cast* shadow (D_2), is the one that we ordinarily think of as beginning at our feet and stretching along the ground. The combination of highlights, attached shadow, and cast shadow gives objects a good deal of their texture and thereby a good deal of their three-dimensionality.

(E) *Detail perspective* is illustrated by the decreased distinctiveness of detail as distances from the viewer increase. You can see much of the fancy stonework on the front of the building at the right, but little or no detail on the twin-domed building at the left. A surface that stretches away from the viewer presents a similar gradient of detail. Look at the floor close to your feet. Note that the texture of the carpet, the boards, or the square tiles is clear and large. Then move your gaze slowly along the floor toward the far wall. Notice that there is a regular, orderly change in the distinctiveness of the texture of the floor. This change in the *texture gradient,* as it is called, is an important cue to distance.

FIG. 2.13 *An artist's use of depth cues to produce the illusion of three-dimensionality. (Antonio Canaletto's "Scene in Venice: The Piazzetta," Metropolitan Museum of Art, Kennedy Fund, 1910.)*

(F) *Aerial perspective* is the last cue illustrated by the painting. This means that because of moisture, dust, and so on, in the air, there is a slight change in the color of distant objects. In normal sunlight they tend to be bluish grey, like distant mountains. In the original color diversion of this painting, the artist used this cue on the more distant domes on the left; they appear bluer than the dome on the right.

One cue that is not illustrated by this painting is that as one focuses on an object in the medium or far distance, objects that are closer to the eye are *blurred*. You probably have seen pictures that have been taken through the leaves of a tree. The cow grazing in the distant field is in focus, but the leaves close to the camera are very blurred. This is a common cue for near objects, but you seldom notice it explicitly.

All of these are distance cues that an artist can reproduce on a static two-dimensional canvas that hangs on the wall. There are other cues, however, that are best reproduced by a movie camera because they involve changes in the retinal image that result from the object or the viewer moving around. The most important of these is *size-distance invariance*, which is essentially the same mechanism as size constancy. If the shape of an object is rigid and its retinal image changes in size, then this must mean that the object has moved either away or toward you. This is illustrated in Figure 2.14. There are three factors involved: The size of the retinal image, the real size of the object, and the distance the object is from you. Knowledge of any two of the three factors reveals the value of the third. Because the retina is part of you, you always know the size of the retinal image of an object. This, plus knowledge of the real size of the object, permits inference of the distance of the object from you. By the same token, knowledge of the retinal image size and knowledge of the distance of the object from you tells you the size of the object.

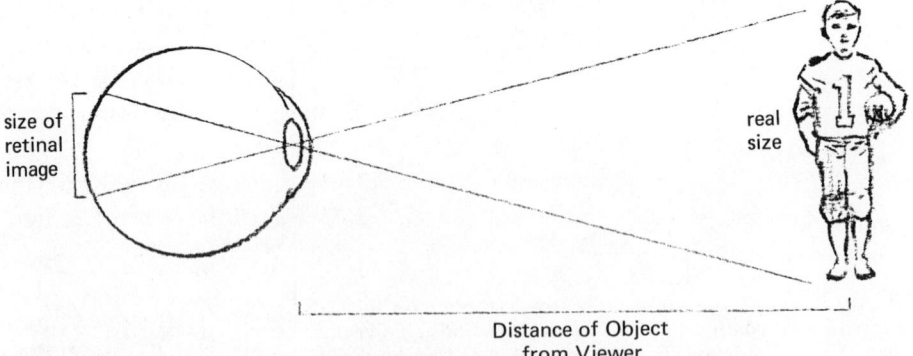

FIG. 2.14   *The three components of size-distance variance: size of retinal image, the object's real size, and the distance of the object from the viewer.*

A less important movement-oriented monocular cue is *monocular movement parallax*—different rates of movement of different objects in the visual field are a cue to which object is further from you. Imagine two cars passing in front of you from right to left at 25 miles an hour. The path of one car passes 50 feet in front of you and the other two miles away from you. The image of the nearer car will have come and gone long before the further car has moved very far across your field of vision.

Binocular cues for depth   Most of us have two eyes rather than just one, and we take advantage of the overlap in what the two eyes see. This permits us to make some rather subtle judgments about three-dimensionality and where objects are located in space.

When an object is fairly far from you, say about 30 feet away, your eyes point straight ahead at the object and the image in each eye falls right in the center of the retina where vision is most sensitive. As the object moves closer, the eyes turn toward each other; that is, they *converge* in order to keep the image in the center of each retina. The tension in the muscles that control this movement of the eyes provides information about the degree of convergence required to keep the images properly located on the retinas. This in turn is used as information about the distance of the object.

There is a second binocular depth cue which is extremely interesting because, until it is demonstrated, most people don't know that it exists. Remember that I said at the beginning of this discussion that three-dimensionality is judged relative to two points in the visual field, you and the place where your eyes are fixated. Because your eyes are about two inches apart, each receives a slightly different image. This difference is called *binocular disparity* and is a cue for the distance of objects. The existence of different images on each of the retinas is easy to see—hold your pencil up in front of you and then fixate on the wall beyond. The pencil will have a double image, one for each eye, and each image is slightly different from the other. If you continue to fixate on the wall and alternately close one eye and then the other, you can make the pencil appear to jump from side to side. These different images in the two eyes provide subtle but reliable information about whether an object lies between you and the place where you are fixating or beyond the point where you are fixating.

The following simple experiment demonstrates how you use binocular disparity as a cue for distance. Hold up two pencils, or your fingers, as illustrated in Figure 2.15. With both eyes open, fixate on B and notice that A appears double. Then without changing your fixation close your right eye and notice

FIG. 2.15 *How to hold the two pencils for the crossed and uncrossed images experiment described in the text.*

on which side of B the image of A appears to be. Now open your right eye, close the left, and again notice the location of A's image. If you did it correctly, you found that A's image always was on the side of B that was opposite the eye you had open. These images are called *crossed images*. In the course of normal vision all objects that lie between you and the point of fixation produce double images that are crossed images.

Now, perform the same experiment again, but this time fixate on A and note the location of the image of B. By alternately closing your eyes you should find that B's image is on the same side of A as the eye with which you are looking. These images are *uncrossed images*. In normal circumstances all objects beyond the fixation point produce uncrossed images. Even though you are seldom aware of the double images in your vision, your brain uses the information about whether they are crossed or uncrossed to make judgments concerning the locations of objects in space relative to you and your fixation point.

This completes our list of cues, or information sources, for three-dimensionality. It is important to realize when looking at this diverse array of cues that you seldom encounter a situation in which only one is available. Rather, most situations are sufficiently complex to provide a large number of the cues, and there is never any problem of being able to correctly perceive the three-dimensional properties of objects or their locations in space. In fact, the monocular cues are themselves sufficient for fairly accurate depth perception. People with only one eye function pretty well, although they may have some difficulty playing badminton, tennis, and the like. These games require quick, accurate perception of an object's location in three-dimensional space, and having two eyes is an advantage. In general, however, the monocular person does quite well.

Seeing:
The Origins
of Depth Perception

There has been a long controversy about whether the perception of three-dimensionality is an innate (inborn) ability of animals or whether it must be totally learned through experience with a three-dimensional world. At the moment, general opinion favors the hypothesis that it is primarily innate. One reason for this opinion is the result of the following experiment.

Figure 2.16 shows the "visual cliff." An infant is placed on the center board where he can look either at the "shallow" side and see the checkered pattern directly under the sheet of strong glass or at the "deep" side where the pattern is three feet or so below the glass. Then the child's mother goes to one side of the table or the other and calls him. If the child cannot perceive three-dimensionality, he is likely to crawl to his mother no matter what side of the table she is on. If he can perceive three-dimensionality, he is likely to be extremely hesitant about crawling out on the glass above the deep side. It is found that children may reach over and pat the glass, but they normally do not go out onto the deep side. They show no hesitancy about the shallow side.

These results are suspect because the children must be at least six months old before they can crawl well enough to be used in the experiment, and it is possible that they already have learned three-dimensionality while learning to crawl. Because younger children cannot crawl, one is stuck with the impossibility of testing very young children to see if three-dimensionality is innate or not. One alternative is to experiment with varieties of animals that can see and walk almost from the moment they are born. For example, when newly hatched chicks are placed on the center board, they *never* go to the deep side. The same is true of kids, lambs, and kittens. White rats, which are nocturnal

glass only

glass over
patterned surface

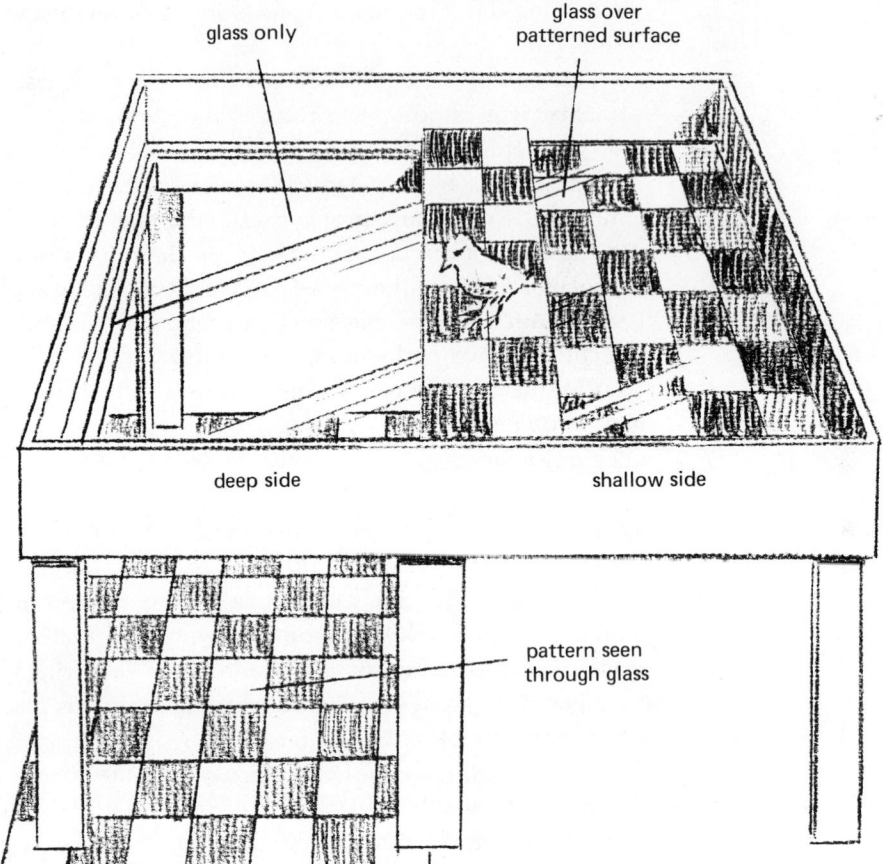

deep side   shallow side

pattern seen
through glass

FIG. 2.16   The "visual cliff" used to test whether the perception of three-dimensionality is an innate ability.

animals and often depend on their long whiskers for information, will walk on the deep side if their whiskers touch the glass; if you clip their whiskers short, the rats have to depend on their vision and they won't go on the deep side. In short, most animals avoid the deep side of the visual cliff, even if they are newly born and inexperienced with a three-dimensional world. This strongly suggests, but does not prove, that three-dimensional perception is innate and that one does not have to depend upon experience in the three-dimensional world in order to develop it. That is, most animals probably are born with the ability to infer three-dimensionality from two-dimensional retinal images.

BOX 2.3

A Blind Man Sees: The Case History of S. B.

Have you ever wondered what it would be like to be blind from the time you were born until you were an adult and then, through some surgical miracle, gain the ability to see? The following is a description of what happened to a man who, after having been almost completely blind (he could barely discriminate light and dark) since the age of ten months, had his vision restored surgically at the age of fifty-two. This description was written by a psychologist, Professor R. L. Gregory, who is in charge of the Perception Laboratory in the Psychology Department at Cambridge University in England.

This case, a man of fifty-two, whom we may call S. B., was when blind an active and intelligent man. He would go for cycle rides, with a friend holding his shoulder to guide him; he would often dispense with the usual white stick, sometimes walking into parked cars or vans and hurting himself as a result. He liked making things, with simple tools in a shed in his garden. All his life he tried to picture the world of sight: He would wash his brother-in-law's car, imagining its shape as vividly as he could. He longed for the day when he might see, though his eyes had been given up as hopeless, so that no surgeon would risk wasting a donated cornea. Finally the attempt was made, and it was successful. But though the operation was a success, the story ends in tragedy.

When the bandages were first removed from his eyes, so that he was no longer blind, he heard the voice of the surgeon. He turned to the voice, and saw nothing but a blur. He realised that this must be a face, because of the voice, but he could not see it. He did not suddenly see the world of objects as we do when we open our eyes.

But within a few days he could use his eyes to good effect. He could walk along the hospital corridors without recourse to touch; he could even tell the time from a large wall clock, having all his life carried a pocket watch having no glass, so that he could feel the time from its hands. He would get up at dawn, and watch from his windows the cars and lorries pass by. He was delighted with his progress, which was extremely rapid.

When he left the hospital, we took him to London and showed him many things he never knew from touch, but he became curiously dispirited. At the zoo he was able to name most of the animals correctly, having stroked pet animals, and enquired as to how other animals differed from the cats and dogs he knew by touch. He was also of course familiar with toys and models. He certainly used his previous knowledge from touch, and reports from sighted people to help him name objects by sight, which he did largely by seeking their characteristic features.

We tried to discover what his visual world was like by asking him questions and giving him various simple perceptual tests. While still in the hospital, before he became depressed, he was most careful with his judgments and his answers. We found that his perception of distance was peculiar. He thought he would be able to touch the ground below his window with his feet if he lowered himself by his hands, but the window was in fact thirty or forty feet above the ground. On the other hand, he could judge distances and sizes quite accurately provided he already knew the objects by touch. Although his perception was demonstrably peculiar, he seldom expressed surprise at anything he saw. He drew an elephant before we showed him one at the zoo [the drawing looked like a very tall spider—Ed.], but upon seeing it he said immediately: "There's an elephant," and said it looked much as he expected it would. On one object he did show real surprise, and this was an object he could not have known by touch—the moon. A few days after the operation, he saw what he took to be a reflection in a window (he was for the rest of his life fascinated by reflections in mirrors and would spend hours sitting before a mirror in his local public house, watching people), but this time what he saw was not a reflection, but the quarter moon. He asked the Matron what it was, and when she told him, he said he thought it would look like a quarter piece of cake!

S. B. never learned to read by sight (he read Braille, having been taught it at the blind school) but we found that he could recognise block capital letters, and numbers, by sight without any special training. This surprised us greatly. It turned out that he had been taught upper case, though not lower case, letters at the blind school. They were given raised letters on wooden blocks, which were learned by touch. Although he read upper case letters immediately by sight, it took him a long time to learn lower case letters, and he never managed to read more than simple words. Now this finding that he could immediately read letters visually which he had already learned by touch, showed very clearly that he was able to use his previous touch experience for his new-found vision. This is interesting to the psychologist, for it indicates that the brain is not so departmentalised as is sometimes thought. But it makes any finding of these cases difficult or impossible to apply to the normal case of a human infant coming to see. The blind adult knows a great deal about the world of objects through touch and hearsay; he can use some of this information to help him identify objects from the slightest cues. He also has to come to accept and trust his new sense, which means giving up the habits of many years. His case is really quite unlike that of the child's.

We saw in a dramatic form the difficulty that S. B. had in trusting and coming to use his vision whenever he had to cross the road. Before the operations, he was undaunted by traffic. He would cross alone, holding his arm or his stick stubbornly before him, when the traffic would subside as the waters before Christ. But after the operation, it took two of us on either side to force him across a road; he was terrified as never before in his life.

When he was just out of the hospital, . . . he would sometimes prefer to use touch alone, when identifying objects. We showed him a simple lathe (a tool he had wished he could use) and he was very excited. We showed it to him first in a glass case, at the Science Museum in London, and then we opened the case. With the case closed, he was quite unable to say anything about it, except that the nearest part might be a handle (which it was—the traverse feed handle), but when he was allowed to touch it, he closed his eyes and placed his hand on it when he immediately said with assurance that it was a handle. He ran his hands eagerly over the rest of the lathe, with his eyes tight shut for a minute or so; then he stood back a little, and opening his eyes and staring at it he said: "Now that I've felt it I can see."

[The tragic end to this case is that as time went on, S. B. became increasingly unhappy and physically ill.] He found the world drab, and was upset by flaking paint and blemishes on things. He liked bright colours, but became depressed when the light faded. His depressions became marked, and general. He gradually gave up active living, and three years later he died.

Depression in people recovering sight after many years of blindness seems to be a common feature of [such] cases. Its cause is probably complex, but in part it seems to be a realisation of what they have missed—not only visual experience, but opportunities to do things denied them during the years of blindness. Some of the cases revert very soon to living without light, making no attempt to see. S. B. would often not trouble to turn on the light in the evening, but would sit in darkness.

From *Eye and Brain* by R. L. GREGORY. © R. L. Gregory 1966. Used with permission of McGraw-Hill Book Company and Weidenfeld (Publishers) Ltd.

Part 4   *THE FOURTH SENSORY SYSTEM, AUDITION*

Now we turn to the sense that is receptive to patterns of sound. Passive reception is called *audition* and active reception is called *hearing*.

Audition: Physical Properties of the Environment

The physical event that we know as sound is the vibration of molecules of air. For example, when you talk over a telephone, your voice causes molecules in the air to vibrate. These vibrating molecules cause the diaphragm in the mouthpiece of the telephone to vibrate. These vibration patterns are then converted to electrical impulses by a small electromagnet behind the diaphragm and your message is sent to the receiver at the other end of the line. Then, at the receiving end, another electromagnet causes the receiver's diaphragm to vibrate, which, in turn, sets the air molecules in vibration and allows the person holding the receiver to hear your message.

Since sound is essentially the vibration of air molecules, many people wonder why they can't feel it as they do a breeze. Perhaps the following analogy, adapted from Dr. Hallowell Davis, will help. Imagine that you are standing beside the pope on a balcony overlooking a tightly packed crowd of people in St. Peter's Square on Easter morning. Across the front of the crowd a cordon of police, locked arm in arm, keeps the people back from the balcony. However, the police are themselves fascinated and awed by the appearance of the pope at the window, and they forget their job from time to time. When they forget, their line becomes slack and is pressed forward by the crowd. This means that the density of the crowd is reduced a bit. But when the police remember their job, they tighten their line and press against the front of the crowd. The people in the front press against those behind them, who in turn press against the people behind them, and so on. In a few minutes, though, the police again forget, the cordon slackens, and the front of the crowd relaxes and moves forward. Then the police remember, tighten the cordon again, and on and on.

From the balcony you would see ripples or waves of contraction and expansion running through the crowd as a result of the alternating tightening and slackening of the police cordon. In general, each member of the crowd will never have moved more than a couple of feet or so. But the waves will still move through the whole crowd.

The individual people in the crowd are analogous to individual molecules in the air. The police cordon is analogous to the diaphragm in the telephone receiver. The waves of expansion and contraction caused by the people pushing each other together and moving away are analogous to the movement of a sound through the air. A breeze, by contrast, would be analogous to the police forcing the whole crowd out of the square. That is, the molecules would all move greatly and in one direction at once rather than in small amounts and in the wave patterns I've just described.

Audition: Structure of the Ear

Let us get back to audition and hearing. Figure 2.17 shows the major anatomical aspects of the ear. The *pinna* is the largest, and actually the least functional, part. Contrary to popular opinion, the human pinna does not do much in the way of "scooping in sounds" as it does in many other animals; perhaps its major service is to hold your glasses in place.

Behind the pinna is the *external canal*, which is a tube leading back into the head. At the end of the canal is a membrane of skin, the *eardrum*. Directly

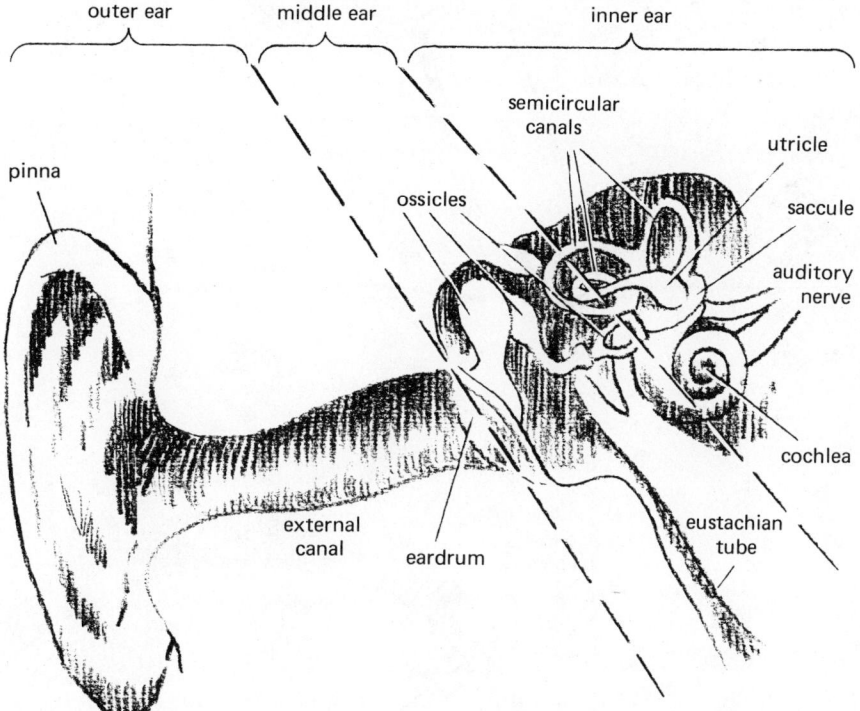

FIG. 2.17   The structure of the ear.

behind the eardrum is a small air-filled chamber called the *middle ear*. This chamber contains three small bones, the *ossicles,* which form a bridge from the eardrum on one side to another membrane, called the *oval window,* on the other side. The function of the ossicles is to mechanically transmit the movement of the eardrum to the oval window.

At the bottom of the middle ear chamber is a small tube, the *eustachian tube,* that leads into the throat. This tube serves to equalize air pressure between the middle ear and the outside world.

The oval window leads to the *inner ear* or *cochlea*. If you took a tube of paper shaped like the one in (a) in Figure 2.18 and rolled it up, starting at the wide end and making 2 ¾ rolls, you would have something that is roughly analogous to the shape of the cochlea—like a small snail shell.

If you looked into an exposed, open end of the cochlea, it would look like (b) in Figure 2.18. The oval window from the middle ear opens into chamber A. The outside of chamber A is bone, but the inner side is a flexible membrane.

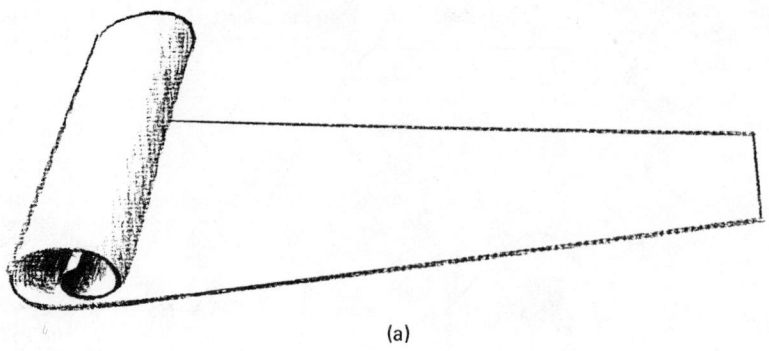

(a)

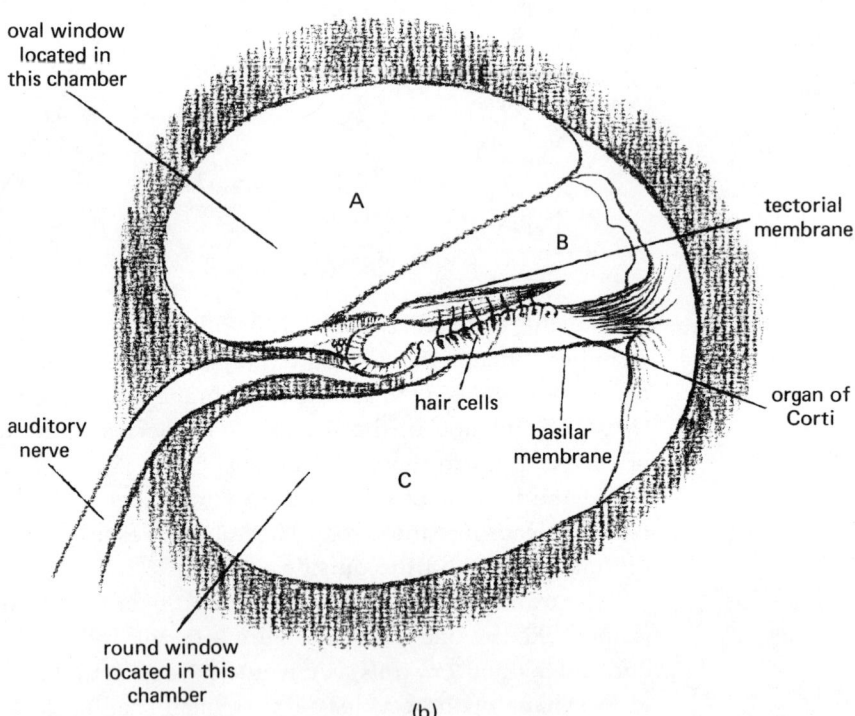

(b)

FIG. 2.18 Part (a) is a diagram of the shape of the cochlea were it unrolled, and part (b) is a cross-section of the cochlea showing its structure.

Chamber A runs the entire length of the tube, and at the far end, in the center of the roll, it connects through a small hole with chamber C. Chamber B is not connected to the other two chambers; it contains the neural elements that send messages about sound to the brain. These elements are in a structure called the *organ of Corti* that stretches along the *basilar membrane,* which is the floor of chamber B. Small hair cells project from these elements and are embedded in an overhanging tissue called the *tectorial membrane.* When the tectorial membrane moves relative to the organ of Corti, the hairs are bent, causing the neural elements to react. These reactions are then transmitted to the brain.

With this rudimentary knowledge of the structure of the ear, let us examine what happens when a sound occurs in your presence. First, the sound source produces waves of alternating increased and decreased density of the molecules in the air. These waves reach your ear and enter the external canal. The alternating increase and decrease in the pressure of the waves makes the eardrum move, which, in turn, moves the ossicles, which then moves the oval window. Inward movement of the oval window increases the pressure of the liquid in the cochlea and backward movement decreases it. Because of a flexible bit of tissue at one end of chamber C, *the round window,* the pressure in the cochlea is not uniform throughout its entire length. Different frequencies of movement of the oval window determine where in the cochlea the pressures will be the greatest. As pressure builds up at various locations along the flexible membrane in chamber A, they distort chamber B, causing the organ of Corti and the tectorial membrane to move. This movement bends the hair cells and causes the neural elements to react, which, in turn, leads to messages being sent to the brain, via the *auditory nerve,* about the locations on the basilar membrane at which the pressure is greatest. And finally, if you can believe it, the brain interprets these messages as sounds of different pitches and "hears" the sound.

The ear is extremely sensitive. A person with healthy, normal ears can hear sound "vibrations" that range from about 20 to about 20,000 Hertz (that is, cycles per second); the latter is far higher than most loudspeakers can reproduce. He also can discriminate very small changes in sounds and can accurately pick out a specific sound from a lot of noise. It is difficult to understand how a relatively crude device like the ear can perform such marvelous feats. Of course, if you'll remember our discussion about the backward construction of the retina, one might have thought that the eye isn't very good either. The problem is not with the construction of the eye or the ear but with our understanding of how they work.

Hearing: Another Active Process

Just as seeing is more than merely the mechanics of vision, hearing is more than merely the mechanics of audition. Hearing is the active attempt to identify the nature of sound sources and to receive meaningful information from the sounds.

There are two categories of sound sources, internal and external. The primary internal source is your own voice, which you hear both through the air like any other sound and through *bone conduction*. When you talk, the bones of your head vibrate. Because the ossicles and the skull each are of a different mass, the ossicles lag behind the skull's vibration, and in doing so they "pump" the oval window. This pumping sets up pressure waves in the cochlea, and the brain interprets these waves as sounds.

The skull is relatively solid and vibrates more readily to low sounds than to high sounds. Therefore, the low components of your voice are the ones most easily transmitted by bone conduction. The result is that your voice sounds lower to you than it does to other people who don't hear those bone-transmitted low components. This is why most people, especially boys and men, are so appalled when they hear themselves on a tape recorder; their voices sound much higher than they are used to hearing because the familiar low components aren't there.

The second category of sound sources consists of external sources. You have pretty fair knowledge of what kinds of external sources can and will produce certain sounds. Big objects usually produce lower sounds than do small objects; a high voice from a big man or a bass voice from a little man are both uncommon enough and unexpected enough to give you a small start of surprise. Or, if the sound of a full orchestra playing Beethoven's Fifth Symphony issued from your mother's mouth when she opened it to speak, you would suspect that it was either a joke or somebody had added something extra to your breakfast food that morning; orchestras and mothers don't sound alike. Even if your mother only sounded like your father, you would be surprised. Thus, not only do you know the sounds to be expected from objects in general (dogs don't talk and cats don't bark and neither of them can sing like a canary) but you also know the specific sounds associated with many specific persons and objects.

Besides knowing what kinds of sounds objects make, you also know what kinds of movements accompany the sounds. A pencil sharpener sitting on the desk spontaneously making a grinding sound would be a bit of a surprise and would lead you to investigate it more closely. By the same token, if an object makes the proper motions during a sound sequence, you are led to infer that it is the sound source. This is how ventriloquism works. When the two figures, the ventriloquist and his dummy, sit closely side by side it is difficult to tell which one is making the noise. So, when the mouth of the dummy moves appropriately and the mouth of the ventriloquist doesn't (at least it doesn't if he is a good ventriloquist), you are led to infer that the dummy is the sound source. Of course, a ventriloquist really can't "throw his voice"; he merely learns to move the dummy's mouth appropriately and to minimize his own mouth movements. Your perceptual inferences do the rest for him. Usually he heightens the illusion by changing his voice when talking for the dummy.

You have another important talent related to identifying sound sources. When you are familiar with a particular sound, you can pick it out of a good deal of surrounding noise. You probably have done this at parties: Listlessly smiling at a boring companion, you secretly listen to the persons behind you discussing something that is probably none of your business while a wild melee of noise, voices, and music swirls around you. The same sort of thing can be reproduced in the laboratory. If the experimenter lets you hear the sound you're supposed to detect before the experiment begins, you can pick it out of noise more easily than if you had never heard it before. In short, you do better if you know what you are listening for.

Hearing: The Ability To Hear

Many of us wear glasses, so we can understand the problems of poor vision. We know that as vision gets worse there is a point at which glasses won't help much; at this point a person is considered medically and legally blind. Beyond this there is total blindness, which means that a person does not react to light at all. The ability to hear has a similar gradation from a slight hearing loss to deafness. People with hearing losses are called hard of hearing and people with virtually no hearing are called deaf.

There are many reasons why people lose their hearing. In some cases, deafness results from some physical malfunction of the ear. For example, a not uncommon problem is the formation of calcium deposits between the ossicles of the middle ear. These deposits prevent the ossicles from properly transmitting movement from the eardrum to the oval window. Often this condition can be corrected through surgery. In other cases, plain foolishness leads to hearing problems. Primary among these is damage inflicted by prolonged exposure to loud noises. Most of us have mild hearing losses as a result of living in a noisy world of traffic, radios, building construction, and so forth. But some people incur serious hearing losses because they place themselves in noisy situations and fail to take proper precautions. Men who work around jet airplanes, for example, run a high risk of developing a severe hearing loss if they don't wear ear protectors—a sort of earmuff that reduces sound. The same is true of men who work on rifle ranges, operate heavy machinery, work in factories, and so forth. Ordinarily, short exposure produces losses that last only a short time. But prolonged exposure to loud noises, or exposure to extremely loud noises for a short period of time, can produce long-lasting effects. It has been found, for example, that one session with highly amplified rock music is capable of producing hearing losses that can last for days or weeks. Indeed, one scientist has suggested that in the interest of preserving people's hearing, ear plugs should be handed out at these sessions before the music begins.

Part 5   *THE FIFTH SENSORY SYSTEM, SMELL AND TASTE*

Seeing and hearing are similar in that they both react to pulses of energy which can be thought of as waves. They are also the senses of which human beings are most aware; our experience is dominated by what we see and what we hear. With smell and taste we move to the senses which play less obtrusive roles in our experience. Indeed, one problem associated with investigating them (and explaining them to you) is that there are fewer English words that clearly describe these experiences than there are for seeing and hearing.

Olfaction and Gustation: Structure of the Senses

Smell takes place when the molecules in inhaled air come in contact with the *olfactory bulbs*. These bulbs are located in the nasal passages above and behind the nose (Fig. 2.19). Apparently, extremely small openings in the surfaces of the bulbs are shaped in such a way that only molecules of the appropriate shapes can enter. When these molecules are present, their entrance into the openings triggers neural elements that signal the brain that they are present. Various classes of molecules give rise to various kinds of odor experiences. The basic experiences may be described as putrid, fragrant, ethereal (like ether), resinous, spicy, and burned. However, if you ask one person to smell something and to describe it in these terms, you will find that his report may be quite different from someone else's. For the most part this results from the fact that people adapt to odors very quickly and therefore find it difficult to focus clearly on the subtleties of their smell experiences. Adapting means that you cease

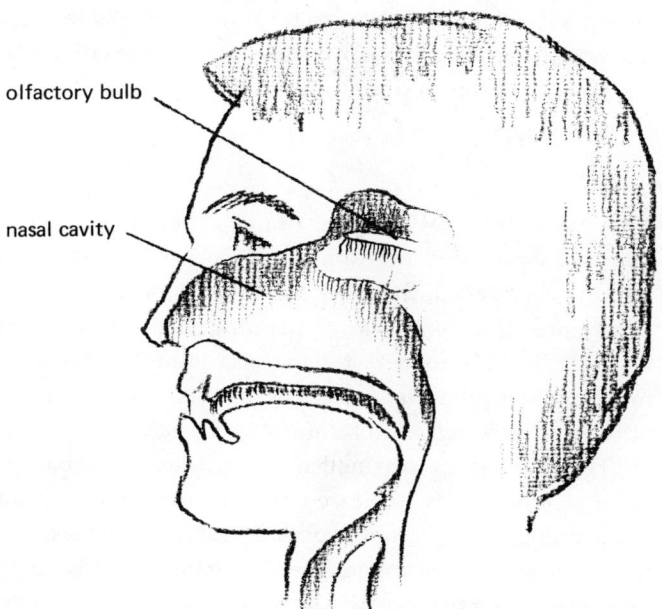

olfactory bulb

nasal cavity

FIG. 2.19   The location of the olfactory bulbs in the nasal cavity.

to be aware of an odor—a blessing in these times of air pollution but a hindrance, nonetheless, to research on smell.

The picture is a bit clearer for *gustation,* or taste. Chemicals in solution, usually either in water or saliva, spread over the tongue, which contains chemical-sensitive elements called *taste buds.* These buds are small cells located in the crevices of the tongue. If you look at your tongue in the mirror, you will see that its surface appears to be covered with fuzz. The sides of each of the little fuzzy structures, called *papillae,* contain the chemical-sensitive taste buds. Depending on the nature of the chemical solution, the buds yield one of four taste experiences: sour, sweet, bitter, or salty. Moreover, different areas of the tongue are differentially sensitive to the chemicals that cause each of these experiences. The tip of the tongue is related to the experience of sweetness, the back to bitter, the front part of the sides to salt, and the back part of the sides to sour. The complex flavors that we ordinarily experience appear to be mixtures of these four basic tastes.

It is easy to examine the differential sensitivity of the various areas on your own tongue. Buy a package of the cotton swabs that are sold in the baby supply section of a drugstore. Dip one in lemon juice and then squeeze it fairly dry. Place it on different parts of your tongue; you will be able to taste it best on the sides and near the back. Then do the same thing using sugar water, salt water, and alum dissolved in water or the commercial quinine water that is ordinarily used in a gin and tonic.

Smell and Taste: Related Processes

We tend to think of the pleasure of eating as involving only taste. However, when you put food in your mouth, molecules escape and go into the nasal passage. As a result, there is a significant smell component to nearly every taste experience. If a person loses his ability to smell, a condition called *anosmia*, he finds that his food tastes flat and is rather dull. In some cases, anosmics find that their food preferences become based on texture rather than chemistry; taste without smell is not sufficient to make food interesting.

The importance of smell in human life is probably not fully appreciated. A large industry is dedicated to the eradication of bad odors, primarily by substituting more pleasing odors. Thus, we have all manner of body deodorants that themselves contain perfumes. We have air fresheners that smell like pine, lime, spice, or flowers. We spend a lot of money to keep our breath smelling like oil of wintergreen or peppermint, and colognes for women and men are a major industry. City governments throughout the country are concerned with the pollution of the air and the bad smells that industry and automobiles create. While we may have ceased to use smell as a source of information, as many animals and less urbanized human beings do, we are sensitive to the negative aspects of smell, and a good deal of our time and resources are directed toward getting rid of them.

Taste, too, is an important part of our lives. Like all animals, we have preferences for certain tastes and these cannot be explained solely in terms of the four basic tastes described above. For example, some animals are meat eaters rather than vegetarians. (It is easy to tell which animals are which by the structure of their teeth and their head. A vegetarian has broad, flat teeth for grinding and large, strong jaw muscles. A strict vegetable diet does not permit storage of much energy, so a vegetarian must eat almost constantly; thus the need for large, tireless jaw muscles. Meat eaters, on the other hand, have sharp teeth for tearing flesh and small jaw muscles, since the energy in meat can be stored, and eating can be periodic rather than continuous.) Human beings obviously are meat eaters, and this fact shows up in our food preferences. We make virtually everything into meat; if something isn't meat, we put fat on it to make it meatlike. The fat is in the form of grease, butter, salad dressing, cheese, vegetable oils, oleomargarines, and so on. Practically nothing we eat is without fat unless we are on a diet, and then we suffer loudly for lack of fats.

Taste preferences are specific to particular kinds of animals. Cats and chickens do not care for candy because they cannot taste "sweet." But dogs, human beings, and rats can taste sweet things and they often crave candy. People can't taste distilled water and usually prefer a more flavorful drink. However, monkeys, cats, and dogs can taste water. It may be difficult to imagine a water taste, as we usually taste only the impurities in the water. But then, a cat might find your fondness for sweets a bit difficult to understand, too.

Closing Comments

This brings us to the end of our discussion of sensation and perception. When a section is so long and detailed, it is easy to lose sight of why it was introduced in the first place and how it contributes to the psychological framework you were promised in Section 1. So, let's pause and review.

Remember that in Section 1 a decision-making view of psychology was outlined. This view rests on the notion that information about the environment is obtained through the senses, is combined with existing information in memory, and that subsequent behavior is planned and executed taking the totality of this information into account. All of the preceding discussion was aimed at giving you a reasonably thorough insight into how the senses procure environmental information.

Moreover, throughout the discussion we have seen that the perceptual system goes beyond the immediately available information to make inferences about what gave rise to that information. Thus, changes in vestibular stimulation are not experienced as mere changes in activity in the utricule, saccule, or semicircular canals; rather, they are experienced as movement of the body. Similarly, changes in the size of a retinal image are interpreted as changes in the distance of an object from the observer. Indeed, the observer isn't even aware that he has a retinal image—he merely "sees" the object. If you'll look back through the section, you'll find that for each sensory system perception involves something more than just the patterns of stimulation of the sense organs. We have some insight into the conditions necessary for these perceptual inferences to occur, but we really don't know how they happen.

If the kinds of perceptual inferences that are illustrated throughout this section seem remarkable, consider the complex perceptual inferences necessary to unify the information (and inferences) coming from each of the different sensory-perceptual systems into what we experience as a dynamic, real-feeling world that is populated by real-feeling objects, people, and events. For instance, when you encounter a close friend on the street, your auditory system receives stimulation from his voice, your touch system receives stimulation from his firm, warm handshake, your visual system receives stimulation from his face and clothing, your olfactory system receives stimulation from his aftershave, pipe, or perspiration. And yet, all these fragments of information are not experienced as separate messages. You don't hear his sound, you hear what he has to say. You don't measure the pressure of his hand on yours nor the temperature of his skin, you feel his eager handshake. You don't see the geometric outlines of his face and body, you see his smiling, friendly face and familiar build. You don't smell chemicals, you smell his accustomed odor. In short, you meet your friend and it seems to you that it is really him that you experience—and yet that very real-feeling experience literally has been constructed by your perceptual system out of all those separate little pieces of information supplied to it by your various sensory systems. Moreover, a large dose of information from memory was used too; how else would you recognize your friend or be able to interpret his actions as friendly? As you can see, it is not an exaggeration to say that your experience of meeting your friend is as much "all in your head" as it is real.

If this all sounds abstract and a bit unlikely, just ponder the fact that it is happening every waking moment of your life. Even now, as you read these words, your eyes merely see black marks on the page, yet you perceive meaning and may even hear a small voice off in the corner of your head saying the words as you read along. I suppose that the big question is whether the meaning you perceive as you read is the same as the meaning I perceive as I write.

Now it is time to turn to what is done with all of this information once it is received by the central computer that we assumed our roving information gatherer to have. This will be the topic of Section Three.

SUMMARY: 1   The human sensory-perceptual system can be thought of as a set of devices that relay environmental information to a central computer, the brain, where it is interpreted and used in the formulation of behavior appropriate to that information.

2   The first system, *kinesthesis,* relays information about the movement and location of the body relative to gravity. Vestibular kinesthesis primarily monitors movements of the head, while touch kinesthesis monitors movements and location of the other body parts.

3   The second sensory-perceptual system, *touch,* relays information about the location, size, shape, texture, and temperature of objects that either touch the skin or that are picked up and held.

4   The third system, *vision,* relays information about the patterns of light that come from objects in the environment. We are sensitive to the brightness and to certain wavelengths of light, which we identify as *color,* as well as to the patterns, which we identify as *objects.* As is true for the other sensory-perceptual systems, vision is not merely passive; that is, we actively interpret light patterns in ways that give them greater meaning than mere patterns. Through this active interpretation process, we see objects that have constancy, wholeness, and location in a three-dimensional space.

5   The fourth system, *audition,* relays information about sounds. As in the case of vision, a major characteristic of the auditory system is that we interpret patterns of sound in ways that give them deeper meanings. We hear music, words, familiar voices, and so on, and we learn what kinds of sounds to expect from the multitude of objects that exist in our environment.

6   The final system consists of both the sense of *smell* and the sense of *taste* and relays information about the air we breathe and the things we put into our mouths. Smell and taste are rather closely related because the chambers in which their primary mechanisms are located are connected. Indeed, smell plays an important role in tasting foods.

7   Of course, all of these sensory-perceptual systems operate in conjunction with one another. An object may be seen, heard, touched, tasted, and smelled all at one time. The central computer integrates all of this information in some unknown way and then uses it as a basis for deciding how to react to the object. In Section 3, we shall see some of the consequences of the interpretation and use of sensory-perceptual information.

Special Topic   Appendix 2: *Brain Mechanisms*

Further Reading   BORING, E. G. *Sensation and Perception in the History of Experimental Psychology* New York: Appleton, 1942, 644 pages.
By tracing the history of many of the topics that have been discussed in this section and placing them in an historical perspective, Boring demonstrates how heavily modern psychological thought has been influenced by the study of the senses and related

perceptual phenomena. A classic, this book is filled with interesting descriptions and possible explanations of a great number of perceptual phenomena.

DAY, R. H. *Human Perception*
Sydney: Wiley, 1969, 193 pages (paperback).
A detailed investigation into human perceptual capacities, stabilities, and instabilities. Although this book was written specifically for Australian students, the author suggests that it will interest any student concerned with the area of human perception and will add a little Australian flavor to his reading diet.

DRÖSCHER, V. B. *The Magic of the Senses*
(Translated by U. Lehrburger and D. Coburn.) New York: Harper & Row, 1971 (c. 1969), 298 pages (paperback).
The visual system of frogs, the olfactory system of dogs, the auditory system of bats, the electric system of fish, and the navigational systems of birds and bees are just a few of the topics touched on by Dröscher in this detailed book about new discoveries in animal perception. Engrossing.

GIBSON, J. J. *The Senses Considered as Perceptual Systems*
Boston: Houghton Mifflin, 1966, 335 pages.
Taking a dynamic view of perception, Gibson treats the senses as *active* mechanisms for obtaining perceptual information about the world and emphasizes the interrelations among these perceptual systems. Although the book contains a great deal of detail, it is well illustrated through use of both figures and examples and therefore is fairly easy to read and understand.

GREGORY, R. L. *Eye and Brain: The Psychology of Seeing*
New York: McGraw-Hill, 1966, 253 pages (paperback).
A well-illustrated and easy to read book about vision, covering such topics as the physical characteristics of light, the anatomical structure and physiological functioning of the eye and brain, and the psychological processes underlying the perception of brightness, color, movement, illusions, and so on. The relation between visual processes and art is also discussed.

GRIFFIN, D. R. *Echoes of Bats and Men*
New York: Doubleday, 1959, 156 pages (paperback).
"Seeing with sound waves" is the major theme of this book. The author, a zoologist, discusses how bats, porpoises, whirligig beetles, and skilled blind people use echo location as a means of finding their way around in the dark.

HANSEL, C. E. M. *ESP: A Scientific Evaluation*
New York: C. Scribner, 1966, 263 pages (paperback).
A good critical examination of experiments on extrasensory perception (perception through channels other than the senses). The author explores all types of ESP (telepathy, clairvoyance, precognition) and psychokinesis and looks at both historical experiments and recent developments.

Kellogg, W. N.   *Porpoises and Sonar*
Chicago: University of Chicago Press, 1962 (c. 1961), 177 pages (paperback).
The results of a careful investigation of how the bottlenose dolphin (or porpoise) "sees with his ears" through the use of a sonar echo-ranging system. Humorous anecdotes, many illustrations, and detailed descriptions of experiments make this a very interesting book.

Vernon, M. D.   (Ed.) *Experiments in Visual Perception*
Baltimore, Md.: Penguin, 1966, 447 pages (paperback).
A book of readings containing classic experiments investigating the perception of form, space, distance, constancy, real movement, apparent movement, and causality as well as experiments investigating the effects of such factors as set, attention, motivation, and personality on perception.

Memory and Rules
THREE

In Section 2, we relied upon an analogy between a human being and an imaginary information-gathering machine that collected environmental information that was subsequently relayed to a central computer. In this section we will press this analogy a bit further by examining an important part of the central computer, *memory*, and the ways in which it contributes to our ability to interact successfully with our environment. Briefly, the notion is that in the course of his or her life, a person develops *rules* for dealing with various situations. These rules, together with records of past experiences and other bits of knowledge, are stored in the person's memory. When a situation is encountered, information about it is sent to this memory; if the situation is *recognized* as a familiar one for which an appropriate rule exists, the rule is *recalled* from memory and is used to produce some desired change in the situation or to predict what will happen next. If the situation is unfamiliar, or if no rule exists, a new rule must be formulated. We will begin with the examination of memory because it is basic to both the recognition of situations and the recall of rules. Then we'll examine the kinds of rules we use and how we acquire them.

Part 1   MEMORY

Memory is the name given to the repository, most likely located in the brain, in which information is stored so that it can be used some time in the future. Thus a taxi driver's memory retains information about the location of specific streets so that he can get there with a minimum of delay. A student's memory retains $(a + b)^2 = a^2 + 2ab + b^2$ so that she can pass an algebra exam. A typist's memory retains the information that the key for the letter a is under the little finger of the left hand so that the job can be successfully performed.

Although common usage implies that to remember something is to be conscious (that is, aware) of the memory, this need not always be the case. True enough, when you remember someone's name you are conscious of it "coming to mind." But when you insert your key into your car's ignition and turn it clockwise rather than counterclockwise to start the engine, you also are remembering, even though the proper way to turn the key may have "never entered your mind." In short, psychologists use the term "memory" to cover a broader range of behavior than is common in everyday language.

Return to the Analogy

Imagine that our roving information gatherer has a memory system located in its central computer that is like the one diagrammed in Figure 3.1. Information about the environment is received through the *sensory units* on the left. It then passes through a *selection device* that gives top priority to the sensory units that are receiving the most important information at the moment. This selected information is then coded electronically, and stored temporarily in a unit called *short-term memory*. The short-term memory unit is of limited capacity, so that if too much information comes in at once, the unit will be unable to store all of it, and some will be lost. The next unit, the *transfer unit,* slowly but constantly extracts information from short-term memory and, by elimination of extraneous detail, simplifies it so that it can be stored more easily. The transfer unit then passes the simplified information on for permanent storage in *long-term memory.*

Whenever the roving information gatherer is required to perform a task or react to its environment, the *retrieval unit* in its memory system obtains the

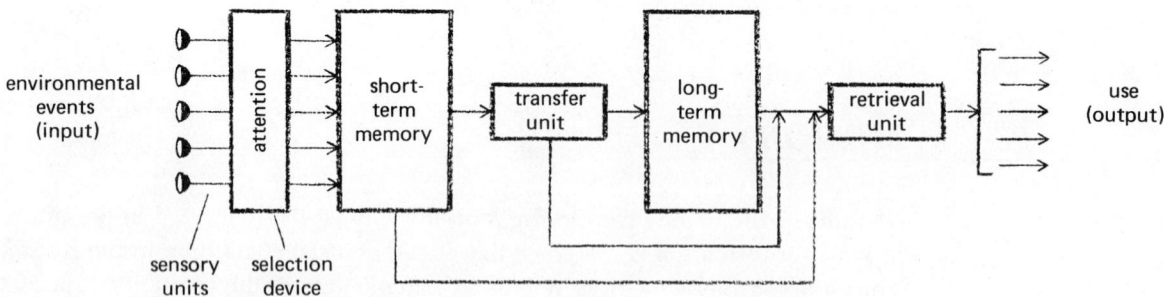

FIG. 3.1   A possible "computer" memory system that is analogous to human memory.

appropriate information from whichever unit the information is in at the moment. However, the required information may not always be available. Remember that if too much information comes in through the sensory units, something relevant may not get into short-term memory; therefore, it will not be available for retrieval when it is needed. Moreover, if the transfer unit distorts some information when simplifying it for long-term memory, the information gatherer will retrieve inaccurate information, and behavior based upon such information may turn out to be quite inappropriate. Keep in mind that, unlike short-term memory, anything, accurate or not, reaching long-term memory will *always* remain there—the main problem is to find it.

Let's return to thinking of the information gatherer as a human being. An individual's sensory input units are his eyes, ears, nose, and so on. His short-term memory is a temporary repository where the hodgepodge of input can be stored until it is simplified for retention in long-term memory. As in the information gatherer's memory system, the human transfer unit is a mechanism that simplifies information and conveys it to long-term memory for permanent storage. The retrieval unit is the device for "remembering" things when they are needed.

Evidence

No one is naive enough to think that human memory is identical to the computer memory system just outlined, but it may prove profitable to think of human memory as computerlike in form in order to study it and learn how it works. Suppose we do think of human memory as being computerlike—do the results of experiments on human memory favor or disfavor the analogy? Well, let's see.

Short-Term Memory

Because its capacity is limited, the computer's short-term memory can accept only a limited amount of information at any one time. This is true of human short-term memory too, and we have a mechanism, like the selection device in Figure 3.1, called *attention*, that helps ease the load on short-term memory by focusing on only part of the available information at any one time. This mechanism can turn off or decrease the flow of information from some of the input units in order to permit others to feed in more information. The limit on the ability of human beings to take things in is well documented. For example, courtroom witnesses often give quite different accounts of the same event. So much was going on at the time of the event that each witness could get only part of the event into his memory; since each witness did not necessarily attend to exactly the same things, each gives a different account of the event.

You can demonstrate for yourself the limits of human short-term memory. Read different-length lists of single-digit numbers to a friend. After you read each list have him try to recall all of the numbers. Use lists varying in length from four to fifteen numbers and write each list on an index card. Make four different lists for each length. You can get the numbers for each list by using the last four digits (not the prefixes) of the telephone numbers listed in the phone book; take the numbers as they come and keep going until you have eight or ten or however many you need to complete the first list. Then start where you left off and keep going until you have the next list completed, and so on. This procedure will insure that the numbers have no pattern that could aid your friend in remembering them. After you have written the lists on the index cards, shuffle the cards and read the first list to your friend at a normal pace. He should try to repeat the list immediately and you should count the number of errors he makes. Do this for each list of numbers. You will find that he does quite well on lists of fewer than eight or nine digits, but beyond this, the task becomes rather difficult. His short-term memory can take in and retain only a limited amount of information in a short time, and therefore longer lists become harder for him to remember completely. (Of course, your friend could resort to a strategy of considering pairs of digits as one number. For example, the ten-number list 1, 7, 6, 9, 5, 2, 8, 4, 3, 1 can be converted to a five-number list, 17, 69, 52, 84, 31; your friend may do better than expected, but in actuality he has changed the task.)

Interference with short-term memory Retention of information in short-term memory is only temporary; unless the information passes on to the transfer unit rather quickly, it will be lost. One way of keeping information in short-term memory for any length of time without losing it is to repeat it over and over to yourself. This repetition process is called *rehearsal,* and you use it quite often. For example, when you look up a telephone number and repeat it to yourself as you reach for the phone, you are using rehearsal. Note how quickly you forget the number if you are prevented from rehearsing by someone talking to you while you are reaching for the phone.

You can better understand the important role rehearsal plays in keeping information in short-term memory if you perform the following little experiment. You will need a watch that has a second hand and two lists of ten numbers each, taken from the telephone book in the manner described earlier. This time have your friend look at one of the lists until he feels he has pretty well memorized it and then remove it from his view. Have him sit quietly for ten seconds and then have him recall the numbers. Next, give him the second list to study, take it away, and ask him to count backwards from 100 aloud. After ten seconds, stop him and ask him to try to recall the numbers on the second list. Because you made him concentrate on counting backwards, you prevented your friend from rehearsing the list, and you will find that he makes more errors on the second list than he did on the first.

If something drastic such as a power overload or short circuit happens to the computer in Figure 3.1, you might well expect it to interfere in some way with the machine's short-term memory. Human short-term memory also can suffer from such interference when a person receives a concussion, experiences specific kinds of severe electric shock, or has certain kinds of illnesses.

Physiological interference   Some people, after having experienced a severe concussion, show a loss of memory. Perhaps you have had the experience yourself—an accident in which you got knocked unconscious. When you awoke, you remembered practically none of the events immediately prior to the accident. Short-term memory seems to have been erased and you remember nothing. Of course, concussions do not always result in a loss of short-term memory, but it is not uncommon for such a loss to occur.

Electrical interference   The same sort of thing happens when people or animals are given an electric shock that is sufficient to cause a convulsion and render them unconscious. Since the nervous system is an electrical device (see Appendix 2), it can be interfered with electrically. The effects of electrical interference are quite interesting because they reveal something about how short-term memory works. Imagine yourself performing the following experiment. First, you teach an animal (say a mouse) to perform some simple task like jumping off a block of wood when a signal is given. Wait a little while and then give an *electroconvulsive shock*, a shock that is sufficient to knock him unconscious.[1] After the animal wakes up, you see if he can still perform the task. You will find that the animal's ability to remember the task depends upon how long you waited after the training period before shocking him. If you shocked him immediately after training, he would retain no memory. If you waited three minutes, he may remember something about how to perform the

---

[1] I do not advocate giving electroconvulsive shock (ECS) to anyone, man or mouse. But lest you think it cruel, someone undergoing ECS becomes unconscious immediately, feels no pain, and apparently retains little or no memory of undergoing the shock. ECS has been used for years in the treatment of some types of mental illness (see Section 5, Part 2).

task. After eight minutes, he would do quite well at remembering, and so on. (For human beings these times probably would be much shorter.) These findings imply that if the transfer unit has time to get to work on the information in short-term memory and move it into long-term memory, the information will be retained and the shock will have little or no effect. However, if the shock comes too soon, that is, before the information has been passed on, it may be lost.

Interference due to illness   There are some people whose brains spontaneously produce electroconvulsions. These people, *epileptics,* apparently have brains that "short circuit" from time to time, and they often report that they have no memory of the events that occurred just prior to the convulsion. (It is important to note that epileptics usually are *totally normal* in all respects except for their attacks, and drugs are now available which help decrease or stop these attacks.)

Short-term memory sometimes becomes impaired as a person gets older and his brain ceases to function as well as it used to. Old people frequently suffer from faulty blood circulation in their brains and, as a result, their brains become damaged. A common effect of such damage is that these people have difficulty remembering the immediate past, although they remember the distant past as well as ever. They often can sit and tell you detailed stories about their early life, yet they cannot remember who you are or where they are. In short, these people give you the impression that their short-term memory is so impaired that nothing is retained in it long enough to be transferred to long-term memory.

Transfer Unit   Psychologists currently are of the opinion that the transfer unit analyzes information in short-term memory, selects the salient parts, and deletes the rest. If this is the case, the effects of the transfer unit might well be revealed through distortions and deletions that it makes in information in the process of passing it along to long-term memory. Thus, if I were to ask you to tell me about a conversation you had yesterday, you could give me the essence of what was said, but you probably could not repeat much of it word for word. Similarly, if you try to visualize the scene of Venice shown in Figure 2.13 without looking back at it, you might get something rather like it, but if you look at the picture again, you will find that your visualization was not accurate—you may have added some things, distorted some things, and deleted some things. In short, most of what reaches long-term memory is a simplified version of the actual information originally received.

Long-Term Memory   Information passed on by the transfer unit to long-term memory probably remains there permanently. This permanence has been most dramatically demonstrated by Dr. Wilder Penfield and his associates, highly respected Canadian brain surgeons. Because the brain has no pain receptors, patients undergoing brain surgery often do not need an anesthetic (except as a "local" on the scalp, which does have pain receptors). Thus, during the course of surgery, the patient is aware of what is going on, and Dr. Penfield has found that when he introduces a very mild electrical current into certain parts of their brains, his patients often have very clear recollections of events that they had long ago "forgotten." Although recollections are quite vivid, the patients are aware that they are just memories and not reality. The scenes, either visual or auditory, are not even like movies or tape recordings of the real thing because not everything that was present at the time is represented. Many of the irrelevant details were screened out, presumably by attention and by the transfer unit, before the information was filed away in long-term memory.

While less dramatic, there are other examples that indicate that much more is stored in long-term memory than one might think. Sometimes, under the influence of hypnosis, various kinds of medical drugs, or while they are ill, people recall things that they could not have remembered under normal circumstances. Then, too, probably everyone has had the experience of hearing or seeing some particular thing and having a long-lost memory come flooding back.

Interference with long-term memory   Loss of long-term memory is known as *amnesia;* it can result from an accident in which the person is hurt, a disease, or in some cases from prolonged psychological stress due to personal problems. Loss of long-term memory means that for some period of time (days, weeks, months, or years) the person cannot remember people or events from his past, although he does not lose his ability to talk, write, or do other things that one assumes must in some way be part of his long-term memory. Why this happens is not entirely clear. It may be that the *amnesiac* has no difficulty retrieving memories of basic skills that he has practiced a lot but has great difficulty in retrieving other kinds of information. This hypothesis is supported by the fact that "cured" amnesiacs often are able to recall all that they supposedly had forgotten.

Amnesia often occurs when people suffer from advanced alcoholism because of alcohol damage to the brain. These people become muddled in their thinking. They lose track of a very important component of memory, *time.* A sense of time is fundamental for finding things that are stored in long-term memory.

For example, if I were to ask you what you did last Sunday, which is a question keyed to time, you probably could tell me without getting it confused with what you did Saturday or what you did Friday. When people lose the time-linked component of memory, they have immense difficulty in keeping their memories straight. Thus, along with other thinking difficulties, advanced alcoholics suffering from amnesia often tend to confuse the present and the past and have great difficulty recalling events in terms of when they happened in time.

Retrieval Unit

The retrieval unit is the key to the extraction and use of information that is stored in memory. It performs two major jobs—*recall*, which we've been discussing all along, and *recognition*. Recall refers to the process of searching memory for a specific bit of information that is demanded by the present circumstances; for example, "Where were you on the night of July 12, 1968?" "What is your father's name?" "What's the capital of Brazil?" Recognition refers to the process of searching memory to see if the specific situation, object, person, or event at hand has ever been experienced before.

The basic retrieval mechanism is probably the same for both recall and recognition, even though recall is ordinarily more difficult and less accurate than recognition. This is because a situation that requires recall usually provides fewer clues about what is to be retrieved than does a situation that requires recognition. If I were to ask you to recall what you did last Sunday, you would have to recall the salient events—for example, going swimming and on a picnic—and then reconstruct the whole day that occurred before, after, and during these key events. However, if I were to show you three detailed descriptions of your activities on three successive Sundays (compiled by a private detective, perhaps), you would have lots of information at hand and could easily pick out last Sunday's itinerary. Recall requires you to pull the detail out of memory, which evidently is fairly difficult, while recognition simply requires you to look at a rich array of information and pick out that which is familiar. To illustrate the difference in difficulty between recall and recognition, notice that while most of us have difficulty recalling people's names (which are merely arbitrary labels), we seldom fail to recognize a face that we've seen before. Similarly, most people find it easier to pass a multiple choice exam (recognition) than to pass essay or fill-in-the-blanks exams (recall).

Forgetting and Recall of Long-Term Memories

If all of the information in long-term memory is stored permanently, what is *forgetting?* The answer may well be that forgetting is not loss of information from long-term memory, but that it is the inability to retrieve information from long-term memory. That is, if information survives attention, short-term memory, and the transfer unit, it is permanently placed in long-term memory—the problem is to retrieve it so that it can be used.

Although we don't know very much about them, there appear to be rather reasonable rules governing what can and what cannot be easily recalled from long-term memory. For example, in 1932, Sir Frederick Bartlett had a group of British men read an American Indian folk story. The story was short but rather complex. Then, at times varying from fifteen minutes later up to two and one-half years later, the men were asked to recall the story. What the men could and could not remember about the story followed fairly clear lines. If a man was asked to recall the story frequently, he soon settled on his own personalized version and persisted in giving it time after time. On the other hand, if a man was asked to recall the story infrequently, each successive recall was different. In this case, the story became simpler, and the unfamiliar American phrases were either deleted or changed to more familiar British ones. Moreover, when a good deal of time elapsed between reading the story and recalling it, the men tended to add their own elaborations—elaborations that made the story more meaningful to them. This meaningful elaboration was usually woven around one or two of the outstanding themes of the original story. In short, the men simplified the story and then made it into something that was meaningful to themselves so that they could remember it better. These results imply that one factor in recall is that information is stored and retrieved in meaningful bundles. While the most salient and coherent information remains relatively amenable to retrieval, any meaningless details soon become inaccessible.

As time passes, more and more details become inaccessible to recall, especially if the information is not used. This makes perfectly good sense. Nonuse of information ordinarily means that it is not very important. Indeed, if old, infrequently used memories did not become inaccessible, all of your past experience would be constantly retrievable. Then, every time you searched for things relevant to the situation at hand, you would receive a huge flood of memories, most of which, being old and outdated, would be of no use to you. If there are limits on the amount of information a retrieval system can handle, and there is reason to believe that there are such limits, forgetting is a valuable mechanism which prevents the system from being constantly inundated. Thus frequency of use is a second factor in the recall of information from long-term memory.

A third factor in recall has to do with the structure of the information. You have probably experienced the *tip-of-the-tongue* phenomenon; a word (piece of information) is right on the "tip of your tongue," but it just will not materialize. The strange thing is that even though you cannot find the word, you know

BOX 3.1

Exceptional Memory: Case Histories of H. M. and V. P.

Psychological investigations of memory usually involve ordinary people, most of whom can remember things reasonably well. Occasionally, however, someone turns up whose ability to remember is either exceptionally poor or exceptionally good. The following are descriptions of two such people. The first, H. M., was studied by Dr. Brenda Milner and others at the Montreal Neurological Institute,* and the second, V. P., was studied by Dr. Earl B. Hunt and Dr. Thomas Love at the University of Washington.†

H. M., at the age of 27, underwent brain surgery in order to curtail frequent and debilitating seizures that had plagued him from the age of 16. After recovery from surgery, it was discovered that while he could still remember things that had occurred before his operation, virtually nothing that happened after the operation ever got transferred from short-term memory to long-term memory. The only way he could retain new information for any length of time was to constantly rehearse it. If he did not rehearse, forgetting occurred the instant he shifted his attention to something else. The result was that even simple things in life became very complex; he could not remember the surroundings of the house to which he moved after his operation (although he managed to learn the floor plan) nor could he recognize his neighbors or remember their names even after he had seen them frequently over a period of at least six years. Because of his

*B. Milner, Memory and the medial temporal regions of the brain. In K. H. Pribram and D. E. Broadbent (Eds.), *Biology of Memory*. New York: Academic Press, 1970.
†E. B. Hunt and T. Love, How good can memory be? In A. Melton and E. Martin (Eds.), *Coding Processes in Human Memory*. New York: Halsted, 1972.

a lot about its structure. About half the time you are in this dilemma, you know how many syllables the word has and you have a good idea which syllable is accented. Moreover, you often may know what the word's initial letter is, and it is quite likely that the first couple of attempts to recall the correct word will result in the recall of incorrect words which have the same first and/or last letter as the correct word. All of this suggests that storage and retrieval of words in long-term memory sometimes rely upon initial and last letters of the words and the number of syllables in the words. In summary, long-term memory storage and retrieval appear to be dictated, at least in part, by the meaningfulness, the frequency of use, and the structure of information.

Mnemonic methods Occasionally you may have noticed advertisements in magazines or newspapers for systems that promise to help improve your

inability to remember what had happened even during the few preceding minutes, he constantly had a vague feeling of anxiety about whether he had just done or said something wrong. While the present looked clear enough to him, he always felt as though he had just awakened from a dream.

In spite of all this, H. M. showed no adverse personality changes after his memory system was damaged, nor was there any decrease in his performance on I.Q. tests (which depended heavily upon the old knowledge he still had in long-term memory). However, he now had extreme difficulty learning anything new, especially anything that required verbal thinking and memory. H. M. has been studied since his surgery in 1953 and no appreciable improvement in his memory has been observed.

At the opposite extreme is V. P., who can play seven simultaneous chess matches blindfolded, who can simultaneously play chess, bridge, and read a book, and who usually is involved in as many as 60 correspondence games of chess for which he keeps no written records. V. P. began to read at the age of five, at which time he memorized the street map of the city in which he lived, as well as the city's railroad and bus schedules. He started playing chess at age eight, and at ten he memorized 150 poems for a contest. He speaks English, Latvian, German, and Russian and can read virtually all modern European languages with the exceptions of Hungarian and Greek. In spite of such accomplishments and even though he has an I.Q. of 167 (which places him in the top .0003 percent of the U.S. population) and has had postgraduate training in history, V. P. prefers to work as a store clerk. His primary interest lies in competitive chess rather than scholarship.

memory. These systems are called *mnemonic methods* (the first *m* is silent and the rest of the word rhymes with "demonic"), and they are all basically alike. If they are diligently applied, many methods actually work because they are based on two of the factors that we have just discussed as being relevant to recall; they teach you how to introduce both meaningfulness and structure into a memory task, thereby facilitating recall.

Some mnemonic methods, for example, require you to learn a series of key words that you can use as "hooks" on which to hang the things you want to remember. You can determine which key word to use as a hook for the word you want to remember by trying to discover (or by creating) some way in which the two words are related. For example, let's say that the first word in your list of key words is *able* and that the first object on a grocery list you want to memorize is *sugar*. If you are of a theological bent, you might say that

V. P. is a well-adjusted man who, unless you were aware of his phenomenal memory, would not appear exceptional to you in any way. However, when given the opportunity to demonstrate his memory, V. P.'s performance is astonishing. For example, recall the experiment described in the text involving the American Indian folktale that Sir Frederick Bartlett gave to the Englishmen to read and remember. The story, which is about 275 words long, was read twice to V. P., after which he was required to count backward by sevens from 253 to 0 (that is, 253 . . . 246 . . . 239 . . .) in an attempt to prevent rehearsal. Then he was asked to recall specific parts of the story 1 minute, 15 minutes, 30 minutes, 45 minutes, 1 hour, and 6 weeks later; he made very few errors no matter how long it had been since the original reading of the story. Moreover, the backward counting that was supposed to prevent rehearsal caused V. P. very little difficulty; apparently he can *both* count backwards by sevens *and* rehearse at the same time, a very rare skill.

When asked about his special ability, V. P. was of the opinion that a good memory is partly innate, partly due to early training and practice, and partly due to the desire and need to remember things. For him, memorization has always been enjoyable for its own sake. And, except for chess, he seldom uses his phenomenal memory for anything of much importance. He suggests that people who actively manipulate situations, rather than passively record them as he seems to think he does, have no need for an exceptionally good memory and therefore they do not develop one. For example, V. P. claims that he is not particularly good at remembering names and faces because it is not very important to him to do so. However, he thinks that if he were a politician, to whom such a skill would be valuable, he would be better at it.

sugar is made from *cane,* which is like *Cain,* who slew *Abel,* which is like your key word, *able.* Thus, when you want to recall the first object on your grocery list, you think of your first key word, *able = Abel → Cain = cane → sugar.* Simple, right? Surprisingly, some people become so proficient at using this technique that they can read a list of words and recall it days later without an error.

Some mnemonic methods apply the principles of rhythm and rhyme to help you remember things. Most of us have used the mnemonic rhymes of "i before e, except after c" or "Thirty days hath September, April, June, and November. . . ." You may even have learned the alphabet by adding a rhythmic pattern as you recited the letters.

One mnemonic method that is commonly used for remembering people's names requires that you reduce the arbitrariness of a name by trying to associate it with some salient feature of the person. Failing that, you can try to imagine the person in some situation that will link him with his name. For example, if a man is large and muscular and his name is Smith, you might think of him as a black*smith*. Or, if his name were Bolles, you might imagine him *bowl*ing. Of course, the risk with using such a system is that you might call the first man Mr. Black or spell Mr. Bolles' name "Bowls," but then, no system is perfect.

Part 2 *RULES*

We move now from the ways in which information is stored in and retrieved from memory to the ways in which it is used in the daily life of the memory's owner. The stored information is of two kinds, *content* and *rules*. Content means the "facts" that are stored in memory, for example, the gist of conversations, things learned in classes, things you see, hear, and read about, and so on. Rules are the links between content and action. Merely recognizing that the thing in front of you is a hamburger is useless to you unless you can also recall a rule or set of rules that tell you what to do with it.

Two Kinds of Rules

Over the past fifty years psychologists have undertaken a vast amount of research aimed at understanding rules, their nature and origins. The findings have shown that there are two basic kinds of rules: what-to-do rules and what-to-expect rules.

What-To-Do Rules

There are two types of what-to-do rules. The first can be characterized as, "In this situation, do such-and-such." This is a rather blind rule that can be schematically represented as $S_1 \rightarrow R_1$, where S_1 stands for a specific situation and R_1 stands for the appropriate reaction, that is, the "such and such" that is to be done.

The second type of what-to-do rule is of the form, "In this situation, if I do such and such, then so and so will usually happen." This is a more elaborate rule than the $S_1 \rightarrow R_1$ rule because the behavior, R_1, is aimed at producing some result, S_2. This second rule can be represented as $S_1 \rightarrow R_1 \rightarrow S_2$, where S_1 is the specific situation, R_1 is the "such and such" that's to be done, and S_2 is the "so and so" that will happen as a consequence.

What-To-Expect Rule

There is just one type of what-to-expect rule. It is of the form, "If this occurs, then that usually occurs too." An example is, "If lightening occurs, then thunder usually occurs too." This kind of rule can be represented as $S_1 \rightarrow S_2$, where S_1 is one event and S_2 is the event that is expected to occur when S_1 occurs. Note that this rule contains no R_1. That is, it does not require any behavior on the part of the possessor of the rule—it is merely a rule about what the possessor can expect about the events that occur in the world around him.

Origins of Rules

If we look across the animal kingdom, we find that every animal shows evidence of using rules. Some of these rules, called *reflexes* and *instincts*, are of innate genetic origin and are near the bottom of the phylogenetic scale. Other rules, called *predispositions*, originate from a mixture of innate and experiential factors. Yet others, called *learned rules* and *imitated rules*, originate sheerly as a result of experience. Finally, there are rules that originate from careful reasoning, called *intellectual rules*, which are limited to animals that are fairly high on the phylogenetic scale.

Figure 3.2 illustrates this array of rule origins. The left end of the array represents automatic, innate rules that persist, even if they are ineffective. The right end of the array represents rules that are based on experience, and reasoning, which undergo change if they don't work. Between these two extremes are rules that reflect various degrees of both innate inflexibility and experience-linked flexibility. Although we are most interested in rules that originate in experience and reasoning because these are the ones that human beings rely upon most heavily, it is worth our while to look briefly at some of the ways the other rules originate.

Reflexes

Reflexes are innate rules that are genetically determined and over which an animal has no control. They are $S_1 \rightarrow R_1$, what-to-do rules; when the proper situation is recognized to exist, the reflex behavior is bound to occur. The success or failure of the behavior is of no consequence—the rule is inflexible and is applied virtually every time S_1 occurs.

For example, a hungry frog will unerringly reach with the tip of its sticky

Reflexes	Instincts	Predispositions	Learned Rules	Imitated Rules	Intellectual Rules
$S_1 \rightarrow R_1$	$S_1 \rightarrow R_1$	? ? ?	$S_1 \rightarrow R_1 \rightarrow S_2$ $S_1 \rightarrow S_2$	$S_1 \rightarrow R_1 \rightarrow S_2$ $S_1 \rightarrow S_2$	$S_1 \rightarrow R_1 \rightarrow S_2$ $S_1 \rightarrow S_2$

FIG. 3.2 *The array of rule origins—from the genetic, inborn rules on the left to intellectual rules on the right. The kinds of rules that result from each origin are given below the line.*

FIG. 3.3   *A reflex; frogs automatically strike with their tongues at passing dark spots which, in the normal course of events, turn out to be edible insects.*

tongue for a small fly moving across its visual field (Fig. 3.3). The rule he is following to produce this reflex behavior is something like, "If there is a moving fly-sized object in my visual field (S_1), then I will try to catch it with my tongue (R_1)." (I hope you'll forgive my putting words in the frog's mouth, but you get the idea.) Because this behavior is so automatic and unchangeable, a frog will strike at any moving fly-sized object, even if it is merely an inkspot on a moving piece of cardboard or even if this inkspot is surrounded by sharp tacks or pins that cut the frog's tongue. Moreover, the dot must be moving; even if a dead fly is placed in front of a hungry frog, he will not reach for it because it is not moving. In short, frogs have an innate rule for handling "moving-dot information," and nothing deters them from using this rule over and over again, even if it doesn't satisfy their major objective of getting food. Because pins, tacks, and moving inkspots normally do not occur in a frog's life, this simple, automatic rule ordinarily works sufficiently well to keep frogs well nourished (although they do miss out on dead flies). Note that the frog's reaction to a moving fly or a moving fly-sized object is not a result of previous experience with flies. Baby frogs don't have to develop the rule themselves; they are born "prewired," as it were, to attack flies.

Instincts

The next part of the array in Figure 3.2 represents rules that are much like reflexes in that they are $S_1 \rightarrow R_1$, what-to-do rules of genetic origin. However, these rules, called *instincts,* are more complex than reflexes, and their application is less blindly automatic.

In the two examples I am about to describe, note that, unlike the frog's simple reaction of striking at a fly or fly-sized object with the tip of his tongue (one $S_1 \to R_1$ rule), instincts usually involve a series of $S_1 \to R_1$ rules which take changes in local conditions into account.

The first example is the mating behavior of the three-spined stickleback, a small fish. In the spring, increased sunlight coming through the water activates the hormonal system of the male stickleback (S_1), setting the conditions for him to apply rules to prepare for mating (R_1). First he digs a shallow pit in the bottom of the stream over which he builds a roof of weeds. After this nest is completed, further hormonal changes cause his belly to become bright red. This red belly serves not so much to attract females as it does to signal other male sticklebacks (who also have red bellies) that this particular mating spot is taken. Studies with wooden models of sticklebacks or stickleback-like objects have shown that the approach of any small object with a red underside (S_1) will elicit an automatic attack (R_1) from a male stickleback. Moreover, the attack will be more intense if the approaching object is in a vertical position, which is the fighting position for sticklebacks, than if it is in any other position. The exact shape, exact movements, and so forth, are irrelevant to eliciting R_1 as long as the red belly and the vertical position are present.

A short while after the nest is completed, a female stickleback, whose midsection is bulging with eggs, appears on the scene. She does not have a red belly like the males and thus approaches without fear of harm. As she approaches, her bulging midsection (S_1) sets up further conditions for application of the male's mating rules. (A bulging wooden model of the female will also serve as an S_1.) The male begins a rather complex mating ritual (R_1) and guides the female to his nest where she deposits her eggs (Fig. 3.4). These eggs serve as an S_1 for the male to fertilize them (R_1). Then the female departs, leaving the male to defend and care for the eggs until they hatch. Note that all of these rules and the complex behavior they involve (it's quite a job for a fish to dig a pit and put a roof of weeds over it) are not based on any previous experience. Next spring all of the surviving males in our stickleback's brood will unerringly apply the same set of rules.

Imprinting in ducklings is another example of an instinctive rule. Soon after a duckling is hatched it exhibits a rule of following (R_1) its mother (S_1) wherever she goes. This behavior is called imprinting. However, the actual mother duck isn't really the important S_1. If the duck egg is placed in another species' nest, such as that of a goose, the duckling will imprint on the mother of this nest as if she were his own and follow her. Indeed, if a human being is present

FIG. 3.4 Male stickleback (left) courting a bulging female. (Adapted from The curious behavior of the stickleback by N. Tinbergen. Copyright © 1952 by Scientific American, Inc.)

at the crucial time the ducklings are ready to imprint, the human being may end up with avid followers.

Just as fake wooden fish can be used to see which S_1 characteristics make the male stickleback attack and mate, fake mother ducks, which vary in size, color, sound, movement, and so forth, can be used to find out what S_1 characteristics are important for imprinting. Such studies show that size is somewhat important; if the model "mother" is too small, the babies peck at it, and if it is too large, they often are frightened by it. Color seems to be important too; a blue "mother" is better than a red one, which in turn is better than a yellow one. Movement of the wings accompanied by rhythmic, rather than sustained, sound also seems to increase the likelihood of imprinting. The best S_1 would appear to be a fake object that looks and behaves like a mother duck.

Timing is an extremely important factor in imprinting. It has been found that if ducklings are hatched in isolation and are brought into contact with a model or a real mother duck at various times after they have hatched, imprinting occurs most strongly at sixteen hours of age. If contact with a model or real mother occurs earlier or later than that, imprinting is less likely to occur. This is because at earlier than sixteen hours the duckling can't walk well enough to follow the mother or the model, and after sixteen hours the duckling becomes fearful of strange objects and tends to avoid them. Under normal circumstances these two factors serve to make a duckling imprint only on his mother because she is the only adult duck present when he becomes able to walk, and the duckling's subsequent fearfulness of strange objects keeps him from applying the rule to other ducks. Thus his mother becomes the only duck to be recognized as the S_1 in his rule about following.

Predispositions

Whenever reflexive and instinctual rules are discussed, the question inevitably arises whether higher animals such as apes and man have such rules. Clearly, we human beings have some reflexes—when your doctor strikes the proper place on your knee, your leg gives a reflexive kick; when an unexpected loud noise occurs, you give a reflexive start and blink your eyes; and when something gets caught in your throat, you cough. However important these reflexes may be to your physiological well-being, they certainly don't play the primary role in your life that the fly-tongue reflex plays in the life of a frog; the frog depends upon his reflex rule in order to keep from starving. We higher animals rely so heavily upon rules other than reflexes that it is safe to say that reflexes, while they are necessary for our physiological functioning, are not all we have to depend on.

While it may be safe to reach the highly qualified conclusion I just did about the reflexive origin of human rules, I'm not so brave when it comes to whether or not we have rules of instinctive origin. For years psychologists were sure about the answer—the question received a condescending smile and a self-assured, "No!" It seemed clear that all human behavior other than reflexes was the result of learned and intellectual rules; no instinctual rules were involved. Indeed, the sheer variety in human activities, the pronounced cultural differences in such things as eating habits, mating rituals, and child care, and even the clear differences in what two people do under the same circumstances, made the notion of human instincts seem remote.

Recently, however, this cut-and-dried answer has taken quite a beating both in scientific journals and in such popular books as Robert Ardrey's *African Genesis*, Konrad Lorenz' *On Aggression*, and Desmond Morris' *The Naked Ape*. The gist of the arguments is that human beings may have some instinctlike rules which are not exactly like the stereotyped, automatic rules we see in sticklebacks or ducks but which are strongly influenced by experience. Indeed, these instinctlike rules may be so heavily influenced by experience that each person's version differs so much from everyone else's version that scientists have failed to detect the basic similarity underlying all these versions. About the only way to get at the underlying similarity is to step back and look at mankind in general—to look at the things we all seem to do time after time, especially those things that make us uniquely human.

When this is done, striking trends emerge. Among these are the fact that we are social animals that develop and indulge in language, create and worship gods, form strong interpersonal loyalties, tend to group together and follow strong leaders (Fig. 3.5), are more aggressive toward other members of our own species than perhaps any other animals in the world, and so on. In short,

FIG. 3.5 *It is quite possible that humans have a predisposition to follow strong leaders; often this has led to disaster. (UPI photo.)*

the list contains most of the things we commonly regard, either proudly or with despair, as "human nature."

Because the origins of these rules are not wholly instinctual on the one hand nor wholly due to experience and/or intellect on the other hand, a new name has been coined for them, *predispositions*. A predisposed origin means that an individual is born with a tendency to do or develop a particular behavior, but exactly how he ends up doing or developing it depends upon his own particular past experiences, the present circumstances in which he finds himself, the culture he lives in, and so on. All of these factors interact to produce a rule that, while we all have it, is unique for each individual. If this sounds a bit ill defined, it is because we just don't know much about these rules yet. That is why there are question marks in this part of Figure 3.2.

Predispositions, particularly in human beings, currently are the focus of a good deal of scientific study and controversy. While many psychologists still cling to old doubts about their existence, recent anthropological data on the evolutionary origins of the human species, zoological data about the behavior of primates other than human beings, and psychological and sociological speculation are all beginning to favor the idea that predispositions exist in human beings. It is yet too early to state that the idea is accurate, but if interest and investigation continue at the present rate, we should know soon.

Learned Rules   Most, if not all, animals are capable of forming rules on the basis of experience. However, the higher the animal is on the phylogenetic scale, the greater the role played by such rules in his ordinary moment-by-moment activities. Their role in human behavior is so large that psychologists' study of human rules has focused almost exclusively on these experienced-based *learned rules* and the process by which these rules are acquired, called *learning*. Because learning is a major origin of human rules, it is proper that the following discussion be more detailed than were the discussions of reflexes, instincts, and predispositions and that it focus on human beings instead of animals. Keep in mind, however, that many other animals use experience to form rules in much the same way human beings do.

What-to-do rules   Learned what-to-do rules are of the $S_1 \rightarrow R_1 \rightarrow S_2$ form; for example, "When Dad's in a good mood (S_1) and I am nice to him (R_1), I can usually convince him to let me have the car for the evening (S_2)"; or, "When the kettle boils over on the stove (S_1), I must turn down the heat (R_1) to make it stop (S_2)."

Note that in these examples the behavior (R_1) is instrumental in attaining some desired outcome (S_2). For this reason, the formation of an $S_1 \rightarrow R_1 \rightarrow S_2$ rule on the basis of whether it works or not is called *instrumental learning* (or *operant conditioning*). Application of the rule is called *instrumental* (or *operant*) *behavior*. The desired outcome (S_2) is called *reinforcement* because its occurrence means that the rule has worked and, therefore, that it is reasonable to strengthen (that is, reinforce) reliance upon it in the future. When the rule does not work and some unpleasant, undesired S_2 occurs instead, the S_2 is called *punishment*.

What-to-expect rules   What-to-expect rules probably never have reflexive, instinctive, or even predispositional origins. They are rules about what follows what ($S_1 \rightarrow S_2$) and they reflect either *cause-and-effect relations* or *correlational relations*.[2] As such, what-to-expect rules are about the things that happen in one's world and depend upon the specific events that are observed there. Thus, expecting a smiling person (S_1) to be friendly (S_2), a barking dog (S_1) to bite (S_2), an object that looks like a fried egg (S_1) to taste like a fried egg (S_2), and a red traffic light (S_1) to stop traffic (S_2) are all examples of what-to-expect rules.

Conditioning   We all form many $S_1 \rightarrow S_2$ rules on the basis of the things we experience, read, and hear. Some are very general—for example, "Medical treatment (S_1) is followed by getting well (S_2)"—and some very personal—for example, "When Dad uses that tone of voice (S_1), I'm in for trouble (S_2)." Note that S_2 often can arouse either pleasant or unpleasant emotional reactions. In the two previous examples, getting well is a good thing when you're ill (S_2 arouses pleasant feelings) and getting in trouble with your dad is usually a bad thing (S_2 arouses fear).

An important aspect of what-to-expect rules is that after the rule is formed, the emotional reactions originally aroused only by S_2 often come to be aroused by S_1 as well. Thus, you may begin to feel better merely by receiving a prescription for medical treatment even though the medicine has yet to be taken. A child may become fearful and begin to cry merely at the sound of his father's gruff tone of voice even though the father has yet to administer a spanking. Thus, past experience from memory can lead to anticipation of

---

[2] Correlation means that S_1 and S_2 are related but that neither causes the other; for example, tall people tend to weigh more than short people, but being tall doesn't *cause* people to be heavy—the two conditions are both aspects of the same thing, being big.

a particular S_2 and a premature experiencing of the reaction that usually accompanies it. The development of this anticipation and premature experiencing is called *Pavlovian* (or *classical*) *conditioning*, and the premature reaction is said to be *conditioned* to S_1.

A well-known demonstration of Pavlovian conditioning, done in 1920 by two psychologists, John Watson and Rosalie Rayner, illustrates how fear aroused by S_2 can come to accompany the occurrence of S_1. The participant in this experiment was a one-year-old boy named Albert. He was a healthy child, emotionally stable, and not given to tantrums or crying. The psychologists wanted to see if Albert could be made to fear a harmless little white rat.

When he first encountered the rat, Albert was not afraid. But after his first exposure, whenever the rat was presented to him, one of the psychologists would strike a steel bar with a hammer (Fig. 3.6). The loud noise frightened Albert and made him cry. After only seven rat-noise presentations, the mere sight of the rat was sufficient to make Albert cry and attempt to crawl away. In short, Albert had developed an $S_1 \rightarrow S_2$ rule; the presence of the rat (S_1) led Albert to anticipate something frightening (the loud noise, S_2), and he began to be almost as fearful of the rat as he was of the loud noise.

Conditions that promote rule learning

(1) MOTIVATION   The whole point of an $S_1 \rightarrow R_1 \rightarrow S_2$ rule is to do R_1 so that S_2 becomes available. This strongly implies that the person who does R_1 must *value* S_2 to some degree or other, and the more he values S_2, the more likely he is to try to formulate a rule to get it. Thus, a child might formulate the rule, "When I'm thirsty (S_1), I must ask (R_1) Mama for a drink in order to quench my thirst (S_2)." Certainly, satiated thirst is a valued state for a child who is thirsty, and he's quite likely to search for, and find, a reliable rule for attaining that state. If the child never got thirsty, however, there would be no necessity (motivation) for such a rule, and he would not bother to formulate one.

Note that motivation has two aspects. First, *it prompts you to formulate a rule.* Second, after a rule has been formulated, *motivation sets the conditions under which the rule comes into play.* That is, the rule is retained in memory until you recognize the current situation as the one that calls for it, whereupon you retrieve the rule and apply it. Thus, the child's rule about asking his mother for a drink gets applied only when he recognizes that he is thirsty (S_1). Note that in this case, the recognition and recall aspects of memory work hand in hand— recognition of S_1 leads to recall of the rule.

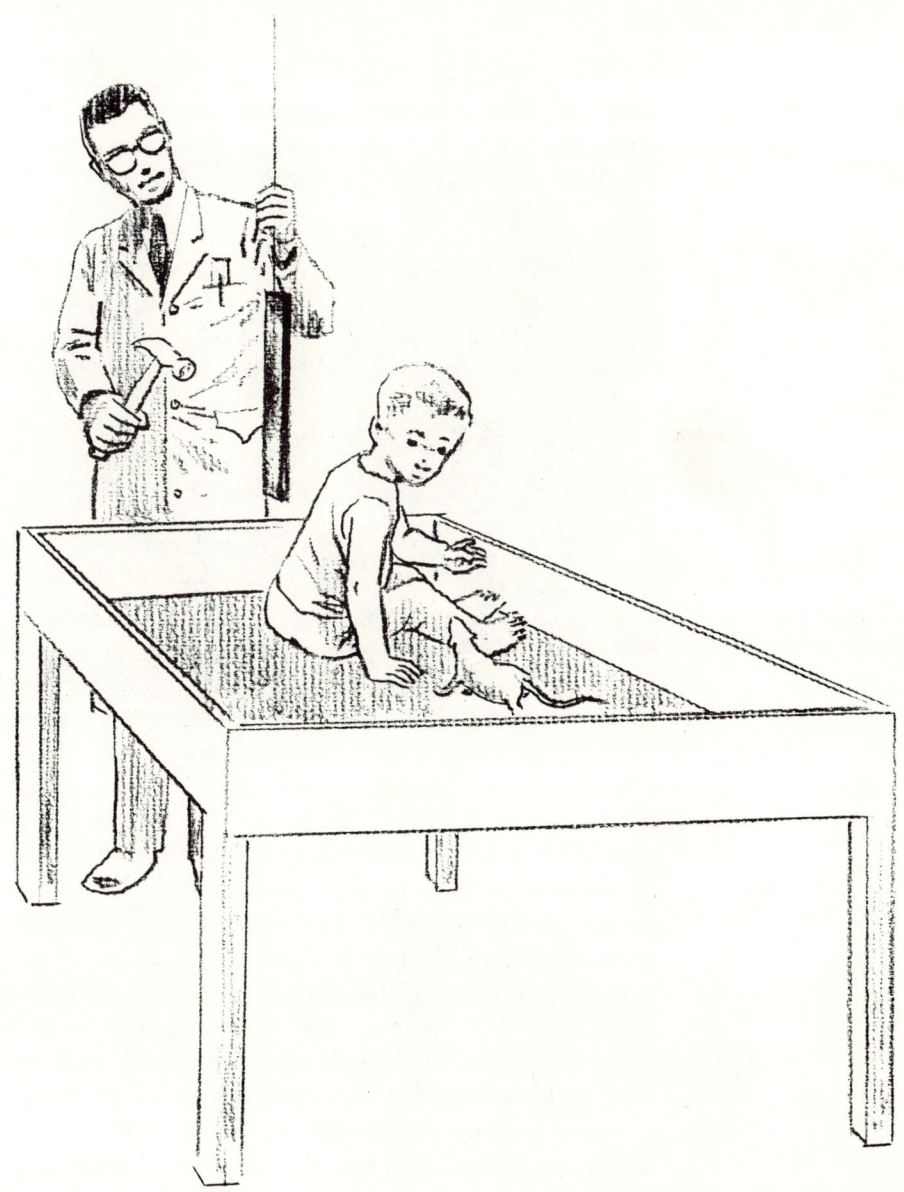

FIG. 3.6 *Little Albert and the rat a moment before the frightening loud noise occurred for the first time. Later, Albert became frightened whenever he saw the rat or any similar object.*

BOX 3.2

Does the Name Pavlov Ring a Bell?

It is quite probable that of all of the researchers who have studied learning, scientific history will remember I. P. Pavlov and B. F. Skinner as the most important. Because of their profound influence upon modern psychology, it is appropriate to briefly describe some of their research and to point out what their findings mean.

The Russian physiologist I. P. Pavlov (1849–1936) was the discoverer of conditioning.* He was dedicated to the view that behavior can be investigated scientifically and that psychological phenomena are simply a product of physiological processes. He regarded the *reflex* as the basic element of behavior. Physiologically, a reflex involves *stimulation* of a sense receptor which gives rise to a nerve impulse that travels along nerves to the central nervous system (the spinal cord or the brain) where it gives rise to a fresh impulse that goes along outgoing nerves to an active organ (usually muscles) where it initiates some *response* to the initial stimulation. Pavlov viewed complex behavior as simply an elaboration and compounding of such elementary reflexes.

Prior to Pavlov, reflexes were regarded as innate and unchangeable aspects of the nervous system. Pavlov argued that under special circumstances, reflexes

*See I. P. PAVLOV, *Conditioned Reflexes*. New York: Oxford, 1927.

(2) *TRANSFER*   If a new S_1 is very like one you already have a rule for, your old rule is a good place to begin in formulating a new rule for the new S_1. Indeed, the old rule may work so well that only minor adjustments are needed for it to evolve into a new rule that is unique to the new S_1. This process of modifying an old rule to fit a new S_1 is called *positive transfer*. Thus, if a man were to transfer those rules that he had formulated for driving his own small, stick-shift car to a large, automatic-shift car that he had rented, many of his old rules would work fairly well and would be rapidly modified into rules that were specific to the idiosyncrasies of the rented car.

Sometimes transfer doesn't work very well. If the old and new situations are highly similar but the old rule is just plain inappropriate to the new situation, transfer may interfere with the formulation of an appropriate rule and thereby make you take longer to get the new rule than if you had started with no rule at all. This is called *negative transfer*. If, for example, you learned to drive a car on the right-hand side of the road, your driving rules are formulated on that basis. If you were to move to Britain, where they drive

could be acquired and lost as a result of experience with the environment. He regarded these acquired reflexes as the rudiments of learned behavior.

Pavlov and his associates performed a large number of experiments to demonstrate the acquired-reflex basis of learning. The most famous of these involved training a dog to salivate to the sound of a bell (Fig. 3.7). Before training the dog, Pavlov connected the salivary gland in the dog's cheek to a glass tube so that the occurrence and amount of salivation could be measured. When he presented food to the dog, salivation automatically occurred as a natural reflexive by-product of the act of the dog seeing food and preparing to eat it; the automatic salivation accompanying the food was labeled an *unconditioned reflex*. Next, a bell was rung each time the food was presented and after several pairings of the food and the bell, the bell alone was sufficient to elicit salivation; the salivation accompanying the bell was labeled a *conditioned reflex*. However, after the bell was rung several times without the food, the bell ceased to bring about salivation, a process that Pavlov called *extinction* of the conditioned reflex.

Pavlov's discovery had a profound effect on psychology because it looked as though he had discovered the physiological basis of learning. And even though the reflex interpretation of learning has been dropped (the modern terms are unconditioned and conditioned *responses*) and many of Pavlov's physiological interpretations have been forgotten, some psychologists continue to regard *Pavlovian* (or *classical*) *conditioning* as the basic mechanism of learning.

FIG. 3.7 *A diagram of Pavlov's famous experiment with the salivating dog (see Box 3.2).*

It is clear, however, that Pavlovian conditioning cannot account for quite a bit of commonly observed learning. Since Pavlovian conditioning involves the elicitation of old behaviors by new signals, how then can it account for the fact that animals and people often demonstrate seemingly new behaviors that uniquely satisfy the demands of new situations? The answer to this question was provided by B. F. Skinner.

Skinner (b. 1904), building on earlier research, is responsible for the careful investigation of a second basic kind of learning, *operant* (or *instrumental*) *conditioning*.† The experiment most commonly used to illustrate this kind of conditioning begins by placing a hungry white rat in a box (appropriately called a Skinner Box) about half the size of a file case drawer (Fig. 3.8). The box has nothing in it except a small dish at one end and, slightly above the dish, a short metal rod that sticks out of a vertical slot in the wall. Once the hungry rat is placed in the box, he begins to sniff around. When he gets near the bar, the experimenter releases a small pellet of food into the dish. From then on, whenever the rat approaches the bar, the experimenter releases a pellet, except that as the experiment progresses, the experimenter becomes more and more discriminating about what the rat has to do before getting the food. At first, merely getting near the

†See B. F. SKINNER, *The Behavior of Organisms.* New York: Appleton, 1938.

on the left-hand side of the road, the old and new driving situations would be highly similar, but your old rules would be inappropriate and would interfere with the smooth formation of new, left-hand rules. Thus, you would have to pay extremely close attention to what you were doing in order to insure that your old rules didn't slip in. (Indeed, should one of these rules slip in and, for example, you found yourself having turned a corner directly into the stream of oncoming traffic, the resulting terror would be sufficient to motivate you to pay closer attention to your new rules.)

(3) *SHAPING* Sometimes transferred rules work more or less well, depending on how closely they approximate the best possible rule. With experience, it is possible to increase a rule's approximation to the best rule by modifying it in light of the results it produces. Reinforcement and punishment of $S_1 \rightarrow R_1 \rightarrow S_2$ rules serve as *feedback* about how well the rules work. If a minor change in a rule leads to a greater amount, better quality, or more immediate feedback, we tend to keep the change. If the amount or quality of feedback is reduced or if it takes longer to occur than before, we know the change we made in the rule was a mistake, and we go back to our former

bar is sufficient. Later, the rat must touch the bar or else he gets no food. Finally, the rat must press the bar downward as far as it will go before he gets any food. This process is called *shaping*, and the end result of it is an animal that will make a *conditioned response* (press the bar) in order to receive *reinforcement* (food). If the response fails to provide reinforcement, it will soon *extinguish*.

As you can see, some of the same terms are used to describe both Pavlovian and operant conditioning, but it should be kept in mind that the kinds of things that are learned are quite different. In Pavlovian conditioning, responses are simply elicited by a signal; the animal plays a rather passive role. In operant conditioning, the responses are emitted by the animal; he plays an active role.

It is highly unlikely that the rat ever saw a bar before, let alone pressed one,

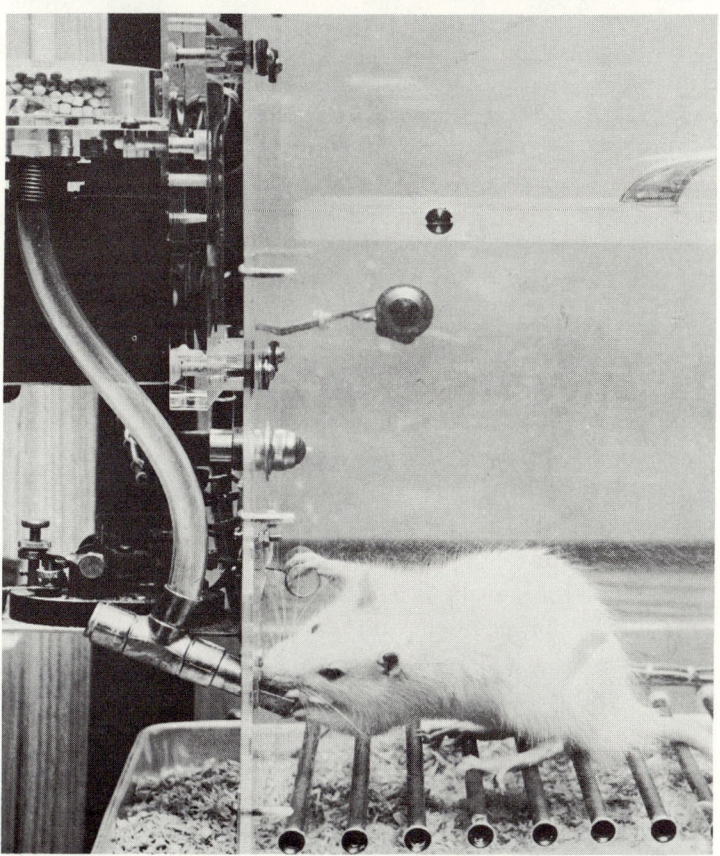

FIG. 3.8   *A laboratory rat in a Skinner Box (see Box 3.2). (Photo courtesy Pfizer Inc.)*

so his having learned to press it cannot be regarded as Pavlovian conditioning; that is, the conditioned response did not come about through elicitation of an old behavior by a new signal. Rather, this kind of learning clearly requires the development of a new behavior, the form of which is molded by the reinforcement pattern provided by the experimenter. In short, the rat had to learn behavior that would *operate* upon his environment, that would be *instrumental* in getting food— hence the interchangeable names, operant and instrumental conditioning.

Even though it sometimes looks mysterious, conditioning is not the automatic, inevitable sort of thing that some popular writers might have you believe. To say that someone has been conditioned to do something does not mean that he has been "zapped" by some magical psychological process which he has no power to resist; people usually cannot be made to do things against their will, although an attractive reinforcement may make it worth their while to do something they ordinarily wouldn't. "Conditioning" is simply a short-hand term for the set of circumstances that promote acquisition of rules (sometimes consciously, sometimes unconsciously). Pavlovian conditioning promotes what-to-expect rules. For the dog, the bell became a signal that food would appear, which led to anticipatory salivation (the conditioned response); if food repeatedly failed to occur after the bell was rung, the bell ceased to be regarded as a signal and the rule was soon discarded (extinguished). Operant conditioning, on the other hand, promotes

version. This process of changing a rule in light of feedback until it is the best rule for the situation is called *shaping*.

Parents commonly use shaping to teach their children such skills as sports, correct pronunciation of words, table manners, and the like. You've probably seen a father teaching his child to pitch a baseball. At first the child has only vague rules about how to hold and release the ball; when he throws it, the ball tends to go just about anywhere. However, with instruction and feedback in the form of the father's encouragement (reinforcement) and the child's own perception of his performance (also reinforcement), the original "grasp-and-fling" rule is shaped into a fairly decent "pitching" rule. As the rule gets better, both the father and the child become more particular about what gets reinforced; wild tosses that formerly would have got praise no longer receive it. Soon, only nearly perfect pitches receive reinforcement, and the child's pitching rule gradually is shaped to produce as many perfect pitches as possible.

(4) *RAPID FEEDBACK*   We formulate $S_1 \rightarrow R_1 \rightarrow S_2$ rules only when we think the R_1 will get us the desired S_2. To know whether this is the case, there must not be much of a delay between R_1 and S_2 or we will fail to perceive

what-to-do rules. For the hungry rat in the Skinner box, pressing the bar (a conditioned response) led to food (reinforcement); if the food ceased to appear after the conditioned response was made, the rule was soon discarded (extinguished).

Recently, generalized versions of operant conditioning procedures have led to some extremely interesting new developments in psychology. One is in a form of psychotherapy called behavior therapy, which is described in Section 5, Part 2. Another is in teaching people to voluntarily control various "automatic and involuntary" aspects of their bodily functioning such as their heartbeat and brain waves; this work is described in Box 3.3.

If the terms used to describe learning seem a bit peculiar to you, it is not without reason. Pavlov used the Russian equivalent of the word "conditional" to indicate that the elicitation of a behavior by a new signal was conditional upon that signal having been paired with an old signal that "naturally" elicits the behavior. When Pavlov's work was translated from Russian to English, "conditional" was translated as "conditioned," and this word has stuck ever since. Even further obscurity is added by the fact that the term "conditioning," which refers to the use of either Pavlovian or operant *procedures* for promoting learning, often is used loosely, as though it were a synonym for learning itself.

a cause-and-effect relation. For example, if punishment (S_2) for a child's bad behavior (R_1) is delayed until his father comes home in the evening, the child may fail to understand what he did that got him into trouble. Dumping his dirty clothes into the toilet bowl has immediate pleasure for him and therefore makes a fine rule. The long delay between the clothes-dumping episode and the spanking may cloud the issue about why the spanking is being administered, and unless the father explains what the punishment is for, the child may never form the rule that dumping clothes in the toilet leads to a spanking.

Timing probably is even more important in $S_1 \rightarrow S_2$ rules than it is in $S_1 \rightarrow R_1 \rightarrow S_2$ rules. Think back to little Albert and his rat. If the loud noise (S_2) had been delayed very long after the rat (S_1) was presented, Albert would never have been able to formulate his "rat $\rightarrow$ noise" rule. Indeed, the things that were consistently present when the noise occurred (the psychologists?) rather than the rat would have become the S_1 in his rule and would have elicited his fear. If nothing consistently accompanied the sound, no rule would have been formed. Indeed, the perception of an $S_1 \rightarrow S_2$ relation is very difficult if there is much of a delay between the occurrence of S_1 and S_2. Think, for example, of the difficulty people sometimes have in finding out what foods they are allergic to because of the delay between eating an allergenic food, say strawberries, and the occurrence of an allergic reaction, say a rash.

(5) *FREQUENCY AND SALIENCE*   The frequency with which an S_1 situation occurs in a person's experience influences whether or not a rule about it will be formulated. But frequency can work both ways. In the case of trying to decide what food (S_1) gives you a rash (S_2), a rule may be more easily formulated if the food is something you seldom eat. Thus when you eat your first spring strawberries and break out in a rash a few hours later, the culprit is easily detected and a "strawberry → rash" rule is quickly formulated. On the other hand, it is sometimes difficult to formulate a rule unless the S_1 situation occurs frequently enough for you to progressively sharpen a rule to fit it or, for that matter, to even notice that there is any rule to be had. To use Albert as an example again, if he had gone into the psychology laboratory only once, he probably would never have formulated his rule; it took seven experiences in the lab to formulate and sharpen his "rat → noise" rule.

Sometimes there is a trade-off between the frequency of occurrence of a rule-producing situation and the salience of the S_1 and S_2 events that compose it. For example, both a rat and a loud noise are salient events to children; a living creature usually fascinates children while a loud noise usually severely frightens them. Thus, in the case of Albert, the rat and the noise were both salient, and the "rat → noise" rule emerged after only seven trips to the laboratory. However, if the rat had bitten Albert the first time he saw it, it is very likely that a "rat → bite" rule (that is, conditioned fear of the rat) would have been formulated even faster because the painful bite would have been even more salient than the loud, frightening noise. On the other hand, if the psychologists had elected to use more familiar, less salient, events for their experiment with Albert, say his wooden blocks (as S_1) and one of the psychologists shouting, "Boo!" (as S_2), a "blocks → Boo!" rule may well have taken a long time to be formulated.

Salient events that actually have no relation to one another sometimes get formulated into false rules that have no real value. This is the basis for superstition. I blush to admit it, but I once found myself unwilling to drive through a certain town near my home because on two previous occasions my car had broken down in the town, necessitating a boring two- or three-hour stopover while expensive repairs were made. The salience of the car breaking down, the dreary wait for the repairs, and my unhappiness about the expense led me to the totally irrational rule, "town → car breakdown, boredom, and expense." Even though I soon recognized the irrationality of my rule and laughed at myself for my foolishness, my next couple of trips through the town were accompanied by anxious anticipation of strange sounds from my car's engine.

Salience also can lead to superstitious $S_1 \rightarrow R_1 \rightarrow S_2$ rules. There is a little rhyme that children sometimes chant, "See a pin, pick it up, all day long, you'll have good luck." For some people, merely one experience of picking up a pin and then, most likely due to chance, having something outstandingly good happen is enough to addict them to picking up pins. The rule may never work again, but the salience of that one experience is enough to keep it operating.

Conditions that promote rule change or abandonment

(1) GENERALIZATION AND DISCRIMINATION The application of learned rules is not a rigid, automatic thing. For example, each time you apply an $S_1 \rightarrow R_1 \rightarrow S_2$ rule, the R_1 may be slightly different, depending upon the circumstances. When you're thirsty (S_1), you can get refreshment (S_2) by drinking water from a glass, a fountain, or your cupped hands, or you can even drink something else such as soda, alcohol, or iced tea (all different kinds of R_1's). The technical term for this interchangeability of behaviors in a rule is *response generalization*.

By the same token, with either $S_1 \rightarrow R_1 \rightarrow S_2$ or $S_1 \rightarrow S_2$ rules, the S_1 situation varies to some degree from one time to another, but you still regard it as sufficiently similar to earlier times to permit application of your rule. Thus, for the $S_1 \rightarrow R_1 \rightarrow S_2$ rule about how to quench your thirst, whether your thirst occurs when you are in the sun, in a stuffy room, or sleeping, or whether it is due to illness, strenuous exercise, or fear, you still apply your "thirst $\rightarrow$ drink" rule. Similarly, little Albert applied his $S_1 \rightarrow S_2$ rule to other fuzzy ratlike S_1's; a dog, a rabbit, a Santa Claus mask, and a fur coat all led him to whimper with fear. The application of the same rule to a variety of similar S_1's is called *stimulus generalization*.

Too great a willingness to regard various S_1 situations as basically similar and appropriate for applying a particular rule can lead to difficulties. For example, when a baby begins to learn to say "Daddy" (R_1) in the presence of his father (S_1) in order to get his father's attention (S_2), he may at first tend to regard any man as a sufficient S_1 for his rule. However, after being rebuked by his embarrassed mother when he applies his rule to total strangers at the supermarket, he becomes more cautious. Because his rule fails to produce the desired S_2 when applied to strange men (and because his mother may even give him a very undesirable S_2 if he doesn't stop it), the child learns to limit the application of his rule to only one S_1, his father. Learning to differentiate

BOX 3.3

Some New Frontiers in Learning

It long has been an article of faith among psychologists that the functioning of our internal organs, our heart, kidneys, brain, and so on, is beyond our own control. True, these organs may react to the occurrence of various kinds of environmental events (loud noise → increased heartbeat), and by manipulating these events a kind of gross control was recognized as possible. But voluntary control of the kind we exercise when we move a finger or arm was regarded as limited solely to skeletal muscles; internal functioning was even referred to as "involuntary." However, two growing areas of research have shown clearly that this psychological dictum is not true. The research has focused on the use of instrumental (operant) conditioning procedures (1) to teach control of the heart, stomach, kidneys, and blood pressure and (2) to teach the control of brain activity as measured by brain waves.

Since 1967, Dr. Neal E. Miller and his associates have performed a variety of experiments in which animals have been trained to modify the functioning of their viscera.* In such experiments it is important to rule out the possibility that the observed modifications are merely the by-product of some other behavior.

*N. E. Miller, Learning of visceral and glandular responses. *Science*, 1969, *163*, 434–445.

between the S_1's that will lead to the desired S_2 and which S_1's will not is called *stimulus discrimination*, and it occurs with both $S_1 \rightarrow R_1 \rightarrow S_2$ rules and $S_1 \rightarrow S_2$ rules.

(2) *EXTINCTION*   Sometimes a rule fails to work simply because it is no longer appropriate. Then the only course is to abandon it—let it become "extinct," as it were. Suppose that a child successfully has been using the rule, "When I'm put to bed (S_1), crying (R_1) will coerce my parents into letting me watch TV for another hour (S_2)." But, unbeknownst to the child, his exasperated parents have gone to a psychologist who advised them to stop giving in to the little nipper and let him cry until he gives up and goes to sleep. The first night that the parents try to follow the psychologist's advice is likely to be a bit rough for everybody as the inappropriateness of the rule slowly becomes apparent to the child. Since the child is quite unlikely to extinguish his rule after merely one night's failure, the next night at bedtime is also likely to be quite noisy. But if the rule again fails to produce results, the child will be a bit less persistent. The third night, he'll probably still give it a try just in case it might work, but if it doesn't, he'll give up rather easily.

For example, if an animal is to learn to increase its heart rate, it could "cheat" by running or jumping around rather than by actually changing some internal mechanism of control. To prevent such cheating the animals are injected with *curare,* a drug that completely paralyzes all skeletal muscles while leaving the internal organs unparalyzed.

When an animal is paralyzed it is difficult to use instrumental conditioning procedures because it is difficult to reinforce the desired behaviors; a paralyzed animal can neither eat nor drink. The solution is either to shock him until the desired behavior occurs (the cessation of shock is reinforcing) or to give him mild electrical stimulation in the "pleasure center" in the brain (see Appendix 2) whenever the desired behavior occurs.

Using curarized rats and either shock or brain stimulation as reinforcement, Dr. Miller was able to train the rats to produce both increases and decreases in heart rate, in systolic blood pressure, in intestinal contractions, in urine formation in the kidneys, in the amount of blood in the stomach wall, and in the amount of blood in the tail. As a little extra touch, they were able to train the rats to increase the amount of blood in one ear while decreasing the amount in the other ear (you can tell how much blood there is in a rat's ear by shining a light through it—the more blood there is, the less the amount of light that will pass through). In addition to all of this, Dr. Miller demonstrated that the rats could learn when

The actual strength of the child's resistance to giving up his formerly successful rule depends on the pattern of his parents' reactions to it in the past. If they have always given in so that crying at bedtime has always led to an extra hour of TV, called *100 percent reinforcement,* their new pattern of never giving in will be in stark contrast to the old pattern, and the inappropriateness of his rule quickly will become apparent to the child. If in the past the parents have been inconsistent about giving in, called *partial reinforcement,* their new pattern will be difficult for the child to detect ("Does their failure to give in tonight mean that my rule is no longer appropriate or is this just one of those annoying nights when they've decided to stand firm?") This difficulty in detecting the new pattern because of partial rather than 100 percent reinforcement means that the child will take longer to extinguish his rule.

Suppose that the parents have given in to their child every second night. This kind of partial reinforcement pattern is called *fixed-interval reinforcement.* As in the case of 100 percent reinforcement, the predictability of this pattern makes any change quite obvious and leads to rapid extinction of the rule. But because the rule has not always been appropriate in the past, its failure is not

to respond and when not to; they learned to increase (or decrease) their heart rates in the presence of a signal which meant that reinforcement would be given and to return to normal when the signal was removed. And, amazingly enough, after a three-month interval without training, the rats still retained the ability to modify their heart rates when the signal was presented again. Finally, using stimulation of the "pleasure center" as reinforcement, Dr. Miller was able to train his rats to either increase or decrease the amplitude of their brain activity, a behavior that is also possible for human beings, as we shall see next.

By placing small electrodes on the scalp, it is possible to record the generalized electrical activity of a living brain. These recordings are in the form of wave patterns that are traced on a moving paper; the recordings are known as *electro-encephalograms*, or *EEGs*. The brain waves vary in amplitude and in frequency, and a number of characteristic wave patterns have been identified and studied. The pattern that recently has been of most interest is an 8–14 cycle per second wave that is called the *alpha wave*. In human beings this wave is observed only when the person is relaxed and peaceful but yet alert. This feeling is called the *alpha state*, and it is regarded by most people who experience it as an extremely pleasant and desirable way to feel—sort of a calm, natural "high." The problem is that alpha states usually are very short—they come and go, alternating with other states as the person's mind wanders or as things happen around him. The research question has been whether people could learn to intentionally produce and maintain the alpha state.

as surprising as it is with 100 percent reinforcement, and therefore extinction is somewhat slower. Note that if the parents were changeable in the pattern of giving in, every other night during some weeks and every third night during other weeks, called *variable-interval reinforcement*, extinction would take even longer.

Now, suppose that the parents have always tried to be firm with the child but have developed a pattern of allowing him to get up and watch TV if he has three crying tantrums in an evening. This kind of a partial reinforcement is called *fixed-ratio reinforcement*. (The child would probably have developed the scheme of having three quick tantrums every evening so he could get up more quickly.) As with 100 percent reinforcement and fixed-interval reinforcement, the predictability of fixed-ratio reinforcement makes any change in the parents' pattern quite obvious, and extinction of the child's rule would occur quickly, although not as quickly as it would have had the rule formerly met with 100 percent reinforcement. And it would take even longer for the child to extinguish his rule should the parents be entirely random with respect to how many crying

A few years ago, Dr. Joe Kamiya decided to see if people could be taught to detect momentary occurrences of the alpha state.† He hooked volunteers to an EEG machine, had them tell him when they thought they were in the alpha state, and then, after checking the EEG record, he would tell them if they were right or wrong (that is, he would reinforce them). He found that after about three hours of such experience the volunteers were able to correctly recognize alpha states 80 percent of the time—they had learned to detect the occurrence of an internal bodily function that few of them probably had ever even heard of before they went to the experiment.

Having demonstrated that people can learn to recognize the alpha state, Dr. Kamiya turned to trying to teach them to produce the alpha state at will. To do this, he again hooked his volunteers to the EEG machine, but this time they were told to produce alpha waves whenever Dr. Kamiya gave a signal. Sure enough, having previously learned to recognize the alpha state, the volunteers were able to produce the state (and, of course, the accompanying waves) whenever the signal was given. This experiment was followed by another in which new volunteers were used to show that prior recognition training isn't really necessary; the EEG machine was rigged so that a tone sounded whenever an alpha wave pattern was occurring, and the volunteers soon learned to keep the tone turned on.

†J. KAMIYA, Operant control of the EEG alpha rhythm and some of its reported effects on consciousness. In C. T. Tart (Ed.), *Altered States of Consciousness*, New York: Wiley, 1969.

tantrums they require before letting their child watch TV, called *variable-ratio reinforcement*.

Thus, a rule's resistance to extinction depends upon how it has been reinforced up to the time it becomes inappropriate. If the rule formerly met with 100 percent reinforcement, the change in its success is quite clear and its extinction is rapid. If it formerly met with fixed-interval or fixed-ratio partial reinforcement, the change will not be quite so clear and extinction will occur somewhat less rapidly, but it still will not take long. Finally, if the rule met with variable-interval or variable-ratio partial reinforcement, the change in its success will be difficult to detect and extinction will take quite a while.

As you might well imagine, the actual length of time (or number of unsuccessful attempted applications) before a rule is completely extinguished depends also upon how many times it has successfully been used in the past. If the child in our example had successfully and frequently been using his rule for two or three years, he is not apt to give it up until it is conclusively proved to be unsuccessful; a rule that has frequently worked successfully in

The alpha state evidently is a very difficult experience to describe, and most people who have learned to control its occurrence do not know exactly how they do it. The most common analogy used to explain how the alpha state feels is that it is like meditation. Some people say that they feel like their entire consciousness is concentrated at a point above their head or behind their eyes. Others feel serene and quiet while still remaining vitally sensitive to everything around them. Still others feel cloaked in peacefulness and become extremely aware of their own feelings. Almost everyone finds that any planned, purposeful thought or concentration on visual imagination quickly ends the alpha state. The validity of the analogy between the alpha state and meditation is strengthened by the fact that EEG recordings of Zen priests and Yogis show that they produce prolonged alpha wave patterns while they are in meditation.‡

‡ See A. Kasamatsu and T. Hirai, An electroencephalographic study on the Zen meditation, and B. K. Anand, G. S. Chhina, and B. Singh, Some aspects of electroencephalographic studies in Yogis. In C. T. Tart (Ed.), *Altered States of Consciousness*. New York: Wiley, 1969.

the past usually is the best bet for the future. On the other hand, a rule that seldom has been used or that has been in use for only a short time is more easily extinguished; it is as though there weren't sufficient evidence on the rule's dependability to make its continued use worth the gamble.

An extinguished rule may be abandoned, but it is not necessarily forgotten. Frequently, after extinction appears to be complete, the rule will suddenly reappear. Thus, the parents of the child we've been discussing might persist in their refusal to reinforce his tantrums until one momentous night he goes quietly to bed and straight to sleep. The parents congratulate themselves and make a mental note to call the psychologist to tell him how brilliant he is and how well his advice worked. But, the next night their peace is shattered; the child reverts to his supposedly extinguished rule and cries with nearly as much gusto as he did when his rule actually worked.

Instead of writing a threatening letter to the psychologist, the parents should merely remain firm in their nonreinforcement of the child's rule because reappearance of an extinguished rule is quite common. This reappearance is called *spontaneous recovery,* and it merely means that for a time after extinction there will be periods during which the child will try the rule just in case it may have become appropriate again. As long as no reinforcement is forthcoming, the rule will quickly extinguish again and soon these episodes of spontaneous recovery will cease.

While we have discussed the work of only two researchers, many others are involved in elaborating and extending the research that has been described. They all tend to be cautious when speculating about the future implications of their research, but two trends seem to be shaping. First, the kind of work Dr. Miller has been doing may someday make it possible for people to be taught to control the functioning of their internal organs as a way of medically treating, for example, gastrointestinal illnesses such as spastic colon or ulcers, reducing high blood pressure, controling irregular heartbeat, and so on. Such control might prove much more desirable than the current practice of using drugs because of the reduced possibility of adverse side effects, the immediate availability of the treatment at the moment it is needed, and the low cost of such treatment. Second, the kind of work Dr. Kamiya has been doing suggests that people might be able to learn to use alpha states to help them to relax and reduce anxiety levels, thereby becoming a "natural" replacement for sleeping pills, tranquilizers, and recreational drugs such as alcohol and marijuana.

Imitated Rules

While it is clear that a fair proportion of a human being's store of rules originate in learning, it is equally clear that learning fails to account for all of them. Learned rules tend to be simplistic in that the events involved are fairly concrete, and the rule is heavily dependent upon immediate feedback if it is not to be abandoned. People, however, also have and use more complicated rules, rules that involve abstract concepts (such as honesty, God, gravity), rules that involve complex events (such as knowledge about genetics or how fulcrums work), and rules that span long time intervals and do not depend upon immediate feedback (such as rules about excessive caloric intake and subsequent obesity). While some of these more complicated rules are based on one's own trial and error experience to one degree or another, far more are obtained from someone else who already possesses them. This method of rule acquisition is called *imitation* and the person from whom the rules are acquired is called a *model*. Both what-to-do and what-to-expect rules can be acquired in this way.

There are two ways of acquiring rules through imitation. The first is by *observation* of a model who is using the rule. Thus, small children acquire many of their rules by observing and imitating the older children and adults around them; when we call a little boy a "chip off the old block," we're merely saying that his father serves as an important model for him. Later, in school, the rules for doing arithmetic and other such procedural skills are acquired by observation and imitation of another model, the teacher. And even for adults, the quickest way to acquire a skill is to watch someone else do it and then to imitate what was done.

The second way of acquiring imitated rules is by receiving written or spoken *instruction* from the model. Thus, we get advice from trusted friends, we find out how to become good cooks by reading the Galloping Gourmet's cookbook, we acquire knowledge of electrical circuitry from a textbook, we discover how to combat body odor from magazine advertisements, and we receive instructions about how to be morally upright from Sunday sermons.

More often than not, imitated rules are acquired through a mixture of observation and instruction—the model both shows and tells you how to do something. For example, if a youngster tries to acquire that favorite childhood code language, Pig Latin, solely by observation, he may never become very good at speaking and understanding it. But he will quickly master it if he both hears it spoken and is told the rule—"Move the first sound of a word to the end and then add *ay* (for example, 'Pig Latin' becomes 'Igpay Atinlay')."

If a rule is complex, observation or instruction may provide only the basic notion and you will have to perfect the rule yourself; for example, observation or instruction will give you a rough idea how to ride a bicycle or how to predict the time it will take for a pot roast to cook, but you actually have to try it yourself and perfect your skill before you can do either task very well. Moreover, successful imitation of a model's rules depends on your having paid attention to the right things while you were observing or being instructed. Initial success in riding a bicycle, for example, depends less on proper pedaling and guiding than upon keeping your balance, something that the model may do so effortlessly that both you and he might not think to pay attention to it.

In general, imitation is a very efficient way of acquiring rules. In one study it was shown that observers acquired an imitated rule in much less time and with much less effort than the observed model required to learn the rule in the first place. This makes sense, of course. Learned rules have to be discovered through trial and error; they are inferred from the results they produce or the correctness of their predictions. By contrast, imitated rules usually are given to you pretty explicitly worked out, and you may even be told how well they may be expected to work.

Imitation is similar to learning in that it not only provides information about *how* to do things (R_1) but it also tells you to what circumstances (S_1) the rule is *applicable* and what outcome (S_2) can be *expected*. However, imitation differs from learning in two ways. First, you need not personally have done the thing or experienced the outcome in order to acquire the rule—it is sufficient merely to have been told about it. Thus, when a friend gives you directions over the telephone about how to get to his house, you acquire an imitative what-to-do rule; when another friend tells you that you'll get sick if you eat fresh oysters during months whose names do not have the letter *r* in them, you may acquire a what-to-expect rule, unless you elect to reject such nonsense.

The second difference between imitation and learning is that not only do you get imitated rules secondhand but you also may never have the opportunity to check their validity for yourself. In learning, the rule initially is accepted or rejected on the basis of how well it works. In imitation, the rule initially is accepted or rejected on the basis of the *credibility* of the model. Credibility means that you believe that the model is knowledgeable on the topic, is generally well informed, is worthy of your admiration and respect, is someone whose advice you habitually depend upon (such as a parent or teacher), and so on. Of course, this is where we often get into difficulties—we sometimes tend to overrate the credibility of a model and uncritically imitate his rules, be it in merely following an older child's lead in doing relatively innocent mischief or, as we get older, in voting for a political candidate because our favorite movie star supports him or in following a popular political leader in calling for war or the persecution of some social, political, or religious minority.

Although we human beings rely heavily on imitation, we are not the only animals that use it. If you've ever observed a puppy growing up around an older dog, you may have noticed that the puppy's behavior often is quite similar to that of his companion. If the older dog plays with a stick or ball, the puppy will too. If the older dog has been taught to "fetch," the puppy quickly acquires this skill. If the older dog delights in chasing cars or barking at the mailcarrier, the puppy (unfortunately) soon evidences the same enthusiasm.

The two most famous examples of animals using imitation involve primates. First, a troop of wild monkeys that live in a Japanese game preserve frequently are fed sweet potatoes by their keepers. Some time ago one of the younger female monkeys began to wash the sand from her potatoes before eating them. Soon almost the entire troop was imitating her and potato washing now is an established custom.

The second example has had fairly broad repercussions because it has necessitated a redefinition of how human beings differ from other primates. It used to be thought that we human beings were set apart from all other animals by the "fact" that we alone use tools. Recently, however, tool use has been observed in a variety of primates. Notable among these is the observation by Dr. Jane Von Lawick-Goodall of wild chimpanzees using sticks to "fish" for termites. The chimpanzees insert a stick into the entrance of a termite nest, wait, and then gently withdraw the stick and lick the dainty morsels from the stick. This skill appears to be passed from the older chimpanzees to the younger by observation and imitation.

Intellectual Rules   The five rule origins discussed thus far account for most of one's workaday store of rules. There is, however, a sixth origin of rules, one that relies upon relatively thoughtful reflection about the kinds of rules that are needed to cope with particular situations and that attempts to "figure out" workable rules. This thoughtful, reflective process is called *intellect,* and the rules we derive from it are called *intellectual rules.*

Unfortunately, psychologists don't really know very much about the intellectual origins of rules. In large part, this is because the peculiar circumstance of the human intellect studying the human intellect makes it difficult for the researcher to keep his subject matter in perspective. Indeed, it often isn't even clear what the subject matter is. Is intellect solely the application of logic and analytic reasoning to the formulation of rules? This is not the case because some very abstract and serviceable rules apparently derive from intuitive processes that are not at all like formal logic or analytic reasoning. In fact, a few of our abstract rules are so grossly illogical (for example, "Friday the 13th is unlucky") that they could not have been derived from careful examination of the facts. So, while logic and reasoning may characterize *some* of our intellectual rule making, they are not the whole story.

Is intellect, then, that little voice you hear in your head when you are considering a problem? If so, what do you call the apparently unconscious processes that sometimes go on when you can't formulate a good rule? For example, you forget about the whole thing for a while and then the rule suddenly pops into your head. Clearly, unconscious activity is as much a form of intellect as is conscious activity, so consciousness and the little voice are only part of the story.

Perhaps intellect is the picture you sometimes see in your "mind's eye" when you are planning something or imagining how a particular rule might work. But since one can also formulate rules about such things as infinity or intransitive verbs without seeing any mental pictures, pictures cannot be the whole story either.

Finally, many people think of intellect as a magnificent, mystical phenomenon about which little can be known. This view often contains a good deal of smugness because its proponents feel that within this mystery lies the beauty of the human soul. They see intellect, and intellectual rules, as representing the creative, intuitive, unbounded aspects of humanity. Unfortunately, while intellect and its products are often beautiful, this view fails to recognize that humanity also can be cloddish and insensitive and that most of us would rather rely upon rules that other people give us than take the pains to formulate abstract intellectual rules for ourselves. These pedestrian aspects of human beings are as characteristic of our intellect as the pleasant ones. Besides, the assumption that intellectual rule making is by definition a mysterious process gives us little hope that we might one day be able to find ways of doing a better job of it.

Since each of these views of intellect repeatedly has been the starting point for unproductive examinations of intellectual rule making, adoption of any one of them runs the risk of getting stuck in an old, well-worn rut. To avoid this risk, many psychologists have decided, in essence, to ignore all of these views and to try a wholly new approach, even though such a plan might overlook some of the important questions that prompted the views in the first place. This new approach consists of regarding the processes involved in intellectual rule making as analogous to the procedures a scientist goes through in attempting to derive rules about the world we live in (Fig. 3.9). Of course, just as no one actually believes that human memory is identical to a computer, no one actually believes that intellectual rule making is identical to science—yet, as in the case of the computer-memory analogy, this intellect-science analogy allows us to use something we already understand as a vehicle for examining something we don't understand.

The scientist as rule maker A scientist's work consists of observing certain classes of events and then formulating a theory about how they are interrelated. He can check on the adequacy of his theory by deriving *hypotheses* about what he expects to happen if he performs a particular *experiment* or makes certain *observations*. The results of the experiment or the observations either *confirm* or *invalidate* his hypotheses, thereby increasing or decreasing his belief in the adequacy of his theory. While increased belief leads to increased reliance on the theory as it is, decreased belief leads to modification of the theory in light of the results of the experiment or observations in order to make it more adequate.

In essence, a scientific theory is a set of $S_1 \rightarrow S_2$ rules, but the rules are usually more complicated than the simple "If S_1 occurs, S_2 will follow" sort of thing that ordinarily derives from learning. An economist, for example, might construct a theory that interrelates the international money market, the U.S. balance of payments, inflation and unemployment, military spending, and the world market in wheat and corn. While some of these S's may be *directly* related to each other, that is, $S_1 \rightarrow S_2$, others may be *indirectly* related to each other; for example, if S_1 is related to S_2, which in turn is related to S_3, then S_1 is indirectly related to S_3. Moreover, the relations may be either *dependable* or *probabilistic*. That is, the relation between the U.S. balance of payments and the price of U.S. dollars on the world money market might be quite dependable;

FIG. 3.9 *The process by which scientists learn about nature can be used as an analogy for studying how people in general formulate intellectual rules.*

a decrease or increase in our balance of payments would dependably lead to a decrease or increase in the price of dollars on the money market. On the other hand, the relation might be probabilistic; an increase or decrease in our balance of payments may only increase or decrease the probability that there will be a shift in the price of dollars. In short, a scientific theory may consist of any combination of simple or complex, direct or indirect, and dependable or probabilistic relations among the events of concern.

Hypotheses are derived from the $S_1 \rightarrow S_2$ rules of the theory; if a $S_1 \rightarrow S_2$ rule in the theory is adequate, and if S_1 (or some specific set of S_1's) can be produced or observed, then S_2 (or some specific set of S_2's) should be the consequence. Such a hypothesis can be tested by making S_1 occur and seeing if the predicted S_2 occurs in the appropriate manner, that is, by an experiment, or by seeking out a natural occurrence of S_1 and seeing if S_2 occurs appropriately, that is, by an observation. If things don't happen in the hypothesized manner, the implication is that the theory is inadequate, at least with respect to this particular $S_1 \rightarrow S_2$ rule, and needs to be modified. In the latter case, the unexpected results of the experiment or observation often provide feedback to help in the modification of the theory.

Hypothesis testing is not limited to formal experiments or disciplined observation. A theory seldom is formulated merely for the pleasure of doing so; it usually is intended to provide rules that will help people deal with particular problems efficiently and successfully. For example, engineers rely on theories from chemistry and physics, government policy makers rely on theories from economics and political science, physicians rely on theories from biochemistry and a multitude of other sciences, and counselors rely on theories from psychology and sociology. Each time one of these people tries to use a theory to help him accomplish something, he is testing a hypothesis and, thereby, indirectly testing the theory. If the test is successful, the reputation of the theory is bolstered. If the test is a failure, the reputation of the theory suffers, and the need for change becomes more apparent to scientists and users alike.

The analogy   Our own intellectual endeavors are like those of the scientist in that all of us observe events that occur around us, formulate theories about how events are related to each other, test hypotheses that follow from our theories, and (sometimes) change our theories in light of the results of our tests.

People's intellectual theories are similar to scientific theories in that they range from simple to complex and involve direct and indirect relations among events, which, in turn, can be either dependable or probabilistic. For example, a man might formulate the simple, albeit weird, theory that increased sunspot activity will be followed by a drop in the stock market. Or he may elaborate upon his theory, taking into account the fact that sunspots are known to cause disturbances in the earth's electromagnetic field, that sunspot activity is cyclical, that the stock market often appears to be cyclical, and so on.

The more complex an intellectual theory becomes, the more likely it is that it will involve indirect relations as well as direct ones. Thus, a simple theory about sunspot activity and the stock market might merely involve the direct relation, "increased sunspot activity → drop in the market." If this simple theory were to be made more complex, it might well involve a set of indirect relations such as, "increased sunspot activity → increased electromagnetic disturbances → disturbed brain waves → erratic investment behavior → drop in the stock market."

Similarly, as theories become more complex, relations tend to be probabilistic rather than dependable. Thus, while the simple version of the sunspot theory might be, "increased sunspot activity *always* leads to a drop in the stock market," the more complex one might be, "increased sunspot activity increases electromagnetic disturbances, which *might sometimes* have a disturbing effect on brain waves, which *might* cause investors to make unwise investments, which, in turn, *could* cause the stock market to go down." All of these evasive words are essentially acknowledgments that the relations are conceived of as probabilistic rather than dependable. (This theory, of course, is nonsense; sunspot activity does *not* influence the stock market and, although increased sunspot activity apparently does increase electromagnetic disturbances on the earth, there is no reason to believe that such disturbances have any effect at all on human beings, especially on their brain waves.)

People's intellectual theories are unlike scientific theories in that they often are ill defined, they often incorporate irrelevant factors, they tend to be resistant to change, even in the light of invalidating evidence, and they frequently are oversimplified. Intellectual theories range between ill-defined hunches at one extreme (like someone's vague feeling that so and so has been spreading rumors about him) to rather sophisticated, well-defined theories at the other extreme (such as a gambler's "system" for betting on horses). In part, the degree of vagueness of an intellectual theory depends on the difficulty people have in isolating and identifying the events of interest. While a scientist has tools that help him measure events precisely (indeed, a major part of a scientist's work involves creation of such measuring devices), the unaided man in the street has to rely on whatever he can get. Thus, intellectual theories about such events as social interactions tend to be pretty vague, since it is difficult to really know what a person means when he does something, and his behavior can be interpreted in many different ways by different people depending upon the circumstances. On the other hand, when events are clear-cut, we often incorporate them into our theories even if they aren't particularly relevant. Thus a "system" for betting on horse races could involve the horses' previous win-lose records, the jockeys' win-lose records, the handicappers' predictions, the betting odds, and so on. Some of these factors may have no relevance to successful betting, but because they are clearly defined and salient, the betting theorist is very likely to incorporate them into his system.

People tend to be much less critical of their intellectual theories than scientists are of their scientific theories. This is not to say that people don't derive and test hypotheses from their theories. Indeed, every time we actually depend upon one of our theories to help us do something, the venture and its outcome constitutes a hypothesis and a test of the hypothesis. However, an outcome that is unfavorable to an intellectual theory may not lead to a change. No doubt you have at one time or another been in a conversation with someone who stated his ideas on some topic and who, when confronted with some contrary evidence or a contradiction in his logic, refused even to consider changing his theory. Cherished intellectual theories tend to be resistant to invalidating evidence. In some cases this resistance is due to the fact that it is humiliating to us to admit we are wrong, especially when we've stated our opinions on some topic. In other cases, we are unwilling to change our theories because it isn't at all clear what changes should be made. This is particularly true when all we get is simple negative feedback; the flat statement that our theory is wrong often provides no information about how to change it to make it more adequate. Moreover, we seldom are willing to reject a theory unless we have a substitute—for most of us a bad theory is better than no theory at all. All of these factors act either separately or together to make our intellectual theories very resistant to change.

Because it is more difficult for people than scientists to focus simultaneously on many events and their interrelations, formulation of adequate intellectual theories is often hindered. When we use our intellectual theories or test them, we tend to get a bit confused: we forget recent changes we've made, we leave out things, or we focus on only one small part of the theory, excluding the rest of it. Although we sometimes try to overcome this confusion by writing things down, by trying to form mental pictures, and the like, we tend to go for the "big picture" in an effort to keep from getting lost in details. The result is that our theories often are grossly oversimplified, which often means that they are not really adequate. But because oversimplification tends to make theories manageable, thereby giving us feelings of mastery and competence, we continue to oversimplify and ignore exceptions to the rules.

This oversimplification process is illustrated by the kinds of simplistic catch slogans that seem to be part and parcel of our private political and social theories. Few of us are capable of clearly analyzing the intricacies of complex political and social issues and of formulating accurate theories about them. Instead, we tend to rely on haphazard (and half-baked) analyses gleaned from swift glances at newspaper headlines. From such information sources we formulate oversimplified theories, which, given a little serious consideration, could easily be condemned. As a result, many of us have formulated such nonsense theories as, "Communists (S_1) are the cause of this nation's social unrest (S_2)"; "Smoking marijuana (S_1) is bound to lead to addiction to hard drugs (S_2)"; "People's laziness (S_1) is the sole cause of poverty (S_2)." A little patient investigation into the facts would show that these theories, and many like them, so oversimplify complex issues that they are patently wrong. (You'll have to look into the Communist question for yourself, but Parts 3 and 4 of Section 6 explain why the simplistic drug and poverty theories are wrong.)

In summary, while not very much is known about the intellectual origin of rules, the use of science as an analogy to human intellectual processes may prove valuable as a guide for future investigations. Even with the little that is known, it is clear that people form theories about the events that are of concern to them, that they test these theories in various ways, and that they sometimes change the theories when their tests reveal the necessity to do so. However, it is equally clear that this intellectual process is not very efficient; theories tend to be oversimplified, include irrelevant factors, ignore invalidating evidence, and they are very resistant to change.

Intellectual development Paradoxical as it might seem, while we lack knowledge about adults' intellectual rule making, we have fairly detailed knowledge about the development of children's ability to make and use such rules. This knowledge has been obtained by observing the changes in children's intellectual rules as they mature. Early in life, a child's rules are simple and involve only the everyday events that immediately surround him. Later he becomes interested in a broader range of events and in how and why things happen, and he gradually begins to acquire more complex theories about the world. He formulates some of his theories himself, but many others are given to him by his parents, friends, and teachers.

A Swiss zoologist and logician turned psychologist, Dr. Jean Piaget (pronounced Pee-ah-jay), is responsible for much of our knowledge about children's early intellectual development. Dr. Piaget obtained most of his information by sitting on the floor observing and playing with babies and by asking older children to solve simple problems and to explain their answers. While his observations have led to a wealth of facts, we will concentrate on only a small part of his findings, the four general *stages of intellectual development* in children. It should be remembered that the ages given with each stage are only approximate because children develop at different rates.

The *first stage* extends from birth to about two years of age. During this stage, the child begins to form rules that permit him to change his sensory-perceptual experiences by moving his body. Thus, he forms rules about how to grasp objects, how to walk, and how to make things happen, for example, "If I want to make a balloon bounce, I must pull the string with my hand." During the latter part of this stage, the child develops the important rule that things continue to exist even if they disappear from sight, the concept technically known as *object permanence*. Thus, while an eight-month-old child will stop reaching for an object if you suddenly cover it with a cloth, a sixteen-month-old child usually will continue to search for it. Having not yet formed the rule of object permanence, the younger child behaves as though the object ceases to exist when he can no longer see it. This is a very *concrete* way of thinking; the world consists only of the experiences of the moment. The older child has made a beginning step toward *abstract* thinking; the world has continuity and existence apart from his own immediate experience. But this is only a beginning step. It takes a long time for truly abstract thinking (rule making) to develop; indeed, many adults never get very good at it.

The *second stage* extends from two to seven years of age and includes the beginnings of language (Section 6, Part 1) and the development of crude rules about logical relations among events. It is during this stage that children are constantly asking "Why?". Since the child's thinking in this stage still is pretty concrete, and because "Why?" to the child means something between "What's the cause?" and "What's the purpose?", he seldom comprehends the complex reasons that underlie events. He really wants simple, descriptive explanations rather than abstract theories. The next time a youngster asks you "Why?", give him a descriptive answer that tells *how* events relate to things he already understands and he'll be better able to understand it.

Children in this second stage reveal the persistence of concreteness in their thinking by their inability to see the world from any viewpoint but their own. If a child were standing in front of an object, say a doll house, and his mother were standing behind it, his answer to the question, "What does your mother

Container A   Container B   Container C

FIG. 3.10 *A child of two to seven years of age is shown containers A and B, which contain equal amounts of water. Then B is poured into C and the child is asked if A and C contain equal quantities. The child ordinarily will say that they do not because the level of the water's surface is higher in C.*

see?" would be a description of the front of the doll house. It probably would not occur to him that his mother's different perspective would make her experience different from his. Another example of concreteness is an inability to comprehend abstract equivalences. If, for example, a child is shown equivalent amounts of water in containers A and B in Figure 3.10 and then sees the contents of B poured into C and is asked if containers A and C contain the same amounts of water, he will say, "No." If asked why, he usually will reply something to the effect that container C has more water because its level is higher. The child has not yet formed a rule to the effect that since no water has been added or taken away, the water in container C must be equivalent to what was formerly in B and is, therefore, equivalent to A.

The *third stage* begins at roughly the age of seven and lasts until the child is about eleven years old. During this stage, the child begins to develop more abstract rules and in doing so becomes capable of cooperating with others because he begins to see other people's points of view. During this stage, the child becomes interested in games with rules, and he develops abstract rules about justice and fair play; for example, he may formulate the rule for baseball that everyone is out after three strikes at the ball except that "little kids" deserve four strikes in order to compensate for their disadvantage in size and skill. This kind of rule is an important step in the child's development because it forms the basis of his later rules for balanced social interactions (Section 4, Part 3). This increasing tendency toward abstract rules also is revealed by the fact that if the child is confronted with the water-container task described in the last paragraph, he now will reply that containers A and C have the same amount of water because nothing has been added or taken away, a rule that is technically known as *conservation*.

It is also during this third stage that the child begins to assign objects and events to classes and to deal logically with the classes. Thus, he sees that all daddies shave, go to work, and so on, rather than these being things that only his daddy does.

The *fourth stage* extends from eleven years onward. During this stage, the youngster begins to formulate theories involving logical relations among abstract concepts and attempts to be systematic in his thinking. School, of course, helps him develop such theories by providing him with the abstract knowledge needed to elaborate upon his simpler theories. While people can formulate fairly abstract theories relatively logically without formal education, schooling tends to help them develop abstract theories in a shorter time by providing them with information they are not apt to experience themselves and by giving them new or alternative theories about the things they think about or experience.

FIG. 3.11   *During the third stage of intellectual development, children become interested in games with rules and in other abstract rules such as justice and fair play. (Courtesy D. Doty.)*

But schools are only one of the ways in which the people around us (our society, as it were) influence the kinds of intellectual rules we acquire and how we use them. Our parents and friends act, perhaps unknowingly, as agents of larger social groups by conveying notions about what are and are not proper rules and what are and are not the appropriate ends that our rules should serve. Through these influences (as well as through the influence of TV, movies, novels, magazines, and our own ingenuity), we acquire a broad range of adequate and inadequate rules. These rules range from elaborate, clear-cut rules about physics and table manners to vague, ill-defined rules about what to expect of people belonging to various ethnic and religious groups and how to best get along with other people. In the next section we will look more closely at social influences on our behavior.

SUMMARY:

1 Memory can be thought of as being similar to a computer system. The sensory units, discussed in Section 2, relay information to *short-term memory* where it is temporarily stored. Then the *transfer unit* simplifies the information and relays it to *long-term memory* where it is permanently stored. When stored information is needed, the *retrieval unit* searches for it, using the mechanisms of either recall or recognition; when retrieval fails, we call it forgetting.

2 Stored information is of two kinds, *content* and *rules*. Content consists of facts and other records of past events; rules are directions about what to do in recognized situations ($S_1 \rightarrow R_1$; $S_1 \rightarrow R_1 \rightarrow S_2$) or about what to expect ($S_1 \rightarrow S_2$).

3 Rules have many origins, the major ones being *reflexes, instincts, predispositions, learning, imitation,* and *intellect.* Learning, imitation, and intellect are regarded as the most important for human beings.

4 Learned what-to-do rules ($S_1 \rightarrow R_1 \rightarrow S_2$) are called *instrumental behavior* and serve to achieve desired goals. Learned what-to-expect rules ($S_1 \rightarrow S_2$) often have the property that emotional responses originally elicited by the S_2 event come to be elicited by the S_1 event, a phenomenon known as *classical conditioning.* The conditions that promote learning are *motivation, transfer, shaping, rapid feedback, frequency,* and *salience.* Conditions that lead to changes or abandonment of learned rules are *generalization, discrimination,* and *extinction.*

5 Imitated rules are acquired by *observation* of a *model* using them, by written or spoken *instruction* from the model, or by a mixture of observation and instruction. Imitation differs from learning in that one need not use the rule oneself in order to acquire it, in which case acceptance of the rule depends on the *credibility* of the model.

6 Intellectual origins of rules are ill understood, but the course of development of a child's ability to formulate rules is fairly clear. There are roughly four stages. In the early stages, the child's thinking is quite concrete and is concerned only with those events that occur in his immediate environment. As the child grows older, his rules become more abstract and take into account events that he does not directly experience and things that he learns in school.

Special Topics

Section 6, Part 1: *Language*
Section 6, Part 2: *Beliefs, Values, and Decisions*

Further Reading

ARDREY, R. *African Genesis*
New York: Dell, 1967 (c. 1961), 384 pages (paperback).
The author argues that human beings developed from carnivorous, predatory killer apes and that our affinity for war and weapons is a result of inherited predispositions. The book contains entertaining, documented examples of human and animal behavior, as well as the results of numerous anthropological investigations.

BAKAN, P. (Ed.). *Attention*
Princeton, N.J.: Van Nostrand, 1966, 225 pages (paperback).
A collection of papers dealing with the concept of attention; the relation between attention and such areas as perception, learning, personality, and psychopathology; the neurophysiology of attention; and current theories of attention. The editor's comments preceding each of the papers help the reader to more clearly understand them.

HALACY, D. S., Jr. *Man and Memory*
New York: Harper & Row, 1970, 259 pages.
The topics include a nontechnical discussion of the history of brain studies; theories of memory; drugs and memory; computers and memory; sleep, dreams, and memory; and ways of improving memory. Very easy reading.

HILGARD, E. R., and G. H. BOWER. *Theories of Learning*
New York: Appleton, 1966, 661 pages.
A detailed and technical introduction to all of the major theories of learning. Also included are chapters on the neurophysiology of learning, the technology of instruction, and other current developments in the area of learning.

HILL, W. F. *Learning: A Survey of Psychological Interpretations*
Scranton, Pa.: Chandler, 1971, 249 pages (paperback).
Less detailed and less difficult to read than Hilgard and Bower's *Theories of Learning*, this book is written particularly for educators; educational and related applications of the learning theories are stressed whenever possible.

HOLT, J. *How Children Fail*
New York: Dell, 1970 (c. 1964), 233 pages (paperback).
A very readable and interesting book on the strategies children use to meet or avoid the demands made upon them in school, the relation between fear and failure, what

children actually learn in school, and how schools fail to meet children's real needs. Holt also has written three other books that deal with the problems children face in school:

HOLT, J.   *How Children Learn*
New York: Dell, 1970 (c. 1967), 156 pages (paperback).

HOLT, J.   *The Underachieving School*
New York: Dell, 1970 (c. 1969), 208 pages (paperback).

HOLT, J.   *What Do I Do Monday?*
New York: Dell, 1971 (c. 1970), 318 pages (paperback).

KÖHLER, W.   *The Mentality of Apes*
New York: Vintage, 1927, 293 pages (paperback).

A report of experiments investigating the intelligence of chimpanzees. From the results of his experiments, Köhler concluded that chimpanzees are nearer to man in intelligence than the lower primates because they show insight behavior in many situations (for example, using sticks to reach bananas outside their cages). A classic work on insight behavior.

LORENZ, K. (Translated by M. K. Wilson)   *On Aggression*
New York: Bantam, 1967 (c. 1966), 308 pages (paperback).

Do human beings have an aggressive, fighting instinct? Konrad Lorenz thinks so and supports his position by examining aggression in various animals and in human beings. Entertaining to read and a good companion to Robert Ardrey's *African Genesis.*

LURIA, A. R.   *The Mind of a Mnemonist*
New York: Avon, 1969 (c. 1968), 160 pages (paperback).

Do you ever think about what it would be like to have an almost perfect memory? This is a book about a man who has such a gift, but who, even though his memories are filled with specific detail and colorful imagery, lacks the ability to go from the specific to the general. The problems he faces are many. For example, because he cannot forget unpleasant childhood experiences, his vivid recollections cause him pain and anxiety. In addition, he has the problem that any voice (or sound) he hears is accompanied by an experience of light, color, taste, touch, and so on, thereby keeping him from paying attention to what is actually being said. A fascinating book.

MONTESSORI, M. (Translated by N. R. Cirillo)   *The Child in the Family*
New York: Avon, 1970, 160 pages (paperback).

First published in Italian in 1956, this book explains the basic principles of the well-known Montessori method of education. Montessori, an Italian educator and medical doctor, stresses that the child is a human being with needs of his own and that he must learn to shape himself (rather than be shaped) in an environment that is free from adult oppression.

NEILL, A. S.   *Summerhill: A Radical Approach to Child-Rearing*
New York: Hart, 1960, 392 pages (paperback).

Based on forty years of experience, Neill argues that education should be aimed at emotional development as well as at intellectual development; emphasis should be placed on freedom and mutual respect between individuals, especially between adult and child.

Norman, D. A.　*Memory and Attention*
New York: Wiley, 1969, 201 pages (paperback).
An interesting book, written in the format of a seminar. Rather than paraphrase, Norman includes many short excerpts from original papers interspersed among his own ideas and comments. Treating the human organism as an information processor, Norman discusses such topics as attention, acquisition of information, short-term memory, mnemonics, and memory storage, ending with a chapter on models of memory.

Phillips, J. L., Jr.　*The Origins of Intellect: Piaget's Theory*
San Francisco: Freeman, 1969, 149 pages (paperback).
A good, nontechnical summary of Piaget's theory of the development of intelligence in children. It ends with a stimulating chapter on the educational implications of Piaget's theory.

Skinner, B. F.　*Walden Two*
New York: Macmillan, 1962 (c. 1948), 320 pages (paperback).
Walden Two is an imaginary utopian community where the principles of behavioral engineering are used to cope with such problems as communal living, child-rearing, work, economics, leisure time, creativity, morality, and free will.

Skinner, B. F.　*Science and Human Behavior*
New York: Free Press, 1965 (c. 1953), 461 pages (paperback).
This is a survey of Skinner's psychological "theory." Emphasis is placed on approaches to the control of human behavior through instrumental learning techniques.

Skinner, B. F.　*Beyond Freedom and Dignity*
New York: Knopf, 1971, 225 pages.
In this book, as in *Walden Two,* Skinner sees man as an organism shaped solely by his environment. Skinner argues that we are kept from moving toward a utopian society that can survive because we cling to the belief that human beings are autonomous, mentalistic creatures that struggle for freedom and dignity. This controversial book includes a discussion of the design of a culture.

Summerhill　*For and Against*
New York: Hart, 1970, 271 pages (paperback).
A collection of papers evaluating A. S. Neill's approach to education and child-rearing. The papers are written by well-known authorities in the fields of education, sociology, and psychology.

Talland, G. A.　*Disorders of Memory and Learning*
Baltimore, Md.: Penguin, 1968, 176 pages (paperback).
Although this book was written as part of a series in counseling psychology, it contains a good introduction to learning, the registration of information, retention, and forgetting. The last half of the book is concerned with memory and learning disorders caused by such things as amnesia, epilepsy, aging, and so on.

Courtesy Robert Kulwin

Social Interactions
and Group Memberships
FOUR

Human beings are social animals. We spend most of our time in the company of others of our species, and their acceptance or rejection of our behavior governs much of what we do. Because our relations with other people are so important, we must consider the dynamics that regulate them. We can get perspective on ourselves by looking at some of the social behaviors we share with other animals. Thus, in this section, we first deal briefly with some selected aspects of animal social relations. Then we examine the human counterparts of the animal social behavior. Finally, we explore the effects that social groups have on the people who belong to them.

Part 1 SOME ANIMALS' SOCIAL BEHAVIOR

Let us begin by examining the social behavior of three species of nonhuman social mammals—prairie dogs, wolves, and rhesus monkeys. These species were selected because the social behavior of each is in some specific way or ways quite similar to human social behavior. As you read these three descriptions notice that four themes will emerge—possession and defense of territorial space, status differences among individuals, the development of social patterns in young animals, and emotional bonding or friendship between individuals.

Prairie Dogs Prairie dogs are found primarily in the western grasslands of the United States. They live in "towns," each of which consists of a vast maze of underground burrows. The entrances to the burrows are located at the top of mounds that are about six feet wide and two feet high. The mounds prevent water from flooding the burrows, serve as lookout towers upon which the prairie dogs can stand and watch for predators, and provide a nice place for a sunbath on pleasant summer afternoons.

Each town, covering slightly less than an acre, is divided into *territories,* each of which is owned and defended by a clan. A clan is a self-contained community. It generally consists of one or two older male prairie dogs, three or so females for every male, and the offspring of these males and females. The territory belonging to each clan is passed on from generation to generation.

As is true in almost all other vertebrate animals, there is a distinct difference between the social behavior of female and male prairie dogs. The females give birth once each year of their four-year lives. They spend a good part of every year caring for their pups, as the young are called. The males, on the other hand, play an important role as defenders of the clan's territory. One of the males in the clan is *dominant;* that is, he is sort of the boss. It is the dominant male's job to patrol the boundary of his clan's territory and to defend it against intruders. Pups can wander freely into the territories of other clans, but as they get older, they will begin to be challenged by the males of these other clans. Thus they soon learn the boundaries of their own clan's territory and remain pretty much within that area.

Social contacts between prairie dogs serve to maintain amicable relations among clan members and to assert territorial rights (Fig. 4.1). The initial social contact between two prairie dogs is known as "the kiss." Whenever two prairie

FIG. 4.1 *Prairie dogs are small animals that occupy "towns" that are composed of numerous burrows, each one occupied by a single family. (Adapted from "The social behavior of prairie dogs" by John A. King. Copyright © 1959 by Scientific American, Inc. All rights reserved.)*

dogs meet, they bare their teeth and touch each other's muzzle as though they were kissing. This *greeting ritual* is so basic that prairie dogs running in terror from a hawk have been observed to hastily kiss each other as they pass in their flight.

The kiss serves as preliminary to further social interaction. When two clan members meet, the kiss is often a prelude to *grooming* (cleaning of each others' fur). After their muzzles meet, one prairie dog rolls over on his back and, still kissing, the other lies down beside him. Then they groom each other until they finally walk off together, their sides pressed firmly together, to find something to eat. Grooming is an important aspect of social behavior in prairie dog clans, and among many other animal groups as well. While for many other animals grooming appears to occur most frequently between males and "their" females, each member of the prairie dog clan seems to groom all the other members.

The kiss also plays a part in keeping neighbors out of the clan's territory. When a clan member meets another prairie dog on clan territory, he bares his teeth in preparation for the kiss ceremony. If the other prairie dog is a member of the clan, they kiss. If, however, the other prairie dog is an intruder from next door, the sight of the bared teeth of the clan member is often sufficient to send him scurrying home. If the intruder doesn't run, the ensuing events are highly ritualized. First, the clan member makes a two-syllable yipping sound that announces the presence of the intruder to the clan. Then the clan member and the intruder rush toward each other, stop, and freeze. One turns around and exposes a scent gland located at the anus. The other prairie dog approaches and smells. Then he turns and exposes his scent gland for the first prairie dog to smell.

This smelling ritual continues until one prairie dog or the other nips or bites his opponent and causes him to move away. Then the bitten one, usually the intruder, either returns or is chased until he stops. The ritual continues over and over again until the boundary of the clan's territory is reached. As the boundary is approached, the intruder gains more courage and soon his aggressiveness matches that of the defender. Where the stalemate in this ritual occurs becomes the new boundary between the territory of the defender's clan and that of the intruder's clan. Thus boundaries are always shifting a bit, but in general each clan's territory remains fairly stable.

Defense of territory is a fundamental theme throughout the animal kingdom. The singing of birds that we so romantically associate with peace and tranquillity is translated by other birds of the same species as, "Stay out of my territory!" If you have a dog or cat, you have probably seen their reaction when their territory is invaded. Perhaps you have noticed that even the smallest dog becomes violent and may drive off a much larger dog. In this simple observation lies a very fundamental fact: the owner of the territory has an enormous advantage. His advantage, courage and ferocity, declines sharply as he approaches the boundary of his own territory.

Usually, defense of territory is directed only at one's own species. For example, prairie dogs will tolerate the presence of rabbit intruders, but they will challenge other prairie dogs. However, unless the animals are caged so the loser can't get away, animals seldom seriously hurt one another. Defense of territory is based mostly on *threat*, and most animals have characteristic threat reactions such as baring of the teeth, assumption of a special posture, and characteristic vocal sounds. Each animal recognizes the threat reactions of his own species and reacts either by going away or threatening right back. Which of these two reactions occurs depends to a large extent upon whether the threatened animal is on his own territory or the other fellow's.

Wolves

While it is easy to sit on a hillside above a prairie dog town and study its inhabitants, the study of wolves presents a problem because they move around a great deal in search of food. Therefore, most of what we know about the social behavior of wolves comes from studies of the packs maintained in zoos. Because a zoo certainly is not representative of wolves' natural habitat, it is possible that our knowledge of their normal social behavior is not wholly accurate. However, the more general findings are probably fairly representative.

The first thing to remember about a wolf pack is that it is a cooperative hunting group which includes both males and those females who have no pups. Hunting appears to have dictated the fundamental form of the pack's social structure: a strong *dominance hierarchy* exists among the male members and a secondary but very important dominance hierarchy exists among the female members of the pack.

A dominance hierarchy is a social status system in which members of low status must *defer* to members whose status is higher. The latter defer, in turn, to those of higher status than they, and so forth. Defer means that the more-dominant (higher-status) member is allowed to go unchallenged if, for example, he crosses the path of the less-dominant (lower-status) member, if he snatches away food, if he takes the most desirable female, and so on. Almost all group-living animals have some form of a dominance hierarchy. In general, the hierarchy exists mainly among the males, the females deriving their status from their mates' place in the male hierarchy. However, for some animals, the two sexes have completely different hierarchies, and these hierarchies are only loosely related to the *affectional bonds* that exist between males and females.

For wolves, dominance is an extremely fundamental fact of life. Exactly how a wolf's dominance is communicated to other wolves is unknown, but it is fairly clear that a wolf's position in the dominance hierarchy of his pack is not related to his size. Nor does he have to fight with others to attain his place or to make his position known.

By and large, dominance is not expressed in the normal run of things. It comes out in times of stress, such as during times of famine when two wolves are in conflict over food or during the mating season when there is conflict over a female. The ritual for dominance follows a pattern something like this. When they meet, the higher-status wolf stands with his head erect, ears forward, and tail straight out behind. The lower-status wolf becomes submissive, his ears back, head low, and tail down and exhibiting a crouching, wriggling walk (see Fig. 4.2). The lower-status wolf tries to get his head under the head of the higher-status wolf and then lick his mouth and muzzle. The latter may take the subordinate's muzzle gently in his mouth or he may just walk off. Note how the behavior of the lower-status wolf parallels that of the dog that has been chastised by his master. The master may think the dog is

FIG. 4.2   *A dominance ritual between two wolves. (From George B. Rabb, Social relationships in a group of captive wolves,* American Zoologist, *7:305–311, 1967.)*

trying to apologize or make up, but more likely the dog (a relative of the wolf) is merely acknowledging his master's dominance or higher status.

The social structure of the pack revolves around the most dominant male. His job is to patrol and guard the pack's territory. In all probability, he also leads the hunt. His mate regulates social relations among the remainder of the pack. The core of the pack consists of these two dominant wolves and all wolves of status. Outsiders are literally on the outside; the lowest-status males and females stay at the periphery of the pack. This peripheral fringe also includes young adult wolves who have yet to mate and who have not yet established their place in the pack's dominance hierarchy. Although the dominance hierarchy changes from time to time, if only by the death of the old and by the entry of the young into the pack, it is generally quite stable. Wolves tend to continue to defer to those animals that were dominant over them early in their lives, and it is difficult to displace an animal from the hierarchy if most of the pack defers to him; it is the behavior of the followers that designates the leaders.

Rhesus Monkeys   The natural habitat of rhesus monkeys is the edge of the African forest and the forests and villages of India. In these areas rhesus monkeys live in middling to large groups in which the males form a rather weak dominance hierarchy; each group of rhesus monkeys tends to be intolerant of the other groups. The rhesus monkeys that I am going to describe, however, live in a laboratory in Madison, Wisconsin. Here Professor Harry Harlow and his co-workers have spent years studying both the normal social development of young rhesus monkeys and the conditions that produce abnormal social development.

Normal   The normal course of social development for these laboratory monkeys is
Development   extremely similar to that which occurs in the monkeys' natural habitat. During the first few weeks of the baby monkey's life the mother feeds him and protects him. She keeps other monkeys away and keeps the infant within her reach at all times. She also holds him and allows him to cling to her, as illustrated in Figure 4.3. Clutching the mother in this manner apparently gives the baby a feeling of security; any new and surprising event in his small world makes him immediately run to his mother and clutch her.

If for some reason the infant becomes separated from his mother for any length of time, a predictable sequence of behavior typically takes place. First, the infant goes through a period of extreme distress during which he calls loudly and is wildly agitated and active. After about two days of separation, depression sets in—the infant sits rolled up in a small furry ball and stops

FIG. 4.3   *A baby Rhesus monkey clinging to its mother. (H. F. Harlow, University of Wisconsin Primate Laboratory.)*

all playing and exploration. Finally, if the mother does not return, the infant will begin to perk up and may be "adopted" by another adult. If the mother does return, there is obvious joy on the part of both mother and infant and for a while they spend a great deal of time clinging to each other. Later their behavior returns to the way it was before they were separated.

The mother begins the baby's integration into the group in which he lives by increasingly refusing to allow him to cling to her, by becoming meaner to him, and by rejecting him from time to time. Thus the young rhesus monkey is forced to become more self-reliant. Now if he suddenly discovers something new, he may not run to his mother and cling to her. Instead, he may approach and investigate the new thing. However, his mother continues to keep an eye on him for some time to come and will rush to his aid if he gets into any serious difficulty.

As the infant's dependence on his mother decreases, his *peer group* becomes more important. His peers are the other monkeys in the group, both male and female, that are about the same age as he is. Since births are seasonal, each infant is usually guaranteed a rather sizable peer group. At first, interaction among peers may consist only of clinging to each other, but this soon gives way to exploring together and more active play. Play is often quite rough and tumble: sham fighting, wrestling, chasing, and so on.

It is during play that sexual differences begin to show themselves. The males play more roughly than the females and, as they get older, the males' play becomes increasingly more aggressive. From this aggressive play emerges the dominance hierarchy within the young males' peer group that will pretty well describe them from that time on. Later, of course, their hierarchy must merge with that of the adults, but exactly how this happens is yet to be discovered.

During late childhood, differences between the sexes become increasingly clear. For example, females seldom are aggressive toward males, although males will attack females. The males grow larger and become much more physically active than the females. Playmates become almost exclusively of the same sex; males play with males and females play with females.

As the monkeys get older and merge into the adult group, playing gives way to more peaceful forms of interaction. Mutual grooming (which can be seen at any zoo at almost any time) becomes a sign of friendship. While a monkey will form new friendships within the adult group, his childhood playmates of both sexes remain his special friends for the rest of his life.

Abnormal Development

The foregoing discussion stressed two sources of social stimulation in the normal development of a rhesus monkey—his mother and his peers. Their relative importance can be gauged by laboratory studies in which babies are raised (1) in isolation, with neither a mother nor peers, (2) with a mother but no peers, and (3) with peers but no mother.

(1) If baby rhesus monkeys are raised in isolation and then put in a situation where they encounter other monkeys, their first reaction is a short period of shock. If they have spent only their first three months alone, they quickly adjust and seemingly develop into normal monkeys. Six months of isolation, however, leads to minor but lasting impairment of social development. Isolation for the entire first year leads to irreparable damage of three kinds. When monkeys who have spent their first year in isolation are first placed with normally reared monkeys, they are extremely timid and they are persistently attacked by the other monkeys; it is as though the isolation-reared monkeys never learned whatever signals monkeys use to express submission, to "say uncle" when they

have had enough. Later, they outgrow their initial timidity and become excessively aggressive. Females will even attack males who are bigger and stronger than they, a form of behavior which is definitely not wise and which is extremely rare among normally reared monkeys. Finally, these isolation-reared monkeys may never learn how to mate correctly. Sometimes a female will finally get the idea if she is placed with a gentle, patient, and experienced male. Usually, however, she just sits and looks at him; as Harlow says, "Her heart's in the right place, but nothing else is." Even if the isolation-raised females do manage to become pregnant and have babies, they don't know how to take care of them. They often are indifferent and rejecting mothers, although they may learn to do a better job after they have had a baby or two. Males raised in isolation seldom learn to mate; they appear to know that there is something to be done, but the mechanics of it escapes them.

(2) Monkeys raised with mothers but without peers for longer than four months have some difficulty adjusting to a peer group. In the long run, however, things appear to work out all right. Given time, they develop appropriate social and sexual behavior. As a variation on this, Harlow raised some monkeys with the fake mothers shown in Figure 4.4. He found that the fake mother covered

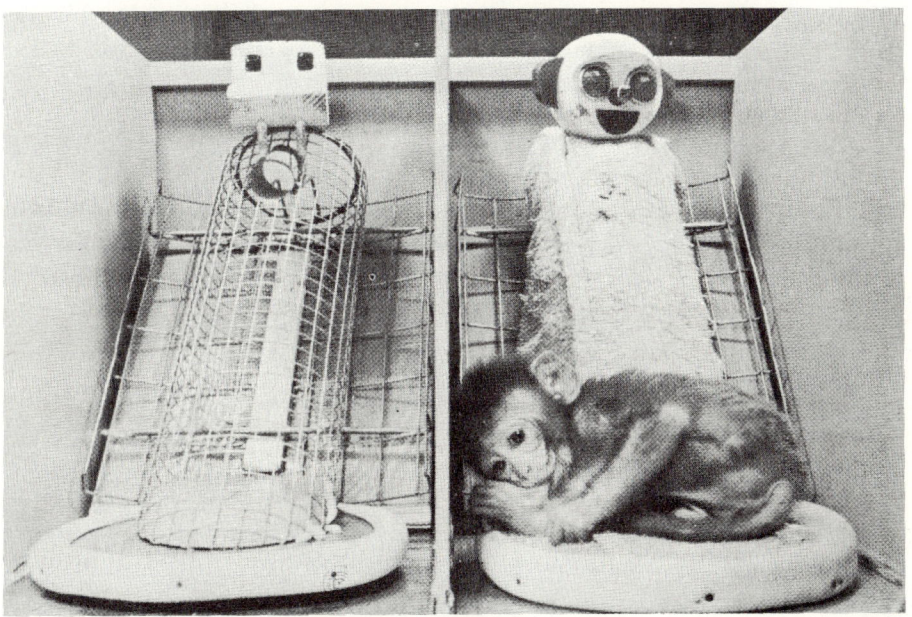

FIG. 4.4 *A baby Rhesus monkey resting in the security of his cloth-covered fake mother; the wire fake mother is on the left. (H. F. Harlow, University of Wisconsin Primate Laboratory.)*

with soft terrycloth is almost as good as the real thing. The baby will cling to "her," run to "her" when he is frightened, and if "she's" removed from the cage, he will show delight when "she's" returned. As you might expect, the clinging behavior with this fake mother goes on much longer than with the real mother, since the fake mother cannot reject the baby and make him take care of himself.

The softness of the fake mother is important. If the baby is fed on the fake mother that is merely covered with wire, he will not cling to it. Instead, he will return to the cloth mother and spend most of his time clinging to it. Indeed, in the absence of a mother, real or fake, a baby monkey will cling to a terrycloth washcloth if it is provided.

(3) Baby monkeys raised with peers but without mothers appear to develop relatively normally. At first, when they're all placed with another group of young monkeys they cower together, but eventually they adjust and begin to play with the "outsiders." By and large these monkeys become sexually mature earlier than normally reared monkeys and begin breeding earlier. It also is interesting to note that when these monkeys have been living as an isolated group and then are separated from one another, they go through exactly the same syndrome that normally raised monkeys experience when they are separated from their mothers—agitation and crying, depression, and apparent elation when they come back together. In a sense, these monkeys fill the parent void for each other.

Recurring Themes

Before exploring the human parallels to the social behavior of these animals, I want to point out some of the themes that keep recurring in the descriptions of behavior of the animals we have just considered.

Territoriality   Common to many different kinds of animals, including various species of fish, birds, and mammals, territoriality is the tendency to claim a specific area and defend it against intruders of the same species. Usually defense of the territory is left to the males, but the females may help defend it under some circumstances.

Within their home territory, many animals command a small area around them that is their own personal space. That they defend this area too is dramatically evident when one sees a subordinate animal "keep his distance" from a dominant animal; if he gets too close, the latter may threaten him.

Dominance hierarchies In almost any group of social animals, some members defer to others. The hierarchy may be quite rigid, as with wolves, or it may be loose, as with monkeys. In either case, males are generally dominant over females, although in some animals, high-status females may be dominant over low-status males. Usually the dominance hierarchy is more clearly defined for males than for females, and the tasks of leadership and territorial defense fall to the most dominant males.

Social development For most social animals, education of the young is a group activity and relies heavily upon help from parents and peers. As we saw with the monkeys, isolation from these influences is devastating; it can produce socially maladjusted animals who later cannot interact properly either with the entire social group or with single individuals.

The general course of social development is fairly similar for all social animals. At first, the helpless infant is closely watched and his needs are taken care of. Then he is given more and more independence and becomes acquainted with his peers. In many animals, sexual segregation takes place during childhood (males associate with males and females with females), as with the monkeys. Then, when mature enough to mate, both sexes become part of the adult group.

Bonding Many animals form strong emotional bonds with other members of their own species. These bonds may last only as long as the mating season, or they may last a lifetime. They may be cross-sex (a male and a female) or same-sex bonds. While cross-sex bonds usually involve reproduction, they need not. Many varieties of monkeys, for example, form cross-sex bonds with specific individuals, but mate with whomever is handy. Same-sex bonds are often indicated by preference for another's company and/or as a mutual grooming partner. Among female rhesus monkeys, as an act of trust, a mother's close friends are permitted to hold her baby a few days after it has been born. Similarly, within some monkey groups strong bonds may develop among a small number of males who then cooperate in defense against predators and the like.

BOX 4.1

Urban Man and Urban Monkeys

Within the last one hundred years or so, there has been a massive movement of Americans from rural areas to the cities. At the same time there has been increasing dissatisfaction about the quality of modern life, dissatisfaction that often is attributed to the "fact" that cities have an unhealthy and dehumanizing influence on their residents. With respect to this "fact," the famous zoologist and social critic Desmond Morris argues in his book *The Human Zoo** that while cities provide many conveniences, they conflict with the natural social patterns of human beings. During the majority of the span of human existence on earth, people lived in small migratory hunting bands. With the advent of agriculture, they settled down and became farmers; yet they still lived in small bands in isolated areas. Then came the cities, a relatively new phenomenon in the course of human history, and Morris claims that they fail to satisfy our fundamental needs for the close cooperative interpersonal relations that were so much a part of our hunting and agrarian "small-tribe" past. Moreover, he suggests that urbanization, and the consequent loss of tribal identity, has resulted in the breakdown of dominance hierarchies that at one time served to impose order on small tribal communities; the result has been a frightening increase in aggression and violence. Morris sees the current interest in communal living and nostalgia for the past as expressions of a desire to return to the old tribal way of life. He feels, however, that having once been urbanized, people are permanently changed and, therefore, a return to a rural life-style will not bring happiness. After the quickening pace of the city, boredom soon triumphs, followed by a tendency on the part of people to either modify the small community to make it more like the city or to abandon it completely and return to urban life.

Whether Morris' analyses and speculations are sound is not as important as the questions they raise. Primary among them is the question of whether urban living actually has adverse effects on human beings. Unfortunately, research on this question is extremely difficult to perform as well as to interpret, so there is no simple answer. There is, however, a provocative study of what happens to rhesus monkeys who opt for living in cities along with human beings. Of course, monkeys are not human beings, and the conditions of their lives in cities are not the same as the conditions of human lives. Still, there is sufficient similarity to provide food for thought, even if no definite conclusions can be drawn from this study.

Rhesus monkeys are native to northern India and are generally found to inhabit forest areas in the countryside. Some of these monkeys, however, have lived in the cities for generations, where they are tolerated in spite of the trouble they

*New York: McGraw-Hill, 1969.

cause because they are regarded as sacred. The study to be described was conducted by a native of India, Dr. Sheo Dan Singh and his associates, who compared rural (forest-dwelling) and urban (city-dwelling) monkeys in terms of dwelling habits, feeding habits, aggressive behavior, and intelligence.†

Groups of rural monkeys spend their day wandering about the forest searching for food and water, and when night falls they sleep in whatever tree is most handy. Groups of urban monkeys, on the other hand, wander through the city during the day, but return to the same abandoned building, housetop, or other protected niche night after night. And interestingly enough, if urban monkeys are captured, taken to the forest, and then released, they immediately make their way back to their urban homes.

When it comes to eating, rural monkeys consume a simple fare of leaves and fruit. Urban monkeys, however, have acquired more sophisticated tastes; they prefer cooked foods such as bread, roasted grains, and spices. While inhabitants of the city often feed the urban monkeys, the majority of the food supply of urban monkeys is obtained from garbage cans and through stealing from shops.

Rural monkeys are fairly aggressive while feeding because of an established dominance hierarchy. The most dominant male usually controls the food supply and allows no other monkeys to eat until he's had his fill. By contrast, city dwelling monkeys are not aggressive with one another about food; the dominance hierarchy is loose, and the dominant males permit others in the group to eat with them. However, urban monkeys are more aggressive than rural monkeys in most other circumstances. An urban monkey will attack a strange monkey (in the forest, threat rather than actual attack is the rule), and unless the loser can escape, one of the two is likely to be severely injured or killed. Indeed, urban monkeys, unlike rural monkeys, are not afraid of much of anything and they will steal food from human children and even attack human adults. During the study, one of the investigators accidentally touched a baby urban monkey. The baby set up a wail and immediately several adult urban monkeys attacked the man and bit him so severely he had to be hospitalized. It is very likely that the reason these extremely aggressive animals are nonaggressive only while feeding is that in order to survive, they have had to learn to share their food, since it is not as plentiful in the city as it is in the forest.

The urban monkeys are wily; they are so difficult to catch that for the laboratory studies on intelligence, the investigators had to pay $7 per urban monkey rather than the mere $2 asked for a rural monkey. In order to see if the wiliness of urban monkeys might be a sign that urban life had made them more intelligent than rural monkeys, a variety of tests that are used to measure monkey intelligence

†S. D. Singh, Urban monkeys, *Scientific American*, 1969, *221*, 108–115.

were given to both urban and rural monkeys; the scores were the same for both groups. However, when curiosity was measured, urban monkeys were found to score higher than their rural counterparts.

The observations made in this study show that urban living influences the sleeping habits, eating habits, dominance hierarchy, aggressiveness, wiliness, and curiosity of monkeys but not their basic intelligence. Like the stereotyped city slicker, the urban monkey is more sophisticated and tougher than his country cousin, but he's not any brighter. While it is debatable whether the results of this study are applicable to urban man, I think you'll agree that they certainly have a familiar ring to them.

Part 2   HUMAN SOCIAL BEHAVIOR

We turn now to the human versions of territoriality, dominance, and bonding. In the course of discussing these three topics, we will discover that some differences exist between human social behavior and the animal social behaviors we have been discussing. We are, after all, different from prairie dogs, wolves, and monkeys. But maybe we are not as different as most people think.

Territoriality

For human beings there are two kinds of territory. The first is *real space*—your yard, your office, or the like. The second is *personal space*—the area that immediately surrounds you wherever you are.

Real Space

There are three types of real space: (1) the space you *legally own,* such as your house; (2) the space you *temporarily own,* such as your office; and (3) the space in which you are a *transient,* such as a table in a cafeteria.

(1) Legal ownership   One of the most obvious facts about most legal systems and their laws is the importance attached to ownership of land and private property. Except in the most extreme cases (for example, murder), a court of law is likely to deal more harshly with someone who violates another's property (burglary) than with someone who violates another's person (assault).

Even without the help of the law, people are quick to defend their legally owned territory and may go to great lengths to prevent anyone from trespassing. Few things are as unnerving as looking out the window and seeing a stranger in your back yard. Even if all the windows and doors are locked, the presence of a trespasser is an affront that seldom goes unchallenged. However, some creatures are considered neutral and are not counted as trespassers. Just as the prairie dogs allow rabbits to wander inside their territory, you allow squirrels, cats, and birds to enter yours (Fig. 4.5). In fact, territories are frequently "owned" by several species—squirrels, birds, your neighbor's cat, and your dog all may regard your territory as their own. Some human beings also receive a right to enter your territory. For example, small children (remember that prairie dogs also permit boundary violations by young pups) are tolerated as long as they cause no damage. Delivery men, mailmen, and meter readers are also tolerated and are called *nonpersons* because their function makes them exempt from some of the usual entry rules of knocking, introducing themselves, and so forth. Indeed, they often wear uniforms to avoid all of the ceremony. It is not uncommon for a milkman to enter a house and put milk in the refrigerator, an entry that certainly would be out of bounds for, say, an insurance man.

Some territories are possessed communally. That is, they are possessed by groups, and the members, both individually and collectively, feel strong territorial rights. Examples are the "turf" claimed by street gangs and the "neighborhood" claimed by the people who live in it. These territories are usually from one to three city blocks in size and have very definite boundaries. Less well-defined, but of equal emotional importance, is the community in which you live (or the state or the nation). Although you do not own such territories in the legal sense, you still resent the presence of uninvited "foreigners." In

FIG. 4.5 *The sign serves to keep other humans out of the owner's territory; but the squirrel's presence is accepted. (Courtesy D. Doty.)*

the extreme case, violation of national borders galvanizes almost all citizens to defense of their "territory."

(2) Temporary ownership   Many of us spend our waking hours in spaces we don't legally own. We work in an office, at a bench, in a truck, and so on. Soon we begin to regard this area as our own by right of use. No one, except the janitor, whom we regard as a nonperson, is permitted to enter without permission; discovery of a stranger in your office is nearly as emotionally upsetting as finding him in your house.

Most people try to mark these temporary spaces as belonging to them by adding things of their own to make the space more personal. Thus, it is common to put pictures of one's family on one's desk, to buy a plant for the office, to hang some object from the rearview mirror, or the like (Fig. 4.6). These objects serve notice that the space belongs to the occupant.

Apartments and rented houses also fall into the category of temporary territory. The residents become as possessive of the space as they would if they legally owned it. Indeed, renting does involve quasi-ownership, since certain rights are legally granted to the renter with regard to use of the rented territory. But it is not really the legality of ownership that dictates the feeling of dominion over a territory. Rather, the important factors are that other people recognize our proprietorship, and that we feel safe and secure there. In short, we feel at home.

FIG. 4.6   *Office workers frequently advertise their territorial claims by placing decorative and personal objects in "their" space.*

FIG. 4.7 *When a stranger sits down at "our" table, we reduce our territorial claim and treat him as almost nonexistent. (Courtesy D. Doty.)*

(3) Transient ownership Finally, there are territories that we own for only the short time that we are using them, but their inviolability is important to us too. For example, at the movies it is highly annoying to go out for popcorn and return to find someone sitting in the seat you formerly occupied. If you had the nerve, you could tell the person that he was sitting in your seat and in all likelihood he would apologize and move. Without thinking about it, people tend to respect even these transient territories.

A good example of transient territory is the space you occupy at a table in a cafeteria. If you sit alone at a table for four, that table becomes yours and it is highly unlikely that a stranger will sit down as long as there are other empty tables in the cafeteria. However, should the cafeteria fill up, some stranger will eventually sit down at your table. Almost invariably he will sit down opposite you because to sit on either side would be too close for your comfort or his. Now each of you own only half the table, and you both try to protect your privacy by treating the other as a nonperson; neither of you speaks to nor looks at the other, except surreptitiously. You withdraw into your remaining territory, read if you have anything to read, or stare around the room—everywhere except at your table partner. Usually you eat faster under these circumstances and attempt to get out of the cafeteria as quickly as possible.

Similar things happen in library reading rooms. Here the point is to achieve as much solitude as possible in order to read. As a result, people tend to sit near one end of the long tables commonly found in such areas, in the hope that newcomers will sit at the other end. In addition, they mark off a space around themselves by putting coats and books on the chairs beside them as well as notebooks and papers on the table in front of them. Indeed, these objects are recognized by everybody else as territorial markers; even if the person leaves the place, no one will sit near it as long as his markers remain.

You can perform a simple experiment to demonstrate the effectiveness of territorial markers in preventing people from sitting near a supposedly occupied chair in a moderately crowded study area of a library. Place a newspaper, paperback books, textbooks, and a jacket at different points around the room near empty chairs. Then note how closely newcomers sit to these objects and how often someone actually sits down in the marked space. In general, you will find the newspaper to be the least effective (someone might have just left it there after he had read it). The paperback books are next in effectiveness, with the jacket next. The texts are most effective in marking the territory.

Personal Space

In addition to the real spaces or territories that each of us lay claim to, we also have a psychological, personal space that we regard as being our own. This space is a portable territory, rather like an imaginary sphere that surrounds us everywhere we go. Unauthorized penetration of the boundaries of this personal space by another person is regarded as a serious act.

Some psychologists and zoologists speak of men and other animals as having two personal spaces, or spheres, one within the other. Invasion of the larger of the two spheres makes the owner want to leave the scene, that is, take flight. Thus, if a stranger sits down beside you in an otherwise empty waiting room, your first reaction is to get up and move. Similarly, if someone stands too close to you, even if it is a friend, you tend to move away. If someone leans over your shoulder to read, you become vexed and either move or ask him to move.

The second sphere is much smaller; for it to be invaded, the other person must be extremely close to you. Only persons for whom you have special affection are gladly permitted this close; intruders are met with sudden hostility. Penetration of this inner space occurs when someone touches you, puts his face very close to yours, or gazes directly into your eyes. All of these can be signs of affection, which, if accepted by you, give you a pleasant feeling. On the other hand, when coupled with various words and gestures, these same violations of your personal space can signify aggression. If the aggressor pokes you, pushes his face toward yours, or stares at you, your reaction, rather than one of pleasure, is one of anger and possibly counteraggression, depending on the circumstances and upon your prudence.

The dimensions of personal space change depending upon the circumstances. For example, in a crowded bus or subway a person may stand so close that he actually touches you. Under these circumstances you accept his violation of your personal space. It is interesting that even when it cannot be avoided, most people are uncomfortable when their personal space is violated. They feel uneasy and dislike being crowded. In fact, we are taught to avoid touching people except under special conditions (men seldom touch each other except to shake hands) and not to crowd others. Most of us resent having people "breathing down our necks." When in crowded situations, such as an elevator or subway, we withdraw into ourselves and treat the other people as non-persons—that way we survive the ordeal. The American custom of everyone facing toward the front in elevators keeps the often crowded occupants from having to acknowledge each others' presence (Fig. 4.8). It also saves everyone

FIG. 4.8 *The custom of facing the front of an elevator permits people to avoid the discomfort of having to look at each other; eye contact is a form of violation of personal space. (Courtesy D. Doty.)*

the trouble of having to find something to look at, since gazing into another person's face at such a short distance would be unthinkable. One way of destroying the composure of a group of innocent people is by boarding a crowded elevator, standing in the front facing the rear, and simply looking at everyone (if you can stand it yourself, that is).

Personal space is not really a standard shape or size. For example, it extends farther in front of you than it does in back. Its size depends on the culture in which you live. People from Latin and Arab countries have a personal space that is much smaller than ours. The result is that they stand closer to each other while talking, they touch each other more, and they appear to be a good deal more tolerant of crowding than we are. These differences can lead to serious misunderstandings when members of different cultures interact, since each person assumes the other person's personal space is the same as his own. In a face-to-face conversation, a male North American tries to maintain a distance of 18 to 20 inches between himself and another man or 14 to 16 inches between himself and a woman. To a Latin or an Arab, these distances are almost like shouting across the room. Consequently, a conversation between an American and, say, an Arab, can be rather uncomfortable. While the American continually strives to increase the distance between them, the Arab keeps trying to decrease it. Both become offended, usually without knowing why; the American decides the Arab is pushy, and the latter decides that the American is cold and snobbish.

This business of establishing a comfortable distance between oneself and another person is extremely important. The distance we select tells the other person a good deal about how we feel about him. We stay further away from high-status persons than from our equals, low-status persons, or children. We stay further from unfriendly people than from friendly ones. And, sad to say, normal persons stay further from persons with physical handicaps than they do from normal persons. So, we see, human beings use distance to communicate respect, friendship, social status, and general understanding of the social rules.

If you want to examine interpersonal distance in more detail, perform the following experiment. Carry a tape measure in your pocket. Whenever you see two people standing and talking, walk up and measure the nose-to-nose distance between them. You'll have to allow for short tempers and short people (the distance between the noses for a short person talking to a tall person will be exaggerated, so you have to adjust your measure), but taking care in both regards can produce some interesting results. A safer procedure is to use yourself as one of the two persons. As another person approaches you to talk, stop and let him or her come up to you and stop. Then whip out your tape measure and measure the nose-to-nose distance. Compare the average distances for conversations between same-sex persons and opposite-sex persons (taking care to avoid affectionate couples in the last group). If you perform this experiment carefully, you will find that, on the average, the latter distance is smaller than the former.

Dominance Hierarchies

Human dominance hierarchies are most familiar to most of us in terms of *status*, which is associated with the occupations and other social functions that various people perform. Status is of two kinds, ascribed and acquired.

Ascribed Status

Ascribed status is given to a person by virtue of the function he or she performs. When a new college graduate is given an army officer's commission, he is given dominance over all enlisted men. Although the new officer may forget it from time to time, this ascribed status does not mean that he necessarily is smarter, better, or more able than the enlisted men. It means that the army requires someone to be in charge; who is in charge is of less importance than the fact that someone is. The army's old saying, "You salute the uniform, not the man," means that whatever his abilities and qualifications, the man has been given dominance and subordinates are expected to defer to him.

Acquired Status

This kind of status is obtained by an individual through his or her own personal efforts or demonstration of ability. Each of us is a member of many groups, and within each group there is some kind of status hierarchy. You are an American citizen, but you probably rank low in the political status hierarchy (I assume that few Congressmen will read this). You are a student, and I will leave it up to you to judge your own place in that hierarchy.

Thus, each aspect of you as a social being—student, businessman, voter, party-goer, friend, or golfer—has a place in the status structure of each of these groups. Moreover, what one person regards as high status may be regarded as low status by another person. While there is general agreement about which occupations have high and low status in our culture, the definition of status may also be unique to the group that is involved. For example, the leader of a streetcorner gang may have fought his way to very high status among his gang, but the rest of society still tends to regard him as a low-status "punk."

Whenever two people meet for the first time, they usually spend the opening moments of their interaction exploring each other's status and establishing dominance. If you'll think about it, you'll realize that you know the clues they use to do it: clothes are a clue, although this is less the case than it used to be in our culture. Manner of speaking and ability to use the language are certainly used to infer relative status. And occupation is still the most important, single clue to status. Soon after two persons begin talking, they— men in particular—usually find out each other's occupation. From that point on, their interaction is relatively predictable. The man with the lower-status occupation will defer to the man with the higher-status occupation by remarking that the latter's occupation must be interesting, rewarding, difficult, or something like that, and that he (or his cousin, wife's uncle, or someone) once considered going into it, but (as a result of low IQ, bad luck, or lack of money) did not do so (Fig. 4.9). The higher-status man will then make some remark about how interesting it must be to be a ditch digger, or whatever, and then the topic will change. The rest of the conversation is likely to be dominated by the higher-status man, if not by his talking more, at least by the lower-status man being careful about what he says so that he doesn't look foolish or offend the other man.

There are many ways in which lower-status individuals defer to individuals whose status is higher than theirs. The low status person will not interrupt when the high-status person is talking, the former will use a certain tone of voice which may sound rather apologetic, and he or she will use many phrases

FIG. 4.9   *It frequently is easy to tell which of two conversing men is the more dominant.* (*Courtesy D. Doty.*)

such as, "I'm not certain but," or, "It seems to me that," rather than the simple declarative sentences that he would use with the people he associates with most of the time. The low-status person is often expected to use the title of the higher-status person; you call your physician Dr. So and So, but he may call you by your first name. In a conversation, a lower-status person gazes directly at the higher-status person less frequently than the latter gazes at him. He seldom, if ever, touches the higher-status person, although the latter may touch him; an employee doesn't put his arm around the boss's shoulders in a display of comradeship, but the boss can put his arm around the employee's shoulders, even if it makes the latter uncomfortable.

With a little work, and some nerve, you can demonstrate the differential effects of high- and low-status individuals on other people's behavior. Find a door that is pretty heavily used, like the front door of a cafeteria or library. Prop the door open and on a post in the middle place an official-looking sign that says, "No entry. Repairs underway. Use side door." (Make sure there is a side door.) Make the sign large enough to be noticeable, but small enough so someone could get through the door with no difficulty.

Although some people will disregard your "official" sign, most people will take it seriously. Now find someone—yourself, if you fit the bill—who is old enough to look "established," and who looks very proper when dressed up and very disreputable when dressed in grubby work clothes. Wait until there are people around and then have the person violate the sign wearing one set of clothes. Then have him or her change and violate the sign wearing the other set of clothes. Violate the sign about five times with each set of clothes, each time when there is about the same number of people around. Observe how many of these people follow the person through the door each time he or she violates the sign. On the average, more people will follow when the person looks proper (high status) than when he or she is in work clothes (low status), even though it is the same person each time. People assume the high-status person knows what he is doing and that the low-status person will get everybody into trouble.

**Bonding
and Social
Development**

Like many other animals, we human beings usually have special feelings about certain others of our species: we prefer their company, we prefer to work with them, and in some cases we prefer to mate with them.

There are three major kinds of bonding systems: (1) cross-sex bonding, which involves persons of opposite sexes and which frequently serves as the basis for marriage and reproduction; (2) parent-child bonding, which involves relations between parents and their children and which normally serves to promote the survival and social development of the young; and (3) same-sex bonding, which involves members of the same sex and which ordinarily serves to promote cooperative activities and social interactions.

Cross-Sex Bonding

While it is fine for zoologists to view mating behavior as the inevitable result of natural forces acting to preserve the species, the situation is not so simple if we look at it from the point of view of those actually involved. As far as we can tell, most sexually mature animals spend some portion of their lives searching for a mate, experiencing very intense emotions, and trying to get things to work smoothly so that a satisfying sexual and social relationship can be established. In human beings this search is called dating or courting, the emotions are called everything from lust to love, and the relationship, when properly sanctioned, is called marriage. As you may have noticed, this whole process takes up a very large amount of our time and attention.

The general pattern of social processes that culminate in human mating are surprisingly similar to those of many other animals. Early in life all infants are treated by their group in much the same way. As the children develop, sex differences become clearer. In some cultures, during middle to late childhood (five years to twelve or thirteen years) the sexes tend to segregate; males tend to associate with males and females tend to associate with females. At this time, adults and the youngsters themselves begin to take sex differences into account, treating males and females differently. And, as sexual maturity is approached (the early teens in humans), there is an increased interaction between the sexes which eventually leads to pairing off into cross-sex couples, courting, and marriage.

A number of fundamentally important factors determine whether a man and woman will be attracted to each other. Initially, physical attractiveness tends to be very important. Attractiveness involves the degree to which the person fits the culture's image of physical beauty as well as how well he or she satisfies the current concept of fashionability (Fig. 4.10). Thus, in the 1920s, fashion and the American image required young women to bind their chests so that their breasts would not protrude; men were entranced. Then, in the 1950s and early 1960s, fashion and the American image required young women to prop and pad their chests so that their breasts would protrude as much as possible; men were entranced. And, in the late 1960s and early 1970s, fashion and the American image required that young women give up binding and propping; men seem to find this entrancing too. During each of these fashion phases, the women who had the flattest or biggest or most medium-sized chests were considered by men to be the most physically attractive and desirable.

FIG. 4.10 *Fashions change and the people who conform most successfully often are regarded as the most physically attractive.*

Photograph above courtesy of McCall's Pattern Fashions Magazine, Fall-Winter 1972 issue.

Photograph at right courtesy D. Doty.

Men's fashions changed too, and with these changes came changes in what was considered masculine attractiveness. In the 1920s and 1930s, clean-shaven young men slicked their hair down with heavy grease and wore bell-bottom trousers. From the 1940s until the early 1960s, equally clean-shaven young men had their hair clipped very short, and their trousers went from baggy to almost skin tight. In the late 1960s and early 1970s, beards and long hair were in and bell-bottom trousers returned. As was true for women, the men who best conformed to the fashions of the times were considered the most physically attractive.

When men and women get to know each other, physical appearance tends to decrease in importance as a determinant of their mutual attraction. Instead, two more subtle factors begin to have effect. The first of these is *need complementarity,* that is, the degree to which the relationship fulfills each individual's private needs. Thus, a timid man may find an outgoing woman attractive because she gladly takes care of the social demands that cause him anguish. The outgoing woman may be attracted to the timid man because she doesn't have to compete with him for the social spotlight. While authorities are not agreed on the degree to which cross-sex attraction is based on need complementarity, it is clear that it is a factor of some importance.

The second factor that influences attraction is the degree of *similarity* between the two persons' values. We will discuss values in more detail later (Section 5), but suffice it to say that the more that people see themselves as agreeing about what things are important, good, moral, desirable, and so on, the more they will tend to be attracted to each other. Indeed, research shows that the chances of a successful, happy marriage are good if the partners really do have similar values (or if their values change to become similar). But if their values turn out to be substantially different, even though each person thinks they're similar, the chances of a good marriage are not very high. This makes sense, of course; if the two are attracted because of incorrectly perceived similarity, they are bound to work at cross purposes because they actually want different things. The strife created in such circumstances often can destroy the marriage no matter how attracted the partners are to each other—they still love each other but they just can't seem to agree about anything. (One function of marriage counseling is to help married couples reconcile their previously unrecognized value differences.) At any rate, it is clear from a great number of investigations into the topic that perceived similarities in values is a basic factor in the development and maintenance of cross-sex attraction and bonding. (This discussion of cross-sex bonding is continued and expanded in Section 6, Part 3, "Love, Marriage, and Sex.")

Parent-Child
Bonding

The two-parent home The behavior of human parents in raising their children is not wholly unlike the behavior of the mother rhesus monkey raising her offspring. The earliest stage consists in large part of taking care of the baby's bodily needs: food, dry clothing, and cuddling—baby people are like baby monkeys in their need to be held. As the child becomes more self-sufficient, the parents allow more and more independence, although supervision is constantly exercised. Soon the child acquires playmates and friends who form his or her first peer group. Then comes the inevitable day when the child's parents find that the opinions of those peers (friends and playmates) count more than theirs do.

With adolescence comes problems of physical and intellectual growth; the adolescent constantly searches for who he is, what he is really like, and what he is capable of doing. It is a difficult period. What is not so often recognized is that it is an equally difficult period for the parents. During this time, it is virtually an axiom that from their offsprings' point of view the parents can do nothing right; parents in these circumstances are best advised to try to think of the whole thing as a character-building experience and to hold out as best they can. This is not to say that the parents actually are always right, but then, neither are their children.

The paradox in all of this, and what often is difficult for parents to realize, is that while the adolescent is trying to change his life-style and to assume independence, he often needs to retreat to the nest, to be allowed to be dependent, childlike, and secure for a time before trying again. As the adolescent changes, the parents, after years of being responsible for their child's behavior, also must change their life-styles. They must learn to allow the adolescent to command his own destiny, even if his new ideas offend their ways of thinking. At the same time, they must continue to provide the love and security the adolescent sometimes so desperately needs. Changing one's life-style is a difficult process, and both the adolescent and his parents face a mammoth undertaking. Is it any wonder that the process is often painful for both parties and that it takes a long time for the wounds to heal?

Aside from sustaining life through food, shelter, and love, the most important function of parents is to educate their children. This does not necessarily mean a carefully planned course of tutoring or anything of that sort. Parents teach their children in large part by serving as *models* which their children can imitate (see Section 3, Part 2). Probably every father has been delighted, or dismayed, as the case may be, when his son has said or done something "just like Daddy does." Until peer influences become strong, parents and older brothers and sisters are of primary importance in shaping a child's behavior, and they do so primarily by being models, by setting an example for the child.

An important, but somewhat strange, set of events dictates which parent has the stronger influence on the child at any one time. When the child is young and helpless, the mother is of primary importance. Babies usually learn to recognize their mothers before they do their fathers; the mother often can comfort the crying child when the father can't, for example. Later, one finds that a little girl will evidence particular affection for her father; she becomes "Daddy's girl." Similarly, a little boy will become "Mama's boy," a situation that often irks the father because he is sure his son will end up being effeminate. Before long, however, everything changes and the little girl, having successfully conquered her father, begins to be her mother's steadfast companion while the father finds his son is constantly dogging his tracks.

This special affection for one or the other parent is called *identification* with that parent. Identifying with the same-sex parent is of primary importance in helping the child establish his own sexual identity. To a large degree, it is by imitating his father that a boy learns to behave in the ways that his culture deems appropriate for his sex (Fig. 4.11). Girls learn their roles in the same way; they begin to play dress-up, use Mommy's cosmetics when Mommy isn't looking, set the table, and make peanut butter cookies.

Shortly after beginning to identify with his same-sex parent, the child starts nursery school, kindergarten, or first grade. Then, over the next two years or so, the children in our society begin to segregate themselves by sex; they begin to restrict themselves in such a way that boys play army, cowboys, and other rough games with other boys, while girls play dolls and hopscotch with other girls.

Sexual segregation continues throughout the grade school years and begins to change only at puberty and the beginning of adolescence. At this time, males and females begin to be attracted to each other and soon courting begins. Along with this change comes a need to re-evaluate oneself and a preoccupation with being socially accepted by one's peers. This, of course, is part of the process of becoming a desirable partner and entering into the courting and mating. It also is the period of adolescent turmoil and striving for self-direction that causes both the child and his parents great difficulty.

The one-parent home   War, death, divorce, and other kinds of difficulties produce single-parent families. The remaining parent usually is the mother because during war men leave and in case of divorce the courts nearly always give custody of children to women. The number of single-parent families is

Courtesy Paul Kopelman.

Reprinted from The Seattle Times with permission.

FIG. 4.11 Children learn many of the behaviors that society deems appropriate for their sex by imitating adults who they observe in real life, in movies, on television, or in books.

swollen by families in which one of the two parents has essentially ceased to participate. Usually it is the father who, because of problems between himself and his wife or because of an overwhelming interest in his occupation, drops out and relinquishes his influence on his children.

It has already been stressed that it is important for the child to identify with the same-sex parent (or some substitute) in order for him or her to develop an appropriate sexual identity. Although there is disagreement about how serious the problem actually is, you can see why some authorities are concerned about single-parent families, particularly those in which the same-sex parent is absent. The fear is that unless an older brother or sister, teacher, relative, or friend of the family can serve as a replacement for the absent parent, the child may have difficulty learning those behaviors that our culture deems appropriate to his or her sex. When left with only a mother, boys may suffer more than girls. Grade school teachers usually are female, and with only their mothers at home, these boys often live in an almost totally female world. Moreover, some mothers have difficulty letting their sons become independent and grow away from them, since, without husbands, their sons often are a major source of male affection. When this happens, the sons may have insufficient opportunity to learn a male sex role. Occasionally such boys become effeminate, develop interests ordinarily associated with women, and, in extreme cases, may have a great deal of difficulty with sexual adjustment later in life. On the other hand, it is not uncommon for such boys to rebel against their overly feminine surroundings and to become almost obsessed with proving themselves masculine, that is, with not being "sissy." Overaggressive boys such as school behavior problems and juvenile delinquents occasionally are examples of this revolt against femininity.

This is not to say that the absence of an adult male in the house can have no effect on girls. To some degree, both girls and boys learn about differences in how men and women behave by the differences in how their parents behave, and they obtain some of their ideas about cross-sex affection by observing their parents' behavior toward each other. In the absence of one parent, these things are difficult to learn, for girls as well as boys. In fact, even with both parents present, cross-sex affection may be difficult to learn. For example, parents who dislike each other but stay together "for the children's sake" may be such terrible models for teaching cross-sex attitudes that they might do their children a service by separating rather than staying together.

Parentless homes   Because of the extreme helplessness and dependency of young human beings, there are very few cases in which children are actually raised without parents or substitute parents. However, children who are raised in understaffed institutions, children who have been separated from their parents, and children who are severely neglected by their parents come pretty close to being parentless.

The necessity of adult care and attention for both the physical and psychological well-being of children is dramatically evident when one looks at infants who have been placed in understaffed institutions such as poorly managed orphanages. Lying helplessly in their cribs, with their basic needs taken care of in an efficient but impersonal manner, these children are more susceptible to disease and death than are children raised by real or substitute parents. If they survive, they are a bit like the baby monkeys that Dr. Harlow raised in isolation; they are retarded in their mental and physical growth. There is even evidence that these children, like the monkeys, can never be normal, but no one really is sure about this yet. One thing is fairly clear, however, if these institutions can arrange to have people hold the babies and play with them, they do not become retarded.

Another parentless situation arises when children are temporarily separated from their parents for one reason or other. When this happens we see yet another similarity between human infants and Dr. Harlow's monkeys. Remember we said that when baby monkeys are separated from their mothers they go through a very predictable syndrome—agitated activity and crying, depression, and eventual recovery if the mother doesn't return or extreme elation if she does. The same sort of thing happens with human babies. A newborn human baby isn't too discriminating about who takes care of him, but starting at about six months of age he begins to recognize the person with whom he has had the most contact, usually his mother. Separation from this person brings on a syndrome that is exactly like that observed with baby monkeys. As the child grows older the syndrome occurs with decreasing duration and intensity whenever separation occurs. If you've ever been at a summer camp that was attended by fairly young children, you've seen the syndrome—the temper tantrum and pleading when the parents prepare to leave the child at the camp, the depression and homesickness that follows, the eventual recovery and, perhaps, enjoyment of the stay, and the happy reunion with the parents at the end of vacation. Of course, that happy reunion sometimes is marred by recriminations and tears about having been abandoned, but this passes and the child usually is quite happy to see his parents again.

The term "neglected children" means a number of things. The institutionalized children we were just discussing would qualify. But sometimes what looks like a good home produces children who should also be regarded as

BOX 4.2

A Little Loving Can Go a Long Way

Although conditions today are considerably different, forty years ago most state orphanages were run down, overcrowded, and way understaffed. As a result, orphans often lived in what amounted to being parentless homes. Thus, in the nursery of one such orphanage in the Midwest, babies spent all of their time in cribs. The small staff was so overworked that the nurses had no time to play with the babies or even to hold them while they were fed—their bottles merely were propped against pillows. Around the age of two, these children were moved to large cottages, where, in groups of about thirty-five, they lived under the supervision of one matron and three or four bored, untrained teenage girls. The children spent most of their time inside except when they went for meals in a central dining hall. All their activities were highly regimented so that the matron could cope with such a large number of children. Clothes for the children were selected each day merely according to whether or not they fit; with the exception of a toothbrush, no child had any personal belongings. This style of life continued for the children until they were either adopted or until they became old enough to leave the orphanage and live on their own. The effect of prolonged institutionalization upon the intellectual and personality development of those children who were not adopted was sad indeed—most of them became emotionally dull, withdrawn, and

neglected. The suburban parents who both work and have a brisk social life and thus employ a succession of nurses and babysitters for their children may neglect their children as much as the slum-dwelling parents who let their children wander the streets. In both cases, the child may not learn properly about affection or about the subtleties of the roles that his society demands of him. The long-term result of such a situation sometimes is a self-centered young person who has no regard for anyone else. His peer group, composed of persons like himself, may provide his only source of support and affection—an unsatisfactory replacement for parents' guidance and love. Sometimes these peer groups, lacking adult influence, have few civilizing pressures exerted upon them, and they may turn to crime and other forms of antisocial behavior.

When, because of neglect and insufficient supervision, Junior ends up at the police station, the neglectful parents, be they suburbanites or slum dwellers, lament that they have done their best with the ungrateful kid and that they are at their wits' end with him. Sadly, this may well be the case—they have done the best they know how. However, Junior may be merely a small edition of his parents, mirroring their self-centered irresponsibility. Tragically, he may

mentally retarded. Few ever completed junior high school, and many ended up in other public institutions for the remainder of their lives.

Until Dr. Harold M. Skeels arrived in 1932, the orphanage had no resident psychologist. (Neither had it a resident social worker or physician.) Our story begins shortly after Dr. Skeels' arrival.

One day two little girls, neglected, undernourished, apathetic, and frail, were committed to the orphanage. Although one was thirteen months old and the other sixteen months, psychological evaluation showed that their mental development was equivalent to that of a six or seven month-old child. So it was decided that it would be best for them to be transferred to a state institution for the mentally retarded. Six months later, Dr. Skeels happened to visit that institution. While there, he noticed two alert, smiling, totally normal little girls and was surprised to find that they were the same two that he had sent there six months earlier. Another psychological evaluation of the girls showed that they were now well within the normal range of mental development for their ages.

Of course, Dr. Skeels was curious about what had caused this marked and rapid change in the girls. His investigation revealed that upon their arrival at the institution, they had been placed with a group of older, relatively brighter women (whose chronological ages ranged from eighteen to fifty years and whose mental ages ranged from five to nine years). Since the girls were the only youngsters

well do the same thing to his children. Like the female rhesus monkeys who became poor mothers because they had no mother to learn from, neglected children may become poor parents because, never having had loving, conscientious parents, they never learned how family bonds normally work.

Same-Sex Bonding   Most of our friends are of the same sex as ourselves. This begins in childhood when the boys and the girls in one's peer group begin to segregate. When subsequent courting occurs, it ordinarily consists of dating only a few members of the opposite sex and, even though this provides an opportunity to get to know these few rather well, the jealousies involved in such relations tend to reduce close contacts with most others. Marriage does much the same thing; the pressures of loyalty to the other person, and his or her jealousy, place constraints on one's friendships with members of the opposite sex. Thus, even later in life most of our friends are of the same sex as ourselves.

As was the case for cross-sex bonding, the similarity between our own and another person's values are the major determinants of same-sex bonding (Fig. 4.12). The people with whom we are most comfortable and that we like best

in the group, two of the women quickly "adopted" them while the other women served as adoring aunts. Even the attendants and nurses showered attention on the girls, taking them for excursions and giving them toys and picture books. Shortly after their amazing recovery the girls were placed in adoptive homes.

This episode suggested to Dr. Skeels that if the other children in the orphanage could be taken from their dull cribs and overcrowded cottages, they too might become as bright and alert as the two little girls had become. Unfortunately, at that time the state had not yet developed a foster parent program and, because adoption procedures were more restrictive than they are now, finding normal homes to which the orphans could go was an impossible task. But it stood to reason that if the two little girls had done so well after spending only a short time with the mentally retarded women, why couldn't it work again on a broader scale?

So, thirteen children from the orphanage who were in the infant to three-year-old age range, healthy, but somewhat mentally underdeveloped, were placed as "house guests" with the mentally retarded women. To fully evaluate the effects

FIG. 4.12   *Similarities in values are an important determinant of friendships.* (*Photo by Merrim, courtesy Monkmeyer Press Photo Service.*)

of such a change, a group of twelve other children from the orphanage (the "control group") were selected for comparison with the thirteen children who went to the institution (the "experimental group"). These control group children were highly similar in all respects to the experimental group children, but, because there was no room for them with the retarded women, they had to remain in the orphanage.

Now the story jumps twenty years forward, to when Dr. Skeels set out to find all twenty-five people from the experimental and control groups in order to see how they had fared in life.* His search was long and difficult because the people had scattered broadly in those twenty years, but finally he contacted all of them (except for one of the control members who had died).

The follow-up showed striking differences in what had become of the members of the two groups during those twenty years. Of the control group, five people were in state institutions for the mentally retarded or the mentally ill, three were

*H. M. Skeels, Adult status of children with contrasting early life experiences. *Monographs of the Society for Research in Child Development*, 1966, **31**, Whole no. 3

are usually rather like us—they enjoy doing what we enjoy doing, their religious and political views are fairly similar to our own, their hopes and hates and fears are like ours. We therefore are comfortable with them and understand them and feel confident that we are understood in return.

Research has shown that similarity is so important to friendships that we frequently tend to overestimate the degree to which our friends are similar to ourselves (while at the same time judging them to be somewhat more social, better adjusted, and more active than ourselves). By the same token we tend to see disliked persons as more different from ourselves than usually is the case (while at the same time judging them to be somewhat less social, more maladjusted, and more aggressive than ourselves). Of course, the effects of value similarity on bonding depends on whether the similar values are very important. If a person agrees with you on unimportant matters but disagrees on the things that are important, you are less likely to regard him as likable than if he agrees with you on a few important values but disagrees with you on the others.

A second determinant of whether you like somebody depends on whether they appear to like you. Few of us can resist friendly feelings for someone with the good taste to recognize our own likability and sterling character. This determinant in conjunction with value similarity can serve to build very strong bonds between two people—when you perceive that the other person has values that apparently are similar to your own, you are inclined to like him.

dishwashers, one was a drifter who took whatever work he could get, one worked part time in a cafeteria wrapping silverware in napkins, and one was a compositor-typesetter who was doing quite well. It is interesting to note that the compositor-typesetter had been a particular favorite of the matron of his cottage and, as a result, he frequently had been a guest in both her home and in her married daughter's home. Moreover, because of a moderate hearing loss, he had been sent to a special high school where he received individual attention and did sufficiently well to go on to complete one year of college. He was the only member of the control group to go beyond the eighth grade. He also was the only control group member who was married, although the drifter had once been married and divorced.

On the other hand, all of the members of the experimental group had done rather well for themselves. The three men's jobs were staff sergeant, real estate salesman, and vocational counselor. The women's jobs were housewife, nurse's aide, teacher, registered nurse, beauty operator, dining room hostess, saleswoman, and office clerk. Only three members of this group failed to complete high school, three completed at least two years of college, and one had graduated from a two-year business college. Eleven of the thirteen people had married (although one later was divorced), producing among them a total of twenty-eight children, all of whom were of normal intelligence.

We must be rather cautious when drawing conclusions from such a small-scale study done under such peculiar circumstances. However, the striking difference between the two groups twenty years after the initial experiment strongly suggests that the love and attention given to the children in the experimental group saved them from ending up like the control group members. It is possible that the major effect of living with the retarded women was to make the children alert, attractive, and bright—good candidates for adoption. And, of course, the adoptive home itself would have a positive effect on the development of the children. This conjecture is supported by the fact that eleven of the thirteen children in the experimental group had been adopted while none of the control group children had been. The lack of a homelike atmosphere, with the care and attention of loving adults, left its permanent mark on the control group children—with the tragic long-term results that we have seen.

Your esteem will prompt him to like you in return, and if your values are indeed similar, his liking will increase even more. His liking of you will strengthen your friendly feelings for him, which in turn will strengthen his liking of you, and so on. Unless circumstances intervene, such as in the case where one of you changes your values, same-sex bonds that evolve in this way may endure for years.

All of the behavior described thus far in this section has involved interactions between two or more animals or persons, that is, social groups. As we have seen, these groups have a strong influence on the individual behavior of their members. Still, we have yet to examine *how* the group exerts this influence and *why* the individual tolerates its interference with his behavior. This brings us to the topics of social pressure, social resources, and leadership.

Social Pressure and Conformity

The threat of a group's disapproval or rejection is called *social pressure.* The individual who exerts such social pressure is acting, in part, as an agent of the group. For example, when you were a child and your mother corrected your table manners she was, perhaps unknowingly, acting as an agent of the culture at large. She spoke for all the people who disapprove of any child who puts mashed carrots in his ear; her disapproval was their disapproval. She was an agent who exerted the necessary social pressure to make you *conform* to the group's rules, or *norms.* The behavior expected of you is called your *role.* The social pressure teaches you how to fill a particular role and also helps form your *attitudes* about how people should behave and how things should happen in any group.

Of course, your mother was an agent for many groups. At different times she may have represented the Methodist Church, the middle class, the United States of America, and so on. The point is that as she guided your growth, and civilized you, she also trained you to conform to the norms of the various groups of which she was a member and of which you, most likely, are now a member.

It may seem as though the group's agent is always gunning for the individual and exercising social pressure on him in a rather heartless way. For the most part, however, this is not the case. Usually, individuals willingly conform to their group's norms because they are well rewarded for doing so. We will discuss these methods in detail shortly, but for the moment note that a major reason for participating in social behavior is to attain acceptance and affection from the other members and, in times of crisis, to be able to rely on the group for *social support.* That is, we expect our groups to back us when we need it.

Social support can take many forms. If the group is a streetcorner gang, support of a member may mean actual physical fighting—"To insult Joey is to insult us all!" At the other extreme, a group's support may merely mean that the group argues the member's right to do something even if they don't like what he does. Academic Freedom is a good example of the latter; the faculty of a school will support a colleague's right to hold the opinion that the earth is square even if most members of the group don't agree with him. It is this kind of support that has allowed scholars to pursue seemingly odd courses of study that have led to important discoveries. In a group that is working toward some well-defined goal, an individual receives social support in terms of personal regard from each member, of aid in doing his job (thereby moving the group toward its goal), and of receiving due credit for his part in the group's enterprise. The point is that a group member ordinarily receives a great deal of support from his fellow group members; this support gives him both a feeling of security and a feeling of being accepted and belonging—feelings that seem to be an important need of almost every human being.

Interactions among people turn on the fact that everyone involved both gives something to the other people and receives something in return. The things that are given and received are called *social resources*. Dr. Uriel Foa, who has studied social interactions in great detail, has found that there are six basic kinds of social resources: (1) love, (2) money, (3) goods, (4) services, (5) status, and (6) information. In a sense, social interactions are like economic interactions—the social resources are the currency.

Love and money Love is interpreted broadly to include any kind of warm, outgoing feeling toward another person. It is possible to convey different degrees of love: through a smile, a compliment, touching, or a simple statement of affection. Similarly, it is possible to withhold love to various degrees: by ignoring the person, by frowning, by a stiff posture and gruff voice, by criticism, or by an insult. Most of us have a strong desire to be loved, and we work hard to see that we get our minimum daily requirement of approval from the people we encounter. We also respond to their needs for love and, depending upon the circumstances and how we feel about the person, we supply this love.

We needn't spend much time discussing money as a social resource. Our economy is based on millions of daily social encounters in which the exchange of money is the main goal of the interaction. Notice, however, that love and money are quite different social resources. Love is very personal in the sense that it makes a difference to whom you give your love or from whom you receive it. The quality of love depends on the persons involved. In contrast, money is an impersonal resource. Money from one person is worth just as much as money from another person. Money is money no matter who the persons involved in the interaction are.

BOX 4.3

Conformity

Few of us like to think of ourselves as conformists, in spite of the fact that both casual observations and scientific evidence clearly show us to be. Our clothes, hair style, manner of speaking, moral convictions, and political beliefs tend to be highly similar to those of our friends. Of course, we seek friends who are like us in these respects, but once we become involved with a group, their ways become our ways.

There have been too many studies of conformity to do justice to them all here. But there are three classic studies that together give a fairly clear picture of the social circumstances that promote conformity. Two of the three studies are laboratory experiments and the third is an investigation of how students conform to their new classmates' views when they leave home to go to college.

The first experiment, carried out by Dr. Muzafer Sherif, demonstrates how quickly conformity to group norms occurs in situations in which the group members have no objective information on which to base their behavior.* The

*M. SHERIF, Group influences upon the formation of norms and attitudes. In E. E. Maccoby, T. M. Newcomb, and E. L. Hartley (Eds.), *Readings in social psychology.* New York: Holt, Rinehart and Winston, 1958.

Goods and services   Goods are concrete objects desired by another person. Services are substantial, concrete types of activities which benefit the person who receives them. The difference between services and goods is that services are personal in that a service is done for a specific person, whereas goods, being similar to money, are likely to be somewhat impersonal.

Status and information   Status and information are symbolic resources rather than concrete ones. Status is a personal kind of resource; when you give status, you give it to a specific person in a specific situation. Information, on the other hand, tends to be somewhat more impersonal. It is not tailored to fit any particular person, rather, it has some sort of value to any number of people.

Just as love and money may be either given or taken away, so too may goods be given or taken away. And services can be performed for a person (that is, given) or they can be taken away (that is, you can do a disservice to or harm the other person). You can provide information that is useful and desired by the other person or you can withhold it or distort it. So too with status; there is a variety of techniques used in face-to-face encounters where

ambiguous situation used in the experiment consisted of having people make judgments about an illusion called the *autokinetic phenomenon*. To see this illusion all you have to do is sit in a room that is totally dark except for a moderately bright *stationary* pinpoint of light about fifteen feet in front of you. If you stare at the light for a few moments, it will appear to move. The illusion is quite compelling; even if you know the light can't be moving, you still would swear that it does. Moreover, if you view the illusion repeatedly, each time the light will seem to move about the same distance and in the same direction, different people having different average distances and directions.

Dr. Sherif's experiment consisted of asking volunteers to make repeated judgments (aloud) about the distance the light moved, either when they viewed the autokinetic phenomenon alone or when they viewed it with a group. The point was to see if peoples' distance judgments would be more similar when they were tested in groups than when they were tested alone. Thus some people were tested alone at first and then assigned to groups and tested again. It was found that soon after group testing began, the group members' judgments became more

one person deprives another person of status or gives him more status so that he stands a bit taller than before.

Clearly, some of these resources are more alike than others. The six different resources can be arranged in the geometrical pattern shown in Figure 4.13, which symbolizes the differences and similarities among these resources with regard to how concrete and how personal they are. Dr. Foa has demonstrated how people regard the relations among the various resources by means of some very clever experiments. In one experiment, people were given a hypothetical description of how one person gave love to another. They were then asked which resource they felt was an appropriate exchange for the love that was given. The answers came out quite consistently. The appropriate exchange for *love* is either to return the love in some way, to do some *service* for the person who gave the love, or to give some sign of respect which would increase the other person's *status*. In other words, when a person is given a resource by another person it is most appropriate for him to return that same resource in some form. The next most appropriate behavior would be to return a resource which lies close to the initially given resource in the diagram in Figure 4.13. Thus, if someone is given goods, most people feel that the appropriate thing to do in return is to offer goods, money, or services. It seems to be much less appropriate to return love or information or to do something to increase their status.

similar than they had been during the individual tests; that is, the group members evolved a group norm and gave up their initial individual judgments to conform to it. Other people went through the experiment in the opposite order, experiencing group testing first and then being tested alone. With this order it was found that the norm established in the group test was carried over into the individual tests—the people continued to conform to the group even when they were alone. Thus, the individual judgments of this latter group of people were more similar to each other than were the individual judgments of the former group of people. Still other people were tested with one other person whom they believed to be a volunteer like themselves. However, the other person actually was a confederate employed by Dr. Sherif and was instructed beforehand about the range of judgments to give. It was found that the real volunteers' judgments nearly always fell very close to the "judgments" given by the confederate. After the experiment was over, the real volunteers stated that they knew that their judgments had been influenced by the confederate's judgments, but, try as they might, they couldn't keep from conforming.

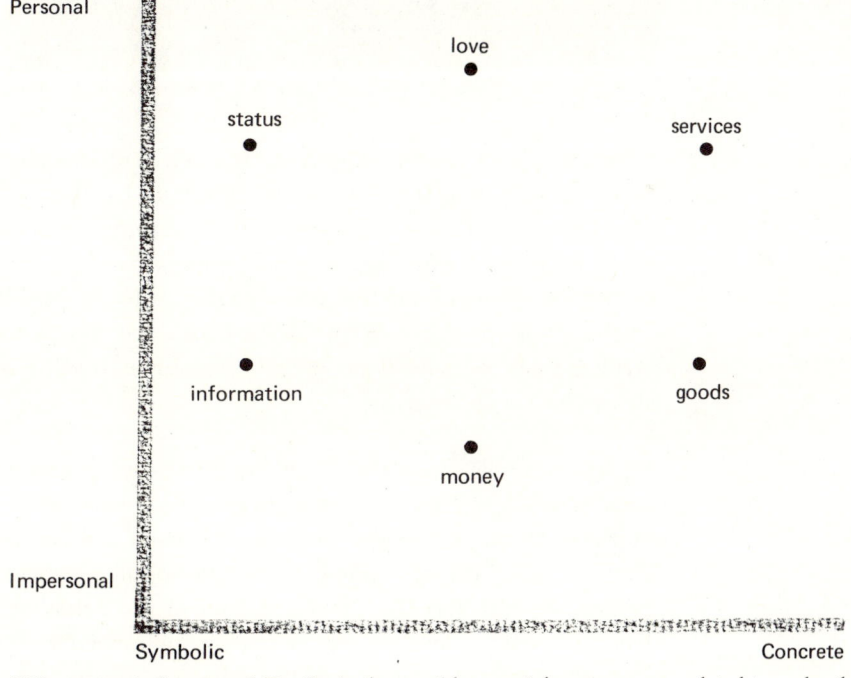

FIG. 4.13   *A diagram of Dr. Foa's theory of how social resources are related to each other and how concrete or personal they are.*

Now you may argue that this study doesn't demonstrate much because of its reliance on a very ambiguous task and that such ambiguity is seldom encountered in everyday life. There is another study, however, that is very similar to Dr. Sherif's experiment but which lacks the ambiguity of the autokinetic phenomenon.

In this second experiment, performed by Dr. Solomon Asch, groups of volunteers were shown a line that was a few inches long and then were asked to say which one of a small set of other lines was the same length as the first.† This task is so simple that under normal conditions, very few errors are made. However, the experiment was not done under normal conditions. Rather, it was done with groups of people (ranging from two to sixteen people per group) in which only one person actually was a volunteer and everyone else in the group was a confederate employed by Dr. Asch. The confederates were instructed to periodically select the wrong answer, and, since the real volunteer always had to state his judgment last, the point was to see under what conditions the volunteer would conform to the obviously wrong answers of the rest of the group. It was found that when there were three or more confederates in the group and they were

---

†S. E. Asch, Effects of group pressure upon modification and distortion of judgments. In E. E. Maccoby, T. M. Newcomb, and E. L. Hartley (Eds.), *Readings in social psychology.* New York: Holt, Rinehart and Winston, 1958.

When people were asked how they felt someone should respond if he was deprived of one of these resources, the pattern illustrated in Figure 4.13 was found again. Suppose someone stole something from you, for example, took goods away from you. Again, most people agree you should take away goods, money, or services from that individual in order to make things come out even. On the basis of these examples, you can see that a social resource is most exchangeable with itself or with the resources that lie on either side of it on the circle in Figure 4.13.

Power

At various times, people are motivated to possess a monopoly on one of these social resources. This monopoly gives the person a source of *social power*, since another person cannot get the resource from anyone except the monopolist. Thus, in the case of money, if the monopolist controls the other person's income, he also has the power to control his behavior. The monopolist can usually count on another person being influenced by his ability to give him love, service, status, or any of the other resources, but this is not always the case. If a person neither needs nor wants the resources the monopolist possesses,

unanimous in their choice of the wrong line, the judgments of the volunteers conformed about one third of the time and remained independent about two thirds of the time. There were marked differences in conformity among the volunteers. At one extreme were those who remained independent throughout the experiment (but were quite puzzled about what was going on); at the other extreme were those who nearly always conformed (as one volunteer plaintively remarked, "They answered with such confidence!"); and the rest were somewhere in between. If there were only one or two confederates in the group or if the majority wasn't unanimous, the volunteers conformed only about one tenth to one twentieth of the time.

I suppose each of us thinks that we would be an independent nonconformist were we to find ourselves in Dr. Asch's experiment. But think for a moment about how you would feel if you were the only person in a group that apparently believed itself to be correct in what obviously is a very simple task. To demonstrate what this pressure would be like, Dr. Asch reversed the group composition of his earlier experiment. This time the group majority consisted of real volunteers and only one member was a confederate. After the majority had given their correct judgments, the lone dissenter gave his wrong answer; the result was undisguised laughter at the ridiculous minority of one. Of course, the laughing majority little realized that they drew their strength from the fact that they all agreed; had any

the monopolist has very little power over him. Thus, there is a difference between *potential social power* that an individual has as a result of being the only supplier of a social resource and the *actual social power* he has when the other person needs or wants the resource which he controls.

As must be clear by now, people enter into social interactions with each other because such interactions give them an opportunity to obtain the social resources they need and want. However, to receive any of these social resources, they also must give some social resources because the other person also wants to receive something from the interaction. If both persons get about as much as they give, the interaction is said to be *balanced*; both persons are happy and the interaction is a good one for all concerned. Sometimes, however, circumstances lead to an *unbalanced* interaction.

Consider the following example. Suppose that we have two people, A and B, who get along well together; that is, they are a balanced group, each supplying the other with some of the resources that he wants. Ordinarily, if either person stops supplying a resource, he will find himself abandoned; the other person will seek someone else to supply the resource that is withheld. But one of them been in the other fellow's shoes, they may well have conformed rather than give a dissenting judgment and risk the extreme embarrassment of being laughed at.

Comparing the results of these two experiments, we see clearly that as the judgment task becomes less ambiguous (length of line versus autokinetic movement), the degree of conformity decreases markedly; still, it doesn't completely disappear. Of course, it can be argued that the mere fact of being in a psychology experiment may exert pressure on people to try to appear as "normal" as possible and therefore to conform if they have even the slightest doubt about the accuracy of their judgments. The third study, as we shall see, avoids this difficulty by examining conformity in a real-life setting rather than in the artificial context of a laboratory experiment.

The third study, by Dr. Theodore Newcomb, examined what happened to girls' political attitudes as they progressed through four years of school at a small eastern women's college.‡ The girls came from wealthy, urban, politically conservative families. By contrast, the college atmosphere was extremely liberal, with students'

‡T. M. Newcomb, Attitude development as a function of reference groups. In E. E. Maccoby, T. M. Newcomb, and E. L. Hartley (Eds.), *Readings in social psychology.* New York: Holt, Rinehart and Winston, 1958.

sometimes this doesn't happen. If, for example, A threatens to stop supplying a resource for B and B cannot find another supplier, B is stuck. He becomes *dependent* upon A for the resource, and as a result, A acquires power over B; that is, B can be made to do things he ordinarily wouldn't do out of fear of losing whatever resources A supplies. Of course, if the cost in terms of having to do unpleasant things gets too high, B may decide that the resource A supplies is not worth the effort and abandon A anyway.

Let us look at a more concrete example, one which is much less like a mathematical equation than the previous one. Suppose a young woman named Alice and a young man named Bill live on neighboring farms in a remote area. Because there are no other young people in that area, Alice and Bill have formed a balanced friendship. One day another boy, Clarence, moves to an adjoining farm. Alice and Clarence soon meet and become friends. From Alice's point of view this is a desirable situation; she has her choice between either of the two boys, and if one of them displeases her she can turn her attention (that is, give love and status) to the other boy. This tactic probably would serve to bring the first boy into line again and Alice would continue to have a choice between the two boys.

popularity and reputation for "community citizenship" being closely tied to being liberal. Thus upon entering college, the new freshmen felt strong pressure to conform to the prevalent liberal point of view if they wanted to be accepted by the other students, particularly the older ones. Dr. Newcomb measured the girls' political attitudes from their freshman through their senior years by having each girl complete an attitude questionnaire every year, and also by interviewing each girl just before she graduated. He then compared the girls' attitudes from one year to the next to see if any changes had occurred.

Analysis of the attitude questionnaires clearly showed a large change from conservative to liberal attitudes for the girls as they progressed from their freshman to their senior year, indicating a marked general trend toward conformity to the prevailing liberal views of the college community as a whole. However, there were distinct differences among the girls in the degree to which they conformed; the interview data revealed why these differences existed.

The interviews revealed that whether or not a student's attitudes changed depended heavily upon what she regarded as her *primary reference group,* that is, the group of people to which she felt the greatest allegiance and whose approval was most important to her. If a girl remained conservative through all four years of college, it usually was the case that she regarded her conservative family, rather than the college community, as her primary reference group. Most of the girls

Clearly, this situation creates two unbalanced friendships, one between Bill and Alice and one between Clarence and Alice. Look at this situation from the point of view of Alice's first boyfriend, Bill, keeping in mind that the same things could be true of Clarence, too. He is lonely, jealous, and unhappy. In order to solve these problems, Bill must either re-establish the balance in his relations with Alice or abandon her. There are a number of possible courses of action Bill could take to solve his problem. First, he might try to prove to Alice that he likes her more than Clarence does (that is, that he is the better supplier of love), or that he is superior to Clarence in his ability to supply some other resource that appeals to Alice. Second, he might re-evaluate Alice's charms and decide that she isn't worth the trouble, whereupon he might spend his life's savings on a car and seek another girl in the next county. Third, he and Clarence might decide to go fishing together and leave Alice to ponder the transience of power.

When Bill and Clarence decide to ignore Alice and go fishing together, they have formed a *coalition* to boycott Alice and to force her to conform to their standards of social behavior. In doing so they have taken her power from her and have now become able to control those resources that she receives. Alice

who became liberal regarded the college community as their primary reference group, either completely rejecting their conservative families or arriving at an "agreement to disagree" with them. Girls at the extreme ends of the continuum in terms of very little or very much conformity were (1) those who were so emotionally or intellectually isolated that they never even realized that their views differed from those of the majority of their fellow students and (2) those who changed their views without even thinking about them because conformity helped them be accepted by the college community.

The general picture that emerges from these three studies (and others like them) is that people usually conform if they have little information upon which to base or defend their divergent opinion (Sherif study). They are less likely to conform if objective information is available (Asch study), although even with enough information the unanimity of a large opposing majority is intimidating. Moreover, the degree to which people conform to a group depends upon whether or not the group is important to them—if it is important, they are likely to change their views in order to be accepted by the group (Newcomb study).

must now give Bill and Clarence something in terms of love, status, or any other resources which appeal to them in order to make it worth their while to continue to interact with her.

Leadership

To one degree or another, all groups exist to achieve a goal, be it pleasant conversation or waging a war. Groups differ, however, with respect to how clearly they define both their goals and the method by which their goals are to be achieved. For example, the goal of a committee assigned to decorate an auditorium for a homecoming dance is rather ambiguous and, as a result, there are numerous ways of achieving this goal. Because the goal has not been defined clearly, the committee is faced with an *unstructured task*. In contrast, the goal of a football team clearly is to win; the methods of doing so are constrained by both the rules of the game and the plays that the team has learned and practiced. Because the methods for achieving its goal are clearly delineated, the football team faces a *structured task*.

Most groups have a *leader*. This leader may be *imposed* on the group from the outside, as in the case of a platoon sergeant whose authority is backed by the army. He may be *elected* by the group, as in the case of a football team captain. Or he may merely come to be regarded as the *informal* leader through tacit agreement of the group, as in the case of an informal spokesman for a student study group. In the first case, imposed leadership, the leader has *power* over his group in that he has the authority to give or withhold social resources if the members do or do not do as he orders. In the other two cases, elected and informal leadership, the leader has little power over his group because he can easily be replaced by the group if he fails to achieve the group's goals and/or deliver those social resources that the group members want.

Leaders differ with respect to their *popularity* among the members of the groups they lead. While a leader with imposed leadership can function rather effectively whether or not he is popular, since he usually is backed by a higher authority, an elected or informal leader depends upon his popularity with the group in order to function well. If he is disliked by his group, he may be ignored or replaced; if he is liked, he may lead the group rather effectively because the group members will put up with a lot before they decide to throw him out and get a new leader.

If you think about it for a moment, groups can be described in terms of the three characteristics we have just discussed: more or less task structure, more or less leader power, and more or less leader popularity. And depending on which combination of these characteristics describes a group, the group can be regarded from the leader's standpoint as a *favorable* or *unfavorable* group to lead. For example, a group that has a structured task, that affords its leader power, and that likes him is a favorable group for the leader. On the other hand, one that has an unstructured task, permits no power, and dislikes its leader would be extremely unfavorable for the leader. Other combinations would be of intermediate favorability. Now, let us look more closely at what favorable and unfavorable combinations of these characteristics mean in terms of the effectiveness with which a leader can guide a group to accomplishing its task.

Leadership and Group Effectiveness

For a long time, psychologists have searched for those characteristics that make a person a good leader. For the most part, their research has been fruitless; some studies suggested one kind of person was best, and other studies concluded that just the opposite kind of person was best. You can imagine the consternation of industrial, military, and social organizations who need methods of telling who will be an effective leader. Things are beginning to change, however. Dr. Fred Fiedler and his associates have examined leadership in all sorts of groups, ranging from bomber crews, sales teams, and surveying parties to the boards of directors of small corporations. From all of this research, they have found that while people behave fairly consistently no matter what kind of group they are leading, different people show different styles of behavior

Box 4.4

Obedience and Disobedience to Authority

Imagine yourself in the following situation: You've volunteered to participate in a psychology experiment. Another volunteer (the learner) has to listen to a list of words that you read to him and then repeat them back to you. Your job is to check the words he repeats back and to give him an electric shock every time he gets one wrong. The two of you go through the word list repeatedly until he gets it perfect, and the longer it takes him to learn the more severe the shocks for being wrong. A psychologist (the experimenter) stands next to you to see that you do everything correctly.

After a few times through the list the shock gets pretty severe and the learner begins to show signs of being in pain. A few more times and he asks to be allowed to stop. At the highest levels of shock he screams. But if you show any signs of wanting to stop the experiment, the experimenter tells you that you have to go on or you'll spoil everything. Now, the question is, would you defy the experimenter and stop the shock?

Dr. Stanley Milgram of Yale University did just what we've described with people of all ages and from all walks of life in both a university setting and in a run-down "private research office" located in a shoddy office building.* Under all conditions the results generally were the same—from 50 to 70 percent of the

*S. MILGRAM, Some conditions of obedience and disobedience to authority. *Human Relations,* 1965, **18,** 57-76.

when faced with being the leader of a group. Dr. Fiedler found these *leadership styles* to range from being extremely *task-oriented* on the one hand to being extremely *person-oriented* on the other, with most people being somewhere in between. The extremely task-oriented leader is very directing, supervising, and controlling. His aim is to get the job done, no matter who gets stepped on in the process; the weak or dissenting group members must either shape up and pull their weight or suffer the consequences. The extremely person-oriented leader is nondirective, considerate, and fairly democratic. His aim is to get the job done while at the same time keep the group members happy and prevent social abrasiveness from developing within the group; the weak or dissenting members are helped and listened to, and the person-oriented leader attempts to take their needs into consideration.

If you have to select a leader for a group, what kind of leader is best? The answer is that it depends on the group for which you are selecting the leader. Using the three group characteristics described above (task structure, leader

participants ended up continuing the experiment to the highest level of shock despite the pitiful pleas of the learner (an actor who was not actually being shocked).

How did the participants feel about what they had done? Awful! But they felt that the experimenter had coerced them into doing it by standing there insisting that they keep on going. Their unhappiness with what they were required to do is reflected in their actions when the experimenter left the room and gave his instructions by telephone; the participants administered very low levels of shock while lying to the experimenter by pretending that they were following his instructions.

If the absence of the experimenter decreased his influence on the participants, so did the absence of the learner, but in the opposite way. When the learner was present in the room, participants were quicker to defy the experimenter and stop the shock than if the learner was in another room where only his voice could be heard. In short, the more removed the authoritative experimenter was, the *less* likely the participants were to shock the learner severely, and the more removed the learner was, the *more* likely they were to shock him severely.

The next step in Dr. Milgram's research was to see how other people's reactions would influence the participants' willingness to continue the experiment.† So he hired two assistants to act as though they were volunteers just like everyone else.

---

†S. MILGRAM, Liberating effects of group pressure. *Journal of Personality and Social Psychology,* 1965, **1**, 127-134.

power, leader popularity), Dr. Fiedler tried to discover which leadership style is most effective with which groups. While the results are complex, the general picture is fairly clear.

In terms of group effectiveness, the task-oriented style works well in favorable groups (where the leader is popular and/or powerful and the task is or is not structured) and in very unfavorable groups (where the leader is unpopular and powerless and the task lacks structure). The person-oriented style works best in groups that are of intermediate favorability. The task-oriented leader's success with favorable groups appears attributable, for the most part, to the fact that his popularity makes up for whatever strife his style may cause. His success for very unfavorable groups may be attributable to his lack of sensitivity to the fact that the group is unfavorable and to his steamroller approach to getting on with the job in spite of everything. The success of the person-oriented style in groups with intermediate favorability seems to be related either to high popularity, which makes the group willing to work with him, or, lacking that,

In one study the real participant and the two assistants all shared the tasks of reading the lists, checking the learners recitation, and giving shock for wrong answers. But midway through the experiment, first one and then the other assistant quit in mock protest against shocking the poor learner. The question was whether the real participants would quit too—90 percent did. In a complementary study the two assistants did not quit but kept going until they were giving the learner the most severe level of shock—only 28 percent of the real participants quit.

Needless to say, Dr. Milgram's findings caused quite a stir. I don't know about you, but they scare me; might I do that? However, the results make sense, although it isn't very pleasant sense. We have many sad examples of people's willingness to comply with the demands of authority—from the Nazi SS soldiers' role in the murder of six million Jews to American soldiers' actions at the My Lai massacre to the National Guardsmen at the Kent State shootings to the policemen at Jackson State and at the 1968 Democratic Convention in Chicago. "But I was only following orders, only doing my job!" is the familiar cry. At a less dramatic level, how many times have you heard a crying child plead innocence with, "It wasn't my fault, he told me to do it!"? All of these were probably fairly nice people; the Nazi troopers had families and friends, the American soldiers were draftees who didn't even want to go to war, the National Guardsmen were the students' neighbors, policemen are usually pretty level-headed, decent men who take more than their share of abuse with amazing self-control, and that crying child probably has been you on more than one occasion.

to sufficiently well-structured tasks in which everybody knows pretty much what is to be done anyway and the leader's job is merely to facilitate activities rather than to actively lead. At any rate, the most important implication of these studies on leadership and group effectiveness is that in selecting people for positions of leadership, it is necessary to take into account both the kinds of group situations they will be expected to lead and the type of leadership style each potential leader tends to use. In doing so, one can avoid ending up with a task-oriented leader in a situation that demands person-oriented techniques, or vice versa.

A major function of a leader is to make dissenting members conform to the group norms. The extremely task-oriented leader relies on threat and coercion to do this. The extremely person-oriented leader relies on reason and appeals to group or personal loyalty. In either case, there comes the time when a member refuses to conform and thereby jeopardizes the effectiveness of the group. Thus he must be rejected by the group. When the leader's power is backed by a large organization such as the army or the law, rejection may be

Dr. Milgram's research fits right in with all we know about these examples—the closer the instructing authority is, the more likely one is to comply with his wishes. The more removed the victim is, the easier it is to do bad things. Removal of the victim is accomplished either by actual physical separation (such as dropping bombs or using guns on him as opposed to close physical aggression) and by making oneself disregard the fact that the victim is a human being (consider, for example, the propagandized hatred of the Jews during World War II, the widespread dislike of the Vietnamese among U.S. soldiers, and the guardsmen's and policemen's anger with "those hippie demonstrators" at Kent State, Jackson State, and Chicago). Finally, if the rest of the group defies the instructions of the authority, it is easy for an individual to defy them too—there is strength in numbers—but if the group sides with the authority, few of us have the courage to revolt.

All of this leaves us with some rather unsettling questions. Is this tendency to comply with authoritarian demands to do dreadful things a result of our particular cultural heritage or is it an inherited predisposition that is universal to human beings? If it is so strong a tendency, are those who commit crimes while "just following orders" guilty of wrongdoing (recall the Nuremberg trials)? How do we help ourselves and others to resist the urge to comply, and would reduced compliance have a disruptive effect on the orderliness of American life? And what about those few people who don't comply, whether in real life or in Dr. Milgram's experiments—how do they differ from the rest of us?

accompanied by additional penalties such as fines, loss of status, imprisonment, or worse. When the leader has no such power, rejection is accompanied by group scorn (withdrawal of love) and loss of the opportunity to participate in the group and to share in its achievements (status, information, money, goods, and services). However, in either case, merely being rejected by the group and losing its social support is in itself extremely painful.

Group Cohesion   Just as groups differ with respect to their goals and the degree to which they satisfy their members' needs, they also differ with respect to how *cohesive* they are. That is, they differ in the extent to which the individual group members cooperate and have a feeling of unity.

Cohesiveness is achieved, in part, by providing adequate communication channels. A group in which all the information is channeled through its leader so that the leader can make all the decisions and be the only source of information for the other members of the group may be productive and efficient, but the members of such a group are not likely to be happy or become close and friendly with each other. On the other hand, a group that encourages communication among its members ordinarily will develop increased cohesiveness without impairing group productivity or effectiveness.

A second way to achieve cohesiveness is to have a very clear-cut goal, one which every member of the group can both understand and discuss with every other member of the group. The fact that a clear-cut goal increases group cohesiveness is illustrated by a study that was done on boys in a summer camp. At the beginning of the summer camp, the boys were divided into two rival teams. As the teams competed with each other in a variety of activities, each team became very cohesive. However, an intense rivalry between the two teams developed. As a result, when they played games, there was a tendency on the part of both teams to cheat and be poor sports. The two teams also played tricks on each other by doing such things as raiding the sports supplies and equipment. Then the people who were running the camp decided to change the situation in the hope of replacing the two highly cohesive groups which were antagonistic to each other with a single harmonious group. Rather than having both teams compete with each other as before, they had both teams work together on important problems. For example, in one situation, the camp's water supply broke down and both teams were enlisted to help search for the trouble and to fix it. In another situation, the camp's truck broke down; again the two teams worked together to get it repaired and moving. After a few days of this kind of unified effort, the teams began to work together smoothly, and the members of the two teams actually became friendly with each other. Thus, at the beginning, when there was very little cohesion in the camp as a whole, the two teams vied with each other. Later, when the situation was changed to permit the members of each team to communicate with the members of the other team, and when both teams began to work together on important tasks, cohesion in the camp as a whole was established. In short, adequate communication channels and a common goal produce good group cohesion.

Some Plausible Speculation about Conformity

The foregoing discussion has rested on the simple premise that people conform to group norms in order to obtain social resources and social support. However, conformity is a bit more complicated than just that; the emotions that promote conformity are much more compelling than mere resources and support ordinarily would justify—the latter usually could be obtained somewhere else with a reasonable amount of effort. The fact is that most of us are much more sensitive to the very unpleasant feelings we experience when we are rejected by another person or by a group than we are to the loss of the resources or support that they have provided us. Indeed, most often it is our unwillingness to risk the possibility of having to experience such feelings, rather than any actual threats by the person or group, that motivates us to try to get along with others as well as we can.

To expand our thinking about peoples' reactions to real and potential rejection, I invite you to join in some plausible speculation. What follows is extrapolated from a theory advanced by Dr. James R. Averill of the University of California at Berkeley, who has studied the factors that contribute to the maintenance of social groups.

While it is likely that human beings and many other animals have *predispositions* to form and maintain social groups, it is not clear what emotions, needs, thoughts, and so on, specifically motivate them to do so. Obviously, this predisposition for forming social groups has survival value for the species in question, but when engaging in social behavior, individuals probably are less concerned with long-range survival goals than they are with satisfying some more immediate needs. As an analogy, consider sexual behavior. At one level of analysis, the effect of sexual behavior is to assure perpetuation of the species. But few, if any, sexually aroused individuals have that lofty goal as their primary consideration; their attention is focused on the more immediate need of satisfying sexual desire. Of course, the pursuit of sexual pleasure ends up accomplishing the long-range goal of perpetuation of the species, but perpetuation is not accomplished because the participants intentionally strove to do so. Indeed, it is rather as though, through evolution, nature has devised a system in which the individual's short-range and immediate interest in sexual pleasure serves, perhaps quite without the individual even realizing it, to assure the long-range survival of the species. Now, if we apply this analogy to conformity, the question is whether there might be a social mechanism that is comparable to sexual pleasure; that is, some feeling or emotion that the individual seeks or avoids that promotes conformity as a by-product and thereby serves to maintain social groups and assure species survival. Dr. Averill's work suggests that there is such a mechanism, the *grief syndrome.*

According to Dr. Averill, the grief syndrome occurs whenever any significant loss occurs—loss of wealth, loss of reputation, loss of self-esteem, loss of valued objects, loss of a secure job, loss of friends, and the loss of someone we love through death or departure (the circumstance with which we most commonly associate grief). In short, loss of virtually any important aspect of one's life can trigger the grief syndrome. And human beings are not the only ones who suffer from it: grief apparently is an *instinctive* sequence of behaviors that is commonly observed in a number of other species of animals.

FIG. 4.14   *The pain of rejection may be a symptom of the first phase of the grief syndrome.*
(*Courtesy D. Doty.*)

Grief must not be confused with mourning. Although grief may well be present during mourning, the latter is essentially a culturally prescribed, ritualistic way of behaving when death occurs. There is some evidence that specific, characteristic physiological changes accompany the grief syndrome, and since these changes do not always occur during mourning, they help to clearly differentiate the two.

In human beings, the grief syndrome consists of three major phases, each phase gradually leading to the next. First, immediately after a loss, there is *shock,* which consists of stunned disbelief followed by extreme agitation. Attention is directed wholly to the loss and the person experiences a high level of general stress. If it is possible to do so, these first-phase behaviors are aimed at recovering whatever has been lost—agitated and relentless searching if it is a material object, or apology, demonstrated remorse, and attempts to make amends if it is a person or social group.

Because most losses are recoverable (for example, we usually find lost objects, and other people and groups usually readmit us to their favor), the grief syndrome usually ends during the first phase. However, we do not soon

forget the unpleasantness of the emotions we felt during the period of stress—
the shock, the fear that the loss might be permanent, the frustration, the guilt,
the anger, and quite often, the desperate feeling of powerlessness and vulnerability. Whenever we suspect that we again are in danger of severe loss,
memory of these emotions reminds us that the cost of taking care of treasured
objects or of conforming to other people's demands may not be as high as
that of the unpleasant alternative, grief. Thus, while social resources and social
support provide positive rewards for conforming to group norms, the speculation is that the fear of grief feelings also is a strong factor in promoting conformity.

Sometimes a loss is permanent, as when someone dies. Because this permanence prevents restoration of the loss, the grief syndrome does not stop
after the first phase and it proceeds to run its full course. So with permanent
loss, the first phase of the grief syndrome gives way to the second, *despair*,
which is characterized by apathy, withdrawal, and depression. It is as though
the overexpenditure of energy during the first phase has left the person ex-
hausted and burned out (and the physiological evidence suggests that this is
a fairly accurate way of thinking about it). Even so, mere rest does little to
help, and it is only with time that despair decreases and the person moves
into the third phase, *recovery*. During the third phase, new objects, persons,
or groups begin to replace the old and, as a result, the permanent loss begins
to occupy less and less of the person's thoughts and emotions.

Grief can last from a few moments (for example, the stab of hurt that results
from a social slight) to many years (for example, prolonged grief over the death
of a loved one). The severity and duration of the grief syndrome depend upon
a number of factors: the person's own nature and background, the importance
of the loss to him, the availability of a substitute for the loss, and so on. And,
depending upon both psychological factors and cultural demands, a person's
grief may either be clear to everyone around him or else be so well hidden
that no one knows that the person is suffering.

Even if death is not involved, the pain of grief is very real. Any rejected
lover or anyone who has agonized about his or her own popularity can tell
you that the grief produced by social loss can be quite devastating and prolonged. What is being speculatively suggested here is that it is the fear of the
pain or grief that encourages us to prevent social losses and makes us carefully
monitor our behavior so that we are not rejected by those persons and groups
that are important to us. This is not to say that we are blind in our conformity;
for example, if its demands violate our values, we may decide that a group
is not sufficiently important to us to make us want to conform. In this case
we may convince ourselves that the group is bad, in order to reduce our loss,

or we may even freely elect to experience the pain of grief rather than conform. Such decisions usually constitute a crisis for us, and often we go through great anguish before we are able to break existing social bonds and move on to new relations. In the next Section we will examine the problems that arise from crises such as this and how we attempt to deal with them.

SUMMARY:

1   Comparison of animal and human social behavior reveals many commonalities, four of which are *territoriality*, *dominance hierarchies*, *bonding*, and *social development*.

2   Human territoriality includes both *real space* (legally owned, temporarily owned, and transient) and *personal space* ("flight" and "fight"). Invasion of either of these spaces by strangers produces emotional arousal in the owner as well as attempts to escape or retaliate.

3   Human dominance hierarchies refer to relative status among persons in any given group. Status can be either *ascribed*, that is, a result of the function a person fills for some particular social group, or *acquired*, that is, a result of the person's own efforts or demonstration of his abilities. To a large extent, how two people behave toward one another in any social encounter depends upon their relative status.

4   Human bonding systems (affectional systems) are of three general types: *cross-sex bonding*, *parent-child bonding*, and *same-sex bonding*. Marriage is the most common example of cross-sex bonding and usually one or more parent-child bonds accompany it. The nature of a parent-child bond is a very important factor in the social development of the child. Same-sex bonding involves friendships with members of one's own sex.

5   All of us are members of a number of social groups. Our behavior is controlled by these groups in that if we want the *social resources* that the group has to offer, we are *pressured* to *conform* to that particular group's *norms*.

6   When someone has a potential or actual monopoly on a desirable social resource, he is said to have *social power*. This means that the interactions of other people with the person with social power are *unbalanced* and that these other people are *dependent* upon the person in power. Most people dislike interactions that make them dependent and will make efforts to restore a balanced relationship or avoid future interactions if possible.

7   The effectiveness of a group often depends heavily upon its leader and his *leadership style*. Styles range from *task-oriented* to *person-oriented*, with different degrees in between. The leader may or may not be *popular* and the group's

task may be either *structured* or *unstructured*. Which leadership style is best for any given group depends upon the leader's power, popularity, and the amount of structure in the group's task.

8   The degree to which a group's members feel *cohesive*, that is, the degree to which they cooperate and have a feeling of unity, is heavily dependent upon adequate communication channels and a common goal.

9   It is possible that fear of initiating the *grief syndrome* is a strong motivation for conforming to the expectations of other people and to group norms. The syndrome is triggered by *loss* and has three phases, *shock, despair,* and *recovery*. When the loss is recoverable, grief stops during the first phase; when it is not, the whole syndrome is experienced.

Special Topics   Section 6, Part 3: *Love, Marriage, and Sex*
Section 6, Part 4: *Psychological Aspects of Poverty*

Further Reading   ARDREY, R.   *The Territorial Imperative*
New York: Dell, 1971 (c. 1966), 355 pages (paperback).
To support his thesis that territoriality is a characteristic of human beings and that it is a result of evolutionary inheritance rather than learning, Ardrey begins by describing various kinds of territorial behaviors in animals. Then he gradually works into territorial behavior in human beings, showing the similarities between man's territorial behavior and that of lower animals. In addition to his zoological interest, the author is a successful playwright and screen writer; the book is extremely readable.

ARDREY, R.   *The Social Contract*
New York: Dell, 1971 (c. 1970), 405 pages (paperback).
Arguing that "equality of individuals is a natural impossibility" and that "every vertebrate born is granted equal opportunity to display his genius or to make a fool out of himself," Ardrey sets out to demonstrate how violation of these "biological laws" has resulted in the failure of social man.

BERNE, E.   *Games People Play*
New York: Dell, 1967 (c. 1964), 192 pages (paperback).
A witty book about the more devious strategies (games) people use in interaction with one another. Berne describes and analyzes 120 of these games in terms of why they occur and what people expect to gain from playing them. Ideas are given about how to free oneself from playing games and to be more socially honest.

BERSCHEID, E., and E. WALSTER   *Interpersonal Attraction*
Reading, Mass.: Addison-Wesley, 1969, 129 pages (paperback).
Much research has been done on the factors that determine why and under what conditions people will like other people. However, it takes skill to summarize this

research without being dull. This book has achieved the goal of being informative and scholarly without being boring.

BROWN, R.   *Social Psychology*
New York: Free Press, 1965, 785 pages.
A well-written, comprehensive book on various aspects of social psychology. Full of illustrative examples and written in a style that is easy to read.

GERGEN, K. J.   *The Psychology of Behavior Exchange*
Reading, Mass.: Addison-Wesley, 1969, 109 pages (paperback).
Examines interpersonal relations from the viewpoint of motivational bases for social behavior, social approval, and interpersonal bargaining.

HALL, E. T.   *The Hidden Dimension*
New York: Anchor, 1969 (c. 1966), 217 pages (paperback).
A study of how human beings use space in public and private. The author investigates the effects of overcrowding and the tension it creates both in large crowds and among individuals in families or offices. Written by an anthropologist, the book also contains a discussion of space-use differences among various cultures and among animals.

LAWICK-GOODALL, J. Van   *In the Shadow of Man*
Boston: Houghton Mifflin, 1971, 297 pages.
This fascinating book is based on the ten years the author spent studying chimpanzees in their natural African habitat. Beautifully illustrated.

LORENZ, K. (Translated by M. K. Wilson).   *King Solomon's Ring*
New York: Crowell, 1952, 202 pages (paperback).
Written by a famous naturalist, this book is full of humorous examples and scientifically accurate descriptions of animal behavior. Chapters on "laughing at animals," "pitying animals," and "buying animals" are particularly interesting.

LORENZ, K. (Translated by M. K. Wilson).   *Man Meets Dog*
Baltimore, Md.: Penguin, 1964 (c. 1954), 198 pages (paperback).
Lorenz first traces the evolutionary history of dogs, then discusses the behavior of dogs and human beings, the training of dogs, and as sort of an afterthought, the relation between dogs and cats.

MORRIS, D.   *The Naked Ape*
New York: Dell, 1969 (c. 1967), 219 pages (paperback).
Morris examines those aspects of our lives that have obvious counterparts in other species (for example, feeding, grooming, fighting, mating, care of the young). He tries to point out through use of illustrations that man, or as Morris calls him, "the naked ape," has certain biological requirements that not even his intellect can change and that these must be met if he is to survive.

MORRIS, D.   *The Human Zoo*
New York: Dell, 1971 (c. 1969), 204 pages (paperback).
Because Morris feels that the modern human animal is no longer living in conditions natural for his species, he sets out to compare the behavior of man with that of captive

animals rather than animals in the wild. While Morris sees the city, or as he calls it, the "human zoo," as yielding many benefits, he also feels it produces many problems and pressures that must be properly solved if the human species is not to be endangered.

MOWAT, F. *Never Cry Wolf*
New York: Dell, 1965 (c. 1963), 176 pages (paperback).
This is a fascinating account of wolves living in the Canadian wilderness. The book not only describes the social behavior of wolves in the wild but it also gives the reader some insight into the difficulties and rewards of studying an animal in its natural habitat.

SOMMER, R. *Personal Space*
Englewood Cliffs, N.J.: Prentice-Hall, 1969, 177 pages (paperback).
An interesting investigation of spatial behavior among human beings. The author discusses the concepts of personal space, dominance, and territoriality as they relate to human behavior. The second half of the book contains a discussion of the relation between human behavior and environmental design and illustrates four different man-environment systems: the mental hospital, the school, the tavern, and the college dormitory.

TIGER, L. *Men in Groups*
New York: Random House (Vintage), 1969, 314 pages (paperback).
A speculative inquiry into the existence and nature of male bonding systems. Written by an anthropologist, this book attempts to answer the question of why males tend to form all-male groups; emphasis is placed on the possible evolutionary bases.

TIGER, L., and R. FOX. *The Imperial Animal*
New York: Dell, 1972 (c. 1971), 308 pages (paperback).
A thoughtful examination of the broader aspects of human social systems, touching on such topics as politics, education, social bonds and relations, sex, and aggression. The authors emphasize our biological nature and evolutionary past and how to understand ourselves as a species, hoping, thereby, to enlighten us as to how we might act to insure our survival. A good companion to books by Robert Ardrey and Desmond Morris.

TOCH, H., and H. C. SMITH (Eds.). *Social Perception*
Princeton, N.J.: Van Nostrand, 1968, 245 pages (paperback).
A collection of readings covering a wide variety of experiments investigating how individuals form impressions of people around them (for example, lipstick and personality, interpersonal perception and marriage, stereotypes). Preceding each reading is a brief discussion of the experiment, its results, and how it relates to other readings in the book.

WERTHEIMER, M. (Ed.). *Confrontation: Psychology and the Problems of Today*
Glenview, Ill.: Scott, Foresman, 1970, 408 pages.
A collection of essays and studies about significant problems facing our world. Articles touch on the problems of identification, conformity and compliance, racism, violence

and aggression, conflict and conflict resolution, control over human behavior, man and technology, and education and creativity.

WHEELER, L.   *Interpersonal Influence*
Boston: Allyn and Bacon, 1970, 119 pages (paperback).
This extremely readable book, written from a historical perspective, focuses on how the actions of one individual(s) influence the actions, attitudes, and feelings of another individual(s). To the point descriptions of experimental results.

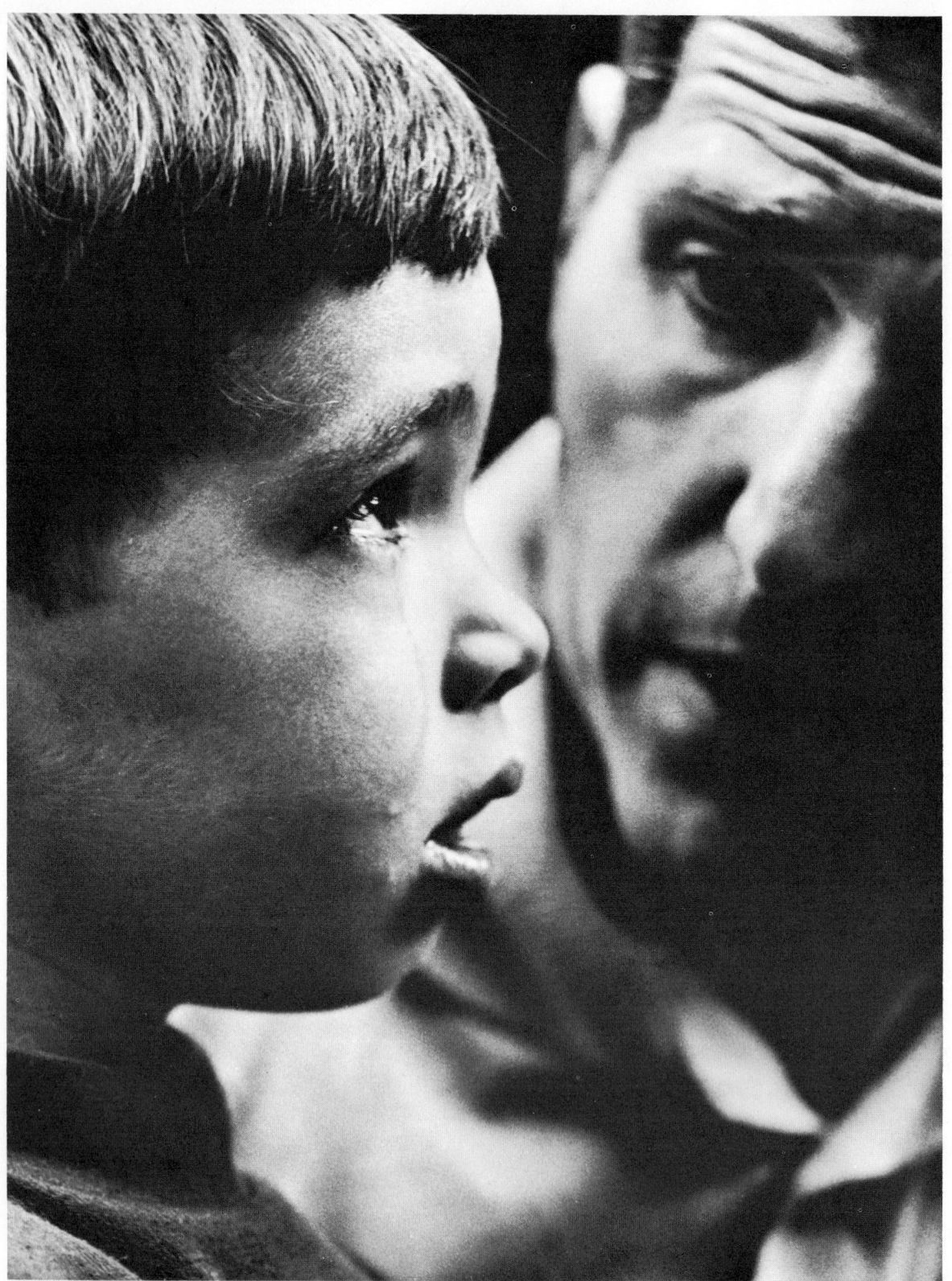

Crisis and Change

FIVE

Certainly, even before reading this book you realized that life can sometimes be a problematic enterprise. I hope, however, that as we explore the topics presented here you will more clearly understand what these problems are and how they arise. In the last section, we focused on problems imposed upon you by external sources—the necessity to satisfy group pressures, to cope with other people's demands, and to conform to cultural expectations and the problems involved in obtaining social resources. In this section, we discuss problems introduced by internal sources; by the fact that you have internal psychological characteristics (knowledge, desires, fears, illusions, dreams, hopes, and so on) that impose constraints both upon how you size up external situations and upon how you select strategies to solve these problems.

Your internal psychological characteristics and the kinds of strategies you habitually use to solve problems are commonly called your *personality*. There are many theories about personality, each of which attempts to help us understand our own internal characteristics. It would be impossible for me to describe all of these theories or to trace in sufficient detail the things they have in common—and it's this common core that probably comes closest to the truth. Therefore, I am going to take another course. To explain how your personality is related to the things that have been discussed in previous sections, I will translate the common core of these personality theories into the language I have used thus far in this book. In doing so, I make no claim to having either the last word or any hold on the truth. I believe, however, that the picture that emerges from my translation is a fairly accurate description (albeit in different words) of what many psychologists currently think about the structure and development of personality.

Part 1 VALUES AND CONFLICT

In the course of growing up, each of us learns a complicated and idiosyncratic system of ideas about what is good and what is not. We learn moral codes, we learn manners, we learn to value social success and to fear social *faux pas*, we learn to trust or to mistrust people, we learn to seek achievement and to scorn failure, we learn to love and hate, we learn that the "good life" requires marriage, children, two cars, and a $60,000 house, we learn that "clothes make the man," we learn that a "normal" person does this or that, we learn that men are strong and women are weak, we learn that democracy is the best political system, we learn that "the bad guys always lose and the good guys always win." In short, we learn a large assortment of truths, myths, and expectations about the world.

To simplify this discussion, I am going to call all of these ideas we have acquired our *values*. This is a good summary word because most of these ideas have a strong evaluative tone—they define what we think the best state of the world is. By the same token, these values are the standards against which we size up external situations; when we come in contact with situations that don't conform to our values, these same values help us decide how to go about dealing with the discrepancy.

Explicit and Inexplicit Values

Values are acquired from many sources—parents, peers, schools, churches, and so on. These sources are fairly clearly understood by most of us: "I was taught that a clean house is a good thing; Mom felt that that's the way it ought to be, and I guess I got it from her." But this clarity of understanding is usually limited to values that are rather explicitly stated by the source—values such as being trustworthy, loyal, helpful, friendly, courteous, kind, obedient, thrifty, brave, cheerful, clean, and reverent. However, we also learned other values at our mother's knee which were never explicitly enunciated and which we would probably have great difficulty identifying. Nonetheless, these partly conscious, *inexplicit values* have as profound an effect as our *explicit values* in determining how we measure a situation. For example, many mothers never mentioned sex to their children, let alone explicitly told them that it is evil. But through subtle expressions of disapproval and discomfort when the topic was brought up (indeed, through failure to discuss sex at all), the notion of wrongness was effectively conveyed. Thus, when they were very young, these people may have come to think that sex is somehow wrong even though nobody

184

explicitly told them that it is. While such individuals may later begin to believe that sex is good, the old, inexplicit values may still remain to raise havoc whenever a sexual situation is encountered.

Of course, we also get some of our inexplicit values from sources other than our parents. One such source is experience. Remember little Albert in Section 3 who came to fear (that is, negatively value) a white rat because it was associated with a loud noise? Many of our negative values come about as a result of such experiences. An adult who as a child was bitten by a dog may still fear and hate dogs even though he does not remember the incident. A woman who was teased by schoolmates for being fat may still value slimness, although she may not realize that she does so because it once implied social acceptance to her. A man who had an overbearing mother may negatively value even mild assertiveness or independence on the part of any woman; yet he may be able to explain his feelings only by saying that for some unexplainable reason he doesn't like "pushy" women. In short, many of our personal likes, dislikes, fears, and pleasures stem from long-forgotten experiences that had a strong effect on our value system.

Another nonparental source of inexplicit values is the mass media. Most of us grew up on a heavy diet of radio, TV, movies, and magazines, all of which tend to uphold values that are considered to reflect the Model American Life. Thus, the typical mass media family lives in a nice house in the suburbs, has two cars and two children, and the father works at a profitable profession. When marriages occur, they are touching and lovely. When children come, they are wanted and cute. When crises occur, they are handled with good humor and good taste. You don't have to be a cynic or a social critic to realize that few Americans actually live the Model American Life; cramped city apartments, a worn-out car, too many children, too little money, and long hours selling in a shop, driving a truck, or working in a factory better describe the actual state of affairs. Even so, the media version has a profound effect on all of us. A great many Americans value the media family ideal and in one way or another strive to attain something like it.

A third nonparental source of inexplicit values is the cultural ideal of what is desirable. These values are the things that "everybody knows" are right and good—like Mom and apple pie. We may not be able to list these values, but we often become upset when one of them is questioned or when we're asked to change or abandon one. For example, when Women's Liberation arguments are presented, there often is a strong reaction from both men and women because their deeply held value that women should be *only* wives, mothers, and housekeepers is being questioned. In presenting their arguments, Women's

Liberation advocates are asking everyone in the culture to change his or her values (as are Black Power advocates, Gay Liberation advocates, Support Your Local Police advocates, and every group that is trying to promote change). The prospect of change is seldom welcomed, especially when our own personal values are involved. Even when the logic of the arguments convinces us, a vague uneasiness remains because our old inexplicit values concerning the roles of women, Blacks, homosexuals, and policemen are being confronted.

Psychological Conflict

Psychological conflict arises (1) when the conditions of the external world do not conform to the conditions that satisfy our values, and (2) when we have inconsistent sets of values that make it virtually impossible for *any* situation to satisfy them. Sometimes the conflict is easily dealt with, for example, you value having a new car, so you work and save to buy one. Sometimes resolution of the conflict is more difficult, for example, you fall in love with (value) a person who doesn't love you. And sometimes the conflict is impossible to resolve, for example, you highly value genius but you are only of normal intelligence. Whatever the problem, an unresolved conflict is stressful because it means a continual discrepancy between how we want things to be and how they really are. The amount of stress arising from such an unresolved conflict depends upon how much we value the things that are involved and how far the situation falls short of being what we want it to be. Often a little stress is tolerable, and so we might decide that we will accept things as they are. When the stress is greater, however, we have to do something about the situation. The manner in which an individual deals with such stressful situations is commonly referred to as the person's *personality.*

Dealing with Conflict: Three Basic Strategies

There are three basic strategies for dealing with psychological conflict and reducing stress. The first is to *change the situation* so that it conforms to your values. For example, if a group to which you belong isn't doing things the way you want them done, you can try to get elected president and change the group. Or, if your boss is sarcastic to you in front of your co-workers, you can go to him and explain how it makes you feel and ask him to stop behaving that way.

The second basic strategy is *withdrawing* from a conflict rather than attempting to change things. This strategy often is wise—if someone at a party is offensive to you, it usually is better to leave him alone than to try to change him (unless you value fights). But in many other instances leaving a situation is not a good strategy. In the two examples in the last paragraph, if the group is very important to you or if you need the job very much, leaving might be self-defeating.

The third basic strategy, *changing your values*, is used when the first two won't work. When we can't make the situation conform to our values (*strategy 1*), and when we can't leave the situation (*strategy 2*), the only way to resolve the conflict is to change our values to fit the realities of the situation (*strategy 3*). This strategy is also important when we have inconsistent values that prevent us from ever creating or finding a situation that completely satisfies them; one or the other of the set of conflicting values must be changed in order to reduce the conflict.

Stability and Change in Values and Strategies

For the most part, each of us has a set of values that is uniquely ours; other people may happen to value the same things, but usually they will differ from us at least in the degree to which they value these things. Moreover, our set of values is pretty stable; while they may change from time to time, the core is fairly solid. Indeed, you can probably describe the major components of most of your friends' values without much difficulty. For example, I know a man who values independence, solitude, physical and intellectual achievement, and complete honesty in his social interactions. This person clearly is different from another of my friends, who values being with people, likes comfort and security, thinks of his job as merely a way to support himself, and feels that it sometimes is reasonable for people to hide their true feelings in order to promote social tranquillity. These two men would obviously evaluate a given situation differently, and the changes that they would try to make in order to deal with attendant conflict and stress would be quite different. Indeed, changes that would make a situation ideal for the first man would make it quite unacceptable to the second, and vice versa.

The general stability of a person's value system is complemented by a fairly high degree of stability in the kinds of strategies he uses to deal with different kinds of situations. Moreover, close inspection often reveals that apparently different strategies may actually stem from the same values. For example, a person who values achievement may approach most situations in a pretty straightforward and energetic manner. But he also may consistently avoid situations in which he knows that the chance of failure is high. Both strategies may be used fairly often by this person, and while they are essentially different, they may both reflect the same value, that is, the need to achieve success and to avoid failure.

Although our values and strategies are fairly stable, we tend to permit small changes to occur depending upon the circumstances of the situation at hand. This is why it is seldom possible to know *exactly* what someone is going to do even if we understand his values pretty well. For example, even a man who has a high value for honesty might lie under some circumstances and be heard to say, "There must be some mistake, officer. I'm sure that I was only going about 35 miles an hour." However, we must not let specific instances of this kind obscure the fact that each of us has a pretty stable value system which is reflected in how we behave.

Crises and Value Changes

It would be inaccurate to suggest that all of your values remain constant throughout your life. Many values remain relatively unchanged, of course, but many change as you mature and go through difficult times. Each of us faces a number of *life crises* during our lives. Life crises are large-scale stressful times such as those associated with starting school, adolescence, leaving home, marriage, children, divorce, death of family members, legal and financial upheavals, illness, career changes, retirement, and aging.

Life crises usually require severe changes in how you live and in how you think about things. These changes reflect underlying changes in your values. You have probably witnessed some of the more obvious examples of such value changes: the person who begins to value religion after the death of a family member, the spendthrift young husband who suddenly comes to value financial security after his first child is born, the conservative young person whose political and moral values change markedly after he leaves home for college, the man who lowers his own value of himself (that is, his self-esteem) after he is prematurely and unwillingly retired from his job. All of these are commonly observed changes in values that occur during times of crisis. Of course, the changes aren't always so vivid, but few life crises pass without having some effect on a person's values.

Life crises are, by definition, situations in which strategies 1 and 2 won't work. If a person could manipulate the situation (strategy 1) to make it fit his values, or if he could escape (strategy 2), there would be no crisis. But adolescence, illness, and aging, for example, are natural facets of life, irreversible and inevitable. Even marriage, usually welcomed by both parties, cannot be made wholly to conform to one's own values—compromises and changes are necessary on the part of both partners; therefore, marriage too qualifies as a major crisis. It is important, however, to note that *whenever it is possible to do so, most people facing a crisis would much rather try strategies 1 and 2 before they resort to strategy 3 and change their values.*

Periods of value change are times of confusion and psychological pain; one doesn't really know what he thinks or wants, and the resulting instability creates a great deal of stress. Adolescence is an example of such a situation. Adolescents often apparently think one thing one day and something quite different the next. This is a result, in part, of their "trying out" different sets of values to see how they work and of their grasping at whatever values they are considering at the moment and behaving as though these values were permanent—only to do the same thing with a somewhat different set of values the next day.

As uncomfortable as life crises may be, and even though we seldom welcome them, they and the resulting value-changing process are a normal, growth-producing part of every person's life. The prospect and the process of change are extremely disquieting to us, even if the resulting change promises to be a better and a happier state of affairs. Even predominantly good crises, such as a marriage or the birth of a wanted child, produce severe stress for most of us. Eventually, however, after the crisis passes or after it becomes the accepted state of affairs, most people settle down with a new set of values, which, while similar to their old set, reflect significant changes as a result of having experienced the crisis.

Crisis and the Ego Defense Mechanisms

As was stated a moment ago, life crises are situations in which strategies 1 and 2 won't work. Yet, most of us persist in trying to use these strategies so we will not have to go through the pain of changing our values. Sometimes this procedure works fairly well if a crisis is not too big or if it's short-lived. But if the crisis is really a major one or if it is prolonged, the inappropriate use of strategies 1 and 2 can lead to psychological trouble.

The specific behaviors that we employ in the inappropriate application of strategies 1 and 2 in times of crisis are called *ego defense mechanisms*. The word "ego" means "the self"—that is, one's value system. Thus, ego defense mechanisms are the behaviors we use, *often without being aware of it*, to defend our values against change. Many of these mechanisms have been given specific labels because they occur so commonly. Indeed, all of us resort to them at one time or another, and most of us rely on one or two of them a great deal of the time. These mechanisms are so common you will surely recognize them, so I will merely list them and give examples. Throughout this discussion keep in mind that many of these ego defense mechanisms are relatively reasonable short-term solutions to minor stressful situations. Things get out of hand when

BOX 5.1

The Aftermath of Crisis

All crises do not have the same impact on our lives. Some crises are relatively minor and we bounce right back when they're over. Others are serious, however, and full recovery from them may take months. The seriousness of a crisis is determined both by the amount of readjustment its resolution normally requires in one's values, style of life, plans for the future, and so on, and by the length of time normally needed for the readjustment to take place. Even though different people may seem to be affected in different ways by apparently identical crises, there is surprisingly high consensus among people about the seriousness of various crises. The purpose of this box is to acquaint you with some recent research about how people perceive the seriousness of life crises and the relation between the occurrence of life crises and subsequent medical problems.

A few years ago, Dr. Thomas Holmes and his associates assembled a list of 43 commonly experienced life crises (both good and bad) and asked different groups of people to rate these crises in terms of their seriousness.* Then the ratings were used to construct an overall Social Readjustment Rating (SRR) scale for each

*T. H. HOLMES and R. H. RAHE, The Social Readjustment Rating Scale. *Journal of Psychosomatic Research*, 1967, **11**, 213–218, by permission of the authors and publisher.

ego defense mechanisms are relied upon too heavily, especially when a person persists in using them even when he's faced with a long-term crisis that can be resolved only by resorting to strategy 3.

Strategy 1 Mechanisms: Changing the Wrong Situation

Strategy 1 calls for changing stressful, unsatisfactory situations. But in a life crisis, no changes are possible (or at least they don't *seem* possible), so we sometimes behave as though *some other issue* were the cause of our stress. As a result, we may—either consciously or unconsciously—use futile, misdirected behaviors in trying to cope with the crisis.

Displacement There are times in life when it is necessary to be somewhat aggressive in order to change a stressful situation, for example, when someone threatens to harm you. However, aggression is appropriate only when it is directed toward the actual source of the stress. When the source is unassailable, people sometimes resort to aggression anyway, but they redirect it or *displace* it, to some inappropriate, usually defenseless, target. Thus, a man who has been called down by his boss and who can't return the aggression for fear

group; each SRR scale consisted of the 43 crises ordered from the most serious to the least serious, with a number indicating its perceived degree of seriousness assigned to each crisis. (See the illustrative SRR scale at end of this box.) Such SRR scales were constructed for adolescent white Americans and adult white Americans, Mexican-Americans, black Americans, Frenchmen, Swiss, Belgians, Japanese, and Malaysians. Comparisons showed that the SRR scales for the different groups of people were remarkably similar. Of course, there were some understandable differences: for example, the Japanese, most of whom are Buddhist, were unconcerned about Christmas, adolescents rated "sex difficulties" as a greater crisis than adults did, and Malaysians seemed less concerned than the other groups were about marital difficulties. But even with the few differences, the most striking finding was the high degree of agreement among these different groups concerning the seriousness of various life crises. In short, life crises are a universal affliction, and most people are quite aware of their relative seriousness.

Let us turn now to a recently discovered aspect of crises—the effects they can have on our health. For a long time physicians have suspected that the stress brought on by life crises can make people more vulnerable to illness, but until the development of the SRR scale there was no way they could measure the severity of crises, and therefore they could not examine the crisis-health relation. Soon after developing their scale, Dr. Holmes and his co-workers, notably Dr.

of losing his job finds himself in a state of conflict; his value for his own self-respect is unsatisfied, and what is more, he cannot defend himself. Since he can't retaliate against his boss, and since he still feels stress due to the "bawling out," the man may displace his aggression (Fig. 5.1). When he gets home he may burst into anger at the slightest provocation, thus getting rid of his stress—to the total surprise and dismay of his wife, children, or dog. To come closer to home, have you ever done poorly on an exam that you truly deserved to fail and then told your friends that the instructor was unfair? It was easier to displace your aggression to the teacher (behind his back) than to devalue yourself for not having done better on the exam.

Sublimation and compensation   Another strategy 1 defense mechanism consists of using the so-called "nervous energy" resulting from a stressful conflict as a source of energy for doing other things. This is called *sublimation.* For example, the agitation arising from frustrated anger or sexual feelings can be directed in other ways: A man who feels discriminated against and, as a result, has a continuous feeling of anger, may become a prize fighter, wrestler, combat

Richard H. Rahe, set out to obtain health information and life crises information from a variety of people in order to see if illness tends to follow crises.† For each individual they studied, they calculated the *sum* of the seriousness values associated with each life crisis experienced during the preceding few years. This sum was used as an index of total crisis. The investigation revealed that illness does indeed tend to follow crises.

In one study of physicians' life crises and illnesses, it was found that 93 percent of the reported illnesses occurred among physicians who had crisis sums of 150 or greater; the rest had been quite healthy. In a similar study, Dr. Holmes asked beginning medical students what crises they had experienced during the two years prior to entering medical school. Then he computed their crisis sums and categorized the students into three groups (without their knowledge, of course). One group was composed of students who had high crisis sums, the second was composed of students with medium crisis sums, and the third was composed of students with low crisis sums. Two years later he asked the same students to recount what illnesses they had had since entering medical school; he found that while 86 percent of the high crisis students had suffered a severe illness, only

†T. H. Holmes and M. Masuda, Life change and illness susceptibility. Paper presented at meetings of the American Association for the Advancement of Science, Chicago, December 1970.

FIG. 5.1 *Displacement of aggressions from unassailable to assailable targets is an inappropriate attempt to use strategy 1.*

48 percent of the medium crisis group and only 33 percent of the low crisis group had been seriously ill. Similar results were found for personnel aboard three U.S. Navy cruisers. And when the crisis sums for college football players were obtained and the number of injuries they suffered during the season were recorded, it was found that 50 percent of the high crisis players, 25 percent of the medium crisis players, and only 9 percent of the low crisis players had been injured during the season.

While all of these results are impressive, it should be kept in mind that this research is still in the beginning stages; the exact nature of the relation between total life crisis and illness and how we might help people avoid illness after they have faced several life crises has yet to be discovered. However, these results strongly suggest that we would do well to think of crises as something other than momentary isolated events that happen and then are over and done with. The fact that next year's health can be predicted from the past two years' crises indicates that certain effects of crises are long lasting; we think that we've resolved them completely but somehow some of their effects linger on. Moreover, the fact that illness can be predicted by knowing the crisis sum indicates that crises pile up; a number of small crises within a certain period of time can be as devastating as one big one. By definition, life crises, whether good or bad, are times of turmoil and change, but scientists are only beginning to understand how deeply they can affect us and how long we take to recover from them.

soldier, or the like. A person who desires sex but thinks that it is immoral may lose himself in studies, religion, athletics, art, and so on.

A mechanism similar to sublimation is *compensation,* which consists of trying to "trade off" for the fact that a situation doesn't fit your values by making some other situation fit extremely well. Thus, a clumsy boy who would like to be an athlete may compensate by being an outstanding student. Similarly, a girl who is not attractive may compensate by being a leader in school activities. In both cases, the individuals find ways of compensating for the unpleasant and stressful fact that an important situation doesn't fit their values by making other situations fit their values very well.

Strategy 2 Mechanisms: Apparent Escape from the Situation

It is difficult for most of us to use strategy 1 mechanisms for very long because they really don't get at the main conflict and their inappropriateness soon becomes apparent. If a man displaces his aggression to his wife, she will soon point out to him that he is being unfair. Anger and desires cannot be kept sublimated; they have a tendency to keep popping up at odd times. The failure of compensation is often strongly felt, for example, when the compensating

The Social Readjustment Rating Scale*	
Seriousness Rating	Life Crisis
100	Death of spouse
73	Divorce
65	Marital separation
63	Jail term
63	Death of close family member
53	Personal injury or illness
50	Marriage
47	Fired at work
45	Marital reconciliation
45	Retirement
44	Change in health of family member
40	Pregnancy
39	Sex difficulties
39	Gain of new family member
39	Business readjustment
38	Change in financial state
37	Death of close friend
36	Change to different line of work
35	Change in number of arguments with spouse

*Based on data from adult white Americans.

good student enviously watches the superior athlete, or when the compensating active girl finds herself sadly sitting at home alone on a Friday evening. When the failure of these mechanisms is recognized, the person is right back where he started; the crisis remains undealt with.

Strategy 2 mechanisms are more extreme than strategy 1 mechanisms because they allow us the illusion of escape from crises, even though crises by definition seem to permit no possibility for escape. Human beings have many ways of mentally "walking away" from unpleasant situations, and these constitute the mechanisms employed when misusing strategy 2.

Denial   One of the simplest mechanisms for evading a crisis is merely to deny that anything is wrong. Many people who are extremely unhappy are quick to deny, both to themselves and to other people, that things are unsatisfactory. Sometimes denial takes this "business as usual" form, and sometimes it leads to a form of *withdrawal* with the person seemingly avoiding the whole situation by removing himself from it completely. Thus, an executive

31	Mortgage over $10,000
30	Foreclosure of mortgage or loan
29	Change in responsibilities at work
29	Son or daughter leaving home
29	Trouble with in-laws
28	Outstanding personal achievement
26	Wife begins or stops work
26	Begin or end school
25	Change in living conditions
24	Revision of personal habits
23	Trouble with boss
20	Change in work hours or conditions
20	Change in residence
20	Change in schools
19	Change in recreation
19	Change in church activities
18	Change in social activities
17	Mortgage or loan less than $10,000
16	Change in sleeping habits
15	Change in number of family get-togethers
15	Change in eating habits
13	Vacation
12	Christmas
11	Minor violations of the law

who is being forced to make a decision that is bound to hurt one of his employees no matter what he decides (a crisis) may simply refuse to even think about the matter.

In most cases denial is not very effective. The person is usually dimly aware of his problem even if he won't admit it to himself. In some cases, however, denial works so well that the person actually believes that there is no problem. This extreme form of denial is called *repression* and usually involves problems that arouse strong emotions. For example, a person who commits a serious crime may repress the whole incident and be unable to remember anything about it. Indeed, he may even regard himself as an innocent victim of senseless persecution because he honestly believes that he is not guilty.

Another form of denial is called *reaction formation*. This mechanism is used when a person has a high value for something that he thinks he really ought to dislike (or, has a low value for something he feels he ought to like). Thus he denies his high value for the thing and behaves as though he actually disliked it. Suppose, for example, that a respected businessman had a strong desire to read pornographic books (sexually explicit literature that is, in the terms of the U.S. Supreme Court, without redeeming social value). This urge might present a conflict, because if people found out his taste in literature, his reputation might be ruined. A crisis would then exist—the man's values for respectability would be in conflict with his value for this particular form of vicarious sexuality. If the stress from the conflict were great enough, the man might resort to reaction formation by completely denying his interest in pornography and taking up the antipornography cause. Of course, everybody who is against pornography does not necessarily espouse the view as a result of reaction formation. Usually it is individuals who fear their own ability to control certain aspects of their behavior who resort to this mechanism. For example, the apparently strong and self-determined man who despises weakness in others actually may fear weakness in himself. The woman who judges the behavior of others harshly may secretly fear her ability to withstand the temptation to do the very things she so condemns.

Projection and rationalization   The second set of strategy 2 mechanisms also involves denial, but it is denial of responsibility rather than denial of the situation itself. The mechanism of *projection* is used in situations in which your values conflict with your immediate feelings, thereby producing a conflict that can be avoided only by attributing your feelings to someone else. For example,  if you value family ties but hate your brother, you have a crisis. A common way of escaping this dilemma is to *project,* that is, to attribute *your* feelings to *him.* After all, if he hates you, you have a perfect right to shun him and you may even be a martyr by going out of your way to do good things for him. Of course, your hidden hatred may subtly make these "good things" more bad than good, but you can point out to yourself, and to everybody else, how hard you tried to overcome his hatred of you and blame any hard feelings on him.

Another common example of projection is the married man who believes that his secretary is in love with him. The truth of the matter may be that he is in love with his secretary, but since he is already married, his own feelings conflict with his value for marital fidelity and, therefore, cause him stress. Rather than face the conflict in a straightforward way, he attributes his feelings to his secretary, who may regard him only as a nice, fatherly man. Thus, he puts the responsibility for his feelings on her shoulders.

The second strategy 2 mechanism consists of making excuses for your actions. This mechanism, *rationalization,* is similar to projection in that it permits you to transfer the blame for the crisis to someone or something else and thereby escape responsibility. Claiming that an exam was unfair relieves you of the responsibility of not having prepared for it. Saying that you lost the race because your shoelace came untied relieves you of the responsibility of not having fulfilled your value for winning. Blaming your companion for your having had a poor evening relieves you of the responsibility of having been socially inept. In short, *rationalizing,* eases your stress and allows you to claim nominal victory in the face of defeat. "I couldn't help it because (the alarm clock didn't go off) (I hurt my hand) (I have a headache) (I thought George would tell you) (I was so drunk I didn't know what I was doing) (I can't afford it) (my mother wouldn't let me) (I've been sick) (the teacher doesn't like me)"—sound familiar?

Fantasy and regression   The third set of strategy 2 mechanisms emanates from our ability to imagine things to be other than they are and to lose ourselves temporarily in our fantasies. Most of us have fairly involved fantasy lives—we imagine ourselves to be successful, witty, attractive, brilliant, and so on, in quiet moments when we are alone. Such fantasy is not necessarily bad. Indeed, it sometimes helps us solve our problems by permitting us to play act how some adventure might proceed; for example, the young man imagines how his job interview will go and thereby rehearses for it. However, fantasy can also be an escape mechanism, a way of slipping out of a crisis into a never-never land where values need not be changed and things are always pleasant and beautiful. The high school drop-out who takes a job that will lead nowhere may imagine himself becoming a rich tycoon to ease his feelings of frustration. The housewife who has fantasies about the romantic life she might live if she were not married to her husband escapes from her unhappiness for a while. While a little fantasizing is harmless, carried to extremes it can become a hindrance to competent living. You may know older people who live in a fantasy about their past, tell stories about exciting adventures that never occurred, and live in such a haze of unreality that they are unable to care for themselves or lead independent lives.

Another strategy 2 mechanism that is aided by our imaginative ability is resorting to childish behavior, *regression.* This mechanism is commonly seen when people are ill—they sometimes become unnecessarily helpless and must be taken care of. In our society, illness is a legitimate excuse to be helpless, peevish, and to go to bed and not have to face the world. At other times we tend to react regressively to crises by becoming dependent on other people, resorting to tantrums, crying, being cranky, and becoming generally childlike in our behavior.

Neurotic Behavior

Virtually everybody uses one or more ego defense mechanisms from time to time, and most of us tend to depend on some of the mechanisms more than is really necessary. To the degree that our behavior can be characterized as *overdependence* on the mechanisms, it is called *neurotic.*

To say that someone's behavior is neurotic is not necessarily to say that it is bad. The term merely means that the person is attempting to cope with a crisis by not actually facing it—either by denying that the crisis exists or by mentally escaping from it. For some crises, defense mechanisms *are* the only way out; the person truly cannot change the situation, leave, or change his values. Usually, however, the situation is not as hopeless as it appears to be. The problem is that the involved person may fail to realize that solutions actually exist, or he may be under so much stress from the crisis that he does not bother to consider alternative courses of action.

The neurotic trap   Neurotic behavior starts becoming a problem when it gets to be so predominant that it blocks a person's happiness. For example, people who are chronically late for appointments may be less forgetful than they are aggressive. By being late and inconveniencing others, such a person, perhaps unknowingly, can express his repressed anger without risking a confrontation. However, when constantly being late for appointments begins to cost him his friends, the advantages of this riskless form of expressing anger are outweighed by the disadvantages of loneliness. The logical solution, of course, would be to find other ways of expressing anger and to stop being late. But since neurotic behavior is rarely logical, what might well happen is that the person will become even more angry because he is losing his friends and will express this increased anger by increased use of his neurotic tactic of being late. This, of course, will alienate people even more, thereby making him even more angry and leading to even more neurotic lateness, and so forth. Such a person finds himself in a vicious spiral called the *neurotic trap.*

The neurotic trap results from the very nature of ego defense mechanisms, especially when they are unconscious. These mechanisms shield us from the unpleasant truth about the crises we're in. They build an insulating wall around us, and when the wall fails to keep out the unpleasantness, we build it higher instead of looking out to see if there is an alternative to the wall. The wall itself soon becomes a source of trouble. Other people begin to react negatively to the neurotic behavior. But our pain from their negative reactions merely brings on more wall building to avoid increased unpleasantness. In time, the low walls of defense mechanisms become the high walls of neurotic behavior, and the overdependence on defense mechanisms constitutes a worse crisis than the one that was being avoided in the first place.

BOX 5.2

Neurotic Behavior: A Case History

During high school and college, Joseph Kidd (a fictitious name) became extremely unhappy and more or less incapacitated for serious effort. He was bothered by severe self-consciousness, always feeling a painful uncertainty about his standing in the opinion of others, and with this went submissiveness designed to avoid conflict with people and win their favor; he could neither control this submissiveness or accept it. With his girl he was equally troubled. He was completely dependent on her affection and very jealous if she so much as danced with someone else. Realizing that he acted toward her "too much like a spoiled child, crying for my own way," he could not bring himself to take a more independent attitude. In consequence, it became increasingly clear that the girl was bored with him and did not really respect him.

Why didn't he take a different attitude? He wanted to, and there was every inducement to do so, but in this respect he was not free. He expected people to give him a great deal of easy appreciation; when they did not do so, he was worried and hungrily asked for it. The young man felt that he had no personality of his own, and he tried the following rather desperate expedient:

I began acting out personalities, and tried observing people and copying them. But these personalities were all short-lived because they pleased some and not others and because they didn't produce that underlying purpose of making people like me; and every time, unconsciously, I would resort to my childish attitude to make myself noticeable.

Varieties of Neurotic Behavior

Extreme and debilitating neurotic behaviors can be roughly divided into four classes. These divisions are not like medical diagnoses, however, in that neurotic behaviors are *not* diseases. The classes merely help us see the similarities and differences among various neurotic patterns.

Class 1: Emotional disturbances   The most common reaction to the stress of a crisis is called *anxiety*. We all know that feeling of fear and apprehension just before taking a difficult exam or on walking into the dentist's office. At times, however, anxiety can become overpowering and exist for much longer periods. Such episodes are called *anxiety attacks*. A person undergoing an anxiety attack feels ill, fearful, depressed, chronically fatigued, and generally unable to face life. He is jumpy, edgy, and may break into tears at the slightest provocation. Often he is unable to maintain interest in everyday activities and is preoccupied with wanting to get away from whatever is causing his anxiety. Unfortunately, the extremely anxious person may not be able to identify the crisis (or crises) that has brought about his anxiety attack. He is fearful and

Clearly Joseph Kidd's problem was not an unusual one. Developing independent adult attitudes is a universal problem. Developing a stable conception of oneself, an enduring sense of personal identity, is also a universal problem. Kidd's case is peculiar not in kind but in degree. It will be noticed that he was satisfied with a "personality" only if it pleased everybody; he was unwilling that anyone should fail to notice and like him. From his own description we can see that he was making a frantic search for esteem. His overwhelming motive was to make people like him, and his well-practiced method, when all else failed, was to make himself noticeable. Failure cast him into despondency and alarm. At times he lapsed into passive daydreaming, but at other times he struggled to learn new and more appropriate attitudes. Eventually, as we shall see, his struggle met with success.

Joseph Kidd was the second son of hard-working, socially ambitious parents. He was a very pretty child and his parents showered him with notice and praise; he was dressed up, shown off, and placed in the center of attention, and he basked happily in this admiration. The effect on his subsequent development was not so happy. For one thing, his constant exposure to the eyes and praises of other people laid the foundation for that intense self-consciousness which later harassed him. For another thing, he was receiving praise for gratuitous qualities—for good looks and fine clothes, or at best, for slight accomplishments—so that he felt little incentive to work for what he got. He formed an habitual expectation of high esteem at no greater cost than making himself noticeable.

apprehensive, but he may not know why—defense mechanisms have kept the problem hidden from him. Neurotic anxiety frequently arises when a person faces an unknown future or is in the process of extreme change, for example, moving to a new city to take on a new job and greater responsibility, graduating from college, entering the army, getting married, and so on. Often this anxiety disappears after the change has been accomplished and the person settles down to a rather stable life again.

A second common neurotic emotional disturbance is *depression*. As with anxiety, we all experience depression every now and then. It often occurs when we feel remorse about something that is important to us. For example, you might feel depressed for a few hours about having written a poor final exam or about having lost some object of sentimental value. Such bouts of depression are short-lived and relatively harmless. Neurotic depression lasts much longer and is so intense that it renders the person virtually incapable of carrying on. A good example of such depression arises when a widow's mourning goes on and on, far beyond the usual length of time. In such cases, it often is found that the depression results less from a sense of loss than from a sense of guilt

In school Kidd progressed well, and through the machinations of his ambitious mother, he was given a double promotion from the fourth to the sixth grade, where he was the youngest and smallest in the group. To keep up his popularity he fell into the role of what he called "a clown and a stooge"; he made the other boys laugh and did errands for them. Upon entering high school, he found these roles no longer productive of esteem; his new companions were contemptuous of his childish ways. Filled with resentment, he began to feel that everyone was against him, so he withdrew from sports and social activities and spent his time at home listening to the radio. Even his interest in his studies dwindled, so that he barely passed his examinations for college.

At college, he found nothing in the curriculum that awakened enduring interest. His failure to make friends soon cost him the esteem of his parents, who looked upon college as a means of social advancement. When his girl began to withhold her esteem, he sought consolation in promiscuous sexual episodes, which gave him at least a momentary feeling that he was acceptable as a man and could get what he wanted. But when he regaled his fellow students with these proofs of his enterprise and manhood, he got much less admiration than he expected. He who had been rich was now indeed destitute of esteem.

Under these circumstances, it is not surprising that Kidd's mediocre academic record went completely to pieces and that he was presently looking for a job. It was at this point that his suffering was most acute and that he fully realized

about not having loved the departed husband enough, about not having made his life easier, or even about being slightly glad the old tyrant is finally dead.

A depressed person is usually listless, tearful, dejected, and withdrawn. All of his attempts to gather himself together seem futile. He cannot concentrate on much of anything and his appetite is greatly reduced. To him, life hardly seems worth living. In extreme cases, he may attempt suicide, although such attempts are often unsuccessful and actually represent a cry for help rather than an honest wish to end it all.

The third kind of neurotic emotional disturbance, less severe than the first two, takes the form of irrational fears, called *phobias* (Fig. 5.2). Some phobias are learned through *traumatic experiences*, that is, through painfully unpleasant encounters such as the one little Albert had with the white rat (Section 3, Part 2). In many cases, however, the origins of phobias are rather obscure. For example, some people are afraid of high places, a fear that is called *acrophobia;* they are afraid that they will impulsively jump or fall if they look over the railing or edge of a high place, although they can fly in a closed-in airplane with no difficulty. Other people are *claustrophobic;* they fear closed spaces such

the failure of the various "personalities" he had been trying to assume. After a while, however, things began to go more favorably. He left home, parted with his girl, and found a small business position in which he acquitted himself well and where he enjoyed the company of other young people. It was a white collar job which met his parents' social expectations, so that he was somewhat restored in their favor. Another girl came upon the scene. Starting the relation on a better footing, he was soon the happy recipient of esteem from her. His life was again moving forward and he began to be mildly satisfied with himself.

He returned to college, from which he ultimately graduated. When he entered military service he found great satisfaction in the comradeship of the other men and resumed the social growth that had been brought to a standstill by his double promotion at school and subsequent estrangement from other boys. Some years later he looked back to his period in the army as the happiest time in his life.

Returning to the family home, he was at first immersed in some of the old conflicts, but the changes he had made in himself proved to be enduring. He was no longer at the mercy of parental desires, nor was he enslaved by his hunger for esteem. When an opportunity arose to reorganize his father's dwindling business, he took charge of the project and carried it to a successful conclusion, substantially increasing his self-respect as well as the esteem he received from others. Throughout these developments his environment was fairly kind to him, but he displayed initiative and took an active part in overcoming his difficulties. Under moderately favorable circumstances he proved capable of developing new channels for satisfying his needs and promoting his growth.*

*Abridged from R. W. WHITE, *The Abnormal Personality* (3d ed.). Copyright © 1964, The Ronald Press Company, New York.

as an automobile, a closet, or an elevator. Still others are *zoophobic*; they are afraid of animals and will go out of their way to avoid being around them. The list of different kinds of phobias is quite long. In part, such fears may reflect past experiences; but they may also represent special forms of defense mechanisms. For example, such fears often represent a form of regression that allows the person to rely on other people, much as a frightened child relies on his parents for patient understanding and protection.

Class 2: Health disturbances　The second class of neurotic behaviors involves real and imagined bodily illnesses that appear to have a physiological basis but that are actually psychological in origin. While the line between physiologically based and psychologically based illness often is not very well defined,

Acrophobia
(fear of heights)

Claustrophobia
(fear of closed spaces)

Zoophobia
(fear of animals)

FIG. 5.2 *Phobias are irrational yet painful fears that can severely restrict a person's activities.*

in some cases it is definitely clear that the illness does not have a physiological basis.

The most common psychologically based health disturbance is *hypochondria*, which is preoccupation with one's own health and a tendency to interpret virtually every minor bodily malfunction as a major illness. Hypochondria is particularly common in our culture because, as was said previously, illness is viewed as a legitimate excuse to be dependent and to avoid responsibility. Hypochondria is an exaggerated version of regression and rationalization with a good measure of fantasy thrown in. It is an excellent way to manipulate other people—the man with "heart pains" and the woman with "chronic headaches" both expect to be shown special consideration because of their "illnesses."

A more serious kind of psychologically based health disturbance is *hysterical symptoms*. In everyday usage, the word "hysterical" means crying and "going to pieces." In psychology, the word means something quite different. Hysterical symptoms, while having no real physiological basis, appear to mimic real and serious physical disorders. For example, in an earlier day, when people were more anxious about sex, there were reported cases in which a person's hand and wrist (but not his forearm) would become completely paralyzed as a result of guilt feelings about masturbation. If there had been a physiological basis for the paralysis, more of the arm would have to have been affected because of the way the muscles of the hand and arm are innervated. In such a case, the paralysis was a neurotic behavior resulting from the conflict (guilt feelings) over persistent desires (positive values) to masturbate (which the person negatively valued as a sin); paralysis made masturbation impossible. This kind of symptom seldom occurs anymore, but even in this day and age soldiers sometimes apparently become deaf while in combat. Subtle tests, however, can detect that there is no physiological basis for this disability. Rather, their deafness is a neurotic behavior resulting from the conflict of a positive value for avoiding combat and a negative value for appearing to be a coward. The apparent deafness provides an excellent honorable rationalization for leaving combat.

A third kind of psychologically based health disturbance consists of *psychosomatic illnesses*. These are real physiological malfunctions such as peptic ulcers, asthma, hypertension, or dermatitis. All of these illnesses have a variety of causes, but in some cases they result from prolonged psychological stress rather than from a strictly physiological problem. When a person is afraid or angry, his body mobilizes to deal with the situation by altering blood circulation, hormone levels, metabolic processes, chemical and mechanical activity of the stomach, respiration, and so on, in order to prepare for battle with the source of the fear or anger. Unfortunately, the source of the stress is not always clear to the person. Continued worry (fear) or frustration (anger) about his job, marriage, poverty, or personal shortcomings may become such a familiar part of a person's life that he ceases to see his stress as the product of real, soluble problems. Instead, he tries to learn to live with the stress, or he tries to get a physician to give him some medicine to treat his physiological symptoms. In such a case, the body's chronic mobilization may begin to cause physiological damage; the high-powered executive's peptic ulcer is a familiar example of this process, and the continually worried student's "heartburn" and upset stomach represents a small-scale version of the same thing.

Class 3: Ritual behaviors The third class of neurotic behavior consists of *ritual behaviors.* The first, *obsessive thoughts,* are recurrent and persistent thoughts that drown out almost all other thoughts. You have probably had the experience of hearing song lyrics run through your head until you thought you'd go wild. Obsessive thoughts are a magnified version of this experience and include thoughts about guilt, sex, fears, hatred, vengeance, religion, and the like. The person is so hounded by his thoughts that he can't think or do much else. Thus, a sexually inhibited young man may be unable to direct his thoughts to anything other than sex. A lonely woman may become so obsessed with the idea of babies that she finds herself continually contemplating kidnapping one at the supermarket. Similarly, we all know people who are so obsessed with their occupations that they think of little else and have virtually no lives aside from their work.

The action-oriented counterpart of obsessive thoughts is *compulsive acts.* These are rituals such as Lady Macbeth's repeated washing of her hands after she engineered the murder of King Duncan in the Shakespeare play; or, on a small scale, your Aunt Grace's perpetual straightening of everything in her living room. *Kleptomania,* compulsive stealing, is also included in this class of neurotic behaviors, as are *compulsive eating* and *compulsive drinking.* In general, both obsessive thoughts and compulsive acts serve as ritualistic behaviors that help people avoid crisis situations. The lady who contemplates kidnapping a child may desperately want adult company. But because she may fear the requirements that are customarily imposed on friendships by other adults, she feels a need for a baby instead. Lady Macbeth tried to wash the imaginary blood from her hands in order to cleanse herself of her guilt (a conflict between a positive value for being queen and a negative value for being a murderer). Aunt Grace may be trying to keep her tedious and fragile world from shattering by keeping everything in its proper place. And frequently the kleptomaniac, the compulsive eater, and the heavy drinker are trying to fill bored, fearful lives while avoiding the risk of having to look at why those lives seem so empty and those fears seem so great. In short, obsessive and compulsive behaviors often are attempts to keep reality at a safe distance.

Class 4: Dissociative reactions   Finally, we come to the most severe neurotic behaviors, *dissociative reactions.* These reactions represent escape in its most obvious form. Although they are depicted in many novels and plays, they do not occur very often. The best known of these behaviors is *amnesia,* a state which involves a person's forgetting who he is. Sometimes this forgetting is so complete that the person wanders off (called a *fugue state*) and begins a whole new life. He can't remember his past and he doesn't know how he got where he is. He may even marry and begin a new career. One day things may start to come back to him, and he will be able to recall the lost period of his life. This neurotic behavior is an exaggeration of repression, and it usually occurs when the person is facing an extremely difficult crisis—perhaps his marriage, job, and health are all crumbling at the same time. It also has been known to occur in men on combat duty. These men merely walk away from their combat unit and are found wandering around aimlessly. Amnesia is very rare, however, and newspaper stories about it are seldom real; it is always a handy excuse for a man to use when he has left his family and begun a new life somewhere else. The classic story about the man who went for a loaf of bread, forgot who he was, and didn't return for fifteen years is more fiction than reality.

Another rare neurotic behavior that belongs in this category is *multiple personality.* We all have many selves; there's the self of you at work, the self of you at school, the self of you as a lover, the self of you playing tennis. For most of us, these different selves all flow together, and we are at least vaguely aware of the others when we are being any particular one. For a person who has a multiple personality, however, these selves may be quite separate. One self can't get along with another self, and so the person may have to become two different persons in order to live with these conflicting selves. Thus, the person who has strongly conflicting values about sex (both desire and shame) might dissociate the sexual and nonsexual episodes of his life. He might think of himself as one person when living a prim and proper life. The "sexual person" may know about the "prim person" (but not necessarily), but the "prim person" almost certainly does not know about the "sexual person." In short, through the mechanism of repression, the person permits himself to lead a Dr. Jekyll and Mr. Hyde kind of life. By doing so, he satisfies his conflicting values without having to face any actual conflict.

Psychotic Behavior

Neurotic reactions to crises can range from mild behaviors such as chronic tardiness to severe and debilitating behaviors such as anxiety attacks and hysterical deafness. There are, however, even more severe reactions to crises, called *psychotic behaviors*.

While the majority of severe reactions to crises are mainly psychological in nature, some psychotic behaviors clearly have physiological origins. Brain damage or toxic reactions to prescribed medications or other chemicals are among the main causes of physiologically based psychotic behavior. For example, a person suffering from mercury poisoning shows such symptoms as loss of control over muscular coordination, a feeling of loss of contact with reality, and an inability to concentrate. You can well imagine the emotional crisis such symptoms would bring about especially at first when the person doesn't know what is causing them. In his frantic and confused attempts to cope with the symptoms and to maintain his concept of himself as physically and mentally competent, the poisoning victim may well appear extremely strange to the rest of us, and perhaps to himself as well. Many experts currently are of the opinion that much of the psychotic behavior that will be discussed below may be a result of similar frantic attempts to cope with reactions to emotional crises brought about by physiological malfunctions, malfunctions that are, in many cases, so subtle that they are difficult to detect and treat. Indeed, medical research has only just begun to unearth clues about the existence of some of these malfunctions, and hopefully when the physiological mechanisms involved are understood, medicine will be able to decrease the incidence of psychotic behavior.

Psychotic behavior can also result from the extreme use of ego defense mechanisms against nonphysiological crises, such as those that have been discussed throughout this section. In some cases, a specific event, often called a *precipitating event*, will mark the beginning of psychotic behavior. For example, suppose that a man is merely getting by in a life that is full of conflict and stress; his defense mechanisms are marginally successful, and he is just at the brink of slipping into neurotic behavior. Then he loses his job. The additional stress brought about by this loss may be too much for him to handle, even with neurotic behavior. So the man may resort to even more extreme measures; he may just sit in a corner and completely withdraw from the world, he may hear the voice of God telling him that he is a failure, he may decide that someone is out to get him, and so on. While such a sequence of events is common, not all psychotic reactions have a well-defined precipitating event. Some evolve in a slow, steady way, merely as a result of prolonged crises and stress.

BOX 5.3

Psychotic Behavior: A Case History

L. Percy King (a fictitious name) has been a patient in a state hospital for twenty-eight years. To his own way of thinking he has arrived at discoveries of revolutionary importance which he does not hesitate to call "the greatest psychological phenomena extant." The doctors in charge of the hospital do not put such a high estimate on his ideas and refuse to return him to circulation in the community.

We shall begin by examining L. Percy King's present beliefs—his great discoveries—arrived at after years of reflection and a long sifting of his experience. He believes that all of his misfortunes, including his long imprisonment at the hospital, have been brought about by the activities of a group of pursuers who have been after him ever since he left his home state thirty years ago and took a job in New York City. These pursuers are equipped with very unusual but entirely explicable powers, which he describes as follows:

> Among these pursuers, I was later to gradually discover by deduction, were evidently some brothers and sisters who inherited from one of their parents some astounding, unheard of, utterly unbelievable occult powers. Believe it or not, some of them, besides being able to tell a person's thoughts, are also able to project their magnetic voices—commonly called "radio voices" around here—a distance of a few miles without talking loud and without apparent

Varieties of Psychotic Behaviors

As you might suspect, psychotic behavior does much the same things for a person as neurotic behavior; it gets him out of a situation that he cannot objectively change or escape, while at the same time preserves the integrity of his value system. As with neurotic behaviors, some psychotic behaviors represent inappropriate use of strategy 1, direct (but inappropriate) action. Some represent an attempt to use strategy 2, escape, but the escape is into an imaginary world, and the person becomes incapable of functioning properly in the real world. Some are a result of a mixture of two strategies, and, therefore, it is difficult to tell exactly what functions they are serving. In general, we can talk about three broad classes of psychotic behavior.

Class 1: Emotional disturbances   Primary in this class are *depressive* and *manic* behaviors. Psychotic depression is similar to neurotic depression, but it is more intense. The person becomes so dejected and withdrawn that it is virtually impossible to talk with him. He may sit and weep, he may quietly stare into space, he may imagine that he hears voices and sees people who aren't there (*hallucinations*), or he may have obsessive guilt thoughts and be convinced that he is being punished for his sins (*delusions*).

effort, their voices sounding from that distance as though heard through a radio head set, this being done without electrical apparatus. This unique occult power of projecting their "radio voices" for such long distances apparently seems to be due to their natural bodily electricity, of which they have a supernormal amount. The vibration of their vocal cords evidently generates wireless waves, and these vocal radio waves are caught by human ears without rectification. Thus, in connection with their mind-reading ability, they are able to carry on a conversation with a person over a mile away and out of sight, by ascertaining the person's unspoken thoughts, and then by means of their so-called "radio voices," answer these thoughts aloud audibly to the person. An uninitiated person would probably be very much startled over such phenomena. For example, what would you think if you were on a level, desolate tract of land without any vegetation or places of concealment upon it, and without a human being within miles, when you hear a mysterious, seemingly unearthly voice answer a question you were just thinking about?

These are the ravings of a sick man. One may be tempted to dismiss them as utter nonsense, but to do so would be to throw away the evidence which upon closer scrutiny allows us to understand what is wrong with L. Percy King. The outcome of his reasoning may be completely absurd, but he is obviously attempting to reason and to make some kind of sense out of his experience. If we look closely, we find consistent themes and a consistent process of distortion. The

Manic behavior, just the opposite of depression, is a caricature of happiness. The manic person smiles too easily and too much. He is too exuberant and too active. He talks too loudly and proclaims his joy too strongly. To an observer, the manic person is like a puppet being jerked through some comic act—but there is an overwhelming sadness in the puppet's manner.

In some cases, people go through alternating phases of manic and depressive behavior; this alternation may occur over hours, days, or weeks. Thus, after a wild show of happiness, the manic-depressive person may sit down and cry for no apparent reason. However, the overall impression you get from observing manic-depressive behavior is that the person is profoundly unhappy. He is so frightened that he has withdrawn from life and can only concentrate upon his lonely fear and his guilt. His attempts to fight his way out, his manic behavior, are a desperate grasp for happiness and vigor rather than effective attempts to deal with his crises.

Class 2: Paranoid behavior   The second class of psychotic behavior, *paranoia*, consists of *delusions of persecution* and/or other delusions. The person may feel that God, the Martians, or the FBI is trying to harm him and that all of his

patient has experienced *hallucinations*—false perceptions—such as hearing voices actually speaking to him or feeling peculiar bodily sensations. From these he has worked out *delusions* or false beliefs. Both of these symptoms, which are common in many varieties of psychosis, show a failure in the patient's contact with reality. He does not engage in sufficient *reality testing*. He does not weigh the possibility that he might have imagined the sound of voices. He uses the device of *projection* to assign to outside forces nearly everything that takes place in his mind. Unless we believe his theory about radio voices, we must assume that when his thoughts are answered, it is by further thoughts of his own. But the patient, for some reason, cannot accept this explanation, and his reality testing breaks down, falsifying the outside world, before the alternative of assuming responsibility for those further thoughts. Going on like this for years, he almost loses the feeling of himself as an active agent; he becomes virtually depersonalized.

Reality testing is such a fundamental process that its disturbance can only indicate some very unusual condition. Healthy people stubbornly persist in testing reality even when real events are going pretty much against them. We can best understand the nature and strength of the forces involved in King's psychosis if we go back to the time in his life, twenty-eight years ago, when reality testing first began to fail.

One day King was taking a walk in New York City. "Being a stranger," he writes, "I was surprised to hear someone exclaim twice: 'Shoot him!' evidently

troubles are the result of this plot against him. He may begin to believe that the people around him are agents of his enemies, and in some cases, if he decides to take action against his enemies, he may resort to violence. Political assassinations are frequently a result of such paranoid feelings, particularly if the person also has the delusion that he is destined to be the savior of the downtrodden (*delusions of grandeur*).

Delusions of grandeur are not uncommon. No doubt, many great men build important and successful lives on such feelings. But when an ordinary businessman begins to believe that he is a famous football star or that he has been selected by Fate to rule the world, he is not likely to be well received by his fellow men. A person with such delusions may be perfectly able to carry on a logical conversation and to explain in intricate detail how he views things, but his behavior is usually too extreme to enable him to function very well in ordinary circumstances. His obsession about being persecuted or his delusions about his special role in the world are far removed from reality; they represent an attempt on his part to mentally restructure the existing situation in order to reduce the conflict that he feels. The person's unsatisfied positive

meaning me." Thinking that gangsters might have mistaken him for someone else he tried to disappear in the crowd and reach the subway. But the gangsters pursued him: "I knew they were pursuing me because I still heard their voices as close as ever, no matter how fast I walked." Back at his lodgings he told no one about his adventure "for fear they would be incredulous."

So far as we know, this was the first time that King hallucinated. Reality testing was by no means abandoned: he himself found the experience so strange that he did not expect anyone to believe it. His whole reaction, however, was peculiar. He instantly assumed that some overheard talk was directed meanacingly at him, and he fled in such panic that there was no opportunity to test this particular bit of reality. Shortly afterwards the same thing happened again. Among the threatening phrases he distinctly heard a woman's voice say, "You can't get away from us; we'll lay for you and get you after a while." Then he noticed that one of the unseen pursuers, "repeated my thoughts aloud, verbatim." This was the beginning of that process of projection whereby he ultimately disowned most of his own thoughts and sensations. At this stage the pursuers merely repeated his thoughts; soon they began to answer them and then initiate them.

King's life gradually turned into a nightmare. He noticed that whenever he entered a room someone would cough twice, then someone else, until everyone in the room had coughed twice. "I would go to the movies where one patron after another would cough twice until dozens had coughed." Reality testing was

value for being important and his negative value for being unable to make himself important produce a conflict that can be reduced only by assuming that there is a plot to keep him from achieving his destiny. The spiral of delusion is accelerated by the logical conclusion that, indeed, he must be important if anyone is bothering to persecute him. Thus paranoid delusions of persecution and grandeur feed upon each other and build a monolithic system that permits the person to escape from his initial conflict into a manageable world of unreality.

Class 3: Schizophrenic behavior The third class of psychotic behaviors is a mixed bag of things. The behaviors are called *schizophrenic* (pronounced "skiz-uh-fre-nic"), and their primary characteristic is profound withdrawal from reality (Fig. 5.3). While there are many variations, schizophrenic behavior usually involves a mixture of fantasy, delusions, hallucinations, and general emotional blandness with moments of strong, inappropriate emotional reactions to particular events. In some cases a schizophrenic person also has peculiarities in his posture, facial expressions, and bodily movements (for example, a

still attempted: "I would have thought everyone had colds had not each one coughed twice, and in summertime with no colds going around." How could he interpret the coughing? "Was there really an organized movement afoot against me?" Coughing and other persecutions at the office where he worked finally convinced him that this was the case, and he resigned from his job.

Now he was completely miserable. Pursuers left him no peace of mind. As he sat in his lodgings, murmurings in the street below told him all too plainly that his murderers were assembling. Voices on the stairs revealed that a lynching party was creeping toward his room, so that in panic he called upon a neighbor to protect him. At last he could stand it no longer and tried to kill himself. His self-inflicted wounds proved not to be fatal, but they led to the summoning of his mother, his return home, and his commitment to the state hospital. During the psychiatric examination he was depressed and indifferent, speaking as little as possible. Later he realized that pursuers had forced this behavior upon him so that he would be judged insane. King's psychiatric diagnosis is *schizophrenia, paranoid type.* There is little reason to suppose that he will ever recover sufficiently to leave the hospital.*

*Abridged from R. W. White, *The Abnormal Personality* (3d ed.). Copyright © 1964, The Ronald Press Company, New York.

stooped posture, halting gait, grimacing and other exaggerated gestures, or constant movement of the legs and limbs). Ordinarily, the person also has difficulty following a train of thought or focusing his attention on anything for very long.

While the behaviors of schizophrenic individuals may vary with respect to overall themes—one may exhibit primarily manic behavior, one depressive, one paranoid, one childishness, and so on—a common thread runs through all of these variations. In general, schizophrenics show a general breakdown in their ability to relate to other people. Some experts believe that this may be a result of exaggerated use of old patterns of interpersonal relations that the person learned at home before he became schizophrenic. This view is supported by studies that have found that the members of families of schizophrenics tend to be less able than the members of other families to cooperate with one another and to carry out planned action together. These findings imply that the families of schizophrenics may never have been very good at interpersonal interactions, thus preventing their preschizophrenic child from learning how to deal well with other people. There is also evidence that mothers of preschizophrenic men are more domineering and inflexible than other mothers. Similarly, schizophrenic people tend to remember their own parents

FIG. 5.3 Sometimes a schizophrenic person will sit in the same position for hours, withdrawn from reality, living totally within a private world. (Courtesy National Institutes of Health, Public Health Service.)

as less supportive and less pleasant than do other people.[1] Thus, it is possible that the childhood experience of schizophrenics may have set the stage for the later development of schizophrenic behavior during times of stress, because it was in childhood that they learned that withdrawal into a world of their own effectively reduces the stress involved in relating to other people.

Even if childhood experiences are a factor in the later development of schizophrenic reactions, we are left with a serious problem: why doesn't everyone raised under "schizophrenic family conditions" become schizophrenic? One possible answer is that inherited (genetic) factors might predispose some people to be more susceptible than others to the stress produced by conflicts and, therefore, cause them to resort to schizophrenic behavior in order to reduce their stress.

---

[1] It is only fair to note the possibility that the preschizophrenic's personality may have been so difficult to deal with, even in childhood, that he caused the family's problems rather than the other way around.

Strong evidence for the genetic argument comes from studies of schizophrenic twins. In about three fourths of the cases studied, if one of a pair of identical twins (who are formed from the same egg and therefore are virtually identical genetically) exhibited schizophrenic behavior, the other twin also exhibited this behavior.[2] By contrast, with fraternal twins (who are genetically different from one another), this happens only in about one sixth of the cases, an incidence that is the same as for nontwin brothers and sisters. These findings imply that when the first twin has a predisposition for schizophrenic behavior, a genetically identical twin tends to share it, but a genetically nonidentical twin does not. This is fairly strong evidence for the involvement of a genetic factor in schizophrenia.

The existence of a possible genetic predispositional factor is further supported by the fact that approximately two thirds of children with parents who are *both* schizophrenic will themselves exhibit schizophrenic behavior at some time in their lives, while only one sixth of children with only one schizophrenic parent display such behavior, and only about one one-hundredth of children of nonschizophrenic parents ever display such behavior. All of these facts strongly suggest that the more genetically similar a person is to someone who exhibits schizophrenic behavior, the more likely it is that he himself will develop such behavior. Even allowing for the fact that a person who was raised in a home with schizophrenic parents or brothers and sisters spent his formative years in a strange environment, the evidence still suggests that at least in some of the cases there is an underlying inherited predisposition to schizophrenic behavior.

It is interesting to note that some recent studies of blood chemistry have indicated that certain chemicals in the blood may be responsible for schizophrenic reactions, although questions have been raised concerning how well the studies were done and how much one can safely conclude from their results.

Where, then, are we left? The picture that is emerging is that in at least some cases, schizophrenic individuals may have a physiological predisposition that interacts with the kind of home they grew up in and the kinds of conflicts and stresses that they encounter. It is as though some people are more vulnerable, through no fault of their own, to the stresses of certain kinds of conflicts—particularly those involving interpersonal relations. The rest of us face the same stresses, but we are not as vulnerable. In times of crisis, we have difficulties,

---

[2] This does not mean that identical twins in general are more likely than other people to exhibit schizophrenic behavior; only that if one identical twin exhibits schizophrenic behavior, the other is likely to also.

but we manage to get through them without having to resort to extreme behaviors, although we may rely heavily upon defense mechanisms, or even neurotic behavior, until we can get back on our feet. The schizophrenically inclined person, however, is handicapped by his heredity and, perhaps, by his past training, and the less extreme defenses do not relieve his stress. Thus, he reaches deeper than most of us have to into the bag of defenses and comes up with more radical methods of getting the world to go away.

It is possible, of course, that the physiological factors we have discussed, and others as yet undiscovered, may not be responsible merely for increased vulnerability to stress but may themselves be the causes of stress. Imagine, for example, that for some reason these physiological factors start causing a person to experience strange, nonspecific bodily symptoms which to him have no apparent objective cause (not unlike what happens to people suffering from mercury poisoning). The person doesn't know what is happening; he begins to experience odd changes in his moods and becomes easily provoked to anger (two common correlates of physiological illness). He goes to his physician, who can find nothing wrong with him because medicine does not yet know what to look for. His increased feelings of strangeness and anger conflict with his values for being "normal" and being kind to other people. He is caught; he can't help feeling the way he does, and yet his feelings are in conflict with his values. To protect himself and his values, he may begin to look for causes of his feelings—maybe people are actually trying to make him angry, or maybe he is being punished for his sins. Soon the conflict becomes so intense that he sees withdrawal from other people as his only alternative. Along with this withdrawal the person begins to reinterpret his experiences in an attempt to give continuity and coherence to the otherwise chaotic, bewildering world in which he finds himself.

People who have had bad trips on LSD and mescaline report experiences similar to what I've just described, but they usually have the comforting knowledge that the drug is the cause of their strange experiences. The schizophrenic person unfortunately doesn't know what is causing his experiences, and therefore he tries very hard to make sense of them—the behavior that we see is a result of what he does to make sense of things. We cannot fully understand the meaning to him of the things he does because we aren't living in his confusing world. To us, the person's claim that he is John the Baptist or Winston Churchill merely seems ridiculous. But if we knew what being these people meant to the schizophrenic person and how such assumed identities help to give the person's chaotic world some kind of order, everything might make a little more sense to us.

The last three paragraphs are mostly conjecture on my part. Science is not certain why some people slip into make-believe worlds and whether these worlds are in fact coherent to them. Some authorities believe that the view expressed here has substance; others would disagree strongly. Some think schizophrenic reactions are totally a result of biochemical and physiological factors and that a person's past experience and present life crises have little to do with them. Others deny that physiological factors play a very important role and contend that the person's childhood experiences and current problems are primarily responsible for producing schizophrenic behavior. The view I described here is a mixture of these two extremes and probably comes closest to the view held by the majority of authorities. However, we are still far from understanding schizophrenic behavior in specific and psychotic behavior in general. Hopefully, the next few years will see advances in this understanding and the development of reliable techniques for helping to bring psychotic people back to a more realistic way of dealing with their crises, conflicts, and stresses.

BOX 5.4

Death: The Final Crisis

Even though we constantly see it portrayed in movie and TV dramas and recorded on newscasts, death has very little reality for most of us. Think about it for a moment. Although you know it intellectually, deep in your heart do you *really* believe that you will die some day?

Inexplicably, preoccupation with counterfeit death in drama and an inability to face it in reality seems to be a common feature of modern, industrialized societies. The dying are usually put in hospitals (where medical attempts to prolong life often go far beyond all reason), which permits the rest of us to be comfortably isolated from what is really happening. We particularly "protect" children from the reality of death, behaving as though the process were some obscene, antisocial act to be hushed up or denied rather than a natural part of human existence. When death comes, we embalm and beautify the corpse in an effort to make it look as it did when it was alive, and then we place it in an expensive protective box in an effort to preserve it as long as possible.

Our attempts to avoid the reality of death apparently are fairly successful. For example, in a recent study of students' feelings about the interrelations among concepts that are central to human existence (goodness, self, reality, and the like), death was found to be unique; that is, it wasn't felt to be integrally related to any of the other concepts.* In short, we push thoughts of death off into a corner. The result is that when we suddenly find ourselves confronted with circumstances that prevent us from avoiding such thoughts, we are caught quite unprepared. In cultures where death is more of a reality, where people die at home among friends and family and where children grow up having seen death and its place in life, fear of death is less intense and people tend to die with a certain amount of dignity. This is not to say that grief and mourning are less intense in these cultures, but actual fear and anger about death apparently are less severe.

Circumstances that force us to recognize and consider the reality of death usually consist of the death of someone important to us, news of the impending death of someone we love, or news of our own impending death. The typical *grief syndrome* brought on by the death of someone important to us was described in the closing paragraphs of Section 4, Part 3. We need not go over it here except to recall that grief has three major phases (shock, despair, and recovery), and that the time necessary for it to run its course varies according to how deeply the grieving person felt for the deceased, how quickly a substitute relationship can be established, social custom, and so on.

Turning to the circumstance in which we receive the news that someone we love is soon to die, we again observe the grief syndrome. First there is shock, denial of the diagnosis, and anger at the doctors for what *must* be a mistaken diagnosis. Then comes despair, depressed acceptance of the diagnosis but an unwillingness to accept the inevitability of death. Finally, there is a form of recovery in that there is an acceptance of both the diagnosis and the certainty of death. However, even though this third phase may include a desire to see the dying person's suffering quickly end, the faint hope that something will happen to save him from death continues to exist until the end. This *anticipatory grief syndrome* takes time. For example, for the parents of a child dying of leukemia, say, the process usually takes about four months; even then, after the child finally dies, the parents go through yet another period of grief.

Until rather recently, very little was known about how we react to our own impending death. We owe our thanks to a small number of scientists for having the courage to find out. Primary among these scientists is Dr. Elisabeth Kübler-Ross, a warm, sensitive psychiatrist who has spent countless hours listening to terminally ill (dying) patients talk about their feelings.† Ironically, some of Dr. Kübler-Ross' findings have to do not with the patients themselves but with the patients' physicians, nurses, and families; the discomfort of being forced to

---

*R. Kastenbaum, Time and death in adolescence. In H. Fiefel (Ed.), *The Meaning of Death*. New York: McGraw-Hill, 1959.
†Elisabeth Kübler-Ross, *On Death and Dying*. New York: Macmillan, 1969.

recognize the reality of death often is too much for the nondying to cope with. If the patient tries either to express his feelings about his impending death or to face it openly, he is quite likely to find himself abandoned by those who are not able to face death. The nurses may drop in to attend to his needs, but then they quickly rush away. His physician (who may regard his own inability to prevent the death as a personal failure) may make only short stops on his daily rounds. And the family may begin to cut its visits to a minimum. Thus, because these people, like most of the rest of us, are unable to face death and, therefore, are unable to help the patient when he needs them the most, the dying patient often has to face the criris alone.

After Dr. Kübler-Ross started listening to dying patients, she quickly learned that they often were eager to talk about what was happening to them, particularly to someone who could accept the reality of death, listen to them, and not run away. She also quickly discovered that there is a sequence of emotions that is experienced by dying patients. These emotions, as we shall shortly see, essentially constitute an anticipatory grief syndrome—the patient grieves for the loss of his future and for the loss of himself.

Although Dr. Kübler-Ross divides the sequence of emotions the dying patient experiences into five phases rather than just three, its similarity to the anticipatory grief syndrome is apparent. First is the initial *shock* followed quickly by *denial* (which allows the patient time to collect his wits after the shock and to mobilize other defense mechanisms). Next comes *anger*, which may be expressed indiscriminately, at family, friends, staff, physician, or even total strangers. Many times this anger stems from a profound feeling of outrage at having been cheated by death, particularly if the patient is fairly young; plans for the future, years of working toward some goal, the joys of having a family, and so on, are all to be brought to an abrupt, unjustifiable end. The major problem arising from this anger is that the innocent people who receive the brunt of it often take the anger personally, and, because of this, become even more inclined to avoid contact with the dying patient.

The patient's anger is followed by *bargaining*, an attempt to postpone the inevitable through good behavior. For example, "I promise to dedicate my life to the Church if I pull through this," or, "Just keep me around until after Christmas, Doctor, and I'll die peacefully" (and after Christmas, Easter becomes the new goal, and so on).

Next, the patient enters the *depression* phase. His strength begins to go, he may grow thinner, he feels worse, his hospital bills accumulate, and his family grows weary. It is now that the reality of his situation begins to be fully realized, and, in a very real sense, he begins to contemplate death and prepare himself to die. This may take a while and he may not be able to dwell too long at a time on what is happening to him, but slowly he becomes more resigned to his fate; unless denial is too strong or death comes too quickly, the reality of death eventually will be accepted. If those around him are unable to accept it too, he may reach this final stage, *acceptance*, without telling them, putting on a mask of optimism to protect them from their own fears. And yet, through it all, he really does retain a thread of hope—a new drug, a new treatment, a miracle of some kind. This small bit of hope provides some slight solace up to the end.

Part 2   *HELP!*

In the first part of this section, we discussed the three basic strategies for reducing stress and resolving psychological conflicts. Then we moved on to a discussion of the misapplication of strategies 1 and 2 to crises that these approaches can't solve, and we saw that the motivation for these misapplications is ordinarily the need to avoid the anguish involved in using strategy 3, value changing. As we have seen, misapplications of strategies 1 and 2 can lead to severe problems. Moreover, such tactics can produce yet another crisis situation; the inappropriate behavior itself becomes a source of conflict and stress because it is not well received by other people. It is not easy for people to put up with a person who chronically employs inappropriate, annoying defenses to "solve" his problems; sooner or later the person's friends are either going to abandon him or exert strong pressure on him to do something about his annoying behavior.

In addition to the problem of other people's reactions to his inappropriate behavior, the troubled person also faces the problem that misuse of strategies 1 and 2 seldom solves his initial conflict. These misapplied strategies merely serve to obscure the existence of the conflict; if the person were to come out from behind his defensive wall, the conflict might be there waiting for him. Of course, unless he at least peeks from behind that wall, he will never know whether the conflict is there or not. So, you see the problem the poor fellow faces—by misusing strategies 1 and 2 he has built a wall to protect himself from the anguish of having to change his values. But in doing so, he has made himself vulnerable to the nonacceptance of the people around him. And if he has built the wall very high, he is never sure whether or not the initial conflict is still a threat. The total burden of all of this is considerable, and it almost always results in the person having an ever-present feeling of dissatisfaction and unhappiness. Unfortunately, by the time he gets this far, the whole problem is so complex that he may not really know why he is unhappy or where to begin in order to set things straight.

Setting Things Straight

Setting things straight requires that the troubled person get out of his endless circle of fear and defense—something that is more easily said than done. When the wall isn't very high, setting things straight may occur spontaneously when the person sees that his conflict has ended. For example, if a man is displacing his anger to his wife because he hates his supervisor but can't express his emotions for fear of losing his job, transfer of the supervisor to another job might resolve the conflict and permit the man to be nicer to his wife. Sometimes even high walls can topple in a dramatic way when, through some accidental slip-up in defensive behavior, the person peeks from behind his wall and finds that his conflict no longer exists or that it is much less stressful then he had judged it to be. For example, a person with a phobia may find himself accidentally caught in the feared situation. If the expected disaster fails to occur (for example, he doesn't jump from the tower, suffocate in the closet, or get bitten by the dog), he *may* begin to realize that his phobia is a useless burden. Of course, this does not always happen; the person's terror may be so great that it alone is sufficient to keep the phobia going—so don't lock your claustrophobic friend in a closet in a misguided attempt to help him get over his phobia!

Setting things straight becomes a more difficult job when the conflicts actually don't go away or when the wall is built too high to peek over. This is the case because, aside from being unhappy, the troubled person may not even know what his problem is. Besides, his defenses, which have hidden his original conflict from him, may themselves be obscure to him. Thus, the soldier who relies on hysterical deafness to avoid combat may actually believe that he is deaf. A man who grossly displaces his aggression may believe it is his wife and children that aggravate him rather than his supervisor. In short, the first stumbling block on the path toward setting things straight is the problem of discovering what the basic conflict is and differentiating it from the conflicts that arise from the defensive behavior itself. This requires a perspective that the troubled person seldom has if his defenses are operating at all effectively.

The second stumbling block toward setting things straight has to do with those inexplicit values we discussed at the beginning of this section. Often people are in conflict because a particular situation fails to conform to their inexplicit values. Because the person doesn't really know what these values are, he can neither change the situation nor change his values. Thus, a woman who truly loves her husband but has inexplicit negative values about sexuality may find herself in a stressful situation; she loves him and knows intellectually that sex is proper, but, nevertheless, she continues to feel guilt and revulsion whenever they have sex. Such stress might, for example, lead to defenses that involve hypochondria; illness could make sex seem impossible. As long as her husband accepts her defense as real and doesn't insist on sex, she may get by pretty well. But if he begins to doubt her illness or begins to look for another woman, her defense becomes self-defeating. As a result, she can develop a new defense (for example, denial that he has found another woman) or she can try to set things straight. To do the latter she has to discover and change her inexplicit negative values for sex.

The third stumbling block is the difficulty of realistically reappraising the conflict situation. To do this successfully requires (1) rechecking to see if there are any effective strategy 1 solutions that have not been considered, (2) rechecking to see if strategy 2, escape, is possible after all, and (3) rechecking to see if strategy 3, value changing, is not less painful than all the pain and stress resulting from use of the defensive or neurotic behavior. The problem is that the person who is caught up in the whole thing is seldom capable of such cool-headed reappraisals. Few of us see very many alternatives for changing the situation when we are faced with a crisis; we tend to focus on the most obvious courses of action and to overlook others that might occur to us were we not under stress. We also tend to rule out escape when it may actually be a plausible and realistic solution. A boy who participates in high school football but hates it may rule out quitting because he thinks his friends will criticize or laugh at him for having quit. If he were to subtly inquire about how they would feel about his quitting rather than assume that he already knew, he might find that his friends couldn't care less about it. We often get ourselves into such situations—we assume that there are high penalties for quitting without bothering to find out if there really are. So too our fear of value changes, our fear of the pain involved in exploring our cherished values and finding them wanting, as well as the assumed anguish of changing them, often appears greater than actually would be the case should we change these values. However, the inconvenience and stress created by defenses frequently come to overshadow this fear of value change. When this happens, the person's defenses are ready to be scrapped and he is ready to re-evaluate his original conflict situation. As before, the basic problem is that, embroiled as he is, he often lacks the necessary perspective for this re-evaluation.

Where To Turn

All of the stumbling blocks to setting things straight have one thing in common: the person who is caught up in his problems often lacks the perspective and courage to try to face them realistically and thereby to change his life. Outside help is needed; the objective eye and supportive sympathy of another person may provide the perspective and strength the troubled person needs.

Family, Friends, and Friendly Strangers

The first and most common source of help is family and friends. Frequently, just talking with someone he trusts about his unhappiness and the things that seem to be wrong can be the beginning of a solution to a troubled person's problems. Merely getting feedback about how other people see his problems and their reactions to his attempts to deal with them may give the individual a fresh perspective and help clarify the issues. Even if a friend can't offer a solution, he can render the greatest service of friendship—he can provide the person with an opportunity to open up and talk. Indeed, if such a heart-to-heart talk does nothing more than convince the person that someone cares enough to listen to him *without judging him,* it may provide him with the courage to look more closely at his problem rather than to continue his defensive behavior.

Unfortunately, family and friends themselves often are too bound up in the troubled person's problem; thus it is difficult to rely upon them for help. A son who feels desperately trapped because he must take care of his aging mother may not be able to express his resentment to his family or friends because they may judge him severely for feeling as he does about his mother. Also, those who know us best often are unable to give us the support we need because our conflicts are their conflicts too. Thus, if the young man were to try to discuss his trapped feeling with his younger brother, he might receive a very disheartening reaction if the brother felt guilt about not sharing the responsibility for their mother's care.

Sometimes, of course, we feel we can't rely on our family or friends because we fear (rather than know) that they might reject us. We value our family ties and friendships, and few of us are willing to risk losing them by admitting our less than acceptable feelings and fears. Thus, a boy who feels guilty about masturbation and erotic thoughts may be unable to talk about his conflict to a friend or a family member because he fears they will lose their respect for him. Of course, his fear might be perfectly justified if the people around him regard such acts as evil, sinful, and perverted. But if the people were better informed, they might be able to alleviate his guilt and reduce his conflict by helping him to understand that virtually every male masturbates and has erotic thoughts, that they themselves have done it, and that medical research finds that masturbation causes no physiological harm. As you can see, the person's dilemma lies in trying to predict how an honest attempt to seek help will be received by the people to whom he tries to talk. If the relative or friend turns out to be understanding and supportive, things will most likely be brought out in the open where they can be looked at and faced in an effective manner. If the one to whom he turns becomes upset, laughs, is shocked, or tells other people what he has heard, the troubled person's problem may be compounded. The risk of the latter is sufficient to keep most of us from going to our family and friends when we need them the most.

The need of people to talk about their conflicts to friendly, supportive people without the risk of being judged has led to the development of a new social phenomenon known as the *encounter group* (Fig. 5.4). An encounter group is a group of friendly strangers who gather together for the expressed purpose

FIG. 5.4   *An encounter group is a group of friendly strangers who meet to talk about their individual problems and to obtain feedback from each other. (Courtesy Preston M. Heller.)*

of talking about their problems and of obtaining feedback from each other. The group might meet for a couple of hours each week for eight or ten weeks or continuously throughout weekends (called *marathons*) or follow any other schedule the group agrees upon.

The ground rules for encounter groups are (1) complete honesty and (2) the mutual understanding that while you may disapprove of another person's behavior, you must not judge the person himself. Thus, a business executive in a group might honestly discuss the pleasure he gets from being overbearing and tyrannical. The other group members are free to express their disapproval of such behavior and to try to help him explore why such behavior gives him pleasure, but they must not judge him as an evil man. The underlying reason for this second rule is that nothing is accomplished by labeling people as evil, sinful, and so on; the labels do not help the individual get any better. On the other hand, the behaviors the person uses to defend himself or even his values themselves may be destructive, and there is great benefit in exploring these behaviors and values and helping the person recognize what they are and what they do. There is an infinite difference between rejecting what someone does and rejecting the person himself.

Encounter groups must have a *trained* leader, a person who is experienced in facilitating interactions among group members and in acting as a referee in order to see that the basic rules, honesty and acceptance, are closely followed. When amateurs try to lead groups, the participants often have very traumatic and needlessly painful experiences because these two rules are easily broken; stay away from groups with amateur leaders!

One of the leader's most difficult jobs is right at the beginning when he has to get a group of from eight to twenty strangers to feel free and safe and to be honest with each other. This usually takes a little time and is seldom easy, but there are ways to overcome the rigid superficiality that usually is present at first. For example, a leader may ask the group to break up into subgroups of three or four people each. The members of each subgroup are told to talk together for three minutes in an effort to get to know each other. After this, the members rearrange themselves into different subgroups of three or four and then do the same thing all over again *except* that they are told not to talk about anything that they talked about in their previous subgroup. This procedure is repeated four or five times, and the results are interesting. At first the talk is very superficial—name, rank, and serial number, so to speak. Then, because these topics are ruled out, the next session becomes more personal—why I'm here, what I expect to get from this experience, and so forth. By the fourth or fifth three-minute session, people have been forced to abandon

conversational trivia; they find themselves talking about things that are important to them *and* listening with interest to what the other subgroup members
are saying about themselves. This *mutual sharing* of important personal feelings
and ideas in a nonjudgmental atmosphere builds a sense of trust among the
members and sets the stage for further exploration.

Many people who participate in a group of this kind find it a good experience, although others are rather unimpressed. Those who profit frequently are
surprised and happy to learn that their particular conflict is not uncommon,
that other group members have similar problems, and that once out in the
open their conflict is not really as scary as it seemed when it was bottled up
inside. The young man who at last feels free to reveal his overwhelming fear
of having to meet people and the elaborate methods he uses to avoid such
situations may be relieved to hear that his fears are shared by others in the
group. Perhaps the other group members can help him find effective methods
of dealing with this fear, methods that they have found to be successful for
themselves. Perhaps a woman who always has been afraid to express her anger
for fear of losing other people's friendship and respect can tell the group about
her conflict and, secure in the knowledge that the group will not reject her,
lose her temper, shout, and scream. Indeed, she may well discover that the
group members are less offended by her anger than she expected and, therefore,
may realize that people do not automatically hate a person if he occasionally
lets off a little steam.

The major value of most encounter group experiences is in getting honest
feedback from people. Defense mechanisms keep us so isolated from our
conflicts that we seldom know how big or how small they really are; we assume
that unless we avoid the entire issue, our world will cave in. Encounter groups
often serve to show us that our conflicts are not as grim as we think, that other
people have survived the same problems, and that not everyone judges us as
harshly as we assume they will. In many cases this reassurance is all that we
need to help us begin to face our problems squarely, to drop or reduce our
dependency upon defense mechanisms, and to begin to make the changes in
the situation or in our values that we previously were so sure we could not
make.

Counseling   Some conflicts are either so personal or so complex that they cannot be solved
with the help of family, friends, or friendly strangers. These more complex
conflicts require careful exploration in order for the troubled person to understand why he is in the quandary he is in and how to get out. We may need
the skilled aid of someone who can both listen objectively and help direct

exploration in the most profitable directions. Such people, called *counselors*, aren't clairvoyant, but through extensive experience and training they have learned how to help people clarify their inexplicit values, evaluate their conflict situations realistically, and understand their defenses. Too, counselors are skilled in supporting people's efforts to face their conflicts and to change their values when that is the proper thing to do. Counselors do not solve problems, they help the troubled person solve his own problems. The job belongs to the person, and the counselor is merely there to give support and a little guidance when it is necessary.

The most readily accessible counselors are physicians. They sometimes have special training in counseling, but even if they don't, they usually have a great deal of experience as a result of situations that arise in the course of treating patients for medical problems. While they are particularly good in dealing with conflicts stemming from medical problems, physicians seldom have the time or the skill to help with complex psychological problems. Thus, a man who is concerned about a lack of energy and constant headaches might profit immeasurably by discussing his problems with his physician. After a physical examination, the physician may be able to alleviate the man's fears; or if something is physically wrong, he may be able to correct the problem. On the other hand, if the man's concerns are fairly deep, have no physiological basis, and are related to his other values and behaviors, the physician usually will refer him to someone who specializes in counseling.

The next level of counseling is done by people who have received special training in counseling as part of their professional training in becoming a nurse, teacher, social worker, minister, and the like, and they usually are associated with service institutions such as hospitals, social welfare agencies, and churches. As with physicians, these counselors ordinarily deal with problems that are specifically related to their own professional areas; nurses work with people who are ill, school counselors work with students and their families, and so forth. While their training and their specialization in counseling allow these people to devote more effort and time to helping troubled people than is possible for physicians, they too, usually do not undertake to help people whose conflicts are deep and when it is evident that the solution will take a long time.

Psychologists and Psychiatrists

Counseling of people with deep, complex problems is usually undertaken by psychologists and psychiatrists.[3] While the techniques vary depending upon the problem, there are essentially three basic approaches to helping people

[3] A psychiatrist is a physician (M.D.) who has additional training in counseling, and his practice tends to be entirely devoted to helping people with psychological problems. A psychologist is a person who holds either an M.A. or Ph.D. degree in

FIG. 5.5   *Psychotheraphy provides support while the troubled person tears down his defenses and learns alternative ways of coping with crises.*

with complex conflicts. The first is *psychotherapy*, the second is *behavior therapy*, and the third is *medical therapy*.

Psychotherapy   While there are many different forms of psychotherapy, all have essentially the same goals—to help a troubled person gain an understanding of his conflict, how he presently deals with it, and why he deals with it the way he does. The belief is that once such understanding is achieved, the person will cease to be a victim of his conflict and will be in a position to actively bring about an acceptable solution to it. The *psychotherapist's* main job is to help the person handle the stress produced by facing his conflict and dropping his defenses and to help him understand why he has turned to defenses rather than more effective solutions. In other words, the psychotherapist is there to support the person as he tears down the walls he spent so long building and to help him see why the walls got built in the first place (Fig. 5.5). Hopefully, the person will then learn to face his problems effectively and not build any more walls.

---

psychology and has specialized in helping troubled people. Unfortunately, unlike the regulation of psychiatrists, many states do not have laws regulating who may and who may not call himself a psychologist. Therefore, there is some danger that you might end up in the hands of a quack. The best way to avoid this is to ask your own physician to suggest the name of a qualified psychologist or to call the counseling center at a nearby university or college and ask them for a list of qualified persons. You should expect to devote from one to five hours each week to counseling by a psychiatrist or psychologist, paying from $20 to $50 an hour if the person is in private practice. Hospitals, community mental health centers, and university and college counseling centers often provide very good service at a considerably lower cost or even free.

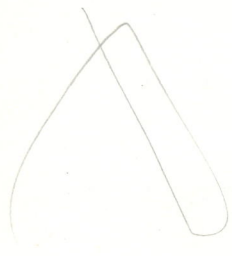

It is difficult to describe what happens during psychotherapy because the process is unique to each person and each psychotherapist. In general, the person's conflicts are imbedded in a morass of denial, confusion, inexplicit values, fear, and a tendency to react to present people and events in ways that once may have been necessary and appropriate but now are no longer so. For example, suppose an unmarried middle-aged man seeks the aid of a psychotherapist because he feels he is so unattractive to women that he is doomed to a life of loneliness. In the course of talking about it, the man may discover that he is not so much unattractive to women as he is afraid of them; he, not the women, breaks up every relationship. Further probing might reveal that his fear of women stems from a tendency to react to all women as he once reacted to his overbearing mother, whom he bitterly resented. His feelings of being powerless to deal with his mother and his conflict between hating her and wanting her love may have been so repressed that he is presently unaware that they ever existed, even though they powerfully affect his reactions to the women he now meets. By talking with the psychotherapist, who mainly asks clarifying questions and tries to point out similarities between seemingly unrelated things the man says and the emotions he describes, the man might be able to see what had been going on all these years and to see his conflict about women for what it really is—old, unexpressed hostility toward an overbearing mother and fear of again being in a similar predicament with another woman.

In the course of making discoveries about a particular conflict, a person may very well find the answers to other conflicts, conflicts that appear, on the surface, to have little or no relation to the issue at hand. For example, the man in the last paragraph might also be bothered by a tendency to lose his temper whenever he finds that even his most casual suggestions are not followed. In the process of exploring his supposed unattractiveness to women, he might discover that he loses his temper because even the slightest failure to be obeyed makes him feel the same frustrated powerlessness that he felt with his mother. As a boy, he repressed this anger. As a man, he expresses it, but it is excessively intense because it is a combination of the appropriate frustration that many people feel when thwarted plus the extra load of anger engendered by his feeling of powerlessness and what powerlessness means to him. Knowing that such situations have this extra meaning for him would allow the man to better gauge his reactions in such situations and thereby better control his angry outbursts.

Much of psychotherapy is devoted to dissecting feelings and values and to looking at them in a new light. The result frequently is that the troubled person sees that his problems are needlessly complex because they are laden with all sorts of extra fears and emotions from the past. Until this "extra baggage" can be identified and unloaded, even simple conflicts are disproportionately difficult to handle. The purpose of psychotherapy is to help the person unload this extra baggage in the context of a supportive, helpful relation with a psychotherapist. The job sometimes takes a while, but there is no reason why problems which have been forming for years should be solved overnight.

Behavior therapy   Within the past ten to fifteen years a new set of techniques have emerged for helping people who have problems. Collectively called either *behavior therapy* or *behavior modification,* these techniques are based on the principles of learning that were described in Section 3, Part 2. As with most innovative developments, something of an evangelical enthusiasm has developed among many of the therapists who have adopted these techniques—an enthusiasm that sometimes obscures the fundamental simplicity and common sense aspects of the techniques. More moderate therapists tend to view the techniques as valuable additions to their store of tools, to be used in conjunction with more traditional methods rather than as wholly exclusive alternatives; it is this view that will guide the present discussion.

One of the major complaints about traditional psychotherapy involves the assumption that insight into one's difficulties necessarily will lead to changes in one's behavior. However, there is not much evidence to support this assumption. Rather, what often happens is that the troubled person comes to understand his problem, how it developed, and how it influences other aspects of his life, but he doesn't really learn what he can do to set things straight. This is not to say that his insight into his problem doesn't provide some degree of comfort and thereby make him happier and better able to manage his life. It is just that insight alone is not sufficient; constructive changes in what the person feels, how he thinks about things, and how he reacts to troublesome situations are the real goals of therapy, rather than insight into why these goals have been unachievable in the past. For example, it is all very well for the man in the example described above to learn that his fears about being unattractive to women and his bad temper both stem from the complexities of his childhood relation to his mother—but what next? In such cases as this, seldom is the person able to throw away his defenses and briskly stride forth to healthy sexual relations and even-temperedness. Rather, now that he understands the shortcomings of his old rules for dealing with various situations, *he has to get rid of those old rules and learn new rules.* This is where behavior therapy steps in.

Let us return to the terminology that was used in Section 3. The whole point of behavior therapy is to get rid of or alter inappropriate what-to-do ($S_1 \rightarrow R_1 \rightarrow S_2$) and what-to-expect ($S_1 \rightarrow S_2$) rules. The assumption behind behavior therapy is that in the course of the person's past experience, he or she has learned inappropriate rules for dealing with and/or predicting various situations. Thus, the solution to the person's difficulties is for him or her to learn new rules. This is done by providing planned experiences that will cause old rules to be abandoned and new rules to be acquired. But while the idea behind behavior therapy is quite simple, in actual practice it often demands a great deal of ingenuity on the part of the *behavior therapist* to plan learning experiences that will promote rapid and effective learning of new rules.

The first step in behavior therapy is to define clearly just what needs to be changed—what the present rule is, in what situations it is used (S_1), and what results (S_2) of using the rule are of sufficient positive value to the person to sustain its use in spite of the fact that it also produces negatively valued results. The methods for doing all of this essentially are the same as the first phases of traditional psychotherapy. However, instead of continuing to focus on the person's past in order to foster understanding of the origins of the unwanted behavior, as traditional psychotherapists do, the behavior therapist focuses on the person's future and begins to look for ways of changing the unwanted behavior. It is here that traditional psychotherapy and behavior therapy go their separate ways.

After the therapist and the troubled person agree on the behavior change that is the goal of therapy, the therapist lays out a plan that hopefully will achieve that goal. If the person's difficulty is very complicated or very severe, the plan often will include a series of intermediate, easily attained subgoals, each of which moves the person closer to the ultimate goal. This series of subgoals is called a *hierarchy.* Thus, if a woman wants to be more socially outgoing and more open with people, the therapist might set up a hierarchy that would help her become more open with the therapist, then with her husband, then with her whole family, then with the people she works with, then with a wider circle of friends, and so on.

The most common way of getting a person to acquire a new and appropriate rule is to *change the results* (S_2) that his old rule produces so that the rule becomes unsatisfactory. At the same time, clear-cut positive rewards are instituted for using a new rule. With this technique the old rule will be abandoned (extinguished), and the effectiveness of the new rule in producing positively valued results (reinforcement) will lead to the acquisition (learning) of the new rule. For example, if a child's rule for getting attention requires that he have a temper tantrum, the parents must stop rewarding such behavior with attention and start giving attention to their child only when he behaves in a more acceptable manner. Similarly, it has been shown that nurses often can aid in the improvement of patients who exaggerate their pain and helplessness. To do so they have to ignore the undesirable behavior and be warm and receptive when the patient remarks that he is feeling better or tries to do things for himself. In short, by making an old rule unprofitable and a new rule attractive, one can induce the person to try a new way of behaving that he might not have considered before. (See the discussion of case histories in Appendix 1 for two additional examples.)

A second way of eliminating unwanted behavior is to *change the situation* (S_1) so that the person's rule is no longer applicable. For example, some cases of childhood asthma are of a psychological rather than a physiological origin; the child, apparently unconsciously, uses his symptoms to cope with or to manipulate his parents. In such cases it often is difficult to change the rewards associated with this rule, because to do so the therapist would have to modify the parent's behavior and their reaction to the child's very severe and very real illness in addition to modifying the child's behavior. Thus, in extreme cases the most effective remedy is merely to remove the child from the situation and to send him or her to live at a school for asthmatic children. In a surprisingly large percentage of cases the asthma disappears as soon as the child gets away from the home situation.

Of course, actual physical withdrawal from the troublesome situation is appropriate only in the most difficult cases. Withdrawal can cause almost as much difficulty as the undesirable behavior itself. Unless things are pretty catastrophic, an adult with family or career responsibilities seldom is willing to pick up and move to a completely new place just to avoid a situation that evokes unwanted behavior. Fortunately, total withdrawal seldom is necessary because it often is possible to help the person see the situation in a new light so that it is *psychologically changed* for him. Because the situation has changed psychologically, his old rule becomes obsolete. This psychological change usually is brought about by having the person learn more about the situation that is causing him difficulty. Sometimes this merely requires him to get up his courage and plunge in. (Remember that the old rules often have served either to keep him out of the situation or to get him out as quickly as possible if he happened to find himself in it. As a result, he often has had little or no opportunity to check things out and see if his interpretations of the situation are correct.) Let us return to the middle-aged man we discussed a few pages back. Suppose the therapist helps him understand that his difficulties with women result from his tendency to interpret even their most innocent demands as the beginning of dominance, that is, that he is replaying his relationship with his mother. The therapist then may suggest that the man take the bull by the horns, so to speak, and have some honest discussions about his feelings with the various women he knows. The results of these discussions may well begin to show him how erroneous his interpretation has been—that reasonable demands and self-assertion on the part of both parties are a normal, non-threatening part of any relationship. With practice and the opportunity to express his feelings to women friends and to his therapist, the man may be able to revise his view of these situations and, for the most part, stop using the old rule that has always caused him to break off with a woman before a deep relationship could develop.

Sometimes things don't work out so simply. If the situation in question arouses a great deal of stress, plunging in may create more problems than it cures. Under these circumstances, behavior therapy calls upon a technique known as *desensitization therapy*. Desensitization therapy is an attempt to extinguish the anxiety that arises in the difficult situation so that the person can bring himself to enter the situation and learn that it need not be as threatening as he interprets it to be.

For example, there are students who chronically suffer extreme anxiety whenever they take an examination; they know the material, but they invariably do poorly on the exam because their anxiety interferes with their ability to concentrate. The desensitization therapy approach to this problem is based on the reasonable assumption that you can't feel both anxious and relaxed at the same time. Thus, the first step is to get the student to relax and the second is to gradually overcome his past history of anxiety in exams. The method of doing this, developed by Dr. Joseph Wolpe, consists of having the student sit in a comfortable chair and become completely relaxed. Then he starts through a hierarchy. First he is told to imagine that he is studying for an exam, then that it is the day of the exam, then that the exams have been passed out, and so on. Whenever the student begins to feel anxious, he tells the therapist, and they both work on getting him relaxed; then they return to the hierarchy and proceed until he again feels anxious. After a few such sessions, the student is able to imagine the entire exam experience without anxiety, and in the process he has learned techniques for intentionally making himself relax. Then off he goes to a real exam, and while he may not be as relaxed as he was in the therapist's office, he ordinarily will find that he can cope quite well with the exam, calling on his newly learned relaxation techniques when they are needed. (These techniques are a mild version of self-hypnosis.) Desensitization therapy reportedly has been successful for a wide variety of anxieties and phobias, including fear of culturally despised animals such as snakes and rats, fear of heights, and fear of enclosed spaces.

Thus far we have focused on psychologically changing threatening situations into nonthreatening situations. However, it is by no means uncommon to find that a person's difficulty results from his being attracted to a particular situation which leads him to do things that he or other people regard as undesirable. Examples are people who buy cigarettes, smoke them, and then bemoan their inability to stop smoking, or people who use every party as an occasion to get roaring drunk, only to repent the next day. Similar examples could be given for sexual indulgences, overuse of drugs, overeating, and a wide variety of practices that generally are regarded as "vices." As was the case for threatening situations, the behavior therapy approach to dealing with this sort of problem requires a psychological change in how the person views the situation, so that what once was attractive becomes unattractive. Or, to put it another way, a nonthreatening situation must be made threatening so the person will avoid it. The technique of behavior therapy used to convert an attractive situation into an unattractive one is called *aversion therapy.*

Aversion therapy involves formation of a new $S_1 \rightarrow S_2$ rule, S_1 being the attractive situation and S_2 an unpleasant event, through use of Pavlovian conditioning. As a result of conditioning, the unpleasant emotional aspects of S_2 come to be elicited by S_1, so that S_1 becomes unattractive and the person tends to avoid it. The formation of a new $S_1 \rightarrow S_2$ rule can be done in either of two ways. The first way, called *conditioned aversion,* requires that a person undergo training in a manner similar to what Albert underwent with the white rat and the loud noise in Section 3, Part 2. Suppose a man wants to stop drinking but feels powerless to stop himself. The behavior therapist might give the man a drug that makes him violently ill. The moment before onset of the illness the man is given a drink of liquor. After a few such liquor-illness pairings, the sight, smell, and taste of liquor may become so repulsive to the man that he will stop drinking. The method does not always work, but if the treatment is repeated over a reasonable period of time, say a year, many people lose their desire to drink. Similar results have been reported for smoking, overeating, and sexual "perversions."

The second approach to aversion therapy is called *satiation.* This requires overindulgence in the attractive situation and its accompanying behavior until the whole thing becomes unattractive. Thus, to stop smoking the person may be required to smoke four or five packages of cigarettes daily until he can't bear the sight of a cigarette.

Although both of these approaches to aversion therapy have been used successfully, behavior therapists are still searching for the most effective ways of applying them. The techniques don't yield 100 percent success, but they appear to be by far the most effective ways of dealing with a variety of unacceptable behaviors that plague so many people and that contribute to their inability to lead effective, satisfying lives.

A good deal more could be said about behavior therapy; it currently is a particularly exciting and growing area of psychology, but the foregoing discussion should give you the general idea. There is, however, one more important question: How lasting are the effects of behavior therapy? The answer is (as usual) that it depends. When the therapy involves changing the results that the old rule produces with the consequent acquisition of a new rule, continued use of the new rule depends on its continued success. For example, if the parents of the tantrum-throwing child continue to ignore the child's tantrums and reward his pleasant behavior, their child's behavior will continue to be pleasant. On the other hand, if they revert back to paying attention only to the child's tantrums, the child will fall back on his old rule.

Similarly, if a real or psychological change in a troublesome situation is maintained, the behavior will remain changed. But, for example, if the asthmatic child is later returned to his parents, the asthma may return, especially if the home situation remains the same. Or if the person who has undergone desensitization therapy to rid himself of his fear of a particular situation subsequently has a few disastrous experiences in the situation, his old rule may be reinstated. And if, after a time, the person who has undergone aversion therapy tries the liquor, cigarettes, forbidden sexual experiences, and so on, and finds them pleasurable once more, he may well re-evaluate the situation as being attractive again and revert back to his old behavior.

Surprisingly enough, in spite of the apparent ease with which it could occur, reversion back to old rules and unwanted behaviors does not happen with the frequency one might expect. It seems that the secret of success lies in being able to eliminate the undesirable behavior for a long enough time to permit the person to acquire alternative ways of behaving and to explore alternative kinds of satisfactions. Once these new behaviors and satisfactions become a customary part of the person's life, he often becomes better able to manage his own behavior so that future difficulties are more easily coped with or avoided.

Medical therapy   We turn now to medical methods for alleviating distressing behaviors such as acute anxiety, deep depression, hallucinations and delusions, unmanageable aggressiveness, and the like. These methods may be used alone or in conjunction with some form of psychotherapy or behavior therapy. The more extreme forms of medical therapy ordinarily are used only when the other forms have failed to produce the desired results.

There are three major forms of medical therapy: drug therapy, shock therapy, and psychosurgery.

DRUG THERAPY   The introduction of drug therapy in the early 1950s constituted a revolution in the treatment of many psychological problems. In fact, the introduction of drug therapy has permitted large numbers of people to leave mental hospitals and to return to relatively normal lives while being treated with drugs on an outpatient basis. No one is completely sure about how these drugs produce their effects or why different kinds of drugs produce different kinds of effects. Many of them apparently influence the transmission of neural impulses in those parts of the brain that are involved in the production and integration of emotions. Some drugs, the *tranquilizers* (such as Thorazine, Compazine, Serpasil, Miltown, or Valium), are effective in alleviating anxiety, extreme forms of overactivity associated with obsessive or compulsive behavior, aggressiveness or destructiveness, and extreme paranoia. Other drugs, the *antidepressants* (such as Tofranil or Aventyl), are used to treat depression, particularly as an early form of therapy. The general effect of an antidepressant is to reduce the person's feelings of worthlessness and guilt and to increase his activity, thereby aiding his overall adequacy and daily functioning.

Drugs do not solve the problems that lead to a person's neurotic or psychotic behavior. Rather, they produce a feeling of indifference to the problem and induce generalized relaxation without undue impairment of intellectual functioning. In cases where the problems are only temporary, drugs help the person through stressful situations with a minimum of difficulty. In other cases, release from depression, anxiety, or overactivity allows the troubled person to "get hold of himself" and become better able to face his problems. In yet other cases the troubled person may continue to take a drug as he would any other maintenance medication, checking with his physician from time to time for regulation of the dosage.

SHOCK THERAPY   There are two common forms of shock therapy, electroconvulsive shock therapy and insulin shock therapy, and no one is certain why or how either of them works. Both are used only for intensely disturbed persons for whom other forms of therapy have been unfruitful.

Electroconvulsive shock therapy consists of passing an electric current through a person's brain, thereby inducing convulsions and rendering the person unconscious for about five minutes. When he awakens, he does not remember having experienced shock; he also is temporarily dazed and confused. After a few such treatments, improvement is often seen in the person's behavior; he becomes better able to comprehend his problems and to profit from psychotherapy. This form of therapy is used primarily with people who are severely depressed, and many authorities claim that it is quite effective. About three quarters of the cases show substantial recovery after only five to ten shock treatments. Electroconvulsive shock therapy is not regarded as an effective treatment for anxiety or neurotic behavior. *Insulin shock therapy* consists of injecting insulin into the bloodstream, thereby decreasing the blood sugar level until the person goes into a coma. The coma is maintained for as long as two hours, and then glucose injections are used to bring the person out of it. When it is used, which is becoming less and less often, insulin shock therapy is limited to people with schizophrenic behavior problems. Both electroconvulsive and insulin therapy have been replaced in large part by drug therapy, and they are now used only when drugs fail to have the desired effect.

PSYCHOSURGERY   The most extreme form of medical treatment for severly disturbed people consists of surgically severing neural pathways between the front part of the brain (behind the forehead) and the brain centers that are involved with emotions. Such an operation, called a *lobotomy*, is used only when all else has failed. It is effective in alleviating the distress associated with extremely acute tension, agitation, depression, aggressiveness, and excited impulsiveness. Immediately after psychosurgery, the troubled person is usually confused, in a stupor, indifferent to his surroundings, and generally out of touch with what is going on around him. Later, he may become more aware of what is going on and even begin to show fairly acceptable social behavior. In some cases, the person apparently becomes quite normal and is capable of working and living a useful life. In other cases, however, there are permanent personality changes; the person becomes calm but he lacks inhibitions, and as a result he may say or do other things that are socially unacceptable. He may be confused and generally fail to care much about anything or anyone. Of course, this new personality, however awkward it might be, is usually an improvement over the old, profoundly debilitating one. Even at that, however, the radical and nonreversible nature of this form of therapy makes it suitable only as a last resort.

SUMMARY: 1   As we grow, we learn that various states of affairs are desirable and "the way things ought to be." These notions are called our *values*. When circumstances are grossly different from our idea of how things should be (that is, they *conflict* with our values), we experience *stress*. A person's characteristic ways of dealing with conflict and stress constitute his *personality*.

2   There are three *basic strategies* for dealing with conflict and stress: (1) *changing the unsatisfactory situation*, (2) *withdrawing from the situation*, and (3) *changing one's values* so that the situation no longer is in conflict with them. The third strategy is the most difficult and the most painful one to use—most of us much prefer to use strategies 1 and 2 than to resort to strategy 3.

3   Sometimes stressful situations arise for which strategies 1 and 2 will not work. These situations, called "crises" are often major events in a person's life, for example, death of a friend or family member, divorce, loss of a job. When confronted with a crisis, people often refuse to "face the facts" (that is, they refuse to reconcile their values with reality). Instead, they resort to futile attempts to use strategies 1 and 2. These attempts often consist of trying to produce changes when none can be made, trying to change situations that are not the actual source of conflict, trying to escape when no escape is possible— often by denying that any conflict exists. All of these tactics are known as *ego defense mechanisms*.

4   When one or more ego defense mechanisms become a permanent part of one's life, they are called *neurotic behavior*. The problem with neurotic behavior is that it often leads to the *neurotic trap*, in which the neurotic behavior begins to alienate people, thereby compounding the person's problems. To cope with the new stress, the neurotic person may intensify his neurotic behavior, thereby making things even worse.

5   *Psychotic behavior* may well represent a person's attempts to deal with physiological changes in his body that are not understood either by him or by medicine. The person has no control over what he is experiencing and sees no apparent cause for it; the psychotic behavior we witness is a desperate attempt on the person's part to deal with his immense crisis. However, this view is merely a hypothesis; research has yet to prove or disprove it.

6   When we get deeply embroiled in conflict and the attendant ego defense mechanisms, we often need help to get straightened out. A trusted family member or friend may be of help, but sometimes professional help is necessary because our family and friends often are part of the conflict in the first place. Professional help can be obtained from counselors, psychiatrists, and psychologists who use such procedures as *psychotherapy, behavior therapy,* and *medical therapy.*

Special Topic   Section 6, Part 5: *Drugs and the Drug Experience*

Further Reading

AXLINE, V. M.   *Dibs in Search of Self*
New York: Ballantine, 1969 (c. 1964), 220 pages (paperback).
This is the story of a withdrawn five-year-old boy who undergoes therapy and eventually is helped. It includes detailed descriptions of his behavior and his therapy experiences. Suspected of being mentally retarded, Dibs was actually an extremely bright boy, and this book follows his search to find himself.

ELLIS, A., and R. A. HARPER.   *A Guide to Rational Living*
North Hollywood, Calif.: Wilshire, 1961, 195 pages (paperback).
Albert Ellis has long held the view that many of our problems in life result from telling ourselves irrational things about what will or will not happen if we do such and such. He claims that we usually exaggerate the seriousness of the consequences of honestly expressing our feelings and opinions and thereby bottle ourselves up. This book is a practical guide for self-debunking one's exaggerations.

ERIKSON, E. H.   *Identity: Youth and Crisis*
New York: Norton, 1968, 336 pages.
Each chapter in this book is a revision of one of Erikson's major essays. Discussions focus on the life cycle and the conflicts one faces from birth to old age, the problems of identity, confusion and negative identity, and the theoretical aspects of the concept of "the ego." The book concludes with three short chapters that deal with the identity problems of contemporary youth, women, and races.

FROMM, E.   *Escape from Freedom*
New York: Avon, 1965, 333 pages (paperback).
An interesting analysis of modern man and freedom written by a well-known psychoanalyst. The book revolves around the idea that modern man is anxious and isolated and is tempted to surrender his freedom to dictators of all kinds or lose it by transforming himself into a well-fed and well-clothed automaton. The question is whether man can advance to the full realization of positive freedom based upon his uniqueness and individuality.

GINOTT, H.   *Between Parent and Child*
New York: Avon, 1969 (c. 1965), 252 pages (paperback).
Although this is a book about how parents can "get through to their children," it also can help adults to communicate better with other adults. Extremely readable and filled with interesting examples of daily parent-child crises and how to handle them. Ginott's subsequent books on communication problems are:

GINOTT, H.   *Between Parent and Teenager*
New York: Avon Books, 1971 (c. 1969), 255 pages (paperback).

GINOTT, H.   *Teacher and Child*
New York: Macmillan, 1972, 323 pages.

GREEN, H. *I Never Promised You a Rose Garden*
New York: Signet, 1964, 256 pages (paperback).
A novel about a sixteen-year-old psychotic girl's three years in a mental hospital. Green's vivid descriptions of the girl's behavior, inner thinking and struggles, and treatment give some insight into the complexity of a psychotic and how she views her life in a mental hospital.

GUSTAITIS, RASA. *Turning On*
New York: New American Library, 1970 (c. 1969), 288 pages (paperback).
The author takes the reader on an odyssey through such topics as encounter groups, sensory awareness, drugs, Zen meditation, communal living, and brain wave control. An interesting and readable book that does not bog down in details.

HALL, C. S. *A Primer of Freudian Psychology*
New York: Mentor, 1954, 127 pages (paperback).
A concise and readable presentation of Sigmund Freud's theories about the organization, dynamics, and development of personality. Includes a discussion of the id, ego, and superego, anxiety and defense mechanisms, and the psychosexual stages of personality development. A good introduction to Freud.

HALL, C. S., and G. LINDZEY. *Theories of Personality* (2d ed.)
New York: Wiley, 1970, 622 pages.
A comprehensive review of the major theories of personality. Fairly technical.

KÜBLER-ROSS, E. *On Death and Dying*
New York: Macmillan, 1970 (c. 1969), 289 pages (paperback).
A fascinating study of how the terminally ill (and their families and physicians) face the major crisis of life—death. The author discusses people's attitudes toward death and gives suggestions about how to help the terminally ill patient when he finds out he is soon to die.

MANN, J. *Encounter: A Weekend with Intimate Strangers*
New York: Pocket Books, 1971 (c. 1970), 208 pages (paperback).
This is a transcript of what happened in an encounter group involving thirteen strangers. It is an interesting exercise to read about their experiences and then to analyze what happened using the guidelines laid down in Carl Rogers' *On Encounter Groups* (listed below).

MASLOW, A. H. *Toward a Psychology of Being*
New York: Van Nostrand Reinhold, 1968, 240 pages (paperback).
Maslow believes that human beings can be loving, noble, and creative and that they are capable of pursuing the highest values and aspirations. Therefore, a major goal of psychology should be to help the individual move toward positive human fulfillment, or "self-actualization"; the book is a blueprint for reaching that goal.

MEHRABIAN, A. *Tactics of Social Influence*
Englewood Cliffs, N.J.: Prentice-Hall, 1970, 152 pages (paperback).
A concise introduction to the principles of behavior modification. The reader is shown

the procedures used to cope with phobias, poor work habits, bad habits in general, and childrens' undesirable behavior.

PERLS, F. S.   *Gestalt Therapy Verbatim*
Lafayette, Calif.: Real People Press, 1969, 279 pages (paperback).
Fritz Perls was a legend in his own lifetime. An overbearing, zestful man who thoroughly enjoyed his own life, he tried to teach other people to enjoy theirs. The first part of this book is his theory about living and about how psychotherapy should be done. The second part of the book consists of examples of therapy, particularly dream analysis. (Frankly, I really like the first part, but the second part leaves me cold.)

ROGERS, C. R.   *On Becoming a Person*
Boston: Houghton Mifflin, 1961, 420 pages (paperback).
This is one of the most interesting books in the psychological literature. Prefaced on the assumption that people can be happy only when they understand and accept themselves and take responsibility for their own lives, this book represents a view that is having an increasingly strong effect on modern personality theory and psychotherapy techniques; much of the rationale of current encounter groups derives from this view.

ROGERS, C. R.   *On Encounter Groups*
New York: Harper & Row, 1970, 172 pages (paperback).
This book deals primarily with what an encounter group is, what really goes on in groups, and the experiences individuals have in groups. Research on encounter groups and the future of the group movement also are discussed.

RUBIN, T. I.   *The Angry Book*
New York: Macmillan, 1970 (c. 1969), 223 pages (paperback).
Rubin, like many other psychotherapists, regards the repression of anger as a common source of many psychological problems (for example, anxiety, depression, insomnia, psychosomatic disorders, alcoholism). In this book he explores ways of recognizing repressed anger and ways of expressing it in an honest, nonharmful manner. People who pride themselves on never losing their temper should read this book.

TOFFLER, A.   *Future Shock*
New York: Bantam, 1971 (c. 1970), 561 pages (paperback).
Future shock supposedly is a psychobiological symptom of change that may become a major crisis in today's world. With the use of numerous insightful examples of how transience and change have already penetrated our lives, Toffler discusses his concept of future shock in the hope that by making us more aware of it we will be better able to meet and deal with it.

WHITE, R. W.   *The Abnormal Personality* (3d ed.)
New York: Ronald, 1964, 619 pages.
A comprehensive yet readable textbook that contains a review of traditional personality theory, neurotic and psychotic disturbances, and the various forms of psychological treatment. Interesting to read because of its many illustrations taken from case histories.

WHITE, R. W.   *Lives in Progress* (2d ed.)
New York: Holt, Rinehart and Winston, 1966, 422 pages (paperback).
Using long-term life histories of three normal people as illustrative vehicles, White discusses the multitude of forces that shape an individual's personality. This book gives the reader a detailed view of how three different people developed and matured as they grew up, how they managed their lives, and the way they learned to deal with their problems.

Doisneau from Rapho Guillumette

Special Topics

SIX

Part 1 *LANGUAGE*

Language is, first of all, a set of fairly complex rules about how to communicate something to someone. In any community of speakers of a language, there are shared understandings about what are and what are not proper rules; "I ain't got none" is scorned in some English-speaking circles and regarded as perfectly acceptable in others. Consider the problem of a child born into a particular language-speaking group. Beginning with no language rules at all, he gradually formulates a set of rules corresponding to those used by the people around him. On the surface at least, the child's task is similar to that of a scientist who sets out to discover the laws of some natural phenomenon: he begins in ignorance, he formulates a simple, rough theory on the basis of informal observations, and then he tests hypotheses derived from his theory, making changes when parts of his theory are not supported and retaining and elaborating the parts that are supported. In short, both the child and the scientist strive to make their theories correspond to some existing external set of rules that are as yet unknown to them. The set the child tries to match are the rules of the language that he hears spoken all around him, while the set the scientist tries to match are the rules that govern the workings of the phenomenon in which he is interested.

The Nature of Language

Language can be analyzed in a number of different ways, and it is not yet clear which approach serves best for the study of how people acquire language. Dr. Noam Chomsky's transformational grammar, however, is currently favored by many psychologists, and, therefore, the following discussion, in general, is cast in his terms.

All languages have four major components, *deep structure, surface structure, grammar,* and *vocabulary.* The deep structure of a language is related to the meaning of the message to be communicated. A variety of differently worded sentences can convey the deep structure, each sentence being an acceptable replacement for the others and all having essentially the same underlying meaning. For example, take the sentences "The boy hit the ball" and "The ball was hit by the boy." These sentences, each consisting of different words and word orderings but still conveying the same meaning, constitute the surface structure of the communication (Fig. 6.1). The set of rules by which surface structure (sentences) is generated from deep structure is called the grammar of the language, and the words (patterns of sounds or written symbols) that are the vehicle for the surface structure are the vocabulary of the language.

While vocabulary is crucial to acquisition and use of language, the grammar is the central mechanism of a language. It is the rules that tell you how to go from deep structure to surface structure, thereby producing communicable sentences. By the same token, grammar tells you how to "decode" a sentence that you receive from someone else, that is, how to go from the surface structure of the received sentence to the meaning the other person is trying to communicate to you.

This is not the place to present an exposition of the complex rules of

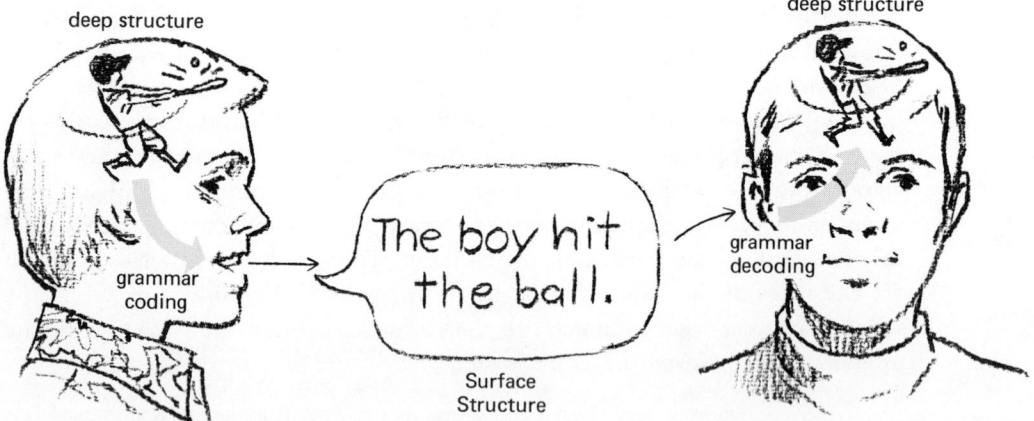

FIG. 6.1   *Use of language to communicate requires the sender to use grammar to transform (code) deep structure into a sentence that has a proper surface structure. The receiver then uses the same grammar to transform (decode) the sentence back into deep structure so that he can understand what was communicated.*

(1) IFYAJIGGLEITALITTLEIT'LLWORK
(2) HOWSABOUTACUPPATEA?
(3) JAEATJET?
(4) ELLAMENOPEA
(5) WANNAWAITASEC?
(6) YAWANNABITE?
(7) DIDDYGWUP?

FIG. 6.2 *People who are fluent in a language can tell where the words in sentences end and begin even though the speaker may run the words together and even mispronounce them. Read the phrases that are listed above to a friend and see if he or she can tell you what the words are. The answers: (1) If you jiggle it a little it will work. (2) How about a cup of tea? (3) Did you eat yet? (4) L, M, N, O, P. (5) Want to wait a sec? (6) You want a bite? (7) Did he go up?*

grammar. Strangely, while most people would find it difficult to state clearly the grammatical rules that people use (indeed, the whole science of *linguistics* is dedicated to this task), everybody in the world "knows" the grammar of his own language, even though we seldom recognize that we know it. You are no exception, as the following exercise will demonstrate. Construct a descriptive phrase using the words (1) "houses," (2) "the," (3) "red," (4) "little," and (5) "two." Most people begin with "the," followed by "two," then "little," then "red," then "houses." We all agree on a set of rules for the order in which articles, modifiers, and nouns should be arranged in English—that is, articles, number, size, color, and noun, and we knew this order before we ever studied English grammar in school. This is a superficial example, of course, since most grammatical rules are much more complex, but it demonstrates the point that you know grammar. Although the rules for English are not ironclad and vary a bit from person to person and from one community to another, they are general enough so that most of us can automatically produce and understand sentences without paying much attention to the grammar involved.

Acquisition of Language

Language is a universal aspect of mankind. Virtually all human beings speak one or more languages with at least some facility, and nearly all live in a world that is flooded with talk. This universality of language raises two important questions: (1) Why don't we all speak the same language? and (2) How do children acquire the language that is spoken in the community in which they live?

The Same Language?   To some degree we all do speak the same language, but let me quickly qualify this statement. The amazing diversity among languages on the earth suggests that all languages are quite different. However, recent findings in linguistics indicate that the *grammars* of all languages are fairly similar in their general form, if not in their specific rules.

Consider a Frenchman, an Englishman, and a Japanese (all grandsons of a Roving Ambassador with a roving eye), each wishing to communicate the same deep structure—the location of their mutual aunt's fountain pen. The Frenchman would consider the pen's location and, using French grammar, would produce a sentence with the proper French surface structure: *La plume de ma tante est sur la table* (literally, "The pen of my aunt is on the table"). The Englishman would do the same thing, except that his English grammar would yield a sentence with a different surface structure: "My aunt's pen is on the table." The Japanese would construct yet another surface structure: *Tsukue no ue ni watashi no obasan no mannen hitsu ga arimasu* (literally, "The table top on my aunt of fountain pen is existing").

While each of these sentences looks and sounds different, the difference is more superficial than it first appears because analysis of the grammars of different languages shows that their grammars are very similar in *form.* That is, while they are not exactly the same from language to language, similar *kinds of rules* are used to turn deep structure (meaning) into surface structure (written or spoken sentences). It is rather like chess and checkers; although the specific rules of these games are different, there is a similarity in the form of the rules for both games. The rules for each game dictate the direction and length of movement, define a player's turn, determine what constitutes a win, and so forth. Thus, even though the two games do not have identical rules, each has a rule that fits into each of the general categories just described, and therefore the games are more similar than they may at first appear. Upon analysis, languages that appear to be dissimilar turn out to have rules in their grammars that are similar in form, thus revealing that human languages have more in common than one might think.

It is clear from these linguistic analyses of human languages that the grammars that actually exist are only a small proportion of the grammars that could possibly exist. That is, if a computer were programed to generate different kinds of grammars, it could generate a far greater range of languages than are actually used by human beings. This possibility, together with the fact of the universality of language and the finding that rules are similar among existing grammars, suggests the intriguing idea that there are *predispositional* (Section 3, Part 2) tendencies for human beings to acquire language, with predispositional constraints upon the kinds of rules that the grammars can have. In short, it may be that the acquisition of language represents a prime example of the predispositional origin of rules that scientists are beginning to suspect underlies a great deal of the behavior that is regarded as universal among human beings.

Acquisition of Language

Even if we tentatively accept the hypothesis that human beings are predisposed to acquire language, learning, imitation, and intellect still play clear roles in the acquisition of language. It is the interplay among all four of these origins of rules that produces the final product—an adult who is proficient with the language of his own group.

Language is most easily acquired in early childhood (another bit of evidence for the predispositional hypothesis). As the child becomes an adult, language becomes more and more difficult to acquire—witness the difficulty high school and college students experience when they try to learn a foreign language. The prime years for language development are between about one and a half and four years of age.

The early stages of language acquisition focus on the rudiments of vocabulary, which is possibly acquired through instrumental learning and imitation. The child babbles something that approximates a word or imitates his parents and they beam with joy and reward him with attention. While learning and imitation may be of importance in vocabulary acquisition, the evidence is clear that neither of them are central to the child's development of grammar. Grammar development, rather than being a result of learned rules, is the result of intellectual rule formulation.

The way in which parents administer reinforcement to their children's verbal utterances is good evidence against the notion that instrumental learning plays an important role in grammar acquisition. Examination of how parents react to their children's utterances shows that they seldom react to the *way* in which something is said; rather, they react to the *validity* of what is said. Thus, if a child were to say, "Sesmie Street at seben o'clock," his mother might reply, "No, at five," focusing on the factual error instead of correcting or negatively reinforcing the child's pronunciation and grammar. (Please be patient with my attempt to write baby talk; I've never tried it before.) If instrumental learning were wholly responsible for acquisition of language, we should expect human beings to be very truthful but unable to speak properly. As you have perhaps observed, the reverse is more commonly the case.

Just as instrumental learning cannot account for grammar acquisition, recent evidence that shows that children actively develop and use their theories of grammar and that they refine these theories as they mature makes it clear that mere imitation also is an inadequate explanation for grammar acquisition. We will review here some of the more outstanding aspects of this interesting evidence.

Beginnings of grammar   Grammar develops as the child begins to formulate and use simple rules to meet his need to communicate with other people. At first, he uses single words, primary among them being the word "No!"—a word that he hears frequently and that often is immensely effective in changing the behavior of the people around him. Then he begins to progress to two-word combinations. These consist of a small set of *pivot words* (often the ones he has been using singly) that can be paired with *open class words* to convey various meanings. Pivot words are words like "allgone," "bye-bye," "more," "see." Open class words are a miscellaneous set that represent the objects and people that are part of the child's life, for example, "boy," "boat," "milk," "Mommy," "Daddy." By pairing a pivot word with an open class word—"allgone milk," "allgone boat," "bye-bye Daddy"—the child begins to have greater versatility and freedom and is on his way to acquiring grammar.

Use of grammar   Use of grammar is revealed first of all by the fact that children seldom use nonsensical sentences. They may say, "That a green doggy," which while not likely to be true, certainly is not the sheer nonsense that "Green a that doggy" is. Second, when imitating what an adult has said, children will usually translate what they hear into their own grammar rather than repeat exactly what they hear (unless they are coached). For example, if a young child were to hear his mother say, "No, you can't color on the wall," he might come up with an imitation like, "color wall," because he is not yet able to deal with negatives, prepositions, long sentences, and so on. Thus, at any given time, a child's imitative speech is seldom more complex than his self-produced speech.

Further evidence that grammar governs their speech is the ability of children to form plurals and past tenses of words they have never heard before. For example, show a child a picture of an unfamiliar cartoon creature and say, "This is a wug." Then show him a picture that has two of the same creatures in it and say, "Now there are two——," and he will say, "wugs!" (Fig. 6.3). Although he has never heard the plural of "wug" as a name for such creatures, by applying his own rules of grammar he can generate the appropriate plural.

Say to a child, "This is a man who knows how to gling. He glings every day. Today he glings. Yesterday he——," and the child will reply "glinged!" That is, he applies his rule for forming the past tense of regular verbs to the

FIG. 6.3   *If a child is shown the single figure and told that it is a "wug" and is then shown the two figures and asked to fill in the blank of "now there are two _____," he will answer "wugs." This reveals that the child is applying a rule for creating plurals to a word he probably has never heard before. (From J. Berko, The child's learning of English morphology, Word, Vol. 14, 1958, p. 154.)*

unfamiliar word "gling." This is strong evidence for use of grammar rather than mere imitation, because adults in this situation usually say "glang" or "glung" rather than "glinged." Thus, even if the child had before come across the word "gling," it is unlikely that he heard an adult state its past tense as "glinged." Clearly, then, the child must not merely be imitating someone when he generates his answer to the question.

Revision   The conclusion that children are constantly revising their grammars is evident from the fact that as they grow older, their spoken language shows obvious, consistent rule changes, even though not all the changes appear to be clear-cut progress toward adult grammar. For example, children usually begin to use the various tenses of irregular verbs before they begin to use the tenses of regular verbs.[1] But as soon as they develop rules for regular verb endings, they often go through a phase in which they apply the rules for regular verb endings to irregular verbs. Thus, after correctly using "came" as the past tense of "come" for a period, the child develops rules for the tenses of regular verbs, such as adding "-ed" to make the past tense, and begins to say "comed" instead of "came." This phase soon passes, but it indicates that the child is relying on a set of rules for generating his own speech rather than merely relying on imitation—he probably never heard an adult say "comed."

Another example of a consistent change in a child's grammar as he grows is the change in the way he asks questions. At first, his questions consist of short declarative statements with a slight rise in intonation at the end. Thus, the difference between "he go!" and "he go?" lies in whether the child's voice rises slightly on the word "go." Later, the child begins to add interrogative words such as "where" or "what" to his sentences in order to form questions (for example, "Where he go?"). Finally, auxiliary verbs are added to make a well-formed question ("Where did he go?"). These orderly changes in the child's method of producing questions are further evidence that he is indeed using rules rather than merely imitating what he hears.

When we speak of a child's grammar becoming progressively similar to adult grammar, we must keep in mind that there are many different adult grammars. The adult grammars, called *dialects*, used by various ethnic, social, and racial subgroups in our culture often differ a great deal from the kind of grammar that is taught in the schools. It is important to remember that, at least from a psychological point of view, one adult grammar is as good as another in that the child's progress toward his parents' grammar is the point of interest, not whether or not he comes to speak Public School Standard English. If you can look at grammars and language in an objective manner, you can begin to appreciate the fact that each dialect is really a language in and of itself, and that while people may "speak poor English," they may also be masters at speaking their own particular version of the English language.

---

[1] Irregular verbs have different words for each tense ("I am," "I was," "I will be") while the tenses of regular verbs are formed by adding regular endings ("I walk," "I walked," "I will walk").

BOX 6.1

"Talking" Chimpanzees

In the fantasy world of literature there have been many human beings who could talk with animals—Rudyard Kipling's Mowgli, Edgar Rice Burroughs' Tarzan, and Hugh Lofting's Dr. Doolittle, to name only a few. In these stories, a gifted person has learned to comprehend the animal's language. Psychologists, on the other hand, while being concerned with whether we can ever have two-way communication with animals, have approached the question the other way: Can animals learn to use human language? (Obviously, pets sometimes learn to recognize specific words and birds can be taught to imitate human speech, but none of these animals use human language as a tool for expressing themselves, for conveying information.) Chimpanzees are the most logical first choice to try to teach language to because they are generally regarded as the animal that biologically, psychologically, and intellectually most resembles human beings.

Early attempts to teach human language to chimpanzees were largely unsuccessful because the investigators tried to get the chimpanzees to imitate the vocalizations of human speech. In the first such study, Dr. and Mrs. Winthrop Kellogg raised a baby female chimpanzee named Gua in their home for nine

Memory and Language

So far, I have restricted this discussion to the acquisition of the rules of language and how the process relates to the rule origins discussed in Section 3. However, if you'll recall, memory also is discussed in Section 3. So, to tie things up in a neat package, let's turn now to some of the recent research findings about how language-encoded messages and words are stored in and retrieved from memory.

Remember that the message of a sentence has two levels, deep structure (meaning) and surface structure (the sentence itself). Which level is stored in memory? Do we store meaning or do we store the sentence verbatim?

The results of studies by Dr. P. H. Kolers at Harvard University and by Dr. S. Bobrow at Stanford University suggest answers to these questions. Dr. Kolers studied bilingual people, people who speak two languages fluently and who often have two very different words, one in each language, to represent the same meaning. Thus, someone who speaks both Spanish and English could speak of his *miedo*, or his "fear," his *sabiduria*, or his "wisdom," his *mesa*, or his "table." Use of this and a second interesting phenomenon enabled Dr. Kolers to examine language storage and memory. This second phenomenon is that when someone memorizes a long list of equally familiar words, he can recall most easily those words that occur more than once on the list. That is,

months, treating her just as they treated their infant son Donald.* While their major goal was to compare the physical development of an infant chimpanzee with that of a human infant, in the course of things they made an effort to teach Gua to speak. The part of the study dealing with development was quite informative, but the effort to teach Gua to speak was completely unsuccessful.

A few years later, Dr. and Mrs. Keith Hayes raised a female chimpanzee named Viki in their home.* They put much more effort into teaching Viki to speak than the Kelloggs had, but they too were largely unsuccessful. After several years of intensive effort, Viki was able to say only four words ("mama," "papa," "cup," and "up"), and, since she spoke very softly and inarticulately, one could not always be sure just which of the four words she was saying.

The first major success in teaching a chimpanzee some form of human language was accomplished by Dr. Charles Ferster, who, in an attempt to analyze the development of language and verbal behavior, taught chimpanzees the language of mathematics.† His chimpanzees were two three-year-olds named Margie and

---

*B. Ford, How they taught a chimp to talk. *Science Digest*, 1970, **67**, 10–17.
†C. B. Ferster, Arithmetic behavior in chimpanzees. *Scientific American*, 1964, **210**, 98–106.

if a word occurs two times on a list, it is roughly twice as likely to be recalled as a word that occurs only once.

Dr. Kolers constructed lists using words from two different languages and asked bilingual people to memorize the lists. Then he had the people recall the words. The important thing is that some meanings were repeated in both languages. Thus, while the words "pain," "fear," and *miedo* (Spanish for "fear") might each occur only once on a list, the fear-meaning would occur twice as often as the pain-meaning. If people code language only in terms of surface structure, all three words should be recalled with equal ease, since each word occurs only once on the list. On the other hand, if people code language in terms of deep structure, then "fear" and *miedo* should be easier to recall than "pain." The latter is what happened in the experiment, indicating that memory coding occurred primarily in terms of deep structure or meaning.

Dr. Bobrow's research findings indicate that the role of meaning in memory storage and recall is not limited to the memorization of lists of words. Dr. Bobrow studied the ability of students to recall words they had seen in English sentences. The logic behind the study was much the same as that used by Dr. Kolers. The students were shown a number of pairs of sentences, both containing the same noun and object, and later they were given the nouns and were asked to recall the objects. In some of the sentence pairs, the nouns

Dennis. Using the binary number system (black and white circles served as the digits 0 and 1, respectively), Dr. Ferster taught the chimpanzees to count and to signify their answers by choosing the appropriate binary symbols. For example, when six objects were present, Margie and Dennis learned to choose OO● (which is the binary symbol for 6) rather than, say, ●●O (which is the binary number for 2). The training, however, was laborious, time consuming, and not very successful; after more than 200 training sessions and 500,000 attempts at counting, Margie and Dennis learned to match the correct binary numbers to only 1 through 7 objects. And it was only after an additional 150 training sessions and 170,000 attempts that they learned to identify accurately up to 7 objects by manipulating ●'s and O's to write the appropriate binary symbol. This is as far as the experiment went. Maybe with more training the animals could have learned to count further, but, at any rate, this experiment showed that with a great deal of training, chimpanzees at least are capable of learning to use symbolic representation, however elementary it may be.

Recently, Dr. Philip Lieberman showed that chimpanzees probably will *never* be able to learn to talk like human beings because the musculature of their throats, mouths, and lips is such that they cannot produce the sounds necessary for human

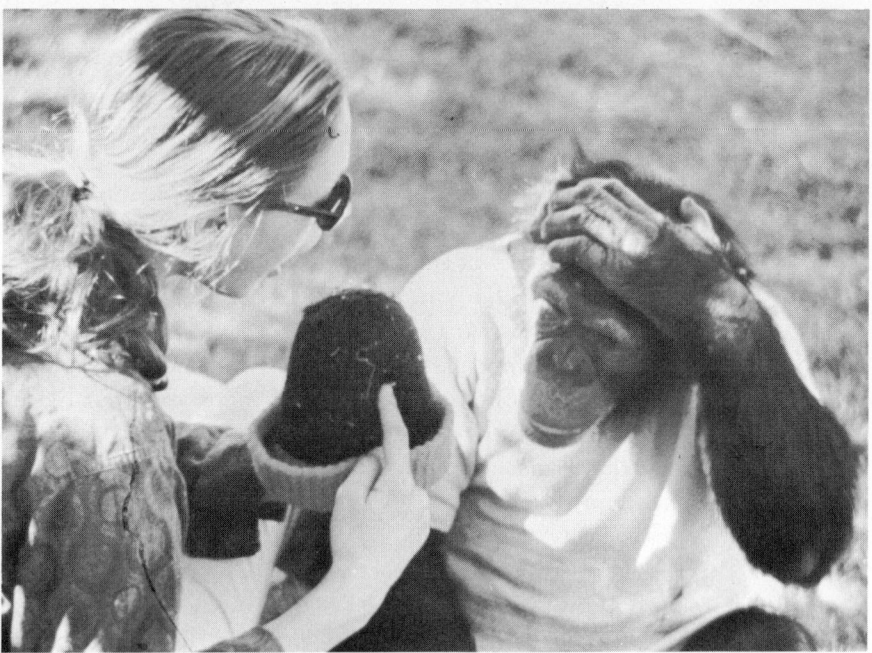

FIG. 6.4 *Washoe using the American Sign Language (ASL) sign for "hat" to name a woolen cap. (See Box 6.1.) (Photo courtesy Drs. Allen and Beatrice Gardner.)*

speech.‡ This finding has given rise to two alternative approaches to teaching language to chimpanzees, both of which have proved successful. These experiments utilized nonvocal behaviors that are part of the natural capacities of chimpanzees. In one investigation, Drs. Allen and Beatrice Gardner raised a female chimpanzee, Washoe, in their home and taught her the American Sign Language (ASL) that is used by deaf persons.§ Relying on such techniques as imitation, encouragement of "babbling" (that is, any form of hand movement), constant use of sign language when around Washoe, instrumental learning (the major reinforcement was to tickle her), and shaping, the Gardners were able to teach Washoe 30 "words" by the end of 22 months of work. What is more, Washoe used these words spontaneously and appropriately, correctly naming pictures of objects as well as the actual objects themselves (for example, dog, flower, hat, toothbrush). She was also able to construct her own combinations of individual signs such as "gimmie-tickle" or "open-food-drink." Later reports indicated that as a result of continued training and experience, Washoe had acquired a vocabulary of 175 words by age seven and that she spontaneously noted anything that interested her; for example, one day while walking with a human friend, a plane flew over and Washoe signed to her friend, "You-me-ride-plane."

Adopting the Gardner's technique, researchers at the University of Oklahoma

‡P. Lieberman, Primate vocalizations and human linguistic ability. *Journal of the Acoustical Society of America,* 1968, **44,** 1574–1584.
§R. A. and B. T. Gardner, Teaching sign language to a chimpanzee. *Science,* 1969, **165,** 664–672.

and objects had the same meaning, for example, "The dog's bark frightened the baseball pitcher" and "The animal's bark scared the big league pitcher." In other pairs of sentences, the nouns and objects had different meanings, for example, "The pine board shored the river bank" and "The securities board shut the mismanaged bank."

In the first pair of sentences, the meanings of "bark" and "pitcher" are the same in both sentences, and therefore occur twice as often as each of the two different meanings of "board" and "bank" in the second pair of sentences. Thus, if meaning is the key to storage and recall, people should recall "pitcher" when they are asked to give the object associated with "bark" about twice as easily as they should recall "bank" when they are asked to give the object of "board." That is exactly what happened. In short, both Dr. Kolers' and Dr. Bobrow's research suggests that memory is keyed to the deep structure of language rather than to the surface structure. Remember from our discussion of the factors that facilitate memory storage and recall in Section 3 that this is precisely the conclusion that other evidence points to.

under the direction of Dr. William Lemmon currently are teaching six chimpanzees to communicate using ASL.¶ One of their chimpanzees, Lucy, has learned 60 words so far, and besides spontaneously identifying objects, she also can answer questions with simple two- or three-word phrases. Lucy learns about 12 signs a month. And, amazingly enough, the youngest chimpanzee in the group (Salome), four months old, already knows two words—"drink" and "food." One wonders if the end result of this investigation will be a group of chimpanzees who will be able to communicate with human beings and with each other in ASL, whether they will invent new signs, and whether they will teach ASL to less sophisticated chimpanzees and to their own future offspring.

In the second successful experiment, Dr. David Premack took a rather different approach.‖ Instead of using hand gestures (signs) to represent words, he used plastic symbols of various shapes and colors, for example, a blue triangle represented an apple, a green M represented the name Mary, and so on. Using instrumental learning techniques, Dr. Premack taught a six-year-old female chimpanzee named Sarah to use these plastic symbols, not only to name objects, answer questions, and express negations but also to understand such general class concepts as color, shape, and fruit. In addition, Sarah learned to form plurals of words as well as longer sentences such as "Sarah insert (the) banana (in the) pail (and

¶Conversations with a chimp. *Life*, 1972, **72**, 55–60.
‖ D. PREMACK, The education of Sarah. *Psychology Today*, 1970, **4**, 54–58; Language in chimpanzees. *Science*, 1971, **172**, 808–822.

You can prove to yourself that coding in memory primarily revolves around meaning. Think back to a poem that you memorized when you were a child. Although you probably cannot recall very many specific lines in the poem, you can remember what the poem generally was about. That is, you remember the meaning. Similarly, you seldom remember specifically what was said in a conversation, but you do remember what it was all about. Of course, this is not to say that surface structure is never retained in memory. Almost any child can reel off the surface structure of the Pledge of Allegiance to the Flag even if he has virtually no understanding of its deep structure, and all of us occasionally are able to recall names of people upon meeting them again years after we've known them. But precise recall of such surface structure is uncommon. It is most likely that deep structure is more readily stored and recalled. But how is it coded in memory if not in words? Think about it; the answer is really quite a mystery. Indeed, this may be the next puzzle for memory research to try to solve.

the) apple (in the) dish." Most important, Sarah ascribes the properties of the object itself to the plastic symbol; for example, when shown a blue triangle (the symbol for an apple) and asked to choose between the alternatives red or green and round or square, Sarah chose red and round, the same alternatives she chooses when she sees a real apple. Latest reports indicate that so far Sarah has acquired a vocabularly of 120 words.

In summary, chimpanzees are capable of learning at least rudimentary human language. Although their throats, mouths, and lips are not suited to humanlike vocalizations, when alternatives such as sign language or manipulable symbols are provided, language learning progresses, however slowly. Moreover, after a reasonable vocabulary has been acquired, chimpanzees are capable of constructing original phrases or sentences and of expressing things that are unique, that is, things they were not specifically taught to say. In the books, Tarzan learned Cheta's language. In reality, chimpanzees are doing a better job of understanding our language than we are of understanding theirs.

SUMMARY

1   All human languages are similar in that they employ basically similar grammars to generate sentences. This similarity among human languages suggests that human beings have a predisposition to develop and use language.

2   Language apparently develops primarily as a result of the child being immersed in it, as it were, and inferring its rules from what he hears. The result is a childish grammar that, with time and practice, comes to be like the grammar of the language he hears the adults around him speak. While learned and imitated rules play an important role in the development of vocabulary, intellectual rules are the primary basis for the development of grammar.

3   Language plays an important role in memory, in that the meaning aspects of language (deep structure) are used in storage and recall of information.

Further Reading

BROWN, R.   *Words and Things*
New York: Free Press, 1968 (c. 1958), 398 pages (paperback).
Brown interrelates linguistic, anthropological, and psychological ideas concerning language. The book begins with the history of a wild boy found in France in 1797 who could not speak or understand language; frequent reference to this case history is made throughout the book to illustrate various points. The discussion covers topics on the meaning of words, reading, animal communication, language and psychopathology, and propaganda.

CHUKOVSKY, K.   *From Two to Five* (Translated by M. Morton)
Berkeley: University of California Press, 1968, 170 pages (paperback).
A fascinating discussion of the language, thought processes, and imagination of the

very young, written by a well-known Russian author of books for children. Chukovsky sees the young child as a linguistic genius—creative and poetic. Full of examples of preschool children's utterances.

DALE, P. S.   *Language Development: Structure and Function*
Hinsdale, Ill.: Dryden, 1972 (paperback).
An interesting, well-written introduction to how children learn to understand and speak the language of their culture. Many good, clear examples and simple explanations.

FURTH, H. G.   *Thinking without Language*
New York: Free Press, 1966, 236 pages.
An investigation into the relations among thinking, intelligence, and language through comparisons of the performance of both normal-hearing and deaf people in such areas as linguistic skill, concept attainment, perception, memory, and Piaget-type tasks. This book suggests that it may be fruitful to use a nonverbal approach to the study of thinking processes in general and concludes with a very interesting chapter on the education of the deaf.

LENNEBERG, E. H.   *Biological Foundations of Language*
New York: Wiley, 1967, 489 pages.
An investigation of the biological bases of language capacities. Part of the discussion is devoted to the language abilities of people who are deaf, mentally retarded, or have some other speech or language disorder. In addition, it covers the physiological correlates of language, the evolution of language, language development, and language and cognition. Heavy reading in places.

McNEILL, D.   *The Acquisition of Language*
New York: Harper Row, 1970, 183 pages (paperback).
A short book that covers early speech in children, the biological basis of language, the role of experience in the development of language, and universals (commonalities) in children's languages.

SMITH, F., and G. A. MILLER, (Eds).   *The Genesis of Language*
Cambridge, Mass.: MIT Press, 1966, 400 pages (paperback).
Proceedings of a conference on "Language Development in Children" covering developmental psycholinguistics, acquisition of Russian as a native language, babbling and its relation to language development, language learning in the deaf, and animal communication (chimpanzee).

THOMAS, O.   *Transformational Grammar and the Teacher of English*
New York: Holt, Rinehart and Winston, 1965, 240 pages (paperback).
A simple and well-written introduction to transformational grammar. Full of definitions of basic linguistic terms and ideas. This is much more easily understood than are most other books in this field.

VYGOTSKY, L. S.   *Thought and Language* (Translated by E. Hanfmann and G. Vakar)
Cambridge, Mass.: MIT Press, 1965 (c. 1962), 168 pages (paperback).
First published in 1934 in Russia, this book is a presentation of a highly original theory of intellectual development and a theory of education and their relation to language.

FIG. 6.5 *Life is full of large and small decisions and for each, one must balance the possible good against the possible bad that each alternative course of action could yield. Then one should select that alternative that looks the most promising.*

Most of us find decision-making a rather unpleasant task. We get confused by the complex considerations that are involved. We vacillate between wanting to get the decision over with and not wanting to risk the consequences of a bad choice. We ponder and think and then, all too often, we end up doing something rash. In short, when we have to make important decisions that cannot be trusted to the blind application of rules, we often find ourselves lacking the rational skills to make the best possible choice.

Because of our lack of decision-making skills, we spend too much time stewing about pending decisions and regretting past decisions. Unfortunately, most decisions involve an element of *risk*, and this in itself means that some of the decisions we make are bound to turn out to be bad ones. There is no way out of this dilemma because we cannot look into the future and see what will prove to be the best decision in the long run. Indeed, all we can do is to calmly attempt to make the best possible decision on the basis of the information that is available at the time and then accept the consequences as gracefully as we can. The major purpose of this discussion is to help you think about decision-making more clearly and to show you how to make the best possible decision. (The ability to gracefully accept the consequences is something that you will have to develop on your own.)

The Components of Decisions

The first steps in decision-making are to clarify exactly what the issue is that you are deciding and to figure out what you want the decision to result in for you. Decision-making is simplified if you can divide the task into manageable parts and then deal with each one separately rather than with all of them at once.

Basically, decisions are *choices among alternative actions.* Actions may consist of any of a range of activities—going to the store versus watching a football game on TV, joining the Air Force versus going to college, getting married versus staying single, taking a psychology course versus taking physics, being pleasant to someone you dislike versus being unpleasant to him. Note two fundamental characteristics of all of these alternative actions. First, they are not ends in themselves; that is, each action is aimed at achieving a goal (called a *payoff* or a reinforcement) that is *valued* either positively or negatively. Thus, you would go to the store in order to buy something you wanted, you would watch football on TV in order to obtain pleasure and excitement, you would join the Air Force in order to get away from home or in order to learn to fly, and you would go to college in order to attain a variety of payoffs (education being one of them, I hope). Second, there is no guarantee that these actions will result in the desired payoffs. Even so, you can fairly well judge the degree to which you *believe* a given action will result in a desired payoff should you decide to choose that action. Thus, while the store might not have the object you want, you believe that it does; while the football game could be dull, you believe that it won't be; while being in the Air Force could be worse than living at home (or you may not get to fly), you believe that it will turn out to be for the better; and while college might not fit your educational needs or live up to your expectations, you tend to believe otherwise.

Deciding between alternative actions merely involves comparing the alternative actions in terms of the *values* of their payoffs and in terms of your *beliefs* that each alternative action will, in fact, lead to the associated payoff; then you choose the action that you expect will please you most in the long run. Note that this strategy is sort of a balancing process—an action that you believe has a low chance of leading to an extremely desirable payoff may be less attractive than an action that you believe will almost certainly lead to a moderately desirable payoff. That is, when you balance the desirability of a payoff against the chances of getting it, you may find that you don't really expect a particular action to be a very profitable venture even though the payoff is of a very high value to you.

One more thing must be added to this balancing process. When you consider the possibility that an action may fail to get a positively valued payoff for you, you also have to consider how you will feel about whatever it actually turns out to get for you instead. For example, if you go to the store to buy something and the store doesn't have what you want, your action has resulted in a negatively valued payoff (fatigue, wasted time, frustration, and so on). Thus, when considering whether to go to the store or to watch football on TV, you have to balance your expectation about the good things that a trip to the store might result in against your expectations about the possible bad things it might result in. You have to do the same for the football game (it *might* be great, but then it *might* be dull). After all of this balancing has been done for each alternative action, you are in a position to decide between the actions by choosing the action you expect to be most promising for you.

Although this process may sound complicated, you should realize that you intuitively make decisions in this manner all the time—you just aren't very precise about it. For example, when deciding whether you want to go somewhere with a friend (action 1), you usually consider what you would do if you didn't go with him (action 2). Then you balance the chances of action

1 leading to a pleasant payoff against its chances of leading to an unpleasant payoff. After doing the same thing for action 2, you select the action that you expect to be the more promising. In order to make this discussion of decision-making a little clearer, we will examine in more detail the components of a decision task and the actual procedures that enable you to perform the balancing process and then make a final choice among the alternative actions.

Beliefs

The word "belief" is used many ways in everyday language. In the present context, as a psychological component of a decision, it is used only to describe *the degree to which a person thinks that something is either true now or may turn out to be true in the future.* By this definition the tenets of a religion or a philosophy would not be called beliefs. Instead, they would be called statements or propositions, and the degree to which the followers of the religion or philosophy hold each of the tenets to be true would be called beliefs. To avoid confusion, keep this distinction in mind as we progress in this discussion.

A belief, then, is a person's *subjective* judgment about the *probability* that something is or may be true. For example, when the weatherman says that the probability of rain is 10 percent, he means that he has only a small degree of belief that it will rain within the next 24 hours. That is, given all the information he has, the weatherman's subjective probability of rain is 10 percent.

Origins of beliefs   Where do our beliefs, our subjective probabilities, come from? In general, they come from an evaluation of the content and rules that are stored in memory. When considering whether a particular action is part of, or similar to, an $S_1 \rightarrow R_1 \rightarrow S_2$ rule that you've already used, you can merely extract from memory the percentage of times that particular rule has resulted in the desired payoff in the past. This *frequency evaluation* is one source of beliefs. It yields a "percentage of successful uses" as your degree of belief—actions that have worked a large (or small) percentage of the time in the past are likely to work a large (or small) percentage of time in the future.

A second source of beliefs is your knowledge of the *constraints* imposed by the nature of the situation. For example, consider the action "If I look for the end of the rainbow, I might find a pot of gold." What you know about the nature of rainbows makes it clear that it would be impossible to actually find the end of one, and for this and other reasons you would have to have a very low degree of belief that you could ever trace a rainbow and find a pot of gold.

A third source of beliefs, *instruction,* is perhaps the source that the majority of us tend to rely upon most heavily. For example, most of us have a fairly high degree of belief that if we properly mix the correct proportions of oxygen and hydrogen, we could produce water, or that if we dropped a heavy object and a light object from a tower, they would both fall the same speed, or that if we placed a small bit of shell in an oyster, we could produce a cultured pearl. We believe these things to be true because someone told us they are true, not because we have any direct experiential evidence of our own. Most of the nonexperiential, abstract knowledge we have has been acquired from other people. The degree to which we believe such acquired knowledge depends upon (1) how much faith we have that our informant knows what he is talking about, (2) how many times we have been told by one or more persons that a given thing is true, and (3) how well new information fits in with the information we already have. For example, in school you usually regard the textbook and the teacher as being fairly well informed. If they both tell you the same thing, and the information they give you is fairly consistent with what you already know, you are likely to accept the new information as being fairly true. On the other hand, if you have reason to believe that either the teacher or the textbook is unreliable, if the teacher and the textbook disagree, or if the information they give you is not consistent with what you already know, you are likely to question the validity of the information, and, therefore, your degree of belief in it will be rather low.

Although the fourth source of beliefs is related to the previous three, it is sufficiently different to deserve separate consideration. This source is *analogy*. If something new is similar to something already in memory, we tend to believe in the new thing to about the same degree as we believe the old thing. Suppose, for example, you do not know if gravity on Mars is different from gravity on Earth, but you know that gravity on our moon is different from that on Earth. Because Mars and the moon are both somewhere "out there," you might by analogy believe that the gravity on Mars is also likely to be different from that on Earth. Similarly, if you do not know whether you can pass a course in physics but you did very well in a course in chemistry, you might regard the courses as analogous in some way and have a fairly high degree of belief in your ability to pass physics.

It is quite likely that there are origins of beliefs other than just these four. However, the sources just discussed should give you an idea of what is meant by degree of belief and how beliefs can have different origins. Rather than explore other origins or belabor the subtle differences and similarities among these origins of beliefs, we must now turn to the second psychological component of decisions, values.

Values

For any action, the value of the payoff is of fundamental importance in determining how a person feels about the action and why he does or does not want to carry it out. For example, "If I get a job, I might be able to pay all of these damned bills" is a statement that reveals a high positive value for getting out of debt. Or, "If I take a calculus course and flunk it, I'm afraid I'll be put on probation" is a statement that reveals a negative value for being put on probation. While it is not uncommon to refer to a person's moral standards as his values, throughout this book the word "value" is used in a much broader sense. For us a person's values are his judgments about *how good or how bad specific situations, persons, objects, or events are for him.*

We all use many different words to tell others about our values. We "love" someone very much, we "hate" to eat liver, we "like" dogs and small children, we think armed assault is "bad," we think charity is "good." Our behavior too reveals our values. We prefer buying a car to buying a boat, we bet that one candidate will beat another, we cut down on lunches in order to save money for a trip, and so on. Through both words and deeds, we reveal to others our values for the things around us.

Levels of values   There are two levels of values. The first, *social values,* consists of those values that large groups of people hold communally. For example, most people in the United States regard the Bill of Rights (the first ten amendments to the Constitution) as an explicit statement of some of their values. These rights are not necessarily valued highly by every individual American, but the group as a whole claims them as having high value and tries to use them as a guide for its judicial system. Of course, many of our social values are not written down like those that are listed in the Bill of Rights. A great many Americans, for example, apparently regard owning a fancy car as something to be valued even though no explicit public statements are made to that effect (except for automobile advertisements).

Clearly, every group and subgroup throughout American society holds some set of values which its members generally agree upon. These social values are usually reflected in the group's goals. Social organizations like the Lions Club or the Kiwanis value friendship and community service. Church groups value charity and devotion to God. Groups of friends value each other's company and mutual interests. In short, social values are a mutually held set of preferences for situations, people, objects, and events.

The second level of values is *personal values.* While some personal values may be identical to the social values of groups, they go beyond that to values for things that groups as a whole seldom consider. For example, a small child may value his beat-up teddy bear long after most other people would have regarded it as worn out and ready for the garbage can.

Differences in values   To understand values, one must recognize that both different groups and different people within the groups often have different values for the same thing. Thus, while Americans value dogs as pets, in some countries dogs are valued as food, and while Americans value cows as food, in India cows are valued as sacred objects. In theory, at least, our economy is based on the fact that because one person values something more than its owner does, he therefore is willing to pay more than the owner thinks it is worth in order to obtain it. The old owner with his money and the new owner with his purchase are both content that they got a good deal because they have different values.

The current strife between middle class young people and their middle class, middle-aged parents about what constitutes the Good Life is one example of different groups holding different social values. The generation that lived through the economic depression of the 1930s still bears the scar. These people tend to place high value on economic security—a good job, money in the bank, an expensive house with lots of lawn around it, two cars, and a college educa-tion for their children represent the Good Life for them. Their children, on the other hand, while they may never have known economic privation, have grown up in a world that could blow up at any moment. They in turn show the effects of their background. They tend to have a lower value than their parents have for security and its trappings; at the same time, their idea of the Good Life is represented by a high value for immediate experience of Life and honest interaction with other people. While each group can be indicted for its apparent unwillingness to look at the other's point of view, their conflict is quite understandable. Parents, not realizing that their children have values different from their own, are truly worried that their children will not make it in the world and will end up in the poorhouse. Children, on the other hand, sincerely believe that their parents have exchanged a vibrant and meaningful life for a house and a station wagon. Extend this kind of misunderstanding and conflict to the level of two nations that have completely different values for economic, social, and political systems and who each think that they know Truth, and you have the makings of a war.

Another thing to recognize about values is that the same group or the same person often values the same thing differently from one time to another. While value changes are less rapid and less pronounced for social values than for personal values, fluctuations in social values within the same group do occur.

Witness how America's values for Germany, Japan, and Russia have vacillated in the last seventy-five years. This is not to say that there have not been reasons for these changes but rather that there have indeed been changes.

Changes in personal values are more rapid and more clear-cut than they are for social values. Your value for a ham sandwich is higher if you have not eaten for a while than it is if you have just had lunch. Your value for borrowing a pair of ice skates is lower in the summer than it is in the winter. If you are a student with a small income, the prestige value of owning a Rolls Royce is a great deal less than the economical value of owning a Volkswagen.

The key to understanding changes in values lies in understanding how the valued thing relates to whatever the group's or person's *goal* is at the moment. Value is related to how *instrumental* a thing, a situation, a person, or an event is in achieving a particular goal. Thus, if your goal is to satisfy your hunger, the ham sandwich can be instrumental in achieving your goal and is therefore highly valued by you. If your goal is economical transportation rather than social prestige, the Volkswagen will aid in achieving your goal better than the Rolls Royce will. The Volkswagen is, therefore, of greater value to you than the Rolls Royce. On the other hand, a change in a goal could reverse all of these values. Thus, if you were thirsty and wanted a drink, the dry, salty ham sandwich might seem repulsive to you. Or, if your goal was to impress a new friend, this objective might override your desire for economy and make you value the Rolls Royce over the Volkswagen. In short, the value of things often depends on how much they will contribute to achievement of a particular goal; if the goal changes, then the value of things may also change.

Origin of values   As with beliefs, memory plays an important role in the origin of values. We all store knowledge about the degree to which various things aid us in attaining our goals. Such knowledge is obtained through both firsthand experience and instruction by parents, teachers, and friends. When trying to attain a particular goal, you use your knowledge to determine what action is necessary in order for you to successfully attain your goal. For example, if your goal is to succeed in school, you know you will have to get good grades in all of your classes and get friendly encouragement from your teachers. You therefore will place a high value on these things; if either one is missing, you will immediately make efforts to see that it is forthcoming. If your goal is to be accepted and loved by a particular person, very likely you will place a high value on behaving in a congenial and loving way toward that person. Moreover, you will value highly any signs of love that you get in return.

Sometimes people develop rather strange ideas about what will help them attain their goals. For example, many people seriously believe that carrying a rabbit's foot will aid them, and as a result, a rabbit's foot becomes a highly valued object to them. So too, people pray to all manner of highly valued spirits and gods because they think that by doing so they can manipulate the future and attain their goals.

Deviant behavior is sometimes the result of peculiar notions people have about what will aid them in attaining their goals. For example, a person may need money very badly, and if he is of the opinion that the best and only way to get it is to rob a gas station, he is likely to place a higher value on robbery than most of the rest of us do. Or perhaps you have known someone who wanted to be liked by everyone but seemed to do exactly the wrong thing every time he was around people. He talked too loudly and too much, he teased insensitively, he dropped names constantly, and all the rest—and he highly valued all of this behavior because he regarded it as reflecting superior social skill! Many times the goal of psychotherapy (Section 5, Part 2) is to help a person see that the things he values are not helping him attain his goals; instead, they often are doing just the opposite.

As explained in Section 5, during psychotherapy people frequently find they do not really know why they value some of the things they value. For example, the man who buys a high-powered automobile may think he merely wants the power of the engine and the feeling that he is making his buddies envious. In reality, however, he may value the car because its power seems to compensate for his feelings of not being as dynamic and powerful as he would like to be. Or a woman who insists on having a large family may think it is because she loves children. On the other hand, the real reason might well be that she is afraid of being left alone in the world, and by surrounding herself with people who depend upon her, she can make herself feel more secure. This is not to say that there is anything particularly wrong with these reasons for valuing cars and families. The point is that people value some things without knowing exactly why they value them. And not knowing why they value the things they do can lead to problems. For example, if the two people in the foregoing illustrations were poor, their respective needs to buy a powerful car and have lots of children could be ruinous. Unless these people are made to realize what goals are being served by the car and the children, they are unlikely to be able to deal with their expensive indulgences in a very reasonable way.

Most of your values are not as devious in origin as the ones that were just described. In fact, day-to-day behavior depends a great deal on pretty straightforward values. You value food when you are hungry, a lover when you are feeling affectionate, and certain objects when they either help you live your life more easily and comfortably or when they provide diversion and entertainment.

Measurement of Beliefs and Values

The best ways to measure how much a person believes that something is true or will become true in the future are to (1) ask him or (2) see how much he will risk on his belief. The first method commonly requires the person to state a number that reflects his degree of belief; for example, "I think the chance that the home football team will win tomorrow is about 80 percent." The second method requires the person to make a bet; for example, "I'll bet you four to one that the home team wins." (Odds of four to one are equivalent to a chance of 80 percent, because the 80 percent chance that the team will win is four times larger than the 20 percent chance that it will lose.) In general, the first method is easier to use.

The best ways to measure how much a person values something is to (1) ask him or (2) see how much he will pay for the thing. The first method commonly requires the person to tell you how much he thinks something is worth *to him*. Since many things are not readily evaluated in terms of dollars and cents (for example, "How much do you value your mother?"), the person is often asked to rate the valued thing on a scale similar to this one:

very
negative————— ——— ——— ——— ——— ——— ——— ——— ———positive
value   −4   −3   −2   −1   0   +1   +2   +3   +4 value

He uses the right-hand side of the scale for things he likes, the middle when he is indifferent, and the left-hand side for things he dislikes. On the right-hand side, he uses 1 for something he values only slightly, 2 for something he values moderately, 3 for something he values a good deal, and 4 for something he values very highly. The gradations on the left side are similar, but the negative numbers indicate dislike and are used for objects that are negatively valued.

The second method of measuring values is a little more difficult to use. It requires that you measure the amount of money, time, effort, or pain a person is willing to pay in order to obtain a positively valued thing. Thus, you can get a fair idea of how much a boy dislikes practicing the piano by keeping track of how long he puts it off or how much punishment he will accept for not practicing (for example, "No TV tonight," which is not too serious, versus "You can't go out of the yard for a week," which is a big price to pay for not practicing the piano for an hour). Similarly, it is fair to say that a student who has considered the situation and elected to work long hours at a job and then study far into the night before catching three or four hours of sleep values his education more than he does his health. A woman who elects to spend large amounts of money for cosmetics values the illusion of beauty more than all of the other things she could buy with that money.

Decisions

We turn now to how beliefs and values help a person to decide to choose one action rather than another. In this discussion, I will speak as though the person makes his decisions rationally, carefully, and systematically. This is usually not the case, of course, but it makes the job of presentation easier.

The first step in making a decision is to review all of the alternative actions that will lead to some particular overall goal. Each action will have both a chance of successfully leading to one or more valued payoffs as well as a chance of failing to lead to the valued payoff and leading to some other payoff instead. The decision-maker's task is to examine each action and then determine which one he expects to be the most favorable for him in the long run.

An Example

Imagine that you are a young man who is trying to decide what to do after graduation from high school. Your overall goal is to put yourself in a secure economic position so you can marry the girl you have been going with for the past three years. You ponder your problem and find two acceptable actions: you can take over your father's pickle fork factory or you can go to college.

No matter which action you decide upon, you stand a chance of succeeding or failing. Suppose you are fairly bright and ambitious, but you aren't really interested in manufacturing pickle forks. Your lack of interest plus your disorderly approach to administrative tasks might easily cause you to fail should you select the pickle fork action. On the other hand, although it would hold your interest, college is no snap, so there is a chance you might flunk out. Besides, you would have to support yourself while attending college (there isn't much money in the pickle fork industry, so Dad can't help).

One reason for taking over the family business rather than going to college is that if you are successful (you would know that in about two years), you will always have a small but sufficient income, and therefore you could marry your girl rather soon. But if you fail, you will have to start all over again in something else and postpone getting married until you succeed at a new job. If you go to college and succeed, you eventually will be able to get a good job and support your wife in style, but you will have to wait at least four years to get married. Should you fail, you will have to look for a job that might not be a very good one.

With all of these thoughts whirling around in your head, you sit down and try to make a decision. Let's assume that you are a methodical, rational person and that you are determined to use all the tools you can find to make the best possible decision. Thus, for each action, you balance the probability of success and the positive value of the payoffs associated with success against

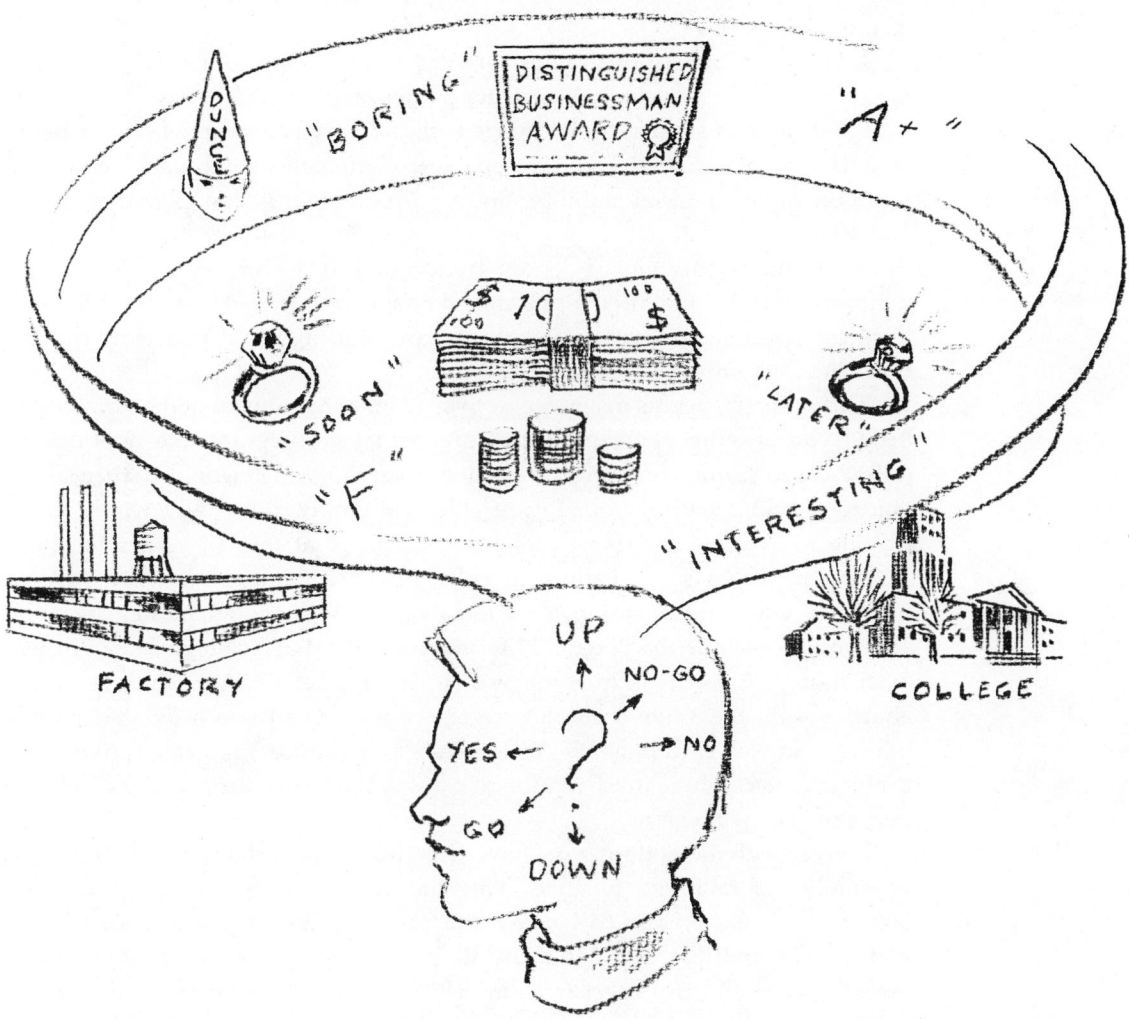

FIG. 6.6 *Because complex decisions are influenced by so many things, we often find ourselves unable to bring them together properly.*

the probability of failure and the negative value of the payoffs associated with failure. Then you select the action that is the more attractive to you. Let's look more closely at how you can methodically accomplish this action selection.

First, you estimate your subjective probability of success and failure for each action. Let's say that you believe that your probability of success in the pickle fork industry is .65 (the decimal point is moved two places to the left to convert percentages to probabilities) and that your probability of failure is .35. And you believe that your probability of success in college is .80 and that of failure is .20.

Next, you consider the values for success and failure for each action and rate them on the scale for measuring values that we discussed a few pages ago. The value of success in the pickle fork industry is tied up with your being able to demonstrate that you have business competence, with your being able to attain rapid financial stability, and with your being able to marry within two years. All in all, let us say that this rates about +2 on the value scale. Failure in the factory means demonstration of your incompetence in business matters (and the potential economic damage it might do to your father's business), prolonged financial instability, and waiting to get married. Let's say this rates −3 on the value scale.

The value of success in college derives from being able to demonstrate how bright you are, the opportunity for intellectual growth, and the opportunity for increased earning potential throughout your life, which would, in turn, allow you to provide well for your future wife and family. But it also would mean waiting four years or more to marry. Let's say that this all comes to about +3 on the value scale. Failure in college would demonstrate your lack of brilliance, would mean looking for a job in order to get enough money to marry, and would preclude the potential lifetime earnings that a college degree brings even though it might reduce the wait to marry. Let's say that this is worth about −4 on the value scale. Figure 6.7 summarizes these estimated probabilities and value judgments for success and failure for each action. The problem is to combine these numbers in a way that will help you make a choice between the two actions.

For each of the actions you have determined a probability of success, a probability of failure, a positive value for success, and a negative value for failure. The next step is to balance the probabilities and values. To do this you merely multiply each value by its probability. Then, to see how much overall good you can expect from an action, you add the product for success to the product for failure; then you select that action with the greatest expected good (usually called the *expected value* of an action). Note that if failure yields

Action	If you *SUCCEED*, you get		If you *FAIL*, you get		Adding the expected good of success and the expected bad of failure yields:
Take over factory 	Belief	Value	Belief	Value	
	.65	+2	.35	-3	
	.65 × (+2) = +1.30		.35 × (-3) = -1.05		(+1.30) + (-1.05) = +.25
Action	If you *SUCCEED*, you get		If you *FAIL*, you get		Adding the expected good of success and the expected bad of failure yields:
Go to college 	Belief	Value	Belief	Value	
	.80	+3	.20	-4	
	.80 × (+3) = +2.40		.20 × (-4) = -.80		(+2.40) + (-.80) = +1.60

FIG. 6.7 *Components of the decision to either take over Dad's pickle fork factory or go to college. College wins.*

a negative value, as in our example, this boils down to subtracting the bad from the good for each action and seeing for which action the good most outweighs the bad. In some cases, determining the expected value may result in your having to choose between two actions which have negative expected values; you should select the action that is least negative.

To illustrate this procedure, let's look back at Figure 6.7. The expected value for taking over the factory is $(.65 \times +2) + (.35 \times -3) = (+1.30) + (-1.05) = +.25$. For college, the expected value is $(.80 \times +3) + (.20 \times -4) = (+2.40) + (-.80) = +1.60$. Since the expected value for college is more than six times greater than that for taking your father's factory, you should decide to go to college.

Review

In summary, then, the best way to make a decision is to think about it for a while. Then, after the goal is clear:

1. Define all the alternative actions and their positive and negative payoffs. In our examples there have always been two actions, each with two payoffs (success versus failure or pleasant versus unpleasant). In real life there usually are more of each.

2. For each action, estimate the probability that it will lead to each of the payoffs. Remember, when you are absolutely certain that an action will yield one payoff and no other, the probability for that payoff is 1.00 and the probability for all other payoffs is .00.

3. Assign a value to each possible payoff of each action, either in money or in terms of the scale that we have been using.
4. Compute the expected value for each action.
5. Decide upon the action with the highest expected value.
6. If the expected values are too similar to permit a comfortable decision, get more information about the various actions so that you can change your probabilities or your values and break the deadlock.

Real Decisions

Clearly, very few people ever sit down and go through the formal procedure just outlined. However, peoples' intuitive decision-making often proceeds along much the same lines even though the beliefs and values are not always explicitly stated and no mathematical calculations are made. If people would learn at least to think about decisions in the way we have just discussed, they would be able to clarify and improve their intuitive decision-making a good deal—they would become more aware of alternative actions, what each action offers, and the uncertainty involved in the whole process. In the long run, awareness of this kind would help them make more satisfying decisions.

One major advantage gained by examining decisions more closely is that it helps people untangle their feelings about the probabilities of actions leading to various payoffs and their values for those payoffs. All too often, people unknowingly let their values influence their subjective probabilities; that is, because they want some payoff very much, they inflate their estimation of an action's probability of attaining it, or, conversely, they underestimate the action's probability of leading to a negatively valued payoff. This is commonly called *wishful thinking*, and it is a very poor basis for decision-making. So, the next time you make a decision, stop and ask yourself if you're distorting your subjective feelings about the likelihood of getting some payoff just because you have a strong positive or negative value for that payoff.

Another advantage of using the decision-making procedure described here is that it helps you keep from relying upon foolish "non-decision-making" tactics. Many of us, because we fear and misunderstand decisions, simply avoid them whenever possible. Sometimes we ask advice of others and essentially let them make the decision for us. This is a handy tactic because if things don't work out well, we can always blame the other guy's poor judgment. We also avoid decisions by putting them off until all of the actions but one become impossible; then we "choose" the remaining action. The nice thing about this kind of procrastination is that if the remaining action does not turn out to be very satisfactory, we can console ourselves by saying that we wouldn't have chosen it had other actions been available. Yet another way we avoid decisions is to choose the action that is currently fashionable rather than take the trouble

BOX 6.2

So Simple Even a Child Can Do It

It is difficult to study real-life decision-making because people often make their decisions so quickly that it is impossible to examine what is going on. Therefore, we must rely on studies that use highly structured tasks which require volunteers to deliberate before making clear-cut choices among alternative actions. The following is a description of an excellent and instructive example of such a study.

The purpose of the study, which was done by Dr. Carol Gray, was to find out if people's intuitive decision-making procedures resemble the formal *expected value* procedure that we have been discussing and that is depicted in Figure 6.7.* In addition, Dr. Gray wanted to find out if such a resemblance existed for both children and adults, the notion being that a similarity between children's intuitive decision-making procedures and the expected value procedure would suggest that the latter is an intrinsically logical and "natural" way of making decisions.

The study consisted of several experiments, each of which involved the following simple task. Cards with arithmetic problems written on them were placed face down in six equal stacks in front of a volunteer; each stack contained problems of equal difficulty, and the six different stacks represented six different levels of problem difficulty. The experimenter showed the volunteer some problems from each stack in order to give him an idea of the difficulty level of each stack. Then the volunteer was asked how many of the problems in each stack he believed he could get right if he had the opportunity to try. These judgments were regarded as the volunteer's subjective probabilities of success and failure

---

*C. A. Gray, Factors in students' decisions to attempt academic tasks. Unpublished doctoral dissertation, University of Washington, Seattle, 1971.

to figure out what action is best for ourselves as individuals. People who base their decisions about drugs, sex, how to dress, how to furnish their houses, what kind of person to marry, and so on, on what is currently fashionable are avoiding decisions even though they may enjoy the illusion that they are self-sufficient and decisive. Seldom do any of these ways of avoiding decisions lead to very satisfactory long-run results. Satisfaction with decisions increases as the method you use becomes more and more like the method outlined above, because it is only then that the decision is tailored to your own personal beliefs and values. In no small part the greatest advantage of the method lies in the necessity for you to consider the various components of the situation and what they mean *to you*—something that most of us don't do often enough in the ordinary course of things.

for each stack. Next, the volunteer was told, for each stack, how many points he would get if he tried to solve a problem from that particular stack and got the correct answer; he was also told he stood to lose the same number of points if he got the problem wrong. Each volunteer then chose and attempted to solve thirty problems, one at a time. The volunteers were told to try to make as many points as they could in the course of choosing and solving the thirty problems.

Note that this decision-making task is fundamentally the same as the college-or-pickle-fork-factory decision described in the text, except that here there are six alternative actions (the volunteer could choose a problem from any one of the six stacks) rather than only two. For each stack, Dr. Gray knew each volunteer's subjective probability of successful solution of a problem and the positive value of success (the number of points that could be won), as well as his subjective probability of failure and the negative value of failure (the number of points that could be lost). This knowledge permitted her to calculate the expected value for each of the six decks for each volunteer, as was done in Figure 6.7. (Note that it is possible for the expected values for different volunteers to be different because each of them had different subjective probabilities of success and failure for each stack.) The underlying logic behind this experiment was that if each volunteer chose his problems from the stack having the highest expected value for him, it would strongly imply that his intuitive decision-making procedure corresponds to the formal procedure.

Third grade children served as volunteers in the first two experiments (Fig. 6.8). The arithmetic problems on the cards were of the kind usually taught in the third grade, some difficult and some easy, but all within the children's general level of competence. In the first experiment, Dr. Gray showed the problems in each stack of cards to the children and got their subjective probabilities of success and failure for each stack. Then she told them about the points to be won or lost, six points for the most difficult problems, five for the next most difficult, and so on, on down to one point for the easiest. Then the children selected and solved thirty problems. Afterwards Dr. Gray calculated the expected values of the stacks and checked to see if the children had selected their problems primarily from the stack that had the highest expected values. They had.

To be doubly certain that the children's problem selections were based upon expected value rather than upon something else, Dr. Gray did a second experiment using these same children. This time she changed around the points to be won or lost in such a way that for each child a new stack became the one with the highest expected value. If their selections were based on expected value, the children should stop selecting from the stack they favored in the first experiment and begin to select from the new stack. They did.

In the final experiment, male college students served as volunteers and the arithmetic problems were taken from a fairly rigorous mathematical achievement test. Aside from these changes, this third experiment was carried out much the same as the first one with the children, and the results were pretty much the same. That is, when students' selections were checked to see if they had come primarily from the highest expected value stacks, it was found that they had.

Even though these experimental results strongly support the idea that intuitive and formal decision-making procedures are quite similar, we must be careful in our interpretation of the results because the experiment involved an extremely simple decision task. For more complex situations, there is a great deal of evidence showing that people have difficulty keeping in mind all the relevant information (for example, all the probabilities and values). As a result, intuitive decision-making procedures frequently are quite unlike the formal procedure. Moreover, in complex situations people tend to take labor-saving shortcuts that work reasonably well but that are very different from the formal expected value procedure. Indeed, even in Dr. Gray's experiments, the volunteers sometimes did things that they would not have done had they been strictly following the formal procedure. The most common breach occurred when a "nest egg" of points had been accu-

FIG. 6.8   Dr. Carol Gray studying how children decide which of six levels of problem difficulty they will select when trying to solve arithmetic problems. (See Box 6.2.) (Courtesy Robert Kulwin.)

mulated; wealth prompted some volunteers to "take a flyer" and select a high payoff problem that they had very little hope of solving. If they got the problem right, they were overjoyed. If they got it wrong, they often selected a few easy, sure-thing problems until they had repaired the hole in their fortune (note the similarity to the way some people play the stock market). Because the formal procedure doesn't countenance wild gambling of any variety, the resemblance between this intuitive decision-making procedure and the formal procedure is less than perfect.

SUMMARY

1   Decisions are choices among alternative actions. Such choices are based upon the relative *values* of the payoffs associated with each action and upon your *beliefs* that you actually would receive these payoffs if you were to select the action.

2   Beliefs, *subjective probabilities,* have their origins in *relative frequencies, constraints of a situation, instruction,* and *analogy.* Values have their origins in your needs at the moment, *personal values,* and in the things that you are taught are important, *social values.*

3   Making a decision requires balancing the good payoffs and their probabilities against the bad payoffs and their probabilities for each alternative action and then choosing the action which appears to be most favorable.

Further Reading

BEM, D.   *Beliefs, Attitudes and Human Affairs*
Belmont, Calif.: Brooks/Cole, 1970, 114 pages (paperback).
A look at the psychological, cognitive, emotional, social, and behavioral foundations of beliefs and attitudes.

EDWARDS, W., and A. TVERSKY.   *Decision Making*
Baltimore, Md.: Penguin, 1967, 412 pages (paperback).
A book of readings on theory and research in the area of decision-making. Articles are written by a variety of people, including mathematicians, economists, and psychologists. While a few of the articles are very difficult reading because of the mathematics involved, others are reasonably straightforward. You'll have to decide which ones you want to tackle.

LEE, W.   *Decision Theory and Human Behavior*
New York: Wiley, 1971, 352 pages.
A comprehensive coverage of theory and psychological experiments in human decision-making. Includes work on subjective probabilities, utilities, decision rules, information seeking, and probability learning. This book is a little steep in places.

ROKEACH, M.   *Beliefs, Attitudes and Values*
San Francisco: Jossey-Bass, 1968, 214 pages.
A strong distinction is made among beliefs, attitudes, and values. Rokeach questions a great deal of the research done on attitudes and attitude change, especially since the majority of findings can be accounted for by more simple explanations.

SCHEIBE, K. E.   *Beliefs and Values.*
New York: Holt, Rinehart and Winston, 1970, 159 pages (paperback).
A very readable and interesting book. The author emphasizes that an investigation of beliefs and values will increase our understanding of a broad range of human behavior. Full of examples and based on a great deal of research.

WILLIAMS, J. D.   *The Compleat Strategyst*
New York: McGraw-Hill, 1954, 234 pages.
An entertaining and informative book about game theory that requires only that you know how to add, subtract, multiply, and divide using both positive and negative numbers.

Part 3   *LOVE, MARRIAGE, AND SEX*

In this chapter we will briefly examine three topics that are of primary importance in most people's lives—love, marriage, and sex. However, our approach is going to be unusual. This discussion, I hope, will make you stop and think, question your attitudes, and look at these topics in a new light. Most people never seriously consider why they search for love, why they want sex, or why they get married. To most of us, the general notion is that love, marriage, and sex represent the "natural" or "normal" course of events. However, I am going to try to convince you that many people's ideas about this "natural" course of events are merely biases that they have learned as a result of living in our particular culture. Instead of making choices for themselves, people let these biases make their choices for them. Therefore, this discussion is aimed at extending your horizons, so to speak, showing you the alternatives so that you can think about your own life more clearly.

Love

Love is an important component of the lives of people in our culture. It is the central theme of our religions, literature, poetry, songs, and drama. Getting and giving love demands a great deal of our time and effort. It behooves us, therefore, to devote a little time to the consideration of love.

Romantic Love

Every culture has its version of when, where, and how one experiences love. Our particular version is called the tradition of romantic love. It is the general version for most of Europe, the Americas, and Australia. It is quite different from the versions of Asia, the Pacific islands, and black Africa except where Christian missionaries have had an influence.

The concept of romantic love is only about a thousand years old. Its roots are obscure, and its history is complex. For our purpose we need only briefly describe this history, and, to oversimplify, we will assert that the two most important roots are Christianity and the social structure of medieval Europe.

Primarily due to the early influence of Saint Paul, Christianity has traditionally been somewhat opposed to sex. This position represented in part a continuation of earlier Jewish attitudes, in part a reaction to the excess of the Romans, and in part a belief that Christ was soon to return and that Christians had best look to getting their souls ready for heaven. Paul's admonitions to avoid sex and his praise of abstinence are still strong influences in our culture. Indeed, the early Church was not in favor of marriage unless one found abstinence too much to bear—"it is better to marry than to burn" (Corinthians 1:7). Later this position changed and marriage became a sacrament of the Church, but the general attitude of antisexuality continued, and a high premium was placed on developing an asexual, beatific love in the image of God's love for man.

This Christian influence was strong in Europe during the Middle Ages, and coupled with the unique social organization of the royal courts, it sparked the romantic tradition that has survived until our own time (Fig. 6.9). Royal courts consisted of a few ladies of rank and many men. The former were the wives,

FIG. 6.9   *The romantic tradition has its roots in European royal courts during the Middle Ages.* (*Bodleian Library Oxford.*)

daughters, and entourage of the noblemen. The latter were ranking soldiers, knights, and courtiers. Because of their relationship to royalty and their social rank, the women were unattainable for most of the men. This unattainability and the Christian virtue of asexual love acted together to create a tradition in which gentlemen devoted themselves and the purity of their love to their noble ladies (although they probably slept with the scullery maids).

The knights and soldiers wore their ladies' colors—a scarf or the like—into battle, and it was fashionable to write elaborate poetry in praise of the lady and her virtue or to hire somebody to write it. This poetry was picked up by the troubadours who, as the court poets and musicians, elaborated upon it and made it part of the unwritten musical literature of the period. (Songs are peculiar things. They reflect how part of the culture thinks about things, and, at the same time, they spread that way of thinking so that it becomes general throughout the culture. Witness how, in the last few years, young people have heard their thoughts and feelings articulated by such people as Bob Dylan and at the same time have been introduced to yet other ideas. Never underestimate the power of songs and poetry—they touch deeply when a person is prepared to hear their message.)

Thus the troubadours and their songs made romantic love a part of the general culture. Of course, this is an oversimplified sketch, but it is roughly what happened. Slowly the idea was assimilated into the courtship and marriage practices of the middle class, who tried to imitate the ways of the royal court. Before that, marriage had pretty much been a business arrangement, but as the idea of romance had its impact, the notion of marriage based on mutual attraction began to emerge.

About this time literature and drama began to move from religious themes to romantic ones. These stories and plays, as well as new songs that drew upon the songs of the troubadours, served to show people how they were *supposed* to feel—they were supposed to "fall in love," be "swept off their feet," and encounter and overcome all manner of obstacles in order to win the person they loved. Because these intense feelings of love were (and still are) regarded as requisite for marriage, most people experienced them. Indeed, every young man and woman had a right to this dream, to this time of intense emotion and romantic involvement. Then they were supposed to get married and settle down.

Other Traditions

There are many kinds of love customs besides the romantic tradition. It is difficult for us romantics to comprehend that the rest of the world does not necessarily share our view of how mating should take place. People who grow up with other cultural traditions believe in them as strongly as we believe in romanticism. Indeed, while we may regard them as emotionally impoverished because of their lack of romance, they may regard us as emotionally unstable for our overinvolvement in what is, after all, a rather simple process.

For most of the world, marriages are not made in heaven. They are sensibly and reasonably contracted to provide a division of labor between two people, a stable home for children, and security in old age. Any emotional ties result from the involvement of the partners with each other over the years and the ties that derive from satisfactory sex. The participants expect no more. They foster no illusions of staying together because of the immutable bonds of enduring love; they stay together because that is the way things are done in their culture. We stay together for much the same reason, but we insist—perhaps unreasonably—that the glow of love last a lifetime.

But It's Real   Just because romantic love is unique to our culture does not mean it isn't real. When people are taught to believe in something and to expect certain patterns of emotions, they usually experience exactly what they expect, and the experience is no less real just because it depends upon having been learned. You have been taught to feel that sunsets are beautiful, to feel a faint stir in your chest when the flag goes by, and to feel a protective tenderness for puppies and kittens. The fact that other people are unmoved by sunsets, flags, and small animals does not make your feelings fake. So too with love; the fact that we're taught to expect to feel it makes it very real for us. And we search for it and find it.

Marriage   The rest of the romantic tradition requires that love lead to marriage. This picture is the mainstay of movies and television. The couple meets, bells ring, they fall hopelessly in love, they become engaged, and they marry. The movie usually stops there, but the assumption is that they settle down in a little cottage where they raise a lovely family and grow old together—always in love, for richer for poorer, in sickness and in health, until death do them part. Then they are buried in adjoining plots.

Is This for You?   What is wrong with this scene? Nothing, really, except that it is only one possible way of living, and many people find that it just doesn't work for them. A lot of damage is done by a stereotyped expectation about how emotions are supposed to occur and how life is supposed to progress. In such important matters as love, sex, and marriage, to seek some sort of cultural ideal is sheer

FIG. 6.10   *The movies' portrayal of the romantic leads one to assume that people fall in love, marry, and live happily ever after. (Courtesy D. Doty.)*

folly. While trying to live this stereotype many people cease to keep in touch with how *they* really feel. Each person is different, and it takes different kinds of lives to satisfy different people.

Marriage and the Alternatives   Since the "normal" course of love and marriage isn't the only way, what is the best alternative? Clearly, I can't answer this question because I don't know you, your moral values, or anything specific about what makes you tick. You have to ask yourself—"Considering my likes and dislikes, and my quirks and qualities, what is the most satisfying love life for me? Will it be the traditional route of love and marriage with sex limited to my mate? or love and marriage with extramarital affairs? a series of marriages? Is it best to remain single and have a succession of deep involvements? Should I merely get sex where I can and avoid involvements? Should I have neither sex nor involvements? Or should I have close friends and no sex?"

Most of these alternatives probably don't appeal to you, but each of them is best for somebody. Some people have great difficulty maintaining a marriage but need sex and want somebody to love. Perhaps such persons should stay single and have one or more lovers who can be seen frequently, lovers who do not demand the responsibility that is usually demanded by a mate. Other people seem unable to become emotionally involved and would do best to have casual sex rather than force themselves to pretend involvement in order to maintain a permanent or long-term relationship. Still others, both men and women, really don't like sex very much and, quite frankly, would be happier if they avoided it instead of forcing themselves to engage in it in order to be "normal." Of course, many people have moral codes that cut their choices down to two— marriage or asexual friendships. Still others regard any alternative to traditional marriage as abnormal, and, even if they thought something else would make them happier, they feel bound to try to be "normal." In any event, it is only when you sit back and consider your own needs and limitations that you can hope to choose something that will make you happy. Otherwise, you'll merely march along like everyone else, trying to force yourself to believe that the synthetic dream you've got yourself into is really the ultimate in happiness and the best you can expect out of life.

Through all of this we've said nothing about children. For many people a prime motive for marriage is to have children. But this presents a problem for a person who wants a life that is not the traditional marriage arrangement. In our culture single people are seldom permitted to adopt children, so they usually don't have the option of raising children outside of marriage unless they are widowers or get custody after a divorce or (for a woman) have an illegitimate child. The stigma of illegitimacy is not as harsh for a child as it once was, but it still exists. Premeditated illegitimacy seems to me a rather selfish thing for a single woman to do to a child in order to satisfy her own need to be a parent. Moreover, as we discussed in Section 4, there may be psychological dangers in raising a child in a single-parent home. Both the stigma of illegitimacy and the possible problems associated with a child's having only one parent make an unmarried woman's choice to have a child difficult to condone.

If you want the pleasure and pain of rearing children in this culture, you had best consider the marriage route. Or perhaps you should re-examine your motive for wanting children (especially in this age of overpopulation): Is it because you are really turned on by children—you want to spend time with them, be part of their successes and tragedies, watch them grow to become responsible adults—or is it merely because wanting children is the "normal" thing in this culture?

It behooves each of us to give some thought to the questions of how we will find love in our lives and how we will balance our needs against cultural demands—the demands for a "normal" life, romantic love, marriage, and children. Acceptance of the traditional course may not be right for you, but then again, it may. At any rate, don't accept it blindly. The high divorce rate in this country (roughly one marriage out of four) is a symptom that the traditional course is not working for a lot of people. Divorce is an emotionally trying experience that can drag on many years after the participants finally realize that they are too unhappy to continue the marriage. It is expensive in terms of money, mental stability, and shattered dreams—one or both parties usually are badly hurt in the process. It is a high price to pay for failure to consider the best way of life for yourself and an unwillingness to give up the romantic ideals that have been so thoroughly ingrained into you.

Unsuccessful and Successful Marriage

In a society like ours that has such a high divorce rate, it is reasonable to ask what factors lead to marriage failure as well as what factors lead to happy and successful marriages.

Many marriage reports have found that the most common source of marital problems is lack of *money*. After the comparative freedom of courtship, the expenses of setting up a household often severely limit the activities of the newly married couple. Usually they begin to have children before they are financially solvent. As income grows, so does the family, and so do expenses. Soon both husband and wife devote a major portion of their time and emotions to resenting the trap in which they find themselves. If they each start blaming the other for their troubles, the marriage is not likely to survive.

Part of the problem has to do with the early age at which people marry. From a physiological point of view, the best age for human reproduction is about ten years before most people are financially able to even consider marriage. As a result, many people marry while still in school, while in the service, or while they are just getting started financially. Lives dominated by financial worries and resentment about wasted youth have little room for love. Indeed, the divorce rate for people who marry before they are eighteen years old is about three times as high as it is for people who wait until their early twenties.

The major factor in marital happiness is also related to age, although more is involved than just age in terms of years. This factor is what is known as *emotional maturity*. First, emotional maturity means the ability to weather personal problems without becoming so upset that you cannot function adequately. Second, it means the ability to put other considerations ahead of your own wants, if that is best for everyone concerned. And third, it is the ability to establish a close, understanding relationship with someone else. These are all valuable assets, but the third is the most valuable and the most difficult to achieve. It requires that you let the other person know you almost as well as you know yourself, and this takes courage. It also requires you to attempt to understand the other person and to help him or her be the best person he or she can be.

Some studies have shown that happily married people *understand* their spouses rather well. Unhappily married persons, on the other hand, tend to assume that their mate is more like them than is really the case. That is, instead of really knowing their mate, they assume that whatever they think or believe also is thought and believed by their spouse. These unhappily married people also tend to be rather shy, sensitive people who are not very good at interacting with others in general. Happily married people tend to be just the opposite; they are outgoing and tend to bring things out and talk about them rather than harboring them away and sulking.

It should not be surprising that one of the best predictors of whether a marriage will be a happy one is whether the partners themselves come from happy families. Happy families make it easy to learn the social skills that are needed to make a marriage work. People from broken homes or from unhappy, tense family situations simply may not know how to get along with people on a day-after-day basis.

Sex

For all of the talk about sex, very little is really said. In spite of recent liberalizing trends, the topic is still out of bounds, and people don't exchange much information about what they think, like, or do. As a result, each of us lives a rather encapsulated life, thinking that the attitudes and preferences that we *assume* that our reference group has (we are seldom sure just what they really are) must be right and universal. The upshot of this isolation is that many people spend unhappy lives trying to force themselves to feel and live in ways that aren't right for them. Witness the woman who has a strong sexual appetite but who, because her reference group says that women shouldn't like sex, feels guilty about her desires and tries to repress them so that she can regard herself as a "good woman." Or consider the man who feels that he is not sufficiently masculine because his reference group urges varied and frequent sex, but he does not feel like a sexual athlete. This frequently happens in the military where young men, away from home for the first time, feel strong social pressures to prove their masculinity even if they don't really want sexual adventurism. Or consider the person with strong homosexual feelings who tries to live "normally" and dooms himself or herself to a lifetime of repression and guilt. In all of these cases, and many more, people have forced themselves to accept one particular view of what is acceptable sexuality. This is unfortunate because, aside from the rather arbitrary standards of one's reference group, there are no absolute standards against which to judge how "normal" or how adequate anyone's sexuality is.

Sex manuals   When most people start to worry that their sex life isn't all it could be, they turn to a sex manual for advice. This source gives them information that is fairly solid and not necessarily limited to a specific reference group. Sex manuals tend to be of two kinds. The first is the how-to-do-it variety. This kind of book will give you a step-by-step method that supposedly assures mutual and unfailing orgasm. It has the charm and latitude of a driver's manual. Unfortunately, the style of this book probably says a lot about the audience for whom it is written; many people approach everything, even sex, as a skill to be acquired and as a task to be accomplished. If the book says spontaneity in sex is good, these people will work at being spontaneous. If the book says that the face-to-face position is most popular in America but that alternatives are important to keep sex interesting, these people will use the face-to-face position on Mondays and Wednesdays and an alternative on Fridays. In short, the how-to-do-it approach is for task-oriented people who are concerned with being great lovers and who are engaged in the search for The Perfect Orgasm. Of course, this approach suits some people, and more power to them. But, as we shall see later, the task-oriented approach to sex frequently causes trouble for people who are caught up in it.

The second kind of sex manual takes the here-is-the-information, do-what-you-want-with-it approach. This type of book gives solid medical and psychological advice but does not pretend that there is any one way to sexual fulfillment. Indeed, one primary point such books make is that sex isn't always great, that you just have to face it, sometimes you won't be pleased, sometimes your partner won't be, but don't crucify yourself or each other—there is always tomorrow. The best book of this variety, to my thinking, is Dr. J. L. McCary's *Human Sexuality* (1967). It is the kind of book about sex which characterizes the following attitude: In order to be an effective person in any area of your life, you have to find out about the alternatives available to you and then select the things that suit you best. Part of being a fulfilled, effective adult means that you cannot depend upon someone else to tell you what is best for you; they can tell you what other people think and what the legal restraints are, both important considerations, but you've got to make your own choices.

Sexual Appetite   When people start to question the *how* of sex, they often begin to wonder if their sexual appetite (sex drive) is "normal." As before, there is no way to answer this question because what is "normal" has no real reference to one's own satisfaction. However, sexual appetite has many components, and it is worth our time to examine them.

First, appetite for sex is much like appetite for food; it has a strong biological basis, but the major component is psychological. In America many people customarily eat three meals a day, but some people eat twice a day and others eat five or six times a day. One of the revelations of the famous Kinsey Report on male sexuality was the tremendous variation among men in average frequency of ejaculations per week—the averages ranged from 0 to 29 or more, with from 1 to 4 being most common. After presenting these data, Kinsey pointed out that most people tend to think that their average frequency is fairly representative of the general population, that is, that they are "normal" and that people with fewer or more experiences are "undersexed" or "oversexed." Because we don't usually talk about such things, most of us don't have an accurate idea about our friends' sexual appetites; we assume that they are like our own and that people who are different must "have problems."

That there is a psychological component in sexual appetite is demonstrated clearly in our cultural assumption that sexual appetite vanishes with age. And, because we believe it, it frequently happens. However, health permitting, a great many oldsters in other cultures lead active sex lives, and many in our culture quietly maintain their sexual appetite, indicating that age isn't as important as we believe it is. It is not improbable that many people use age as an escape from a very boring sex life. An uninterested male frequently is unable to maintain an erection, and it is easier to blame the failure on age than to admit that sex with his wife bores him. Also, many people who have always regarded sex as a task to be performed well can use age as an excuse to retire.

Male sex appetite is a variable thing. It seems to be highest when sex is available, and it can decrease markedly when a man is isolated from women (for example, when he is aboard ship or when he is out hunting). However, after periods of deprivation the availability (or possible availability) of a partner quickly increases his appetite. Then, once sex is again available, the appetite returns to its usual level. Of course, the greatest curb on sexual appetite is sexual satiation; there is seldom any danger of a man doing himself physical harm by overindulgence in sex because he will be unable to maintain an erection or have an orgasm after he is satiated.

Very little is known about the sexual appetite of women. Most women can passively engage in sex and enjoy it even when they aren't highly aroused. This, together with cultural training to be nonaggressive in sex and to wait for the man to initiate it, makes it extremely difficult to learn much about female sexual appetite. However, some research data indicate that female and male sexual appetites are not basically different, only that the two sexes have been taught that their appetites are supposed to be different.

The whole business of culturally determined sex roles has a lot to do with sexual appetite. A woman who has been taught that it is her role to be "pure" and that sex in marriage is merely a necessary evil may restrict her sexual appetite to the vanishing point, and she and her husband may be happy that way. Or she may be unhappy, revolt, and develop a strong appetite. Again, she and her husband may be pleased with her change. The bad part, of course, is when the two people have incompatible appetites—someone has to yield and the result is seldom very satisfactory. If the stronger appetite is neglected, clandestine extramarital sex may be sought. If the weaker appetite is forced to increase, the person may feel used. One solution is for the person with the stronger appetite to masturbate from time to time.

The final comments on sexual appetite are about the problems of people who try to fit some sort of sexual image. Thus, it is not unusual for both men and women to behave as though they have stronger sexual appetites than they really have. Indeed, they sometimes even convince themselves. In such cases, the person usually is trying to reassure himself of his sexual adequacy. The man who propositions every woman he meets may enjoy sex less than the man who has sex less frequently but who has it because it is right and good for him. The notion that a "real man" is always on the make, always ready for sex, is part of America's James Bond-Mike Hammer-Playboy syndrome. The argument against this syndrome, and its counterpart for women, is that it is a role that many people force themselves to play. And to assume a life-style without considering what it means to you is to place yourself in bondage.

Varieties of Sexual Experience

There are four predominant patterns of sexuality in our culture: (1) masturbation, (2) premarital sex, (3) marital and extramarital sex, and (4) homosexuality. Other patterns exist, such as sexual experience with animals, but they are relatively uncommon, so we will not discuss them here.

Masturbation In a society such as ours that does not permit free sexual contact between unmarried young people, masturbation is usually the first sexual outlet experienced. For men, masturbation ("jacking off") involves grasping the erect penis and rhythmatically slipping the loose outer skin back and forth until orgasm ("coming") is achieved. For women, masturbation usually involves rhythmic rubbing of the loose skin around the clitoris or insertion of a finger or some other object into the vagina and rubbing it back and forth in imitation of a penis. For both men and women masturbation is usually accompanied by sexual fantasies of various degrees of vividness.

Many young men begin masturbation not only because it feels good but also because they find that if they don't, they have sexual dreams while asleep that end up in spontaneous ejaculation ("wet dreams"). The mess created by the ejaculation and the embarrassment caused by their mother's discovery of the soiled sheets causes many young men extreme discomfort. Thus they begin a regular pattern of masturbation. About 94 percent of the males in the United States who have been asked admit to having masturbated (and someone has suggested that many of the remaining 6 percent are liars). For a few, masturbation remains the major sexual outlet throughout their lives. Some masturbate only once or twice in their lives. Most men resort to masturbation when a sex partner is not available.

Masturbation is much maligned in our culture—indeed, two common judgmental labels for it are "playing with yourself" and "self-abuse." This negative view results from the general antisexuality of Christianity, specifically from the biblical story of God's anger with Onan for "spilling his seed upon the ground" (Genesis 38:9), which some scholars have interpreted as a prohibition against masturbation (another name for masturbation is Onanism, in reference to this story). Other biblical scholars say that God was angry because Onan refused to have children by his brother's widow, the custom of the time, and that masturbation was not the issue.

This is not the place for theological arguments, but there certainly is no evidence that masturbation is physiologically harmful. However, because people have been taught that it is evil, the guilt arising from masturbation can be psychologically troublesome. In fact, children used to be taught that masturbation would make them go blind, cause insanity, and make them incapable of sex in later life. Too many children were subjected to this kind of frightening nonsense by well-meaning parents, physicians, and ministers. Then, scared, but unable to control their impulses, these misinformed children gave in to their desires and went through agonies of guilt and terror. What a needlessly awful burden to place on youngsters just so that the parents could enjoy the illusion of having raised clean, innocent, sexless children.

Because boys are usually aware that their friends masturbate too, they feel freer to do it, and their guilt is usually less severe than it otherwise might be—they have the consolation of knowing that if they are going to be blind and insane, their whole generation will have similar problems. Girls, however, seldom discuss masturbation as openly as boys do. As a result, fewer girls feel free to engage in it (about 25 percent of U.S. women over twenty-five years of age have never masturbated), and when they masturbate the guilt is frequently quite severe. Because they have learned that to touch themselves "there" is nasty and disgusting, many women have strong feelings of degradation and guilt after masturbation and develop negative feelings about any touching of their sexual organs—an attitude that may adversely affect their later sexual activities with men.

Some authorities regard masturbation by adults as a symptom of sexual maladjustment. Perhaps it is—it really depends upon how the individual himself feels about it. If he or she really wants sex with a partner but for some reason is unwilling or unable to find someone, then masturbation might be regarded as such a symptom. Of course, masturbation isn't the problem, the problem is loneliness, unhappiness, and a hang-up about seeking a partner. And if no partner is available, masturbation is a reasonable substitute.

Sometimes people worry that they masturbate too much. As was said in the discussion of sexual appetite, what is enough or too much really depends upon what the individual wants. Of course, the person who does virtually nothing but masturbate might want to consider *why* masturbation plays such a large part in his life. The fantasies of masturbation and the other-worldliness of orgasm can be an attractive refuge from reality, and a very unhappy person may be using them to keep the real world out.

In general, unmarried men masturbate about as frequently as they would have sex if they were married; and if they have an occasional sexual experience, they masturbate just that much less. That is, the frequency of men's sexual outlets remains about the same, but the kind of outlet may change from time to time. Many married men masturbate when they are away from home on trips, when their wives are ill, just before and after their wives give birth, or if they are in the mood for sex and their wives aren't.

Single women masturbate less frequently than men and less frequently than they would experience sex were they married. Many single women seldom masturbate or may do so only two or three times a month, usually just before or just after their menstrual period. Others report greater frequency. So, you see, the frequency of masturbation varies a great deal depending on the person and the circumstances. The point is, however, that masturbation is a legitimate part of almost everyone's sex life; it is more predominant when no partner is available, but even then it often plays a role.

Premarital sex   Traditionally, Americans have professed to believe that premarital sex (sex before marriage) is wrong and that both men and women should practice *abstinence* (no sex) until they marry. For the most part, this profession has a hollow ring to it because we actually practice a *double standard* (to a degree men are permitted premarital sex but women supposedly aren't). That is, men are *told* not to engage in premarital sex, but subtly they are encouraged to do so—a male is usually hesitant to admit he is a virgin unless he is strongly religious and/or exceedingly honest. At the same time women are discouraged from engaging in premarital sex, and the fear of being branded immoral has prevented a good number of them from doing so.

If men are encouraged to have premarital sex and women aren't, with whom are the men having sex? In the past, the major source was prostitutes. Young men still may go to a prostitute for the adventure of doing so or if they know no eligible women (for example, soldiers or sailors on leave in a strange city), but as a rule they no longer resort to prostitutes. Sometimes young men have premarital sex with a casual acquaintance or with a woman they meet at a party or a bar. This *sex without affection* is satisfactory for some people who want sex without any emotional ties. For others, this kind of sex is unsatisfactory and merely provides a method to relieve sexual tension until a person can be found with whom a deeper relation can be formed.

The usual alternative to the double standard and to abstinence is *sex with affection.* Most commonly this involves engaged couples; of the women who have premarital sex, about 75 percent have it with the man that they will later marry. Somehow the notion that everybody's intentions are honorable and that marriage is in the offing seems to make premarital sex less of a "sin" than it would be otherwise. The couple might not openly admit that they are having sex, but the fear of discovery is decidedly less than if they were not engaged to be married.

Sex with affection is probably the most common pattern for nonmarital sexual relations of any duration, whether or not the couple is engaged. In our culture it is generally believed that love for one's partner enhances sex—and the belief probably makes this true. This belief has its basis in the idea that to love is to marry and that sex is proper only in marriage. But for many people the attitude also generalizes to nonmarital sex, and for these people affection is a prime prerequisite for sex.

INCIDENCE OF PREMARITAL SEX The incidence of permarital sex in the United States varies among different kinds of people. First, men engage in it more than women do. Second, men with at least one year of college are less likely to have had premarital sex (about 65 percent by the age twenty-five) than men who have had only an eighth grade education or less (about 90 percent by the age twenty-five). On the other hand, about 60 percent of better-educated women have had at least one premarital sexual experience by

FIG. 6.11 *Public statements of appreciation are a common part of affectional bonding.*

age twenty-five compared to only 30 percent of less-educated women (however, about 80 percent of less-educated black women have had premartial sex by age nineteen). There are two reasons for these patterns. First, less pressure is put on lower class black and white men and upon lower class black women to remain virginal. Second, lower class women marry quite young and, among whites, the woman's virginity is very important to her prospective husband; he, of course, is expected to be sexually experienced.

Religion also plays a role in whether people have premarital intercourse. A study done in 1963 found that in Catholic marriages only about 30 percent of the couples had had sex while they were engaged; in Jewish and Protestant marriages only about 40 percent had done so; and in marriages where the two partners had different religions or no religion at all, about 60 percent had had premarital sex during their engagement.

In another survey, about 75 percent of the women who had had premarital sex, whether or not it was with the man they later married, said that they felt no regrets. What's more, 70 percent of these women said that under the same circumstances they would do it again. Of the engaged couples who had had premarital sex, 93 percent of the men and 91 percent of the women said that sex strengthened their relationship.

Marital sex   In our society, marriage has a variety of meanings. For the middle class it means an economic union with friendship, a long-term sexual relation, and children. For the white lower class and for various nonwhite and ethnic subcultures, it may mean something quite different; in some cases the woman is required to limit herself to sex with her husband while the male is free to engage in sex wherever he can find it. In some cases the marriage is merely a formality for legitimatizing whatever children the wife may bear, and the couple may live together only from time to time. In most cases, the middle class ideal of a close friendship between the partners is unthought of. In fact, the latter is true in most cultures; the mate is an economic and sexual partner and friendship is formed with persons of one's own sex.

SUBPATTERNS   Even within the middle class romantic marriage, a variety of sexual patterns exist. Some couples, through preference or as a result of sexual problems, live a life of near *abstinence.* These couples may engage in sex from time to time in order to beget children or because one or the other feels the need, but in general their marriage does not include a sexual relationship. In some cases such a pattern is satisfactory to both partners, and when this is so, they are probably doing what is best for themselves. However, when the pattern is imposed on one partner because of the other's dislike of sex, health problems, or the like, the toll on the deprived partner often is too much to permit the marriage to endure.

Usually, married persons restrict themselves to sex with their mate; between 85 and 90 percent of the sexual activity for married people in general is with their mates, and a good deal of the rest is masturbation. However, circumstances arise in the lives of many married people (about 50 percent of the husbands and about 25 percent of the wives) that lead to at least one sexual experience with some other person. As with premarital sex, more men engage in this *extramarital* sex than women, more lower class men do so than middle class men, more middle class women do so than lower class women (this is true for whites, but probably the reverse is true for blacks), and more nonreligious people do so than religious people.

Part of the motivation for extramarital sex often is sheer boredom. We like to believe that a prolonged, loving relationship will keep sex vital throughout a lifetime, and this may be the case for many couples. However, for many others, a lifetime seems very long and sexual boredom may overcome even the most sincere love. In a culture that worships the advertising agency's version of youth, youthful sexuality, and sexual adventurism, fifty years of sex with just one person may seem a little grim. An affair often seems to offer excitement, adventure, a tantalizing touch of the forbidden, a renewed feeling of youth, and another chance at our cultural pot of gold, romance.

Whether or not extramarital affairs destroy marriages is an open question. Certainly, in some cases the affair allows the participant to experience the feeling of vigor, excitement, and so on, that is needed to get through a time of difficulty or boredom within the marriage, and as such it tides him or her over and may actually save the marriage. In other cases the affair may show the participant that the marriage is unsatisfactory and lead to its dissolution. In the latter case it is really difficult to know whether an affair is the symptom of a disintegrating marriage or whether it contributes to the disintegration.

Extramarital sex, *adultery,* is considered a sin by most major religions (particularly for women), is illegal in most states, and is grounds for divorce virtually everywhere. In part, this taboo stems from the notion that women are the property of their husbands and that property is supposed to belong solely to its owner. Few societies have regarded the male as particularly blameworthy in the case of adultery. This attitude has changed in recent years, and now adultery is regarded as a breach of trust that makes either person equally responsible for his or her actions. Of course, many marriages survive adultery, and, in some cases, the couple agrees to countenance or even to encourage it. Such cases are relatively rare and authorities constantly debate the wisdom of such arrangements. However the meaning of marriage is changing as a result of women's increased independence and the impact of contraception, and it is to be expected that there will be fundamental changes in the ground rules of marriages.

Homosexuality Masturbation is sex with oneself. Premarital, marital, and extramarital sex ordinarily are heterosexual, that is, involving a partner of the opposite sex. Homosexuality is sex with someone of one's own sex. While most people are willing to admit that the other patterns are common and normal, few regard homosexuality as either common or normal. In making such a judgment, they are ignoring the fact that roughly one third of American males and one fifth of American females have, at least once, engaged in sex to the point of orgasm with someone of their own sex.

SOME TERMS Let us first define some terms so we will know what we're talking about. *Homosexual* describes the fact that two persons of the same sex are sexually attracted to one another or that they have sexual relations with one another. It also is used to describe sex relations between men, while the term *lesbian* is used for sex relations between women. Unfortunately, the terms "homosexual" and "lesbian" are also used as nouns and adjectives to label and describe the people who engage in such relations—labels that have a particularly damning quality in our culture. Too frequently they are inaccurate; they imply that the person engages exclusively in homosexuality, which is not necessarily the case. *Bisexual* is the term used when people engage in both heterosexual and homosexual relations.

INCIDENCE OF HOMOSEXUALITY   About 4 percent of American males (roughly three million) engage almost exclusively in homosexual relations throughout their entire sexual lives. Another 31 percent (about 20 million) have had periods of at least three years of occasional to exclusive homosexuality some time after puberty. Of course, some of the three-year periods of activity were during adolescence and were motivated by curiosity rather than by a preference for men, but the experiences were, nevertheless, homosexual.

Lesbianism is less common. Only about 1 to 3 percent of American women (about one and a half million) engage exclusively in lesbian relations. Roughly another 15 percent (about ten and half million) have had one or more homosexual experience. Altogether, out of a total population of about 140 million people over the age of 15, about 35 million American men and women have had homosexual experiences—a number too large to permit one to regard homosexuality as a particularly uncommon sexual pattern.

The incidence of homosexual activity, as for heterosexual activity, differs for different groups of people. Homosexuality is roughly twice as common among men as among women. Social class doesn't make much difference, but homosexual relations occur more frequently among nonreligious people than among religious people. People who are heterosexually married seldom engage in homosexuality, although it does occur more often than is generally believed.

SUBPATTERNS   Homosexuality reflects some of the same subpatterns as heterosexuality. *Abstinence* is practiced by a large number of people who have homosexual feelings but do not yield to them. Roughly 50 percent of the men and 28 percent of the women interviewed for the Kinsey Report said that they had experienced homosexual feelings at one time or another. In view of our cultural taboo against having such feelings or telling someone about them (even Dr. Kinsey), it is likely that these figures are unrealistically low. The fact that Americans support thriving businesses in homosexual pornography implies that a great many people are fantasizing even if they are abstaining.

Sex without affection is a relatively common pattern within homosexual relations. Many bars, particulary in large cities, cater to a clientele that is primarily interested in meeting prospective partners for homosexual relations. The meetings are casual, and the people seldom see each other again. Too, homosexual prostitution exists to provide a means for immediate, noninvolving sex.

The *sex with affection* pattern also is common. Indeed, many people engage in homosexuality because they feel a strong sexual affection for a person of their own sex; they may never engage in homosexuality again after that relationship ends. Longer-term homosexual "marriages" are not very common but they do occur; the two people live together and are regarded as married by themselves and by their friends. Such relationships tend to be somewhat unstable and shortlived, but sometimes they last as long as a heterosexual marriage. The absence of the legal and social sanctions that ordinarily seal a heterosexual marriage and inhibit its dissolution are absent in a homosexual marriage and may contribute to its greater instability.

WHY HOMOSEXUALITY? When considering homosexuality, it is common to ask where things went wrong. This, of course, assumes that something went wrong, that heterosexuality is the pattern that would spontaneously emerge if a person were not "messed up" in some way. However, it is a great deal more reasonable to assume that for human beings a generalized sexuality is all that emerges spontaneously and that people learn what they "should" regard as "correct" objects for this sexuality. Many cultures countenance homosexuality, particularly between unmarried males, in addition to heterosexuality. In such cultures people learn that both men and women are appropriate for sex, and as a result there is no shame, no notion of guilt, and no source of worry. Officially our culture dictates that the only acceptable sex object is a marriage partner of the opposite sex. Homosexuality is forbidden, and it is reasonable to ask why some people engage in homosexuality when it is subject to such strong disapproval.

One answer to this question is that people who engage in homosexuality are genetically and biologically different from everyone else—"they were born that way." But there is virtually no evidence to support such a view, in spite of a great deal of research.

Another answer is that some people engage in homosexual relations because they were victims of homosexual assault or homosexual pornography during their formative years. This view has even less supporting evidence than the genetic view; many people have had various forms of homosexual experience as children, forcible and otherwise, and have emerged as well-functioning heterosexuals. Moreover, there is little reason to think that pornography has a damaging effect on anyone, except insofar as it misinforms. These answers, then, are unacceptable.

The third answer is that the pattern of family interactions while one is a child sets the tone for an individual's later sexual identification. Probably different patterns of family interactions work in different ways to produce sexual orientations, but there are three generally dominant patterns that can be described. In one, the child's treatment by his parents, from the very beginning, is appropriate to his sex. His parents dress him in the kinds of clothes that are currently acceptable for his or her sex. They expect, tolerate, and subtly encourage boisterousness and aggressiveness from their sons and passiveness and daintiness from their daughters. In the course of this treatment, the requirement to be a "normal" boy and a "normal" girl is communicated, and subsequent behavior tends to stay on the same track into adolescence and actual sexual activity.

The second pattern is one in which the parents' treatment of the child is in opposition to the culturally appropriate role or is not very well defined. The result is that the child learns an incorrect or ill-defined role that is inappropriate or only semiappropriate. From this there may well arise a confusion in sex identity and/or inappropriate sexual behavior.

The third pattern is one in which one parent is extremely dominant and the other is either weak or absent. In such cases the dominant parent may treat the child in either a seductive manner or a repressive manner, both of which may later lead to a homosexual pattern. If a dominant mother establishes very strong ties with her son, he may never want to break them to establish ties with another woman—so he avoids other women, turns to men for sex, and stays "true" to his mother. On the other hand, a mother of this type may so dominate her son that he develops a fear of women in general and turns to men. A dominating and disapproving father may inadvertently teach his son that he is incapable of being the man that his father is and that he cannot expect to hold the respect and love of a woman. By seeking only men, the son avoids failure with women and also obtains the masculine approval that he did not get from his father. For women the same sorts of patterns occur, but with the opposite parent.

Thus, the *why* of homosexuality is not clear. It probably has different origins for different people—just as heterosexuality is different for different people. Homosexuality is not necessarily an "abnormal" pattern if you look at it from the viewpoint of all of human cultures and across history; but in our culture it is not an acceptable sexual pattern. However, to judge from the recent increase in homosexual themes in movies, books, and theater, we may be witnessing the beginning of a change in our cultural attitudes toward homosexuality (Fig. 6.12). Sympathetic treatment in these media, with less emphasis on the "those poor sick people" theme, might free many people from the nagging fear about their own homosexual urges and permit greater freedom for every person to consider rationally what sexual pattern is best for him or her.

FIG. 6.12   *The militance of the Gay Liberation movement is an indication that many homosexuals are unwilling to continue being ashamed of their desires and that they demand the freedom as citizens to live as they see fit. (UPI photo.)*

The "Sexual Revolution"   The popular press is constantly flooded with stories about a "sexual revolution" that is supposed to be occurring among high school and college-age people. To read these newspaper and magazine stories, you would think that everybody is having sex with everybody else, all the time, anytime. Some readers of these articles look upon this revolution as a release from moralistic oppression, while others look upon it as a sign of moral decay and impending social catastrophe. The fact is, however, that the press has created a myth.

For example, if you look at the surveys taken among college students over the years, you find that a little more than 50 percent of the unmarried men have had sex at least once and that roughly 25 to 30 percent of the unmarried women have. These percentages have remained about the same since the first survey was taken in 1929. Although recent surveys have shown some increase in premarital sex for college women, it is difficult to know whether this is actually the case because there are variations from one survey to another and the results are not all the same. In addition, there is a question about whether there has been any increase in the number of women who are engaging in sex or whether there has merely been an increase in the willingness to admit it. At any rate, these survey results show that if there is a sexual revolution of the variety that the press reports, it is a very timid revolution and hardly worth all the shouting.

Sources of the myth   The myth of the sexual revolution has two probable sources, one new, one old. The new one is the recent increase in the mobility and independence of young people and their freedom to congregate in what might be called "youth ghettos." The old one is the old feeling of alienation and mistrust between the generations, the "generation gap." Let us look at each source in turn.

In the late 1960s and early 1970s a totally new phenomenon appeared in Western society. Throughout Europe and North America highly mobile young people flocked to places like Haight-Ashbury in San Francisco. Almost any large city had such a youth ghetto where alienated, angry, bored, and unhappy young people went to be with their contemporaries and where they could feel that they were part of a cultural revolution. A central theme in these ghettos was defiance of the supposedly suffocating moral and legal impositions of the straight society (the "establishment"). Thus, the group encouraged drug use and sexual freedom, and its members, like all of us, were sensitive to the pressure of their peer group and followed its rules to one degree or another. The press, in its zestful search for a good story, projected this phenomenon as an image of all youths. Of course, such projection was inaccurate; only a small proportion of youths seriously became part of the phenomenon. A beard, long hair, a bead necklace, or granny glasses and a long skirt did not make a person part of it, although many young people affected such attire and enjoyed feeling that they were defying society.

What happened was that the phenomenon of the youth ghetto served to bring together large numbers of people who had very liberal ideas concerning sex and who didn't mind talking about them. Thus, their sexual attitudes and practices were visible, as was also the case with their drug attitudes and practices. Although there are no data that I know of, I suspect that even at that there was more talk than action. Just as few young men would admit virginity in a locker room conversation, few residents of a youth ghetto would tell their friends that they didn't approve of promiscuous sex. In both cases the person tells his peers what he thinks they want to hear so he can avoid disapproval. At any rate, the press listened to what was said, seemingly took it seriously, added a liberal portion of wife-swapping stories, and garnished the whole thing with a dash of group marriage tales; the result was the myth of a raging sexual revolution.

The second contributor to the myth is not unlike the first except that it has always been with us. The so-called generation gap has always existed and is always being rediscovered; our oldest historical records contain lamentations that the younger generation is on the high road to Hades. This has been a popular theme in our day because the dramatic increase in population has resulted in a large proportion of young people; in fact, about 47 percent of the U.S. population today is made up of persons under twenty-five years of age. As was the case with the youth ghetto, the increased proportion of young people in the population has made their behavior more visible than it was in the past. The result is that older people can more easily contrast their attitudes with those of their children and then sadly shake their heads.

Evidence suggests, however, that young people today are not much wilder than their parents were at the same age, the parents are simply more conservative than they were when they themselves were young. Actually, the fact of getting older is not necessarily what makes people become conservative; many people over thirty are very liberal. But when the issue for people is *their children,* for whom they feel responsibility, the story is different. There is something about being responsible for another person's behavior that immediately evokes a conservative tendency. After all, poor behavior may result in harm to that person, and it reflects a failure in responsibility on the part of the parents. Given this difficult set of circumstances, most parents end up setting rather high standards, so if their children fall a little short they won't be very badly off. The result, of course, is that the parents require better behavior of their children than they required of themselves at the same age. The children, with the support of their peer group, set somewhat more realistic standards for themselves and therefore fall short of their parents' demands. Consequently, the parents decide that "young people today" are morally lax, and the children decide that their parents are old-fashioned and "up-tight."

Is there a revolution? All of the foregoing has not been to say that a sexual revolution is not taking place. A vast change is indeed underway today in people's attitudes toward sex. This revolution, however, did not start in the seventies or the sixties or even the fifties or forties. Rather, it began about the time of World War I—in short, with your grandparents.

The sexual revolution is a complex mixture of things. First, it is characterized more by a change in attitudes toward sex, sex roles, permissible sex, and so forth, than by an actual increase in nonmarital sexual activity. Much of it centers around the changing role of women in U.S. society as increased educational and economic opportunity afford women greater independence to determine their own lives rather than exist as chattels of their husbands and fathers. Too, the greater availability of contraceptive devices, starting with the mass production of condoms ("rubbers") in about 1920, has allowed American women to separate sex from reproduction, thereby giving them more freedom to plan their own lives.

Since the pioneering efforts of your grandparents, there has been a gradual liberalization of attitudes toward sex, and, as might be expected, young people are in the vanguard. Although sexual behavior itself has not changed very much, people are less harsh in their judgments about other people's sexual attitudes and about nonmarital sex, even if they don't themselves indulge. This relaxed attitude toward other people's sex lives, however, does not always extend to the person himself. That is, people seem to think that a sexual revolution is raging around them, but they don't feel part of it. If you asked college women if premarital sex is common among their classmates, about three quarters would say it is, yet, as we have seen, only about 25 to 30 percent of college girls engage in premarital sex. On the other hand, many a college girl who occasionally has intercourse doesn't even use a contraceptive because she is afraid that it will look like "premeditated sex" or that her roommate will discover the contraceptive and think that she is immoral. In short, many of these girls think that everybody else is having sex, and they don't judge harshly, but they don't consider themselves part of the group.

Sexual Intercourse   This book is not intended to be a sex manual. McCary's *Human Sexuality* and others are good, and they do a much more thorough job than can be done in the space available here. However, a few physiological facts might interest you and will provide necessary information that can be referred to in the subsequent discussion of the psychological aspects of intercourse.

Based on the recent research of Dr. W. Masters and Ms. V. Johnson, the sexual response cycle can be thought of as having four phases: (1) excitement, (2) plateau, (3) orgasmic, (4) resolution. We will examine these stages in rough detail for both men and women and then discuss their psychological implications.

Excitement phase This phase corresponds to the early stages of sexual arousal on the part of the two partners, the initial kissing, undressing, and the beginning of sexual play. For most men, sexual excitement, through fantasy or the beginning of sexual activity, causes the nipples to become erect, brings on a flushing of the skin starting on the belly, and produces a general increase in muscular tension, heart rate, and blood pressure. The penis becomes erect as a result of the engorgement of spongy tissue in the shaft with blood. The excitement phase in women brings on erection of the nipples and enlargement of the breasts. A flush may appear, often beginning on the belly and spreading to the neck and breasts, and muscle tension increases, as does blood pressure. The clitoris swells slightly as the blood in it increases, and so do the lips surrounding the opening of the vagina. The internal walls of the vagina secrete a clear lubricating fluid, and the barrel of the vagina increases in length and width in preparation to receive the erect penis.

Plateau phase After the partners are sexually aroused, there is a phase of sexual activity that consists of manipulation of the sex organs, soft stroking, and other sexually stimulating behavior. This phase moves toward the orgasmic phase and in large part consists of actual intercourse that culminates in the orgasmic phase. In men, the plateau phase involves further increase in muscle tension, and possibly a spread or the late appearance of the flushing of the skin. Blood pressure increases, and the pulse may increase from its normal 70 beats per minute to over 100 beats per minute. As orgasm is approached, the head of the penis fills with more blood and the testes increase in size and are drawn closer to the body. For women, the plateau phase involves an enlargement of the area immediately surrounding the nipples, a spreading of the skin flush, and an increase in muscle tension, particularly in the buttocks as the woman approaches orgasm. The pulse rate and blood pressure increase. The clitoris withdraws under the fleshy hood that normally is directly above it; this means that the movement of the penis in the vagina stretches and moves the skin surrounding the clitoris as well as the overhanging hood. The friction of this skin against the clitoris brings the woman closer to orgasm.[2] The friction of the vaginal barrel against the penis, particularly on the head of the penis, brings the man closer to orgasm.

Orgasmic phase For the man, orgasm consists of a loss of voluntary muscular control and an increase in blood pressure, pulse, and breathing rate. The seminal fluid ("come"), composed both of sperm and other fluids, is spurted out through the tube that lies along the underside of the penis by the contraction of muscles at the base of the penis. This is accompanied by an extremely pleasurable sensation and momentary oblivion to anything else. For the woman the heart rate increases, as does breathing rate. The clitoris stays under its hood, and the vagina begins a series of strong contractions. As with the man, orgasm is extremely pleasurable for the woman, and she is usually oblivious to all else during it.

Resolution phase Immediately after orgasm the strong physiological excitement evident in the earlier phases begins to decrease. The man's nipples again become soft, his skin flush begins to fade, his muscles begin to relax, his heartbeat, blood pressure, and breathing become normal, and the testes return to their normal position and size. His penis rapidly decreases to about one half its erect size and then slowly decreases to its normal size unless sexual stimulation persists. The first decrease usually occurs within minutes after orgasm. Even with prolonged stimulation that successfully maintains the erection, most men must wait a while before they are capable of a second orgasm.

The woman's resolution phase consists of a slow return of the breasts and nipples to their normal size, the disappearance of the skin flush, muscular relaxation, and return of pulse, blood pressure, and respiration to their normal state. The clitoris descends from under its hood and slowly returns to its normal size. The vagina returns to normal, as do its external lips. During this phase many men and women report feeling warm and loving toward their partner and a desire to hold and be held. Both partners often feel closer to each other, feel more in harmony after mutually satisfying sex than at any other time; it is a time of tranquillity after having *both* given and received extreme pleasure.

Deterrents to satisfying sex The phases just described, and what happens during them, are characteristic for people engaged in satisfying sex, although

---

[2] For many women the stimulation resulting from the movement of the penis in the vagina is insufficient to cause orgasm. In such cases, direct stimulation of the clitoris by the man's hand often is an acceptable solution.

minor variations occur for different people. The problem is that many people never fully experience satisfying sex. To understand why, at least for the most common problems, you have to draw on a number of the things discussed thus far in this book.

Sex is complex for human beings. Other animals seem fairly capable of doing it without too much trouble (although monkeys sometimes have problems, if you'll remember the discussion in Section 4, Part 1). The physiological components of human sexuality are fairly automatic if they aren't interfered with by the psychological components. However, because the psychological components, starting with attraction and ending with the loving feeling during the resolution phase, essentially control sexuality, frequent interference with the physiological component is not surprising.

The major psychological problem that can interfere with sex is *fear:* fear of being immoral, fear of failing to perform properly, fear of pregnancy. Note that the first two of these fears refer to a set of standards that the person assumes are the "right" way to proceed with sex.

Women usually are most affected by fear of immorality—after roughly twenty years of hearing sex talked about only in terms of good and evil, it is difficult to think of it in any other way. However, just because women are frequently victims of this fear does not mean that men are immune. For both sexes, after having been taught that sex is to be avoided, attitudes cannot be expected to change merely because love is found and/or a marriage ceremony takes place. Long-standing attitudes don't change that easily; a person has to be aware of them and work on changing them.

Fear of immorality also can influence the freedom of sexual expression even after fearful feelings about intercourse are overcome. Variations in sexual position, oral-genital contact, use of fingers and teeth for erotic stimulation, all are part of the arsenal of lovemaking. Many people feel that such practices are degrading and immoral and refuse to engage in them even if their partner would like to. Of course, if a person actually feels this way, he or she would be as unwise to do them because "one should" as to not do them because "one shouldn't." However, these variations in sexual stimulation can be extremely pleasurable and can keep sex interesting and satisfying.

The second fear, fear of inadequate performance, is a problem faced by more men than women. Our cultural ideal for a male is that he should be sexually knowledgeable and that he should take responsibility for initiating sex and seeing that both he and his partner are satisfied. The desirability of being a "good lover" or a "stud," or whatever term you prefer, is conveyed to him through his peer group, through the jokes and stories he hears during adolescence, and through the kinds of male stereotypes (like movie stars) that our society worships. The notion that a "real man" is strong (but gentle), is demanding (but never resorts to rape), can make a woman beg for more, and can go all night has little basis in actual human example and even less in physiological fact. But even though they may try to take all of this idealistic nonsense with a grain of salt, many men have a deep need to fulfill this impossible image. For a man in this predicament, each sexual encounter is a performance—he must prove his masculinity to himself, his partner, and to some unseen set of judges (his peers and all the people they represent). Some women get caught in this same trap and feel that they must perform well in order to show their partners—and the unseen judges—that they really like sex. These people often get so caught up in the performance that they fail to enjoy sex except as physical exercise or as one more success or failure at a task that they have set for themselves.

The third fear, fear of pregnancy, is shared by both women and men, although women most frequently are aware of it. For unmarried partners the possibility of pregnancy is a real threat to the future. If conception occurs, there are only four alternatives, none of them easy. First, there is marriage, the most common and perhaps the least satisfactory solution; unless marriage was already planned, the mutual resentment of having been forced into an unwanted marriage can make both partners miserable. The second solution is for the child to be placed for adoption, a solution that often leaves the mother with strong guilt feelings as well as the social stigma of having borne a child out of marriage. The third solution is for the unmarried woman to keep the child, which, as has been pointed out before, is usually an inadequate solution because of the potential effects of having only one parent and of the label of illegitimacy for the child. The fourth solution is abortion. Depending on one's moral feelings, this can be the best solution in states where it can be legally performed by a knowledgeable physician in a clean medical clinic. Back-alley abortions are dangerous and may leave a woman physically and psychologically damaged—at best the woman usually is quite ill after one of these illicit abortions.

For married couples the fear of pregnancy usually involves such tangibles as the threat of another birth to the mother's health, hospital expenses, and the long-range cost of feeding, clothing, and housing another child. Often intangible values are of even greater importance; another baby often means that the wife will be tied to the house for a few more years and that she will have to go through the same trials and tribulations with the new child that she has already gone through with one or more previous children. As the couple gets older, they may look forward to the day when they can travel or relax without being concerned about dependents; another child puts that day off still further.

Many young couples want to delay having children, or to avoid it altogether, so they can spend their time with each other, establish themselves financially, travel while they are young, and so forth. For them, pregnancy requires a complete change in life-style and in their plans.

With all of these consequences hanging in the balance, it is little wonder that people can be haunted by the fear of pregnancy. Of course, contraception reduces the likelihood of pregnancy, but the fear often remains, and not without reason. No contraceptive, with the possible exception of the Pill, is really foolproof, if only because many people do not use them correctly. The point is that the fear of pregnancy is a real and reasonable fear and that it can keep people from enjoying a satisfying sex life.

All three of these fears (moral, performance, and pregnancy) can lead to a spectrum of sexual problems ranging from minor and nondebilitating ones to quite severe problems that make sex virtually impossible. If both partners share the same fears and are satisfied with the sex life that these fears dictate, no one can question their choice. However, the more common case is for one or the other partner to feel restless and resentful and to feel that there ought to be more to sex than what he or she is experiencing.

For women, fears about sex can lead to a general lack of interest in it. Indeed, the old-fashioned notion of a woman being "frigid," that is, unable to experience sexual arousal or orgasm, often results from just this; the woman becomes so fearful that she represses her sexual feelings. Of course, such fears are seldom clear to the woman, partially because today it is unfashionable to be fearful about sex. Because there seldom is a physiological basis for the woman's lack of interest in sex, doctors in the past were unable to trace the source of the "frigid" woman's dysfunction and generally regarded it as an incurable problem. The modern approach is to work on the source of the fears; psychotherapy and a very patient, supportive partner can overcome these fears and permit the woman to be sexually alive.

Some men also react to these fears by losing interest in sex. However, men also evidence other symptoms, primarily an inability to attain an erection (called *impotence*) or an inability to attain orgasm and ejaculation (called *ejaculatory incompetence*). The clinical subtleties of these problems need not concern us here. The point is that the man's sexual problems may be more obvious because his sexual apparatus may not work correctly; a woman with similar fears can still engage in sex and, if she wants to fool her partner, she can pretend to have an orgasm. She may not be happy with her sexual experience, but unless she tells him that things aren't the way she would like them to be, her partner may not realize that she is sexually unhappy. On the other hand, a male's sexual dysfunction is painfully obvious both to his partner and to himself if he cannot attain and maintain an erection or if he cannot ejaculate.

The tragedy is that many men don't realize that occasional impotence or inability to ejaculate is not uncommon. Fatigue, too much to drink, drugs, worry about business or finances, illness, depression, and so on, can prevent a man from having satisfactory sex. But many men panic when this happens because of their fear of failing to perform well. They think that they should always be able to deliver and that a failure is a reflection on their manhood. So, the one failure strengthens their fear, which feeds the fear still more. This increases the chances of yet another fear-produced failure, and on and on until the poor fellow is so tense and scared that he either gives up (with the resulting damage to his self-concept and marriage) or seeks professional help. Until recently the therapeutic outlook for impotence and ejaculatory incompetence was bleak. However, new therapy techniques are becoming available, primarily through the efforts of two previously mentioned researchers, Dr. Masters and Ms. Johnson, at the Reproductive Biology Research Foundation in St. Louis, Missouri. These techniques consist of the husband and wife working together to reduce the sexual fears that prevent them from attaining satisfactory sex and helping each other attain the pleasure of full, free sexuality.

One of the primary lessons to be learned from the Masters and Johnson work on sexual problems is that satisfactory sex requires that one get the "spectators," those unseen judges, out of the bedroom (Fig. 6.13). That is, fears of immorality and of performance are fears related not to what the person himself wants to do and experience but rather to what he thinks "they" expect. (It is much like the first time you ever stole anything. Maybe nobody saw you, but even so, you felt as though someone somewhere knew. The feeling was not based on your reaction to whether or not you wanted the thing you stole. Rather, it was related to that great big "they" that is composed of your parents, your friends, the police, society at large, and, for some people, God.) In short, many people limit their sex lives to what they think would be approved of by all those spectators; they never do what they themselves want. Their fears that these illusory spectators might disapprove of their practices, their performance, or their uninhibited enjoyment renders them less capable of full and unhampered involvement in sex than would otherwise be the case. The unfortunate result is a failure to experience full sexual satisfaction.

So far, the focus has been on three fears that can interfere with sex. There are others, of course, and their effects are much like those described in the

FIG. 6.13 *Imaginary judgmental "spectators" frequently are a deterrent to satisfactory sex.* (By permission of Voices—The Art and Science of Psychotherapy, *Vol. 1, No. 1, Fall 1965, drawn by John Severin.*)

last few paragraphs. Some people fear venereal disease. Some think that because the sex organs are also used for urination that they are unclean (not necessarily true). Some people fear being discovered while having sex, or they fear that people will know that they do it. Some people are so afraid of members of the opposite sex that, though they may marry, they can't trust their mate or feel strong sexual attraction. Some people are afraid that they like sex too much and will wear themselves out (a fallacy), or that they don't like it enough and must be odd. Most of these fears reflect a certain degree of the "spectator" problem, but some, such as the fear of venereal disease, are well founded under certain circumstances.

Sex is a natural function that, with a little thought and cheerful communication, can proceed with ease and be extremely pleasurable. However, we live in a culture that teaches us to be pretty tense about sex. The things we learn over the years are hard to look at objectively—they become unconsciously accepted "truths" and vaguely defined values. For all their ghostly qualities, these things can cause a good deal of pain. As was said before, we all are encapsulated, in a sense, because no one talks freely and honestly about his or her sexuality. We all fear that we might reveal some inadequacy or abnormality. As a result, in this encapsulated vacuum, our vague, ill-defined attitudes and fears can operate freely, unencumbered by any opposing, corrective information from other people. We can read books that describe technique and sexual positions, but seldom can we find anything that convincingly corrects our maladaptive and disruptive attitudes and values. Sometimes it takes psychotherapy to change attitudes. Sometimes it takes a patient and better-informed partner. But first, it takes an honest self-appraisal and a willingness to admit that there are problems that have to be faced and evaluated. Then, if these problems are causing trouble, you have to decide how to change them and if it is worth it. If it is worth it, you must work on it. A therapist or your partner can be of aid, but it is your life and it is up to you to get the most out of it that you can.

SUMMARY

1   Every culture has its version of when, where, and how to experience love. Our version is the *tradition of romantic love,* which had its origins in Christianity and the European social structure of the Middle Ages. Its primary legacy is to lead most of us to expect to "fall in love," marry, have a family, and thereby lead fulfilling and contented lives.

2   Few of us give much consideration to what kind of love life is best for us—we just drift along looking for the romantic ideal. However, increasing divorce rates and other indications of social change make such a passive course less satisfying than it may have been in the past.

3   There are four predominant patterns of sexuality in our culture: *masturbation, premarital sex, marital* and *extramarital sex,* and *homosexuality.* Most people engage in one or more of these patterns throughout their lives.

4   The so-called sexual revolution is not a recent event; sexual patterns have not changed appreciably for the last forty years or so. The current revolution has to do not so much with sexual behavior as with the liberalization of attitudes toward sex, sex roles, permissible sex, and so on.

5   The major deterrent to satisfactory sex is fear—fear of *immorality,* fear of *failure* to perform adequately, fear of *pregnancy,* and so on. Such fears must be faced and overcome if a person is to achieve sexual fulfillment.

Further Reading

BACH, G. R., and P. WYDEN.   *The Intimate Enemy*
New York: Avon, 1970 (c. 1968), 375 pages (paperback).
This book describes how to fight fairly in love and marriage. The authors suggest that fighting is good for an intimate relation if it is done fairly. They show you how.

Cox, F. D.　*Youth, Marriage and the Seductive Society*
Dubuque, Iowa: Brown, 1968, 131 pages (paperback).
This is a fairly straightforward examination of young Americans' sexual attitudes and behavior. It is a textbook with down to earth advice and some good insights into the problems of early marriage. A bit traditional but well worth looking at.

Ellis, A.　*Sex without Guilt*
North Hollywood, Calif.: Wilshire, 1970 (c. 1959), 190 pages (paperback)
A self-help guide to guiltless sex. Covers a variety of aspects of sex, among them masturbation, homosexuality, frigidity, sex education, sex censorship, and myths about love.

Fromm, E.　*The Art of Loving*
New York: Harper & Row, 1962 (c. 1956), 146 pages (paperback).
This is the modern classic on love—brotherly love, motherly love, erotic love, self-love, and love of God. It is an insightful book with the theme that loving is necessary for human fulfillment. Its one flaw is that while it tells you that you must be a loving person if you are to be happy, it doesn't give you even a glimmer of how to become a loving person if you don't happen to be one now.

Katchadourian, H. A., and D. T. Lunde.　*Fundamentals of Human Sexuality*
New York: Holt, Rinehart and Winston, 1972, 514 pages (paperback).
A book written specifically for a course in human sexuality. Contains a wealth of information about the biological, psychological, behavioral, and cultural aspects of human sexual behavior. Sections on the erotic in art, literature, and film are particularly interesting. Informative and easy to read.

Kirkendall, L. A., and R. N. Whitehurst (Eds.).　*The New Sexual Revolution*
New York: Brown, 1971, 236 pages (paperback).
An insightful book on a newly emerging morality about sex which emphasizes individual choice over societal demands. Contains a collection of papers by various authors delving into such topics as obscenity and pornography, homosexuality, sex education, the relevance of marriage, and population and birth control.

Lieberman, B. (Ed.)　*Human Sexual Behavior*
New York: Wiley, 1971, 444 pages (paperback).
Books of readings often are spotty in their coverage, but this one does a very good job. It contains both research studies and essays by experts, so it is well balanced and fairly thorough. The first section surveys what famous psychologists have had to say about sexuality—which could be good except that most of what is surveyed is very old. The rest of the book is more to the point—what people actually do and think—and is much more interesting. The reviews of the Masters and Johnson research and the earlier Kinsey work are particularly valuable.

Masters, W. H., and V. E. Johnson.　*Human Sexual Response*
Boston: Little, Brown, 1966, 366 pages.
The only thorough study of human physiological processes before, during, and after sexual intercourse. This is a fairly technical book, apparently intentionally so in order

to avoid any taint of sensationalism. However, if you've had a biology course and are willing to tolerate some vagueness in places, it would be well worth your time to look through the book.

MASTERS, W. H., and V. E. JOHNSON.   *Human Sexual Inadequacy*
Boston: Little, Brown, 1970, 467 pages.
The Masters and Johnson technique for treating sexual problems are famous by now. This is the book in which the techniques were revealed to a waiting world. These techniques are widely used and seem to have fair success. The book is difficult to read in places—it seems to be written in "social science doubletalk" in an effort to obscure and confuse—but if you are determined, you'll make it and it probably is worth the effort.

McCARY, J. L.   *Human Sexuality*
Princeton, N.J.: Van Nostrand, 1967, 374 pages.
If you dared to ask about everything you ever wanted to know about sex and found that the answers were shallow, hysterical, or nonexistent, McCary's excellent book is for you. It is interesting, up to date, and informative, but it also is solid enough and sufficiently well documented to put it head and shoulders above the usual sort of sex manual.

REISS, I. L.   *Premarital Sexual Standards in America*
New York: Free Press, 1960, 286 pages.
Delves into the sexual nature of man and the history of sexual standards. Discusses various types of sexual permissiveness, the positive and negative consequences of sexual permissiveness, and future trends in premarital sexual standards.

REISS, I. L.   *The Social Context of Premarital Sexual Permissiveness*
New York: Holt, Rinehart and Winston, 1967, 256 pages.
A systematic study of premarital sexual attitudes among students and adults in America. Describes techniques used to measure premarital sexual permissiveness and delves into the relations between premarital sexual permissiveness and such factors as race, religion, social class, dating characteristics, and family and peer attitudes.

Part 4 *PSYCHOLOGICAL ASPECTS OF POVERTY*

Most of us don't spend very much time thinking about poverty. We may lament being broke, if we are. We may decry the injustices suffered by the poor, if we know about them. And we may resent welfare payments to those "lazy bums," if we are ill informed. But few of us really understand the various components of poverty or their implications for the poor themselves, for their children, or for society as a whole. The necessarily limited purpose of the following discussion is to outline some of the psychological implications of poverty in as dispassioned a way as possible. It will be dispassioned because there is not space in this book to convey fully the emotional toll of poverty (*The Grapes of Wrath* by John Steinbeck, *Manchild in the Promised Land* by Claude Brown, or any of the flood of recent books about poverty do a better job than could ever be done here). And, too, this discussion will be dispassioned because there is a strong need for solid information about poverty if something constructive ever is to be done about it.

What Is Poverty?   Contrary to popular opinion, poverty is not merely the absence of money. Even the poor usually have some money; they would be totally unable to survive without it. Indeed, a poor man in America might be quite well off compared to a poor man in Mexico or India. As a matter of fact, Mexican laborers willingly come to the United States to work for what we consider low wages, because, compared to the wages they receive at home, they do not have a bad deal. Similarly, Spanish, Italian, and Yugoslavian workers migrate to northern European countries to perform labor that the local residents don't want to do, and they do it for pay that the local residents consider too low. But the general standard of living is lower in the migrant workers' home country than in the country to which they go to work—and therein lies a clue to what poverty is.

Above some ill-defined point of deprivation, whether or not a person is poor depends upon his economic standing relative to other people around him. People who at least have enough to eat may never think of themselves as poor if all of their neighbors are in the same boat. For example, a farmer who lives in a rural area in India and who has sufficient food is not likely to think of himself as terribly poor. On the other hand, someone who has the exact same resources as the Indian farmer but lives somewhere else in the world, say the midwestern United States, might regard himself as poverty stricken. The *first factor* that defines poverty, then, is that, above some minimum level, it is not how little you have that makes you poor, it is how little you have relative to what other people around you have.

The *second factor* that defines poverty involves the fact that many people choose to live on meager means. No one considers such people as being poverty stricken. Many religious orders practice renunciation of personal wealth. Persons dedicated to social service, such as Peace Corps volunteers, VISTA workers, and many of the people who work for social agencies in the slums all willingly limit their incomes. Yet these people aren't poor in the usual sense. Why? Because they are "broke" because they choose to be so—a truly poor person doesn't choose to be poor.

The *final factor* that defines poverty is the most fundamental one. Consider a twenty-two-year-old college student and a twenty-two-year-old high school dropout, both working as dishwashers in a restaurant. The difference between them is that the college student is going somewhere. He isn't considered poor because he has hope of better things to come. The high school dropout may have dreams, but his dreams are a sad substitute for hope. Uneducated, unskilled, and unrealistic because he cannot afford to be otherwise, the dropout, and others like him, is likely to have come from poverty, to stay in poverty, and to die in poverty. Thus, the final factor defining poverty is that the poor have neither the personal resources to effect change nor the economic capital upon which to build a better future; therefore, they have very little realistic hope.

Who Are the Poor?

Who are these people whose resources are low relative to the economy as a whole, who do not choose to be poor, and who are trapped in their poverty? If we take the government's unreasonably low figure of roughly $3,500 a year for a family of four as the cut-off point for defining poverty and count all the adults who have lower incomes,

—20 percent of the 47 million families in the United States are poor
—45 percent of the single people in the United States are poor (this consists mainly of old and young people, all of whom make less than $1,750 a year).[3]

What are these poor people like? About 78 percent of them are white. And, although they constitute only about 12 to 15 percent of the general population of the country, nonwhites constitute 22 percent of the poor. Roughly half of the poor live in cities where their life often is more difficult than that of the rural poor, since the rural poor can supplement their diet with home-grown foods. Many of the urban poor are a result of the agricultural revolution that has been taking place over the past 70 years. One of the major effects of this revolution has been a reduction in the percentage of the U.S. population (down to 5 percent) that is needed to grow the food for the entire country. Thus, many agricultural workers have been forced to go to the city to get jobs—and jobs often do not exist. Many of the poor are old persons who live on fixed retirement incomes or older workers who have been laid off and can't find a new job. Some are widowed, divorced, or deserted women who must care for and support their children. Some are uneducated young people with mar-

---

[3] Depending on the criterion used to define poverty, the figures vary a great deal. However, the point is that there are many more poor people than most of us realize.

ginal jobs. And many are nonwhites who, because of discrimination and/or lack of skills, are unable to get permanent employment and therefore are forced to hold one low-paying job after another, often with periods of unemployment in between. In short, there are many kinds of poor people, and to talk about "the poor" as one group is to oversimplify.

All of the poor fare badly. They die younger than the affluent, have a higher infant mortality rate, have more diseases, do hard labor that wears out their bodies, eat less well, live in homes that are overcrowded, and suffer from a chronic economic instability that prevents remedy of these ills. The poor are the last hired and the first fired. They tend to form a human cushion which absorbs the ups and downs of our economy. The next time you hear that a mild recession is needed to stop inflation, remember that the resulting increase in unemployment will be due mainly to the laying off of these marginal, poor workers.

Poverty in the United States includes all kinds of people—whites, blacks, Mexican-Americans, Indians, Asian-Americans, and so on. All of these groups have members who are considered to be upper class and middle class, but each also has members—the poor—who are on the bottom of the heap. While there are differences among the poor depending upon which ethnic or racial group they come from, these differences are much less significant than you might think. A poor black is much more like a poor white than he is like a middle class black. The same is generally true of other groups—economic and social class differences greatly outweigh racial or ethnic differences. Differences among the poor also depend upon whether one is talking about the young or the old, the settled or the migrant, the urban or the rural. Because we cannot possibly cover all of the picture, the following discussion is based mainly on the young and middle-aged poor people who live in the poorest sections of large American cities.

How Do They Get By?

Consumption

The major method of getting by when you are poor is to cease to consume whenever and wherever possible. Poor families stretch their money by buying cheap food, which means lots of starches and occasionally a little fatty meat. They work hard to retain whatever credit they have by paying just a little on each bill every month; credit is necessary in case of emergency. If you lose your credit, there is one thing to keep in mind: Don't get sick! Without credit, there is no cushion to fall back upon when things really get bad. Even with credit, the poor cannot afford to see a doctor or buy medicine.

Shopping and the use of credit are expensive undertakings for the poor.

FIG. 6.14 *Some of the many faces of poverty.*

Courtesy Office of Economic Opportunity.

Courtesy Fred Weiss, photographer.

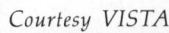

BOX 6.3

An Unfinished Poem

The following poem was given to me by a friend, Dan Donaldson, who found it one morning sticking out of a typewriter in the Skid Row drop-in center where he worked. The anonymous author evidently discovered the typewriter the previous evening and sat down to compose this poem. He was either interrupted or he lost interest in the poem (it is unfinished). Even though it is short, the poem conveys a little of the down-and-out loneliness of the people who live on Skid Row. It is reproduced here exactly as it was written.

"WHO'S HE?"

To see a person on the street
wondering just what or who he is,
An addict? A hood? Or cop on the beat?
Maybe a psycho, or perhaps he's gay;
Let me tell you, friend, on the street you'll meet 'em all
Whether it's night time—or day.
There's a lot of difference, though,
between day and night,
between peace and violence,
being friendly or uptight.
Daytime it isn't quite as bad,
though sure, you get your pushers, your bums, your loners,
your high-class people, or your ones on Skid-row.
Every walk of life turns up during the day,
but at night-time the "high-classers" lock their door
to the world—home with their families and T.V.;
　There they stay.

The poor seldom have the mobility to comparison shop or to buy elsewhere, so merchants in poverty areas often sell goods at higher than normal prices or sell inferior goods. The merchants claim that their high prices make up for theft and shoplifting, which may be true in part, but their high prices often do better than merely make up the loss. Also, the poor are bad credit risks and, as a result, few stores outside the poverty areas are willing to extend credit to them. However, while merchants within the poverty areas may extend credit freely, their generosity is often an illusion. First, unless local laws prevent it, credit and interest charges are often very high and either falsely represented by the merchant or ill understood by the poor. Second, merchants frequently

But that's when another kind of life surges up,
up all night, all night to stay—
your bums, your winos, your down-and-outers
who bummed all day.
Like your winos, and alcoholics who live from
one bottle to the next, night and day,
your pushers come out—double force—
to sell their "Kicks" to a certain source.
Your prostitutes come out—to whom they may
they sell their "love",
It's not love for love's sake;
nor do they give love away;
A few workers go out for a party
but when the bars close, they,
like the "high-classers", go home.
Home, to leave the unfortunate walk the streets,
To, like the rest, roam.

The loners—who don't run with any one group,
here now, later gone . . . who's somewhat afraid
to get involved, who's nervous around people
'cause they've perhaps, been burnt or hurt
one too many times by people, or are used to
institutions, and not the "outside" world;
but who are night people
because you don't have to worry what Mr.
High. . . . .

sell something, say a television set (America's most economical babysitter), on contract to a poor customer and then sell the contract to a bank. If the television set goes haywire or if he can't make a payment, the customer goes back to the merchant only to find that he actually must deal with the bank. While the merchant might fix the television set or allow time for the payment, the bank tends to be more impersonal. So, the poor person may well end up with a nonworking television set for which he must continue to pay or else have it repossessed—neither of which were part of his understanding at the time he made the purchase. Similarly, rents, interest on loans, product quality, and all the rest are disproportionately bad in poverty areas. The worst part is that even when they are cheated in some outrageous way, poor people seldom report it because they don't want to get involved with the police. So they continue to be cheated.

Here is a simple experiment you can do to see how expensive it is to be poor. Go to a supermarket in a middle class neighborhood in your city. Note the quality and prices of meats, for example. Then compare these with the quality and prices of meats in a similar store in a poor neighborhood. You will find the quality is lower and/or the prices higher in the poor neighborhood. This discrepancy is greatest when both the poor neighborhood and the city are very large and when there is inadequate public transportation (even when transportation is good, very few people are willing to pay 35 cents to ride a bus twenty blocks to save 50 cents on a few groceries). In smaller cities where it is easier to get around or where the store is likely to encounter public ill will for overcharging the poor, quality and price discrepancies are smaller.

Welfare

A major source for getting by when you are poor is some form of welfare. Because welfare programs are continually changing, it would be useless to try to give specific details about them here; the information would be wrong by the time you read it. However, a few general comments about welfare are in order.

Americans have a peculiar attitude about poverty and welfare. The citizens of most industrial countries regard poverty as unfortunate but understandable and view welfare as a part of the poor person's right to survive at a tolerable living level. In contrast, Americans regard poverty as a sign of failure (which is a major sin in the eyes of most of us) and welfare as a gift, condescendingly given, for temporary relief until the poor person gets himself together. The notion of being our brother's keeper seems to escape us when welfare is involved. Indeed, many taxpayers actually believe that the majority of people receiving welfare payments are using the money as a way of avoiding work, that the poor enjoy living on taxpayers' hard-earned dollars, and that welfare recipients are laughing behind their hands at "honest, hard-working men." Certainly, there are some abuses of welfare, just as there are "working men" who don't earn their pay, but the abuses are slight compared to the need that is filled.

The notion that the poor should pull themselves together and work their way up and out of poverty is an inspiring idea, but it fails to recognize the facts. First, many of the poor are old; we provide various forms of welfare to keep them alive in their last years, and it is unrealistic to expect them to move upward and onward. Second, many of the poor are mothers who must care for and support children, and it would be harsh indeed to deprive the children because of their parent's poverty. (Contrary to rumor, there are not so very many illegitimate children in this category, and even if there were, is the child to be hungry because he or she was born to an unmarried mother?) These mothers have too great a job as it is to expect them to pull themselves up economically at the same time. Third, most of the poor lack education, and, as we shall see in a few moments, this deficiency is not easily remedied in order to help the poor help themselves.

All of this is not to say that welfare is good, at least not as it works now. Our welfare system is grossly inadequate—the money is insufficient, the red tape is unbelievable, and the humiliation that the recipient often tolerates in order to get his pittance is grim testimony to the magnitude of his need. If most of us faced the cold indifference, condescending superiority, and the dehumanizing treatment these people receive at the hands of the lower echelon employees of many welfare agencies, we would tell the whole system to take the money and stick it in its ear.

A major reason for the failure of the welfare system is that many taxpayers, congressmen, and agency administrators seem convinced that the recipients are trying to cheat the public. As a result, there are so many safeguards and requirements that the whole system breaks under its own weight and does a great deal of damage in the process. A classic example of this is the infamous "man in the house" clause that was once part of the Aid to Dependent Children Program. This clause stipulated that child support could not be paid if there was an able-bodied man living in the house. Hapless social workers were rumored to have had to go around at night to make sure that no man was living in the recipient's home. As a result, many men who in fact worked but who earned very low wages found it expedient to move out of their homes so that their wives could receive child support payments; this money, together with the man's meager wages, provided a subsistence living for the family. However, in numerous cases the seeming windfall of child support payments effectively broke up the family. Poverty and the foolish "man in the house" clause economically coerced the father into leaving his family. For too many families this was the beginning of the end, and the children who the support program was supposed to aid ended up without a father.

The inconsistency in American views of government payments to its citizens is shown by the fact that many people who would be among the first to damn welfare receive many benefits themselves. For example, many farmers have survived for years on various forms of farm subsidies and land-bank payments, a form of welfare for the overproducer. The Oil Depletion Allowance gives oil well owners tax relief because the natural resource they are exploiting is being depleted and will someday be gone, a form of welfare for the rich. Or consider the large number of students who receive Social Security payments while they go to college, a form of aid to dependent children, except that the father is dead rather than merely living somewhere else. These are all forms of welfare for people who are not poor. To qualify for them you have to have had money in the first place to have bought the farm or the oil well or to have made Social Security payments. The welfare programs that are actually labeled as such are designed for people who may always have been too poor to buy their way into the system. These forms of benefits logically are not all that different; the difference is in how Americans feel about them. Somehow we think that Social Security payments that help a young man or woman through college have greater virtue than child support payments that permit a woman to stay home to care for her baby. When measured in terms of human need, however, the difference is difficult to calculate.

Education and Urban Poor Children

The fact that slightly over one third of the people on welfare come from welfare families themselves implies that to be born poor is to stay poor. The problem is how to break this cycle. One obvious answer is education. However, the children of the poor seldom do well in school, so we are right back where we started. We must ask, then, what prevents their success in school and can anything be done about it?

Motivation

Two basic aspects of success in school are motivation and ability. Motivation frequently is lacking in poor children because they see little or no relation between the things they are expected to learn in school and the things that comprise their everyday world. Thus, teachers of poor black students complain that their pupils can't read, although the students spend their leisure time pouring over the writings of Malcolm X. In short, the material they get in class has no apparent relevance, so they expend no effort. Malcolm X had something of importance to say to them, so they are motivated to read his books. It is hard to estimate the total waste of an educational system which fails to engage its students on their own intellectual ground. All schools commit this crime to some degree, but middle class students are groomed from birth to fit into middle class schools, and thus they tend to survive somehow. Poor children or youngsters from other subcultures within our society are not groomed to fit the middle class educational system; therefore, they have little chance of survival in it. This is doubly tragic because both the poor parents and their children believe that education is the only way out—but they frequently cannot cope with the system.

Ability

In order to talk about ability, as contrasted with motivation, we need some way of deciding how much potential ability a child has. The standard measure of this potential, especially for school success, is IQ tests. These tests consist of series of questions or tasks of increasing difficulty, and the child's IQ is determined by how far up the series he can go relative to other children his age. (The average IQ score in the United States is 100; about two thirds of the population scores between 85 and 115.)

IQ tests do not measure intelligence in the sense that most of us use the term; they merely predict a student's likelihood of success in white middle class schools, and all the other uses they are put to are questionable. Poor children by and large score lower on IQ tests than middle class children, indicating that poor children will experience greater difficulty in school than other children. This prediction is quite accurate.

Even after you have been through all the arguments about how IQ tests are biased because they do not tap what poor children (or minority group children) really know, the fact still remains that the tests accurately predict the failure of these children in school. This is partly because both the tests and the schools have a middle class bias, but griping about the schools really solves nothing, because for the poor to extricate themselves from poverty they had best learn such middle class skills as reading, writing, and, perhaps, understanding physics. Let us face reality, then, and assume that the schools *are not* likely to change. Then the question becomes, Can the poor change? There are two answers to this question: no and yes.

The No answer   The no answer relies on skimpy but fairly reasonable evidence. The first argument is that by and large the poor are poor because they are stupid: Over the years the less able people have slowly sunk into poverty, married other less able people, and produced less able children. This argument is weak for several reasons. First, there is no evidence that such a large-scale downward migration has indeed taken place. Moreover, the notion that ability is genetically determined and fixed for all time is probably nonsense. While the ranges within which a person's abilities can develop may be limited by genetic factors, there is ample evidence that experience plays a very large role in the development of these potential abilities. We will return to this last point when we discuss the yes answer to whether the poor can change to fit the schools.

The second "no" argument relies on evidence which suggests that poor children may do poorly because they are generally not very healthy. Their poor health is due, for one thing, to the fact that before giving birth the mother cannot afford either good nutrition or proper medical care for herself, and after giving birth she cannot afford them for the child. Too, she may not know how to take care of her baby, and this ignorance may contribute both to the child's malnutrition and to his general exposure to unhealthy situations. At any rate, these factors, especially in the early months and years of the baby's life, may cause profound and lasting damage. Studies with laboratory animals show that extreme protein malnutrition in the early part of life can lead to permanent mental retardation. It is difficult, of course, to know how much to generalize such results to human beings, but these studies suggest that early malnutrition possibly may cause permanent impairment of some poor children's ability to learn.

The Yes answer   The yes answer to the question of whether the poor can be changed to fit the school system rests on the assumption that abilities are not rigidly fixed and that proper training and experience can increase those abilities.

When poor children start school, it is generally found not only that they have low IQ's but also that they lack other skills that contribute to classroom learning. For example, they frequently cannot count, name colors, identify pictures of animals, or do all the other things that we normally assume are the stock in trade of a six-year-old. Moreover, the degree to which they lag behind middle class children increases each year until finally, in the eighth grade, they are about three years behind. In short, poor children start with a deficit and keep falling further behind middle class children as time goes on.

All of the evidence suggests that the poor child's basic problem is that he lacks the background upon which to build school success. His experience at home may have taught him all there is to know about how to feed four people on $2 a day or what to do when your little brother is bitten by a rat, but this kind of knowledge doesn't help much when it comes to classroom learning. Thus, the poor child needs first to develop an appropriate experiential base upon which he can build his education. Most of this base must be obtained at school because the child's home is still the way it has been all his life. But in a middle class school, which is not geared toward helping him obtain this base, the poor child progresses slowly and falls further and further behind.

The obvious solution to the problem, if this skill-deficit explanation is true, is to put the poor children, before they begin school, in an enriched program that focuses upon developing the skills they require. In short, some kind of compensatory education program is needed.

Several small compensatory programs have been established, more or less as experiments, and the federal government has sponsored a large-scale project called Head Start, which is available to the poor throughout most of the country. A Head Start program usually consists of a year or, in some cases, a summer of training for four-year-old children who are to enter kindergarten the following September. The program varies from one school to another, but the overall objective is to broaden the children's experience through taking them on field trips (many poor children have never been out of their own neighborhoods), reading stories to them, having them play counting games, engaging them in supervised play, and so forth. The benefits of the program are difficult to assess, but it is generally found that there is about a ten-point increase in the children's IQ scores as a result of their participation in a Head Start program. Unfortunately, however, the effects of the program do not appear to last. At the end of the first grade, Head Start children are indistinguishable from other poor non-Head Start children, and, like the latter, they lag behind the middle class children.

Some people believe that in order to avoid the fading of the Head Start effects a follow-up program should be instituted to continue enrichment throughout the lower grades. Such a program (called Follow Through) has been instituted, but it is too early to assess its effects.

Other people believe that the full potential of Head Start has never been realized. The program was set up with great haste and little planning because everyone was afraid that hesitation would lead to the loss of the funds that had suddenly become available. The end result was a program with little uniformity in the methods used throughout the country and only vague ideas about what was to be accomplished. The vagueness of the goals often resulted in the development of very low-keyed programs rather than rich educational experiences that were prescribed by the logic that underlies the idea of Head Start. Learning to play "Run Goose Run" and to color within the lines cannot be expected to do much to an IQ score, let alone prepare a "disadvantaged" child for success in school. Perhaps if the program were more intense, longer-lasting results would be obtained.

Evidence from a number of non-Head Start experimental programs clearly shows that very intensive training has a profound and lasting effect on the IQ's of poor children. One such program was carried out at the University of Illinois by Dr. M. B. Karnes and his associates. Fifteen three-year-old children participated in three twenty-five minute sessions each day for ten months; one of the sessions covered mathematics, one covered language and reading readiness, and one covered science and social studies.

In the mathematics sessions, the children developed counting ability and number concepts, some skill in manipulating numbers, number vocabulary, identification of geometric shapes, and the idea of dimensions and the ordering of objects along dimensions. Objects used included candies, bottle tops, poker chips, peg boards, and so forth.

In the language and reading readiness sessions, the children learned to identify pictures, to hold a book right side up, and to turn the pages of the book one at a time in a right to left progression. They learned to relate the pictures in the book to the story as the teacher read it. Afterwards, they were asked questions about the story in order to teach them to pay attention to its content. These story-time sessions were also used to expand the children's vocabularies and to expose them to standard English.

In the science and social studies sessions, experience with natural phenomena was stressed. The children learned to identify the parts of their bodies and such objects as food, clothing, and furniture, as well as to classify things on the basis of color, size, and shape.

At the beginning of the program the average IQ of the group was 94.5. By the end of the program the average had gone up to 111.4, an increase of 16.9 points. Six of the fifteen children showed an IQ increase of 20 points or more, and four gained from 10 to 15 points. Four did not show much gain, and one child failed to gain at all. However, no child lost IQ points.

Compare these results with the test scores of fourteen similar children who were not enrolled in Dr. Karnes' training program. These children were tested at the same times the children in the program were tested, but they stayed at home and continued their usual everyday lives. At the beginning of the program the average IQ for this group was 91.3 (not really different from the program group's 94.5). At the end of the ten months the average was relatively unchanged at 88.5 (as compared with the program group's increase to 111.4). One child gained between 10 and 15 IQ points, five stayed roughly the same, and eight showed losses of from 4 to 14 points. Clearly, the training program significantly increased the IQ's of the children who were in it. The IQ's of the other children were, with one exception, either unchanged or lower at the end of the ten months—not a very encouraging prognosis for just staying at home.

Results similar to these have been obtained in the studies of other non-Head Start experimental programs, some less dramatic to be sure, but still much the same. In one recent study, the IQ gains were found to still exist when the children were beginning the third grade.

The key to all of the successful programs is *intensity*. It seems necessary to immerse the child for from one to three hours a day in a very structured setting in which he is expected to perform and in which, at the same time, he receives help to do well. While time is allotted for fun and games (although even these are made into learning experiences), the rule is that the child must work. The freedom of the typical nursery school will not do. The child is fighting a very important battle, one that may well determine his entire future, and for the teacher to approach it as anything less than a battle is unrealistic and irresponsible. Given the alternatives, an intensive program is clearly the only way, and Head Start programs should be bolstered to meet these requirements if they are to be of much use.

What does compensatory education compensate for? Why do these intensive compensatory programs work? Clearly, their success implies that the arguments about inherited IQ deficiencies or health impairment (the no answers outlined above) are either wrong or not sufficiently large factors to fully account for poverty. If so, then what is being compensated for by compensatory education?

First, the programs are compensating for the child's ignorance. It is difficult to imagine how little intellectual stimulation there is in the home of a poor family. Some children grow up in homes in which there are no books; they have never seen anyone read anything—other than a comic book—for the sake of enjoyment. Moreover, the language used in such homes is seldom standard English. While people may be talking all the time, few grammatically correct sentences are spoken. There also is a tendency to use short or incomplete declarative sentences, and heavy reliance is placed upon the use of expletives and slang. This is not to say that such language fails to communicate—"Like, man, wow!" may convey a great deal but it is hardly appropriate preparation for reading a book or understanding a teacher.

A poor child's ignorance is also partly a result of his surprisingly limited range of experience; poor children do not get around much. Few have ever been to a zoo, a museum, or an art gallery. Seldom do they go to a downtown shopping area or just ride around on a bus. Many have never been in an elevator or on an escalator. Rural poor children know little or nothing about the city, and city poor children don't know where milk comes from or what a live chicken looks like.

A second thing that successful compensatory education programs do is help the child learn to question things instead of depending entirely upon authority. With poor children especially, this is no small task because quite often the child-rearing practices of the poor unintentionally stifle the development of this questioning attitude.

Studies show that the mothers and fathers of poor children, even though they love their children very much, tend to put a high premium on obedience and that this obedience is obtained in an authoritarian way. The child is expected to do precisely as he is told, without question, just because an adult says so. Certainly, one could argue that poor mothers often are harassed, worried, and too busy to take time for explanations, but it really goes beyond that. All mothers are busy, but they don't all consistently resort to authoritarian demands for obedience. Middle class mothers have a much greater tendency to explain *why* they make a demand rather than merely issuing an order with no explanation. In doing so, middle class mothers teach their children to question things and to resist blind acceptance of authority. Thus a middle class mother might say, "Fasten your seat belt so you won't hit your head if I have to stop the car quickly." This is a long, complex sentence that contains both a demand and a reason for the demand. When the child complies, he knows why he should do so. On the other hand, a poor mother would be much more likely to say, "Fasten your seat belt!" to which the child might reply, "Why?" and she would answer, "Because! Now fasten it!" In other words, a poor mother tends to issue short, direct commands and give no reason other than authority.

A study that illustrates the difference between how poor and middle class mothers interact with their children was done by Dr. Helen Bee and her associates at the University of Washington as part of an evaluation of a Head Start program. The researchers observed the way the mothers behaved toward their children both in a waiting room and in a subsequent experiment that required the children to build a block house like a completed model that was on a table in front of them. The differences between the behavior of the poor and the middle class mothers was quite clear. In the waiting room the middle class mothers talked with their children, answered their questions, and generally helped them pass the time with a minimum of anguish. The poor mothers tended to pay less attention to their children, with the exception of issuing direct commands ("Stop that and sit down!") or of occasionally answering questions.

In the house-building task all of the mothers were told that they could give their child as little or as much help as they liked—to do whatever they felt would help their child do his best. Again the two kinds of mothers behaved in markedly different ways. The middle class mothers helped by asking helpful questions ("Where does this yellow block go?"), by expressing lots of approval for successful progress, and by showing very little concern over errors. Moreover, the middle class mothers seldom told the child specifically what to do next, nor did they actually do the next step themselves. By contrast, the poor mothers gave their children fairly specific directions about what to do and when to do it, showed about equal amounts of approval and disapproval (and a good deal less approval than the middle class mothers expressed), and they frequently handed their child the correct block for the next step or even reached over and placed the block in its proper place themselves. In short, the mothers of the poor children were far more directive and authoritative than were the middle class mothers.

A similar difference between poor and middle class mothers is revealed in studies of the things they think they would tell their children as they sent them off to school for the first time. Middle class mothers come up with things like, "You will meet lots of other nice children and your teacher is going to help you learn, but remember she has to teach all the other children too, so you can help her by doing as she says." The child is made to look at school as a good thing with new friends and a teacher who wants to help. Good behavior is demanded, but a reason is given for the demand. On the other hand, poor mothers tend to say, "Remember to be a good boy and do exactly what the teacher tells you to," that is, to give no explanation, just an admonition to comply with authority.

Given five or six years of being taught to not question, the poor child goes off to school rather like a soldier marching to battle with all the wrong weapons. The child has been taught not to ask why, to always accept what he has been told. He has been taught that sitting quietly and causing no fuss is the ultimate in being a good boy (and will usually please adults, both parents and teachers). He has never been taught to value learning except insofar as it might help him get a good job some day. He hardly understands the teacher's language and often he is almost unable to speak it himself. His authoritarian upbringing tends to leave him unable to initiate inquiry on his own; unless the teacher tells him what to do, he is at a loss or afraid to try anything new for fear of getting in trouble with the teacher. In short, the poor child is preprogramed for failure in school. It is small wonder that his frustration may build until he becomes a behavior problem that the teacher cannot cope with or until he starts skipping school and finally drops out altogether.

Clearly, until methods are found to overcome this preprogramed failure, poor children will grow up to become poor adults who will raise yet another generation of poverty, and on and on. A ray of hope seems to lie in good, intense compensatory education. But until the present programs are strengthened and extended, even this isn't enough, and many of the poor are destined to remain trapped by their poverty.

The Groups and
The Values
of Urban
Poor Youths

While compensatory education may help poor children succeed in middle class schools, there are yet other difficulties that bar their escape from poverty. In large part, these difficulties arise from a profound difference between the social behavior and values accepted by some poor people and those accepted by the middle class. These differences give rise to mistrust and misunderstanding on both sides. And because economic resources usually are in the hands of the middle class (a fact that almost defines "middle class"), the mistrust and misunderstandings make it difficult for the poor to have access to jobs and the like. In the following discussion, the values of one subgroup of poor people, poor urban males, are examined in order to give you an idea about how discrepant these values can be.

Social Groups

Almost all adolescents, poor or affluent, tend to gravitate toward groups of special friends. This is a normal extension of involvement with peers, and it is intensified in adolescence as the youngster begins to grow away from his parents and become an autonomous individual. Among middle class youths, these groups are composed mainly of same-sex members during the early years. Later, they become increasingly composed of both males and females, until the members finally leave for college, get married, get jobs, or move away. If the group members stay in the same locality, the group may endure in some loose form throughout the members' lives.

The same kind of thing happens among urban poor youths, but their special needs result in the formation of somewhat different kinds of groups. We will look primarily at males in this context because the females, as a rule, do not form groups with their own same-sex peers. Females tend to move toward the males' groups and exist as satellites rather than as true members. Marriage, which comes at an early age for poor females, removes them from the male group. From then on, their primary social groupings focus on female members of their own families—their mothers, aunts, sisters-in-law, and so on.

To understand the importance of a male group to its urban poor members, it is necessary to keep in mind that a large percentage of the males in these groups come from homes in which the mother is either the sole parent or the only one active in taking care of the children. This is true in both black and white households. The result is that the adolescent turns to his peers for aid in developing his self-concept as a male (Fig. 6.15). Of course, almost all adolescent males depend upon their peers in this matter, but the self-concept problem is exaggerated in the case of an urban poor youth. Living conditions at home often are difficult and restrictive. The boy is trying to escape his mother's authoritarian child-rearing style, he is bored in his restricted environ-

FIG. 6.15 *The violent behavior of urban poor youths results less from maliciousness than from a desire to demonstrate their masculine toughness.* (*Courtesy Tom McCarthy.*)

ment, he longs to be treated as an adult, and finally he longs for adult male companionship and respect. The "street-corner gang" provides the relief and social support he needs.

Values

Street-corner gangs and their value systems have been studied in great detail by Dr. Walter B. Miller and his associates at Boston University. The following discussion is based on this work.

It is difficult for most people to imagine the world of a poor urban youth. Whereas a middle class youth learns a set of values that puts a high premium on achievement (economic and intellectual), self-sufficiency, and honesty, a poor youth learns a very different set of values. Because of these different value systems, the middle class and the poor often come into conflict. The poor youth's behavior follows quite logically from *his* set of values, but when viewed through middle class eyes, it looks illogical and somewhat demonic. Indeed, many of our laws are written to curb the behaviors of people with different values and to extend at least the basic ideas of the middle class value system throughout the entire society.

Avoiding trouble Many poor people respect the law and teach their children to be law-abiding for the same reasons middle class people do, to promote social order and general tranquility. For many urban poor youths, however, the motivation to abide by the law is quite different. To them the law is another example of the external authoritarian pressure that they have experienced since they were born—first through their parents, then through their teachers, and now through the law. Their tactic for dealing with the law is much the same as the one they have used all along for dealing with authority: do everything you can to *stay out of trouble.* This does not mean that you don't break the law so much as it means that you don't get caught. Indeed, prestige can be gained by successful law-breaking because it satisfies some of the other values that will be discussed in a moment. The point here, however, is that these young men, and their parents, place high value on not getting into trouble, on conforming to the letter of the law if not to its spirit.

Toughness and "smartness" Toughness is a highly valued sign of masculinity for poor adolescents. It consists of many things—bravery, physical strength, and athletic ability, as well as a stereotyped "masculine" manner of non-sentimentality, nonintellectualism, treatment of women sheerly as sex objects, and an appropriate style of dress and bearing. "Smartness" is important, too, but it does not correspond to the middle class notion of intellect. Rather, a "smart" person is one who can outfox someone else, a person who can live well merely by using his wits with little or no physical effort. A smart man does not work; he figures out how to get money from the man who does. Smartness is reflected in excellence in snappy repartee—semiritualized ways of telling about events or a joking exchange of insults. Many styles of such repartee exist, each style having rather specific goals. There is a style for subtle aggression that focuses on insulting the other person's mother, a style for propositioning a woman, a style for getting out of trouble, and so forth. The smart person is the one who can use these styles inventively and successfully. To be both tough *and* smart is success itself, but if you can't be both, being smart is somewhat more important than being tough.

Excitement and fate When you are poor there isn't much money for entertainment. Life can be very boring when you're just standing on the corner waiting for time to pass. So, excitement is called for from time to time. The time is usually the weekend when the bars are busy, when there's music, dancing, and all the rest. The excitement may take the form of drunken evenings spent in bar hopping, fighting, and trying to pick up women, or it may take the form of fighting with another gang. At any rate, excitement is periodically sought.

Fate is part of excitement in that many poor people regard themselves as being lucky or unlucky. This leads to gambling or playing the numbers as a form of excitement and a feeling of lucky self-confidence in fights. The belief in fate—that whatever you do has little bearing on what will happen to you—is another example of the poor person's feeling of being at the mercy of external influences—parents, teachers, the law, and luck. The winning hand is to be tough, smart, *and* lucky.

Independence Part of the poor adolescent's masculine role is both to appear and to feel free of strings, to be his own master. This idea is generally shared by all Americans, but it takes on a special meaning among urban poor males. Their need for independence is expressed in a great deal of talk ("I'll tell that bastard boss to go to hell!") but only occasional action. Much of this, however, is merely a smokescreen. Valuing independence but having spent all of their early lives learning unquestioning obedience, these males find themselves in a peculiar situation: they resent authority, but, at the same time, they tend to put themselves in positions of having to submit to it. They may do so because being controlled has come to signify to them that the controller cares about them (just as their parents showed that they cared by being authoritarian). Many of these youths seem to gain a sense of stability from being controlled. This is one reason, aside from the need for a job, that so many poor young men enlist in the army, a large number making careers of it. They may gripe about the army the entire time they are enlisted, and their need to assert their independence by occasionally breaking the rules may keep them from attaining much rank, but the army's strict rules, its tough all-male environment, and its willingness to tolerate Saturday night sprees makes it a good home for people who have a need both to be independent and to be controlled by authority.

So, too, you can see how this value for independence makes marriage of little interest to poor males. Their marriages tend to be short, or the male may live at home only from time to time. His wife raises the children the way she and her husband were raised, and so the cycle goes on.

Values and the Group

We now see that the poor adolescent often lives in a world in which his primary reference group is a group of other boys who are much like him and who hold much the same values. They have all been taught to avoid trouble with authorities, that for the most part their future is only partly under their own control, and that luck is important. The masculine image they strive for is toughness, smartness, and independence. They spend long hours just hanging around talking. Occasionally they go out for a little excitement, which often provides the opportunity for them to demonstrate how tough or how smart they are.

Within the group, a dominance hierarchy develops based on toughness and smartness. A brush with the law, while a violation of the don't-get-in-trouble value, often serves to prove toughness and will increase a member's status in his group. So, too, the superior ability of a smart member to put everybody else down and to outsmart nonmembers will give him status.

The conformity pressures within these groups are very strong, and violations of group standards will lead to expulsion. Because the group often is his main social contact, fear of expulsion provides strong motivation for a member to go along with the group even if he personally disapproves of what it is doing. These strong group pressures also serve to signal to the member that the group cares about him and that he belongs. As we have seen, for such a youth it is of prime importance to belong; he knows he belongs when he experiences the group's strict control over his behavior.

Psychological Problems and the Urban Poor

Throughout this discussion we have repeatedly seen how the poor are at the mercy of numerous environmental and psychological pressures. Aside from sheer economic want, they are the last hired and the first fired, they pay more for the things they buy, they don't eat properly, they are subject to ill health, they often are dependent upon welfare with all of its uncertainties and administrative complexities, their children don't do well in school, and, to top it all, their authoritarian upbringing leaves them overly susceptible to pressures from people they regard as authorities. As you might expect, all of these pressures take their toll. The poor are diagnosed as having more psychological problems and are institutionalized more frequently than are middle class and upper class people.

Before continuing, a clarifying remark is needed. There is a difference between being mentally ill and being *diagnosed* mentally ill. Psychiatrists and psychologists are nearly all from middle class backgrounds and, as you can see from the foregoing discussion, their values and attitudes often are vastly different from those of the poor. As a result, they may interpret some kinds of behavior or some kinds of answers on psychological tests as evidence of mental illness when, in fact such behaviors or answers are reasonable for a person from a poverty background. This is not to say that the poor are constantly being railroaded into mental institutions by a group of insensitive or diabolical doctors. Rather, it is merely to point out that mental health problems among the poor may not be quite as extreme as the following data suggest.

The best study of psychological problems and social class was done by Dr. A. B. Hollingshead and Dr. F. C. Redlich in New Haven, Connecticut. New Haven is a large industrial city that has a fair proportion of poor people and it also has a large middle class. The researchers obtained information about virtually everyone in the city who was undergoing some form of treatment for psychological problems. Of course, the psychologists and psychiatrists didn't reveal names or anything personal about their patients; they just reported objective things like occupation and amount of education, in addition to the diagnosis and type of treatment the patient was receiving. On the basis of the objective information, the researchers decided to which social class each patient belonged. To simplify the discussion we will consider only the results for the middle class and for the very poor.

At the time of the study, the middle class represented roughly 30 percent of the population of New Haven, and the very poor represented about 18 percent. However, only 20 percent of the psychiatric patients were middle class, while 37 percent were poor people. In other words, there were about twice as many poor people as you would expect if both the middle class people and the poor people were equally likely to have severe psychological problems. On the other hand, there were only about two-thirds as many middle class people among the psychiatric patients as you would expect. In short, the poor appear to be more likely to have psychological problems.

When the researchers looked at the diagnosed severity of the problems, they found that about 45 percent of the middle class patients were diagnosed as having mild problems (neurosis) and 55 percent were diagnosed as having severe problems (psychosis), while only 8 percent of the poor were diagnosed as having mild problems and 92 percent as having severe problems. When they looked at the patients with the most severe problem (schizophrenia), they found that 13 percent were from the middle class while 45 percent were from among the poor. In short, poor people were diagnosed as having more serious problems than were middle class people.

Next, the researchers turned to the kinds of treatments these patients received. The various kinds of treatments were grouped into three categories. The first category was psychotherapy. The second was organic therapy, which included medication, electroconvulsive shock treatments, and insulin shock treatments. The third category consisted solely of custodial care—maintenance at home or in a hospital with no attempt at treatment (Fig. 6.16). Of the middle class patients, 62 percent got psychotherapy, 23 percent got organic therapy, and only 15 percent received custodial care. In contrast, only 16 percent of the poor patients received psychotherapy, 33 percent received organic treatment, and 51 percent received custodial care only. In short, the poor patients got less help than the middle class patients.

Two reasons may account for these differences in the kinds of treatments for the two kinds of patients. First, more of the poor patients were diagnosed as having severe problems, and doing psychotherapy with severe patients is extremely difficult. Psychotherapy is more often used to help neuroses rather than psychoses. If the patient is really extremely disturbed, custodial care often is about all that can be done for him. Second, most poor patients have to go to overcrowded and understaffed public hospitals because they can't afford private doctors. The shortage of psychiatric personnel in such hospitals makes it virtually impossible to do therapy with any but the mildest, most promising patients; the rest end up as custodial cases.

Even if the findings of this study need to be interpreted with caution, they clearly demonstrate that the poor have a greater propensity to psychological problems, their problems are diagnosed as more severe, and they receive less adequate treatment than the middle class.

Conclusion

The purpose of this discussion has been to introduce some aspects of poverty that are not commonly recognized but which are of central importance in dealing with poverty. As you are well aware, poverty is a major problem in this and almost every country, a problem that seems elusive and difficult to solve. The questions we have reviewed may help you to better understand the reasons for this elusiveness and for the difficulty in finding clear-cut, workable solutions. Clearly, the poor are a diverse group with diverse needs. In some cases merely making more money available would fill those needs; in others the problems run much deeper. It is these deeper problems, the internal and external barriers that prevent many of the poor from controlling their own lives and realizing their potentials, that constitute the unrecognized tragedy of poverty and, perhaps, that present the greatest obstacle to the eradication of poverty.

SUMMARY

1   Poverty is not merely a lack of money. Rather, it is defined by how little money a person has relative to other people around him, the lack of choice about being without money, and the lack of hope for better things to come.

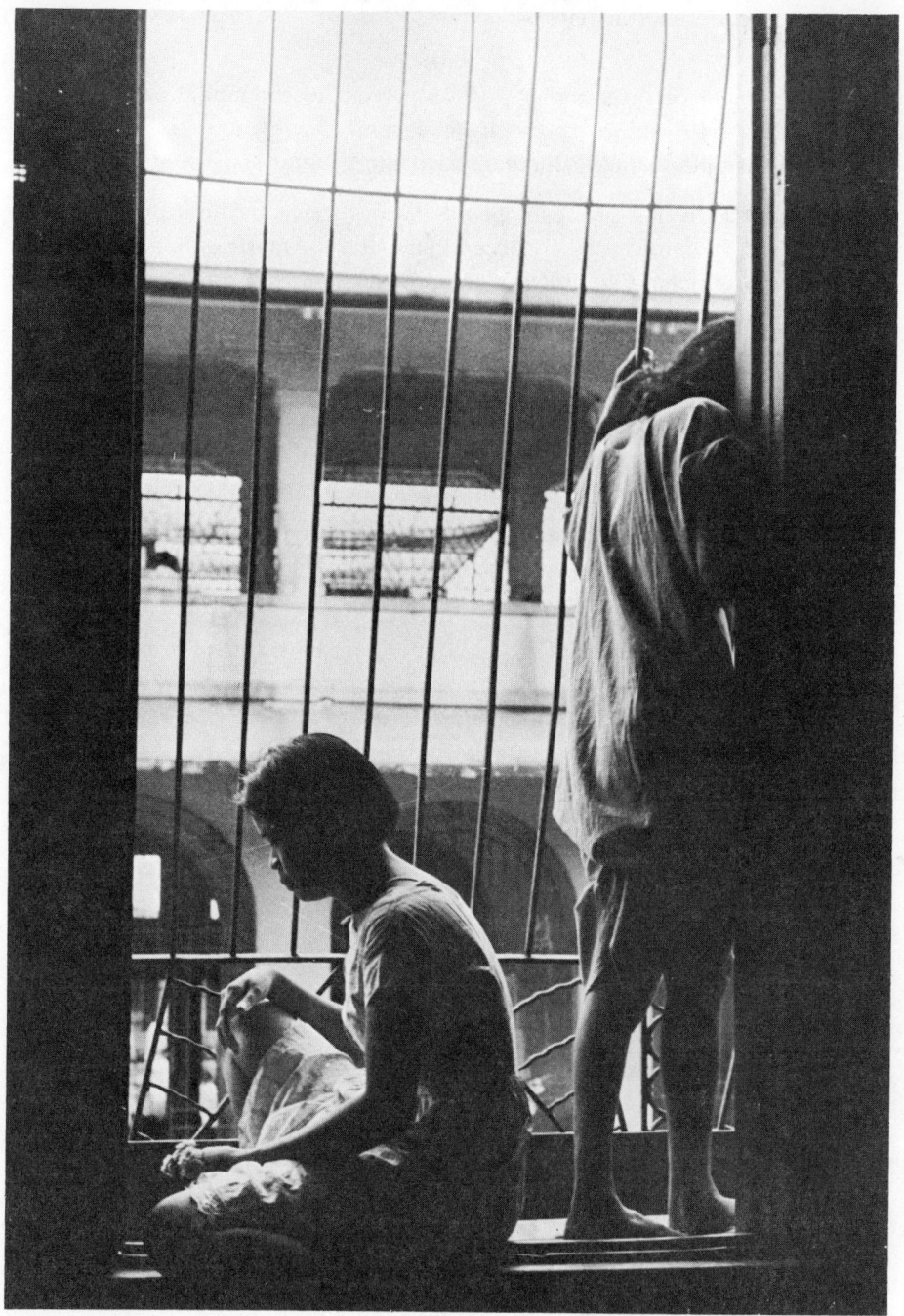

FIG. 6.16 When they have psychological difficulties, the poor, even though they are diagnosed as having more severe problems than the nonpoor, often receive very little treatment other than custodial care. (UPI photo.)

2   About 20 percent of the families and 45 percent of the single people in the United States are poor, even by the government's low criteria for poverty incomes. These percentages fluctuate with the general state of the economy.

3   The poor are a diverse group of people who survive by limiting their consumption and, in come cases, by accepting welfare. American hostility toward welfare has produced a complex, frustrating system that does not work well and is in great need of reform.

4   Education is an apparent key to helping people lift their children out of poverty. However, diverse factors in the child's poverty background conspire to make him unable to profit from the usual public school educational process. There is hope that compensatory educational programs will be of help in overcoming this obstacle. Of course, education is but one attack on the problem. Many of the poor are old, some are ill, some are mothers who must support and care for their families, and so on. Education holds no hope for alleviation of their poverty.

5   Examination of the values of poor youths reveals other stumbling blocks besides education to full participation in the economy. One, for example, is a tendency to both resent and relish submission to authority. These conflicting feelings sometimes make it difficult for poor youths to hold steady jobs.

6   As a result of all of the pressures they experience, the poor are diagnosed as having psychological problems more frequently, have more severe problems, and are institutionalized more frequently than are nonpoor people.

Further Reading

BINSTOCK, R. H., and K. ELY (Eds.).   *The Politics of the Powerless*
Cambridge, Mass.: Winthrop, 1971, 340 pages (paperback).
This book represents a collection of papers that revolve around the struggles of powerless groups to better the conditions of their lives in America. Some of the powerless groups discussed are the Blacks, the Indians, the Chicanos, and the poor.

BROWN, C.   *Manchild in the Promised Land*
New York: New American Library, 1965, 429 pages (paperback).
An absorbing autobiography of a man who grew up in the midst of gang wars, stealing, dope pushing, and killing. A very "live" description of what life is like in a slum. The book makes you admire people like Brown who somehow survive.

GINSBURG, H.   *The Myth of the Deprived Child*
Englewood Cliffs, N.J.: Prentice-Hall, 1972, 252 pages (paperback).
A discussion of the psychological research and theory concerning the intelligence, language, and intellectual development of poor children; the author analyzes and

evaluates the attempts made to improve the quality of poor children's education. A good compilation of some of the research done in this area.

HARRINGTON, M.   *The Other America: Poverty in the United States*
Baltimore, Md.: Penguin, 1971, 202 pages (paperback).
This book presents one of the clearest pictures of what poverty is like in America. It is an angry book, but the anger is justified by the facts.

KEISER, R. L.   *The Vice Lords: Warriors of the Streets*
New York: Holt, Rinehart and Winston, 1969, 83 pages (paperback).
About a youth gang living in a slum in Chicago. Written by an anthropologist, this book explores a life-style that is prevalent in many depressed areas of large American cities.

LARNER, J., and I. HOWE, (Eds.).   *Poverty: Views from the Left*
New York: Morrow, 1965, 319 pages (paperback).
A collection of papers covering economic, political, sociological, and practical investigations of the war on poverty. Covers topics such as housing, aging, food programs, and the Head Start program.

STEINBECK, J.   *The Grapes of Wrath*
New York: Bantam, 1970 (c. 1939), 502 pages (paperback).
The story of a family of Oklahoma farmers who, upon being thrown off their farm, migrate to California. The story takes place during the Great Depression of the 1930s, but the message is very modern.

TIFFANY, D. W., J. R. COWAN, and P. M. TIFFANY,   *The Unemployed*
Englewood Cliffs, N.J.: Prentice-Hall, 1971 (c. 1970), 180 pages (paperback).
Using case histories, interviews, and research with unemployed men and women, the authors examine who the unemployed are and why it is so difficult for them to hold jobs. The last part of the book deals with various types of vocational rehabilitation programs.

Part 5   DRUGS AND THE DRUG EXPERIENCE

Most people hold strong opinions about drugs and their use, opinions based on little or no factual knowledge. At one extreme are those who are unsympathetic to the drug scene. They see drugs as being uniformly dangerous and a symptom of moral decay which will undermine society. At the other extreme are people who view the use of drugs as a relatively harmless attempt to expand one's own experience and to get more out of life. As is usually the case, when you get things in perspective by looking at the facts, the truth lies somewhere between these two extremes.

I have tried hard to obtain solid information about drugs to present here. In my search I was struck by two things: (1) the small number of clear-cut facts available and (2) the vast amount of personal opinion that parades as fact. Few people stand ready to defend the unlimited use of drugs, but many are happy to damn them in any and all forms and to press for strong legislation aimed at reducing their availability. It is striking that in this area, as in so many controversial areas (for example, sex), people who believe that they know Truth seem convinced that the rest of the population isn't bright enough to govern its own behavior and therefore must be controlled by laws. It is perhaps more charitable, as well as more accurate, to believe that people are bright enough but that they lack the information upon which to base intelligent decisions. In the face of no information, most of us rely on our reference groups for making decisions rather than consider the unanswered questions for ourselves. In order to help you think about answers to the drug question for yourself, I will present as much solid information as is reasonable in a book like this. It is difficult to be objective about drugs given the spirit of our times, but what follows is as near the truth as I can make it.

An Old Phenomenon

Throughout history, virtually every culture has had one or more ways for its members to dope themselves. In some cultures, opium and its derivatives have been commonly used and, when used in moderation, have been generally regarded as acceptable. In some tropical cultures, it has long been the custom for people to chew betel nut, a mild drug that is used to help take the drudgery out of hard, repetitive labor. In the southwestern United States, various Indian cultures used peyote in their religious ceremonies. And even in ancient times most cultures produced alcohol, in forms similar to beer and wine, by fermentation of grain and fruit. Most of these alcoholic beverages would offend the palate of today's fancier of extra light beer and aged wine, but like their latter-day counterparts, they doped the people who drank them—and that, after all, was their job.

Why have countless generations of people doped themselves? Perhaps they did it to stop sadness or pain, to forget, to drop their inhibitions, to feel free, or to take the edge off strained social relations. There are probably many other reasons, too, but basically they all boil down to the fact that, by and large, drugs alter your experience and make you feel good. To one degree or another and from one time to another most people indulge in various alterations of their normal moment-to-moment experience.

If this sounds odd, just look around you; people actively seek unusual experiences. Sky diving, ferris wheels, light shows, scuba-diving, fast cars, loud music, religious experiences, cocktails, adventure movies, seances, and sexual arousal are all examples of things that temporarily change one's usual state of experience, and most people who experience them find them pleasurable. Of course, some of these activities appear to be more "natural" than others (for example, sexual arousal versus sky-diving), but the fact remains that the pleasant thrill and the other-worldliness, a change from the ordinary, is an incentive strong enough to lead most of us to engage periodically in such activities.

Drugs: Use and Abuse

One way of altering experience is to introduce various chemicals into your body. The chemicals that are used this way are called drugs, and very few of us fail to partake of at least some of them. If you are ill and the doctor gives you a pain killer, you have altered your experience with a drug. If you smoke a cigarette to "calm your nerves," you have altered your experience with a drug. If you take a diet pill to curb your appetite, you have altered your experience with a drug. If you drink a cocktail to relax after a long day, you have altered your experience with a drug. For most of us it is not a question of *whether* we use drugs or not; rather, it is a question of *what kinds* of drugs we use, what function they serve, and how often we use them (Fig. 6.17). We will turn to the question of what kinds of drugs in a moment, but first let us look at the notion of use and overuse (that is, *abuse*) of drugs.

Most articles about drugs use the word "abuse" in two ways. For socially acceptable drugs such as alcohol or diet pills, abuse means overuse and addiction. For less socially acceptable drugs such as LSD or marijuana, it means virtually any use at all. This is unfortunate because it implies a double standard of evaluation, and there is no place for a double standard in an objective consideration of drugs and their role in modern life. Therefore, I have elected to avoid use of the term "abuse" and to rely on your understanding that the use of any drug to the point that it interferes with one's day-to-day ability to function is overuse. For example, alcohol hangovers interfere with normal functioning, and therefore frequent hangovers are an indication of alcohol overuse.

Addiction

A person is said to be addicted to a drug when he feels that he cannot get by for very long without it and he consequently becomes preoccupied with making sure that it is readily available. Most of us know persons who are

FIG. 6.17   *All of us use drugs; it is merely a question of which ones, why, and when.*

addicted to either the nicotine in cigarettes or to alcohol, and some of us know persons who have died as a result of these addictions.

There are two kinds of addiction. The first is *physiological addiction*, in which various physiological functions of the body become dependent upon the presence of the drug. Withdrawal of the drug leads to physiological symptoms that can range from the relatively mild effects of giving up smoking to the very painful withdrawal symptoms of a heroin addict. In some cases it is possible to substitute some other chemical to stop the withdrawal symptoms until the body can adjust to the fact that the original drug is no longer being supplied. But then there is always the danger of becoming addicted to this other chemical.

The second kind of addiction is *psychological addiction.* While many people fail to believe it, psychological addiction is, in its own way, as painful as physiological addiction. The notion that "it's all in your head," and therefore not real, is sheer nonsense. Psychological symptoms after withdrawal from nonphysiologically addicting drugs can be a nightmare. Indeed, the fear experienced by a person who cannot get the drug to which he is psychologically addicted can be every bit as dreadful as the fear experienced by a person who is physiologically addicted to a drug.

A powerful component of psychological addiction is dependence upon the paraphernalia, rituals, and life-style of drug use. That is, some addicts are just as much caught up in the process of obtaining, preparing, and taking the drug, as well as with their friendships with fellow addicts, as they are with the drug itself. There are a few reported cases in which people have become addicted to fake heroin. These people exhibit many of the usual psychological symptoms when they withdraw from the fake drug but none of the physiological symptoms. Some of these people continue to take the fake heroin even after they have been told that it is fake—and their "habit" costs them from $50 to $150 a day! Clearly, something other than the "drug" itself is the attraction for these addicts.

Most often the attraction is the need to be accepted by members of their chosen group. Such "fake" addicts have friends who are part of the drug scene. These friends have dropped out of straight society and have placed high value on drug use. To remain accepted by their friends, these fake addicts must conform to their friends' values about drugs. This often leads to the development of psychological addiction to a harmless substance (either because these addicts didn't want to take real drugs or because they didn't know they were being given fake heroin) so that they will be accepted as "one of the gang." The major danger of becoming addicted to a harmless substance is that the addict does not build up a tolerance for real heroin. Thus, if he accidentally is given real heroin, he may inadvertently give himself a lethal overdose.

Most cases of drug addiction consist of both physiological and psychological addiction. The symptoms experienced by a person who gives up smoking are in part a result of his physical dependence on nicotine, but they also are partly a result of psychological dependence. Cigarettes have become an important part of the smoker's life—governing how he holds his hands, what he does after eating, how he fills empty moments in conversation, and so forth—and

FIG. 6.18   *Cigarettes become an important part of a smoker's life—how he holds his hands while talking, how he fills the gaps in conversations, what he does while relaxing, and so on. Drugs and the rituals and paraphernalia associated with them fill much the same role, and more so, for those who become deeply involved in the drug scene. (Courtesy American Cancer Society.)*

their absence is not an easy thing to ignore (Fig. 6.18). Similarly, a person who has dedicated every day to seeking out money for heroin and going through the ritual of buying and using it has built his life-style around the drug. His life and his related values have to change when he gives up the drug, and a change in one's life-style and values is not easy to endure.

The avoidance of the agony of withdrawal symptoms, both physiological and psychological, is the addict's most pressing problem. To do this, he must always have access to his drug. Because the sale of most "unacceptable" drugs, drugs which we will discuss in a moment, is against the law, his only source is illegal channels where the price usually is extremely high. In order to obtain the necessary money, many addicts turn to crime. It has been estimated that every day in New York City alone addicts commit more than one million dollars in crimes in order to buy drugs. To ignore the addicts' needs, whether you sympathize with their addiction or not, is both cruel to them and expensive for society at large. Clearly, what is needed is a system that permits addicts an alternative to crime for obtaining drugs without simultaneously increasing the general availability of drugs to potential addicts. England, for example, has instituted a system by which addicts can legally obtain the minimum necessary doses of drugs. This makes committing crimes unnecessary and at the same time allows the addict to obtain appropriate medical aid. In this country and others, methadone, a drug which can be prescribed legally, is often substituted for heroin. This substitution method permits the addict to withdraw from heroin without going through the pain of the withdrawal symptoms. Even methadone use must be closely supervised, however, because it too can be addicting.

Acceptable Drugs

Our society permits relatively free access to a variety of "acceptable" drugs. Only the most familiar, nicotine, alcohol, pain killers, and pep pills will be considered here.

Nicotine

Nicotine usually is taken by smoking cigarettes, cigars, or pipe tobacco—snuff and chewing tobacco are no longer very popular and, as a result, ashtrays have replaced spittoons in public buildings. Even nonsmokers are expected to provide ashtrays for guests who smoke. Smoking is a good example of how strongly most of us react to social fads; it is amazing that so many people ever began smoking in the first place—the illness induced by one's first cigarette must be one of life's most uncomfortable experiences. Of course, now that smoking has been linked to cancer, more and more people are attempting to break the habit or even to avoid beginning it.

Nicotine is a poison found in tobacco leaves. It is absorbed by the body in very small amounts when the tobacco is smoked. The first few puffs gives the smoker a lift, but with subsequent puffs the nicotine acts as a depressant and, if tolerance has not developed, can produce headaches, an upset stomach, nausea, and profuse sweating. After tolerance has developed through prolonged and determined use, the user usually derives a calming effect from smoking. This calming effect may be as much due to the ritual involved in smoking and the smoker's expectation that such effects will occur as it is to the physiological action of the drug itself.

Alcohol

In moderation, alcohol produces a pleasant feeling. Often it is the primary method of oiling the wheels of social interactions; a large segment of our population would find a party without alcohol as impossible as a ski meet without snow. In large amounts, alcohol produces such effects as disorientation, slurred speech, undue depression or happiness, sleep, and hangovers. The effects of alcohol, however, vary from one time to another, depending upon the expectation of the person involved. For example, alcohol intoxication occurs with greater ease in a party setting than in a business setting even though the same amount of alcohol may be consumed at both times. Tolerance to alcohol develops if you drink it habitually—that is, it takes more and more to produce the same effect a smaller amount used to produce. Indeed, in many cultures, our own included, the ability to drink large amounts of alcohol without exhibiting symptoms is prized as a masculine virtue: "He sure can hold his liquor."

Alcohol addiction, *alcoholism,* ranks as the fourth major health problem in the United States. About seven million U.S. citizens are alcoholics. Prolonged alcoholism results in damage to the brain, liver, and other organs of the body and results in the death of about twelve thousand Americans every year. Nearly ten billion dollars are spent in the United States every year for alcohol, and taxes on its production and sale are an important source of income for both the federal and the state governments.

Relaxants and Pain-Killers ("Downers")

"Downers" include tranquilizers (such as Miltown, Equinol, Librium, and Valium) and barbiturates (such as Nembutal, Seconal, and Amytal). They are usually prescription drugs issued by physicians to people who really need them to get through temporary periods of stress and to people who can convince the physician to let them become habitual users of the pills. The major effect of all of these drugs is to make the user feel relaxed and, in large doses, to make him go to sleep. Small doses give the user release from worry and a feeling of well-being. Most tranquilizers are not necessarily physiologically addictive, but the development of psychological addiction is common. In large doses, barbiturates are physiologically addictive; abrupt withdrawal from a high rate of consumption of barbiturates can lead to convulsions, hallucinations, and even death. Barbiturates and alcohol are a deadly combination; both are depressants and the user may go to sleep and not wake up again.

Amphetamines ("Uppers")

"Uppers" are most commonly found in diet pills or pep pills. When sold on the street, amphetamines are called "speed." The drugs are "acceptable" only in the diet or pep pill form; we will discuss "speed" in a moment.

Amphetamines (Benzedrine, Dexedrine, and Methedrine) are used medically to wake up the user and keep him energetic and alert or to abate his hunger. No one knows how many straight, ordinary people have come to rely on amphetamines in the form of diet or pep pills to get through the day. Such pills are easily obtained, often without prescription, through legitimate sources. Physiological addiction does not occur, but because the pill gives the user a pleasant lift, it is easy to develop relatively mild psychological addiction to the small amounts of amphetamine in these pills.

Unacceptable Drugs

To facilitate discussion, "unacceptable" drugs will be divided into two classes: "hard drugs" such as narcotics and "speed," and, for want of a better term, "soft drugs" such as LSD and marijuana.

Hard Drugs

With the exception of "speed," hard drugs are seldom used by students, except as an occasional experiment, so we won't devote much space to them. People who use them usually inject the drugs directly into their bloodstreams with a syringe and needle. This practice is, in itself, extremely dangerous, since contaminated needles can transmit hepatitis (a disease of the liver), infections of the blood, heart valves, and lungs, and other serious diseases. Indeed, these diseases constitute almost as much of a health threat as the drugs themselves.

Narcotics This class of extremely powerful and addicting drugs consists of heroin, codeine, morphine (all of which are derived from opium) and meperidine (which is a synthetic but similar in its effects). All of these drugs lead to a very withdrawn, happy feeling that is sort of a "cop-out" high. Prolonged use and heavy doses lead to the development of tolerance and addiction; the happy feeling goes away, and the person needs the drug just to feel normal. Withdrawal from the drug results in two or three days of muscle pains, twitches, sweating, nausea and vomiting, and diarrhea. Less severe symptoms may continue for up to six months.

Overdoses of narcotics can be fatal; they affect respiration and make the user stop breathing. Indeed, most drug deaths are a result of overdoses or general physical deterioration that leaves the addict vulnerable to fatal diseases. Overdose is common because the user is never sure of the strength of the drug he purchases.

"Speed" "Speed" is the hard drug that the reader is most likely to encounter. It is usually taken in the form of pills, but heavy users sometimes dissolve the pills and inject the liquid into their bloodstreams with a needle. This practice runs two dangers: first, it involves all the dangers of using a needle, and, second, if some of the substance in the pills does not dissolve, there is the danger that it may end up floating around in the bloodstream.

"Speed" depresses fatigue and hunger, and, in large doses, produces palpitations of the heart, nervousness, headaches, and dizziness. However, for the most part, it gives the user the illusion of being alert, acutely sensitive, full of well-being, and very efficient (but he is not necessarily any of these things). "Speed" is not physiologically addictive in the usual sense, but tolerance develops quickly—the user must increase the dosage in order to continue to get the desired effects.

The physiological mechanism that leads to the need to keep increasing the dosage of "speed" is simple to understand. The drug apparently causes certain natural chemicals in the nervous system to be released. These chemicals, in turn, cause the nerves to become very sensitive and to be easily stimulated into action. The end result of this action is to give the user the alert, sensitive feeling that he's seeking. However, continued large doses of "speed" deplete the supply of natural chemicals. Since the body cannot replace these chemicals quickly, more and more of the drug must be taken in order to squeeze out every possible drop of them. When they are virtually all gone (usually after the person has been awake and without food for a long time), the user begins to exhibit symptoms of anxiety and extreme depression and feelings of paranoia. There are cases in which "speed" users have become so depressed and fearful that they have locked themselves in closets where, because "speed" depresses the appetite, they have starved to death. More often, however, the user merely collapses from fatigue and sleeps for a long time. Upon awakening, he feels bad and experiences a strong desire to take the drug to relieve this feeling. Thus the "speed freak" gets into a cycle that leads to psychological addiction, emotional and physiological deterioration (brain damage), and, in some cases, death.

Soft Drugs

LSD (D-lysergic acid diethylamide)   This is a very powerful synthetic drug; it is synthetic in the sense that it does not occur in nature but is produced in a laboratory. It is a liquid that is usually taken by placing a very small amount on a sugar cube and then eating the cube. Tolerance develops, but LSD is not physiologically addictive. Withdrawal symptoms do not occur, and people seldom develop psychological addiction. LSD is generally used only for an occasional "big trip." Frequent use can lead to a deep involvement in one's own experience, virtually excluding the outside world. People sometimes report recurrences of their trip several days, weeks, or months after taking LSD, an experience that can be quite frightening and lead the person to believe that he might be becoming insane.

A typical LSD trip lasts about eight hours and usually involves altered perceptions of color, size, and shape and feelings of happiness, love, goodness, and a strong sense of the beauty of surrounding objects. The user often becomes mentally detached from events that are going on around him and focuses entirely on his own thoughts and experiences. Such involvement with one's own thoughts under LSD frequently leads to feelings of profound insight and self-understanding; some users claim that their lives have been substantially changed by such insights.

But there is another side of the coin. Not all LSD trips are good ones, and a bad trip is an experience that few people want to repeat. Indeed, there are even a few reported cases of psychosis following LSD. Suicides and other drastic behaviors have also been attributed to the drug.

Bad trips, psychoses, suicides, and such things may not be caused by LSD itself. Many authorities suspect that people for whom these grim things occur are strongly predisposed to such experiences before they take the drug. The hypothesis is that LSD, like alcohol and many other drugs, strips away one's protective defenses and turns attention inward. For a person who has no serious problems at the moment, this dropping of inhibitions and inward focus may be extremely pleasant. For a person already in some sort of psychological turmoil, inhibitions and defenses may be necessary for maintenance of stability; loss of defenses may be sufficient to precipitate bizarre behavior, and the inward focus may reveal things with which the person cannot cope. Even if this explanation is true, the problem is that a person may not know that he is psychologically unprepared for the drug until he's already into a bad trip.

LSD AND CHROMOSOMAL DAMAGE Recently there have been reports of LSD causing chromosome damage. As you may recall from biology courses, the nucleus of each cell in your body contains forty-six chromosomes, each consisting of a string of genes. These genes control your hereditary characteristics and dictate the functioning of the cell. Early research indicated that taking LSD often appeared to lead to fragmented chromosomes, and fear developed that this would lead to premature aging, abnormal offspring, and possibly even to leukemia. However, this research is often difficult to interpret. Some studies used laboratory rats that were given massive doses of LSD, doses proportionately far greater than most human users ever take. The rats' chromosomes became fragmented, which may mean that large doses of LSD cause fragmentation or that rats are particularly susceptible to chromosome damage, or both. Other studies found chromosome fragmentation in human beings who used LSD frequently. However, these people probably were users of more than one kind of drug, and it is hard to know whether LSD was the main or the only cause of fragmentation. Newborn babies of heavy users sometimes have fragmented chromosomes, but this fragmentation clears up soon after birth, and it is yet too early to tell if any permanent damage has been done to such babies. And, to complicate things, some studies have failed to find any fragmentation at all. So the picture is quite unclear. Indeed, many common chemicals in large quantities can fragment chromosomes with no apparent physiological repercussions. Thus no one can be sure whether LSD really leads to problems or not.

It seems to me that because no one knows exactly what LSD does or what its long-term effects are, it is wise to abstain from taking it. From the point of view of this book (particularly Part 2 of this section), one should approach the question as a rational decision-maker and ask oneself if the possibility of a good trip outweighs (1) the possibility of a bad trip and (2) the possibility of some kind of serious genetic damage.

Marijuana This is the drug most widely used by young people, aside from alcohol and tobacco. While fewer young people use it than the popular press would like to believe, more of them use it than their parents would like to believe. One survey in San Francisco found that among those between eighteen and thirty-four years old, one third of the males and one fourth of the females reported having used marijuana at least once. More female college students had used it than female nonstudents, and, surprisingly, more male nonstudents had used it than had male students. By and large, users were fairly conventional people, although, as you might expect, many tended to reject some of the traditional American values. In the population as a whole, the President's Commission on Marijuana estimated that 24 million Americans had at least tried marijuana.

Marijuana has been around for a long time (its first recorded use was in 2700 B.C.), but until recently it has not been used much in the United States. It is the dried stems and leaves from the Indian hemp plant *Cannabis sativa,* a weed that grows readily almost everywhere. *Hashish,* which means "grass" in Arabic, is a concentrate of the resin found in the delicate top leaves of the hemp plant and is much more powerful than marijuana. Because the law against growing *Cannabis* in the United States is as strictly enforced as possible, most of the marijuana used here is smuggled into the country.

Marijuana is usually smoked as a cigarette or in a pipe. When smoked it has a very distinctive odor—which accounts for the continued record sales of pungent incense as a cover-up. Sometimes, instead of being smoked, it is baked in cookies or brownies and eaten.

Marijuana is not physiologically addictive, although psychological addiction is possible. It increases the pulse rate, causes the eyes to become bloodshot, and, in some people, increases thirst and appetite (the latter phenomenon is affectionately known as "the munchies"). No adverse physiological effects have been reported. There are no withdrawal symptoms, and tolerance, in the usual sense, does not develop. Indeed, a sort of reverse tolerance is often reported; frequent users find it takes less to get high than when they first began using the drug. When marijuana is smoked the high is fairly self-limiting in that the user reaches a plateau and can get no higher. When it is ingested in cookies or the like, the high may get out of hand and become rather like hashish high. No deaths have been attributed directly to marijuana, and bad trips are infrequent.

The psychological effects of marijuana depend a good deal on the user's expectations, his personality, and the setting in which it is taken. Most people report a contented, peaceful, dreamy state in which they are quite aware of perceptual experiences and in which they feel slightly withdrawn from other people while still maintaining a feeling of pleasant communication with them. Frequently, very mundane events seem extremely funny, and large doses of marijuana can lead to vivid, usually enjoyable, visual hallucinations. Often people experience distorted perceptions of distance and time; five minutes may seem like a half hour. A feeling of insight, similar to that experienced on LSD, is sometimes reported, and an increased awareness of the beauty of music, color, and objects is common.

With all these good things going for it, it is small wonder that many people develop a decided taste for marijuana. However, aside from the law, which we will discuss in a moment, there is some danger in its use. First, because of its illicit source, there is no telling what the buyer may be getting besides marijuana; there have been many cases in which poor-quality marijuana was artificially "improved" with a variety of strange chemicals, any of which might be dangerous. The second danger is psychological dependency; for some people the pleasant illusions of marijuana may replace the unpleasant realities of life. Such persons may continuously use marijuana, drifting off into a haze and ceasing to be functional, self-reliant persons. The third problem with marijuana is, as with LSD, that it may be that people who have a predisposition toward psychosis, depression, suicide, and so forth, may find that the drug is sufficient to push them beyond their limits of stability.

SOME FEARS ABOUT MARIJUANA   Two commonly expressed fears about marijuana are, first, that it leads to heavy drug use (for example, heroin) and, second, that it interferes with judgment so that the user might kill himself or someone else while driving a car. The first fear is the result of sloppy logic and has no basis in fact. While many people who end up on heroin may have begun on marijuana, this in no way proves a cause-and-effect relationship. People who are predisposed to drug addiction (often people who simply cannot cope with reality) ordinarily begin with the more easily obtained and less powerful drugs, and marijuana happens to fill the bill. Once into the drug scene, such people may seek the more powerful effects of hard drugs in order to escape from life. To say that marijuana *leads* to heroin addiction because most addicts began with marijuana is a bit like saying that a child's milk drinking *leads* to adult alcoholism because most alcoholics began by drinking milk. Such an argument, of course, overlooks the fact that a lot of people who did not become alcoholics also drank milk.

The second fear, that marijuana interferes with judgment, and particularly with driving skills, has greater substance than the first. There is not very much research on the subject, but that which exists presents a very interesting picture. First, it appears that marijuana can affect tasks that require close, active attention and short-term memory. For example, if a person who is unused to marijuana is asked to assign symbols to rows of randomly arranged digits on a page (that is, each 2 on the page gets a ⌐, each 3 gets a], each 7 gets a Λ), he does a poorer job when he is high than when he is not. So too, his performance is worse on a task that requires him to keep a stylus touching a small spot on a rotating disk, a task requiring very close attention. Marijuana leads to impaired performance on tasks that tax the person's short-term memory, such as doing arithmetic problems in his head (for example, "start with 106, subtract 7, add 1, 2, or 3 to the answer, then subtract 7 from the new answer, add 1, 2, or 3 to that, and so on, until you reach a number between 46 and 54"). Also, if you read strings of digits to a person and immediately ask him to recall them, he can correctly repeat strings of up to about nine digits when he is normal and only up to about eight when he is high on marijuana. If you ask him to give the string back to you in the reverse order, he can repeat strings of up to about eight when he is normal and only up to about six or seven when he is high. These tasks all require close, active attention and short-term memory; poor performance under the influence of marijuana suggests that these faculties are impaired.

On the other hand, marijuana does not impair one's ability to perform tasks that merely require passive attention, for example, pushing a button whenever

Beware! Young and Old—People in All Walks of Life!

This  may be handed you by the <u>friendly stranger</u>. It contains the Killer Drug "Marihuana"-- a powerful narcotic in which lurks *Murder! Insanity! Death!*

WARNING!

Dope peddlers are shrewd! They may put some of this drug in the 🫖 or in the cocktail or in the tobacco cigarette.

WRITE FOR DETAILED INFORMATION, ENCLOSING 12 CENTS IN POSTAGE — MAILING COST

Address: **THE INTER-STATE NARCOTIC ASSOCIATION**
(Incorporated not for profit)

53 W. Jackson Blvd.　　　　**Chicago, Illinois, U. S. A.**

Reprinted with permission from *Marihuana Reconsidered* by L. Grinspoon.

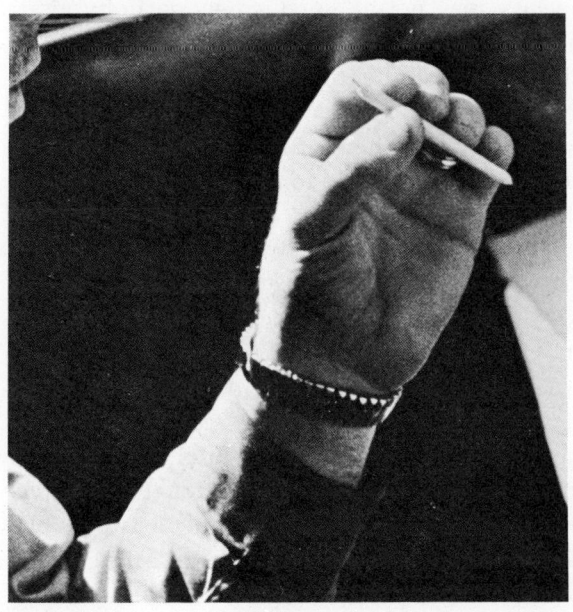

FIG. 6.19 "Official" reactions to marijuana have tended to be rather hysterical. Perhaps the 1972 report by the President's Commission on Marijuana and Drug Abuse, which reached conclusions similar to those presented in the text, will contribute a more reasonable tone to future considerations of marijuana use.

some specified letter appears in a sequence of letters that are flashed on a screen. This kind of attention serves to detect events rather than to search actively for things; as such, it probably represents the kind of attention (for good or for bad) that most of us rely heavily upon when driving a car.

One recent study rather directly examined the relation between marijuana and driving. There is good evidence to believe that a reliable method of differentiating safe and unsafe drivers is to have people "drive" a laboratory mock-up of a car. A film containing various normal and emergency driving situations is projected on a screen in front of the mock-up, and the experimenter measures the person's driving performance in terms of whether or not he accelerates or decelerates when he should, steers appropriately, uses turn signals correctly, and the amount of time he spends monitoring the speedometer. When experienced marijuana users performed this task, their scores were virtually the same on marijuana as when normal, except that on marijuana they did not monitor the speedometer as much as they normally did. When these same people were high on alcohol (0.10 percent alcohol concentration in the blood, the amount which legally is intoxicating), they made significantly more errors; out of 405 possible errors in the course of the test, the average was 84.46 when normal, 84.49 when high on marijuana, and 97.44 when high on alcohol. These results *suggest* that passive event detection, the kind of attention that characterizes some aspects of driving, as well as people's ability to react appropriately to the events, may not be impaired seriously by marijuana. However, get it straight, safe driving also requires active attention, especially in emergencies, and that kind of attention probably is impaired by marijuana, so I am *not* saying that it is all right to drive while under the influence of marijuana. Moreover, no one knows what the time and distance distortions that marijuana users commonly experience may do to driving ability—finding out by trying it yourself might turn out to be an experimental investigation that is deadly to yourself or to someone else.

Some Important Considerations

A few more things need to be said because they are relevant to making a decision about the use of drugs. These have been saved for last because they are general and can be applied to almost all of the drugs discussed.

First, no one is sure how any of these drugs interact with other chemicals. Many people are legitimately on one or more forms of medication (for example, tranquilizers, birth control pills, insulin, anticoagulants). While it is possible, even likely, that there would be no harmful effects, few people have the courage or foresight to ask their physician about possible drug interaction, and even

BOX 6.4

Some Common Drugs: Uses and Effects

Drugs	Pharmacologic Classification	Medical Use	Potential for Physiological Addiction	Potential for Psychological Addiction	Tolerance	Possible Noticeable Effects When Overused	How Taken When Overused
Morphine (an opium derivative)	Central nervous system depressant	To relieve pain	Yes	Yes	Yes	Drowsiness or stupor, pinpoint pupils	Orally or by injection
Heroin (a morphine derivative)	Depressant	To relieve pain	Yes	Yes	Yes	Same as morphine	Sniffed or by injection
Codeine (an opium derivative)	Depressant	To relieve pain and coughing	Yes	Yes	Yes	Drowsiness, pinpoint pupils	Orally (usually as cough syrup)
Paregoric (preparation containing opium)	Depressant	For sedation and to counteract diarrhea	Yes	Yes	Yes	Same as morphine	Orally or by injection
Meperidine (synthetic morphine-like drug)	Depressant	To relieve pain	Yes	Yes	Yes	Similar to morphine, except that at higher doses, excitation, tremors, and convulsions occur	Orally or by injection
Methadone (synthetic morphine-like drug)	Depressant	To relieve pain	Yes	Yes	Yes	Same as morphine	Orally or by injection
Cocaine	Central nervous system stimulant	Local anesthetic	No	Yes	No	Extreme excitation, tremors, hallucinations	Sniffed or by injection
Marijuana	Hallucinogen	None	No	Yes	No	Drowsiness or excitability, talkative-ness, laughter, hallucinations	Smoked or orally
Barbiturates (e.g., amobarbital, pentobarbital, secobarbital)	Depressant	For sedation, sleep-producing, epilepsy, high blood pressure	Yes	Yes	Yes	Drowsiness, staggering, slurred speech	Orally or by injection
Amphetamine drugs (e.g., amphetamine, dextroamphetamine, methamphetamine— also known as desoxyephedrine)	Stimulant	For mild depression, anti-appetite, narcolepsy	No	Yes	Yes	Excitation, dilated pupils, tremors, talkativeness, hallucinations	Orally or by injection
LSD (also mescaline, peyote, psilocybin, DMT, STP, THC)	Hallucinogen	(Medical research only)	No	Yes	Yes	Excitation, hallucina-tions, rambling speech	Orally or by injection
Glue (also paint thinner, lighter fluid)	Depressant	None	Unknown	Yes	Yes	Staggering, drowsiness slurred speech, stupor	Inhaled

SOURCE: *Drug Abuse: Escape to Nowhere*, Philadelphia: Smith Kline & French Laboratories, 1971. Used by permission.

if they did, it is doubtful that he would know. Certainly, you should never take two stimulant drugs (for example, pep pills and methedrine) or two depressants (for example, barbiturates and alcohol) at the same time. It is likely that there are many drugs that should not be mixed, and since most of us do not have the necessary information to permit a safe decision, we should be cautious.

Second, the drugs that are bought on the street are not necessarily what they are represented as being. Indeed, many drugs turn out to be LSD, in spite of what they are labeled. Also, strychnine and other such dangerous substances are sometimes added to low-quality drugs in order to increase their punch. Remember, even if you know the person you purchase a drug from, you have no idea where he got it, and where that second party got it, and so forth. Needless to say, the kitchen chemists who make LSD do not have to comply with government standards for sanitation and purity of product. No doubt their wares are often hazardous to your health in more ways than one.

Third, almost all drugs, even marijuana, can be psychologically dangerous (1) to people who are having difficulty coping with some serious psychological conflict or crisis and (2) to people who generally have difficulty coping with the demands of reality. In the first case, the strangeness of the drug experience can "push the person over the edge." That is, psychotic episodes have been reported with almost all of these drugs, although, as was said before, in most cases this is probably because the person was strongly predisposed rather than because of an actual effect of the drug. In the second case, even the mildest drug can be psychologically addictive to a person who needs a crutch. Of course, this does not happen overnight, but it is a far greater danger than most people realize. For many people, even mild release from stress can be such relief that they can come to depend upon the drug that gives such relief to them.

Fourth, and last, the use of almost all of these drugs is regulated, if not prohibited, by law. In theory at least, minors may not purchase tobacco or alcohol, prescriptions are needed for tranquilizers, barbiturates, and amphetamines, and narcotics, LSD, and marijuana are strictly prohibited. Violations of these laws carry different penalties in different states, but all can bring more serious retribution than most people realize. As of this writing (early 1973), the state of Washington, which is where I live, prohibits the possession, manufacture, sale, or distribution, except through legitimate channels, of a long list of drugs, including prescription drugs, and LSD. The law prescribes up to six months in jail and a $200 fine for a first offense, and any transaction involving a minor results in up to twenty years in prison and/or a fine of up to $50,000.

Moreover, it is a felony to "traffic in narcotics," and a first offense can result in from five to twenty years in prison and a fine of up to $10,000. If a minor is involved, the prison term is from twenty to forty years and the fine can go as high as $50,000, or both. In some states, the sale or use of marijuana is considered a felony.

The federal law concerning the sale, possession, and so on, of narcotics and marijuana requires a prison term of from five to twenty years and a fine of up to $20,000 for a first offense. Selling heroin to anyone under the age of eighteen is punishable by life imprisonment or death.

Even if you're not convicted, or if you get only a light or suspended sentence, drug charges can have a very serious effect on your future. Many professions that are either licensed by the states or have similar permit requirements (for example, the practice of law) require that you be of sterling character, and a drug charge is definitely tarnishing. Security clearances and commissioning as a military officer require similar high standing. Moreover, conviction of a felony can result in the loss of voting rights, the right to a passport, and the right to hold public office.

SUMMARY

1   Drugs are broadly used in our culture, only we don't always recognize and admit that things like aspirin, diet pills, coffee, alcohol, and so on, are drugs.

2   When a person cannot get by without some specific drug, we say that he is *addicted* to the drug. Addiction can be physiological, psychological, or both.

3   Unacceptable drugs include hard drugs such as narcotics and "speed" and soft drugs such as LSD and marijuana. Hard drugs clearly are dangerous. There are questions about the long-term effects of LSD, and while evidence about its negative effects is weak, it does exist. Even though many authorities state that marijuana is dangerous, there is little evidence to date to substantiate such a claim. Use of marijuana, however, is illegal, and because the consequences of arrest and conviction for its possession are *very* negative, one should consider carefully whether or not its use is worth the possible risks.

Further Reading

CANADIAN GOVERNMENT COMMISSION OF INQUIRY (Interim report). *The Non-Medical Use of Drugs*
Baltimore, Md.: Penguin, 1971 (c. 1970), 448 pages (paperback).
Although this book contains research specifically on the extent and pattern of drug use in Canada as well as the issues of control of drugs and treatment techniques, it also presents a good deal of factual information about the various kinds of drugs used nonmedically and their physiological and psychological effects.

Drug Abuse: Escape to Nowhere
Philadelphia: Smith Kline and French Laboratories, 1971, 104 pages (paperback).
Written primarily for teachers, this book covers the various drugs and their effects, the methods of therapy for drug addicts, educational approaches to the topic of drug use, and how to recognize overuse of drugs.

FORT, J.   *The Pleasure Seekers: The Drug Crisis, Youth, and Society*
New York: Grove Press, 1969, 254 pages (paperback).
An evaluation of the use of mind-altering drugs and their effects on the individual and on society in general. The book has a pro-drug tone and uses only those critics who condemn drug use (but who favor existing use of alcohol and cigarettes) as hypocrites. Opinionated but very readable.

GRINSPOON, L.   *Marihuana Reconsidered*
Cambridge, Mass.: Harvard University Press, 1971, 443 pages (paperback).
This well-documented book on marijuana covers a variety of aspects of marijuana use all the way from the history of its use in the United States and its use in medicine to its various psychological and physiological effects.

HORMAN, R. E., and A. M. Fox (Eds.).   *Drug Awareness*
New York: Avon, 1970, 478 pages (paperback).
An interesting collection of papers on marijuana and LSD, prepared specifically to make the reader aware of the possible consequences of nonmedical use of these drugs. Each chapter has an introductory comment in the beginning to explain the inter-relatedness of the papers in that chapter. Covers both psychological and medical effects.

NATIONAL COMMISSION ON MARIHUANA AND DRUG ABUSE.   *Marihuana: A Signal of Misunderstanding*
New York: New American Library (Signet), 1972, 233 pages (paperback).
This is the Presidential Commission's report on marijuana use in the United States. It is a reasoned, if conservative, examination that recommends changes in our overly restrictive and unrealistic legal attempts to deal with increased marijuana use.

RAY, O. S.   *Drugs, Society, and Human Behavior*
St. Louis: Mosby, 1972, 299 pages (paperback).
Written from three points of view, historical, pharmacological, and psychological, the book begins with an elementary introduction to the nervous system and pharmacology and moves on to discuss all of the major drugs in use today, from alcohol and cigarettes to tranquilizers to hallucinogens.

YABLONSKY, L.   *Synanon: The Tunnel Back*
Baltimore, Md.: Penguin, 1967 (c. 1965), 408 pages (paperback).
An absorbing account of a unique program for treating and rehabilitating drug addicts. Interesting to read because much of the book is based on case histories and recorded conversations.

Tools for
Psychological Research
APPENDIX 1

Throughout this book there are numerous references to research that serves to clarify some important point or that demonstrates some psychological phenomenon. Frequently it is difficult for a nonpsychologist to conceive of how such research is conducted; the techniques of physics and chemistry seem vaguely comprehensible to most people, but the methods for studying psychology are more difficult to imagine. This appendix is intended to show you how psychological research is done.

Two Approaches   There are two approaches to the study of psychology. The first, the *armchair approach*, consists of watching people or events around you, examining your own thoughts and feelings, and then sitting down in a comfortable armchair and drawing general conclusions from your observations. The value of this approach is that it focuses where the action is, on your own psychology, and on the psychology of other people; it can contribute important insights into understanding people's feelings and behavior. Indeed, from the inception of psychology (when the first caveman wondered why another caveman did what he did) until quite recently, the armchair approach was the sole method by which psychological knowledge was obtained.

The problem with this approach is that there is no way to determine whether the general conclusions based on one's observations are right or wrong. Suppose you and I were to move our armchairs so that we could sit side by side and watch people at a carnival. You, being of a cheerful disposition, conclude that the happy atmosphere of the carnival derives from the fact that people who are happy in the first place come to a carnival in order to express their happiness. I, being of a more gloomy turn of mind, conclude that the happy atmosphere derives from the fact that people who are desperately unhappy flock together to hide their unhappiness in a mantle of joy. Whose conclusion is right? We have both sat and watched the same people, yet we have reached opposite conclusions.

Part of the difficulty is that we both were influenced by our own personalities; we lacked objectivity. Of greater importance, we can't decide whose conclusions are right or wrong until we get some decisive information; to do this we must walk over and ask a few people if they were happy or unhappy before they came to the carnival. When we ask this question we've started to employ the second approach to obtaining psychological knowledge—*research*.

Research, like the armchair approach, begins with observing, pondering, theorizing, and stating tentative conclusions which are called *hypotheses*. Then it goes one crucial step further and requires that these hypotheses be checked against the facts in order to decide whether they are reasonable or not. I said *reasonable* in that last sentence rather than true because the "knowledge" encompassed in any science is only the set of hypotheses that the scientists believe at the moment; today's truth may be tomorrow's folly. Thus, the point of research is not to demonstrate truth. Rather, it is to marshal evidence that will increase or decrease scientists' belief in a hypothesis. The strategy for marshaling such evidence is called the *scientific method*, which we will discuss in a moment.

It is important to recognize that research is a human endeavor that involves creativity in conceiving hypotheses, in devising ways of testing them, in interrelating the results, and in fitting these results in with other things that are already known. Psychological research involves human beings learning about themselves and about other animals. It is not the inhuman, cold, chrome-plated mechanical monster that many nonpsychologists fear it is. No one is trying to find ways to control men's minds or make them puppets that automatically respond to the appropriate tug on their strings. The aim is to find out enough about ourselves to help alleviate the human misery that plagues us and to help us attain the best that is in us. For these reasons it is important to know about such things as how we see and hear, how people learn, how we make decisions, how we react to each other in social groups, and how our values determine our behavior. By understanding these things we can learn how to help people see and hear better, learn more efficiently, make more effective decisions, have more satisfying social interactions, and cope better with their personal problems.

The Scientific Method in Psychology

The "scientific method" is a general term for the set of attitudes and the group of techniques that have evolved to guide research and aid in the interpretation of the results of the research. Each discipline has its own special subset of these techniques, but the attitudes of objectivity, honesty, and scholarship are held in common by scientists in all disciplines.

Steps in the Method

In general, the scientific method consists of five steps.

1. *Careful observation* of the events of interest (as when we sat at the carnival and watched the people).

2. *Formulation of a hypothesis* (my notion or yours about the prior happiness of the people, for example). The criteria for a suitable hypothesis are that it be interesting and that it be amenable to examination. For example, the hypothesis that the human mind is green won't do for two reasons: (1) the color of the mind would be of no more than passing interest, except at a very dull party, and (2) there is no possible way to investigate the color of a human mind because no one ever saw one.

3. *Execution of the research* (as when we asked people if they had been happy or unhappy before they came to the carnival). In psychology there are four basic methods of doing research. These will be outlined in detail in a moment.

4. *Interpretation of the results,* which is very difficult because it is here that one's biases are most likely to have their full effect. If 13 people at the carnival said that they had been happy before they came and 10 said that they had been unhappy, would your belief in your hypothesis be increased or decreased? Certainly 13 is more than 10, but then again it is only 3 more. If we continued asking people, who knows but what the 10 might climb to 20 and the 13 increase only to 14. Thus, the question is whether the difference between these numbers is merely due to chance or whether it really tells us something about the moods of people who go to carnivals. The techniques used to answer this question and to help us keep our own biases from answering the question for us are called *statistics.* We'll briefly discuss the primary ideas underlying statistics when we discuss the four methods of psychological research.

5. *Communication* of the hypothesis and experimental results to scientists and other interested persons. This step involves scientists discussing their work among themselves and publishing periodic reports in scientific journals. Then specialized scholarly books and more general texts (like this book) take the published research reports and try to fit together "the big picture." So, the things that are in this book, other psychology books, and books in other disciplines started as observations and ideas, were subjected to scientific research, were published in short journal articles, are brought together by textbook authors, and, in the case of psychology, presently are being transmitted to you. You are the final consumer of the work of many, many scientists.

*Strengths
and Weaknesses*

This, then, is the scientific method as it works in all disciplines, not just in psychology. Its strength lies in the attempt at objectivity and in the emergence of the broad picture from the multiplicity of studies conducted by many different people; one poorly done study or a wrong conclusion on the part of one scientist cannot distort the broad picture very much.

The weakness of the scientific method lies in the fact that there are many important questions that it is not suited to investigate and answer. This is because the method relies on clearly stated hypotheses that permit objective, repeatable observations to be marshaled as evidence for or against them. An untestable hypothesis cannot be examined using the scientific method: How does one test the existence of God or of ghosts? How does one test the power of astrology or the beauty of a painting? You may be able to find out how many people believe in God, ghosts, the power of astrology, or the beauty of a painting using the scientific method, but you can't resolve the more basic questions, for example, that God exists. By the same token, it is foolish to disbelieve in God, ghosts, and so forth, merely because science cannot demonstrate their existence—to misquote Hamlet, "There are more things in heaven and earth, Horatio, than are dreamt of in your [Science]."

Four Psychological Research Methods

The four methods most commonly used for psychological research are (1) experiments, (2) simulation, (3) naturalistic observation, and (4) case histories. Each is particularly appropriate for studying certain kinds of questions, and each will be discussed in turn.

Experiments

The essence of an experiment lies in the experimenter intentionally and carefully varying some important aspect of a situation and observing what a person (or animal) does as a result. Traditionally, the varied aspect is called the *independent variable,* and the part of the person's behavior that is watched for change is called the *dependent variable.* The exact amount of change in the dependent variable is called the *datum* (plural = *data*). Thus, if for some reason a person's acquaintances write him spiteful letters (the independent variable) and I observed the degree of decrease (datum) in the friendliness he accords these acquaintances (the dependent variable), I might be able to infer that the person had become angry. This inferred factor, his anger, is unobservable. You never see anger because it is inside a person; all you see is the person's behavior. But you infer that the independent variable (the letters) did *something* to the person. This "something" is reflected in the dependent variable (the decreased friendliness) and is called an *intervening variable.* In this example, the intervening variable is anger. In other cases it might be IQ, talent, schizo-phrenia, love, and so forth—all those unobservable qualities that we infer about people from how they behave.

You can see from the foregoing discussion that an experiment has three major parts—the experimenter-manipulated independent variable, which in-fluences the unobservable intervening variable, which is reflected in changes in the dependent variable. In psychology the intervening variable is usually the thing we are interested in knowing about. By using experiments, psycholo-gists have been able to carefully study things like IQ or happiness—things that have never actually been seen, weighed, touched, or smelled—a not unimpressive accomplishment when you stop to think about it.

How to perform an experiment   To perform an experiment you begin with some circumscribed task that involves the variables you are interested in; then you manipulate the independent variable and see what happens to the de-pendent variable. The point of a circumscribed task is to make sure that the only aspect of the situation that is changing is the independent variable. Otherwise you don't know if changes in the dependent variable are the result of what you did or the result of some other, extraneous, changes in the situation. In short, you must *control* the other aspects of the situation so that they do not influence the person during the experiment (Fig. A1.1).

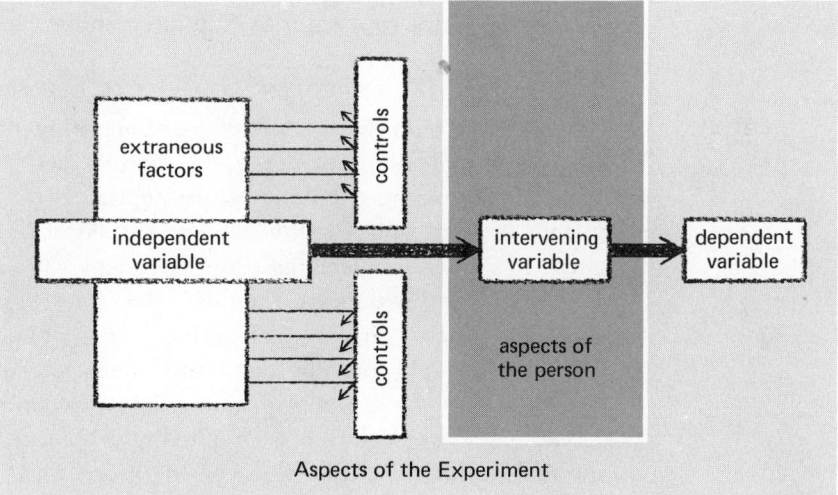

Aspects of the Experiment

FIG. A1.1   *A schematic illustration of the logic of an experiment. By use of proper controls, the independent variable is the sole influence on the intervening variable; this influence is then reflected in changes in the dependent variable which are observed and recorded by the experimenter.*

Now that you're armed with some of the technical terms, let's look at three hypothetical experiments and identify their tasks, variables, and controls. At the same time, we can use these experiments as vehicles for introducing some other technical concepts you should be aware of.

HYPOTHETICAL EXPERIMENT 1, MEMORIZATION Suppose your hypothesis were that people can memorize meaningful material more easily than they can memorize meaningless material. You give two similar groups of people material to memorize (the task). One group gets the first three stanzas of T. S. Eliot's poem "The Lovesong of J. Alfred Prufrock" in its usual printed format (meaningful material) while the other group gets the same material printed in the same format but with the words jumbled up (meaningless material). Each group has received one of the two conditions of the independent variable: meaningful and meaningless material. Both groups are given four minutes to read through the material and try to memorize it, after which they are asked to recite all they can remember. Then they are given another four minutes to memorize and another opportunity to recite all they can remember, and so on until they get it perfectly. Each "memorize it-recite it" opportunity is called a *trial*, and each person continues until he can recite perfectly the material he was given to memorize. Then you find out which group took the larger number of trials (the number of trials for each person is a datum) to attain perfect recollection (the dependent variable). If the group with the meaningless material took more trials, you could infer that meaningless material is more difficult to memorize (the intervening variable) than meaningful material.

HYPOTHETICAL EXPERIMENT 2, DIETS AND DEPRESSION Suppose your hypothesis were that people who are on stringent "crash" diets increasingly experience feelings of depression as the diet progresses. You go to a hospital where overweight patients are kept in bed and fed a minimal diet intravenously, and you ask the patients to take a psychological test that is sensitive to depression feelings (the dependent variable; each person's "depression score" is his datum). There are two ways you could manipulate the independent variable, that is, the length of time that people have been on their diet. First, you could give the test many times to the same person, starting on the first day of the diet and repeating it at various times thereafter. Second, you could give the test once to each of many people, but give it to some people on the first day of their diet, some on the seond day, some on the third, and so forth. The advantage of the first way of doing the experiment, called the *longitudinal method*, is that it permits you to observe changes in an individual person's depression feelings as the diet progresses. Its disadvantage is that when they repeatedly take the same test, people unintentionally tend to repeat the answers that they gave the last time (so you couldn't detect a change in depression even if it occurred), or they tend to ponder the questions and dream up answers that they think you would like them to give (which might make it look as though there was a change in depression even when there wasn't).The advantage of the second way of doing the experiment, called the *cross-sectional method*, is that the people take the test only once, so you don't run the risk that repeated testing involves. Its disadvantage is that you can't observe changes in an individual person's depression feelings throughout the course of the diet.

HYPOTHETICAL EXPERIMENT 3, DREAMING AND REST Suppose your hypothesis were that the amount of dreaming that people do during the night influences how well rested (that is, calm and unanxious) they feel the next day. Of course, you can't make people dream, but you can either let them dream naturally or prevent them from dreaming. You might attach small electronic sensing devices to people's scalps and near their eyelids, devices which will detect the specific patterns of eye movement and brainwaves that occur when people are dreaming (this is not science fiction, it really can be done). Then, by flipping a coin, you *randomly* designate one half of the people to be in the *experimental group* and the other half to be in the *control group*. No one should know which group he is in or what your hypothesis is. Then, whenever anyone in the experimental group starts to dream, you prevent it by awakening him (the independent variable). You don't keep track of the dreaming of the people in the control group. Instead, you let them dream naturally, but every so often you awaken them until you have done it as often as you awakened the people in the experimental group. This controls for the fact that merely being awakened from time to time will decrease the degree to which people feel well rested the next day.

The next morning you have all of the people rate how well rested they feel on a scale from 1 to 7, where 1 is "more tired than I was when I went to bed last night" and 7 is "very rested." Then you compare the ratings (the data) given by the two groups to see if your hypothesis is supported. Note that in this experiment only the experimental group actually receives the independent variable; the control group is included for purposes of comparison. The whole situation of sleeping with wires attached to your scalp and being awakened throughout the night is peculiar. The control group represents what "normal" people did in this strange set-up, while the treatment of the experimental group is identical to that of the control group in every respect but one, and that one respect is the one you're interested in—the independent variable, prevention of dreaming.

Describing the data In each of these hypothetical experiments we were rather vague about what you would do with the data and how you would use them to decide whether your hypothesis was reasonable. However, data analysis and subsequent decisions about the hypothesis are a very crucial part of the research. Experimental data are seldom so unequivocal that the decision about the reasonableness of the hypothesis is clear and unquestionable. The data are that way because people are that way; the people who participate in experiments differ in the way they are when the experiment begins, in the degree to which they are affected by the independent variable, and in the degree to which they understand and try to comply with the task the experimenter asks them to do. Thus, in our memorization experiment, if a person has a poor memory or if he thinks the experiment is really a subtle intelligence test rather than a study of memorization, he is likely to give results that differ from what the other people give. For these reasons, and for reasons specific to other experiments, psychologists have learned to live with equivocal data. But we still must make decisions about our hypotheses. Thus we have adopted a set of techniques, *statistics,* for helping us make these decisions.

Statistics can be divided into two types. The first is called descriptive statistics. The second is called inferential statistics.

DESCRIPTIVE STATISTICS These statistics are used to summarize the data you get from a group of people. In the first and third examples of experiments, each group yielded a variety of numbers—some people in the memorization experiment took more trials for perfect recollection than other people in the same group, regardless of which group they were in. Some people felt less rested than others after the dreaming experiment, whether in the experimental or control group. Because of this, decisions about the hypotheses must depend on the groups as a whole rather than upon the results for individuals; therefore, some way is needed for summarizing each group's data. The three important summary statements are about the *central tendency* of the group data, about the *variability* of the group data, and, in some cases, about the *correlation* between two sets of data for a single group.

Central tendency means the average, but there are three different commonly used kinds of averages:

1. The *mean* is the sum of the individuals' data divided by the number of individuals in the group. This is what most people mean when they talk about "the average." Suppose that the number of memorization trials for a group of seven people were 3, 5, 5, 9, 11, 15, and 43 trials. The mean would be $(3 + 5 + 5 + 9 + 11 + 15 + 43) \div 7$, which is $91/7 = 13$. We would say that the mean of the group data is 13 and use this number to summarize the group's performance.

2. The *median* is the datum that lies in the middle of the group of data. Thus, the median number of trials is 9. Three of the seven people memorized in fewer trials and three took more trials to learn. Because it falls right in the middle, it seems reasonable to use the median as a summary of the group performance.
3. The *mode* is the datum that occurs most frequently. Thus the mode for the seven numbers is 5 because two people memorized in that many trials. While it is not compelling in this particular example, you can see intuitively that it might be reasonable to regard the most "popular" datum as representative of what a group does.

Now, all three of these descriptions of central tendency yielded different numbers. Which is right? The answer depends on what you want to say about the group. The mean is the balance point of the data and is best when it is important that every datum be taken into account in determining the group "average." That is, if the data were put on a seesaw like the one in Figure A1.2, the mean would be the point where the fulcrum would be placed so the seesaw was perfectly balanced. It says that the one big number down at 43 is important and can compensate for a lot of low numbers at the other end of the scale.

Sometimes, of course, very deviant numbers are peculiar cases and not at all representative of the rest of the group. The person who took 43 trials to memorize his assigned material probably was not trying very hard or perhaps did not understand the task. At any rate, taking his datum seriously rather distorts the picture because everybody else memorized in fewer than 15 trials. In such a case it might be best to use the median (which is 9) to summarize the group performance. For the hypothetical data we have been considering here, the median gives the clearest picture.

The mode is not used a great deal in psychological research, but when it is, it is usually to describe data that can't be meaningfully added, subtracted,

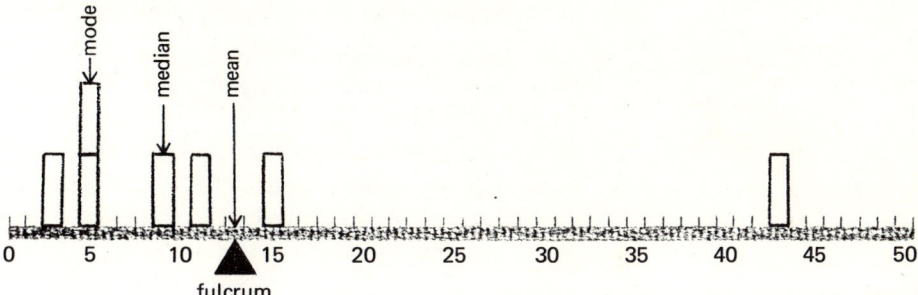

FIG. A1.2 *Hypothetical data for the memorization experiment placed on a teeter-totter. Each block represents the number of trials required by each individual in the experiment to recall correctly all of the memorized material.*

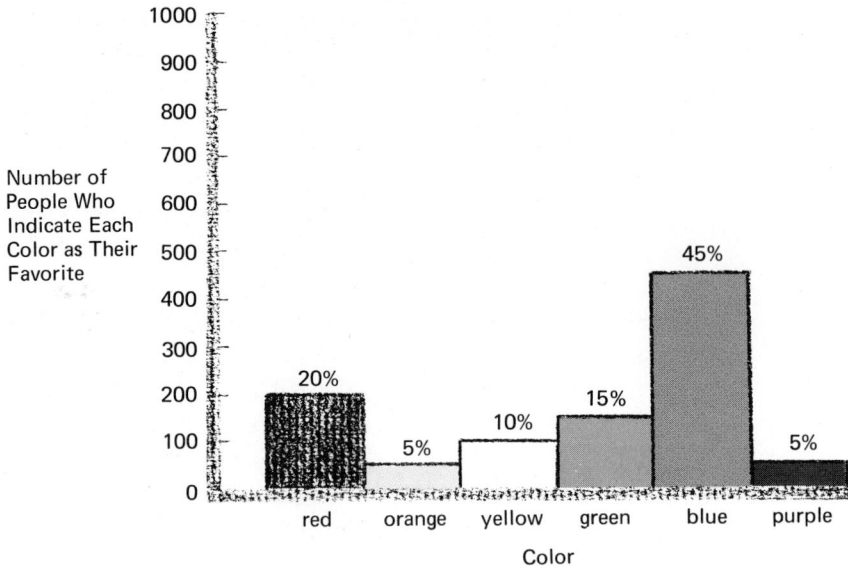

FIG. A1.3   *Hypothetical color preference data for 1000 people at Disneyland. Mode = blue.*

divided, and so on. Suppose I asked one thousand people at Disneyland (which would give me a good cross section of America) to tell me their favorite color and got the hypothetical results shown in Figure A1.3. It would be nonsense to compute a mean color or a median color; there is no way to do it. But I can say that the most frequently obtained datum (color statement), the mode, was blue. In a sense, then, blue could be regarded as the favorite color of that group as a whole.

Variability means how much or how little consensus there was among the data. To describe the data adequately it is necessary to know more than merely the central tendency of the group; you also need to know something about how much or how little similarity there was among the data.

1. The *variance* is essentially the average of the distances between each datum and the group mean. That is, if you found how far each datum is from the group mean and then calculated the mean of these distances, you would have a way of expressing how variable the data were—how "spread out" they were around the group mean. Unfortunately, this simple procedure leads to some problems. If you look at Figure A1.2 again, you will see that if you subtract the mean from the low numbers, you will get negative-numbered answers (for example, $5 - 13 = -8$), and if you subtract the mean from the high numbers you get positive-numbered answers (for example, $43 - 13 = +30$). When you add these positive and negative numbers together to calculate the mean distances, you get

a pretty odd answer. In our example the average distance would be $[(-10) + (-8) + (-8) + (-4) + (-2) + (+2) + (+30)] \div 7$, which is $0/7 = 0$. This answer implies that there is no variance among the data, which clearly isn't true. To avoid this sort of nonsensical result, each of the distances is squared before they are averaged. This gets rid of negative numbers (squared numbers are always positive, because if you'll remember your rules of algebra, a negative number multiplied by a negative number yields a positive number). This squaring procedure also attributes more importance to large distances than to small distances (for example, the square of 2 is only 4, the square of 5 is 25, and the square of 10 is a whopping 100). The point in giving more importance to the large distances is because it is appropriate to acknowledge that a few large distances more clearly imply a lack of consensus among the data than do a few small distances. Thus, squaring solves two problems; it gets rid of the negative numbers, and it makes large distances contribute more heavily to the statement about the nonconsensus among the data. For our example, variance $= [(-10)^2 + (-8)^2 + (-8)^2 + (-4)^2 + (-2)^2 + (+2)^2 + (+30)^2] \div 7 = (100 + 64 + 64 + 16 + 4 + 4 + 900) \div 7 = 1152 \div 7 = 164.57$. We might say, then, that our hypothetical memorization group had a mean of 13 trials and the variance among the data was 164.57, but that is not very intuitively meaningful, is it? That is, to say that data that range from 3 to 43 have a variance of 164.57 seems a bit odd. So, it is customary to use the square root of the variance, called the *standard deviation,* as the measure of nonconsensus among the data. The standard deviation puts the measure back into numbers that are the same magnitude as the data, and therefore is more intuitively meaningful. The standard deviation for our hypothetical data is $\sqrt{164.57} = 12.83$. Isn't that better?

The standard deviation has another characteristic that makes it important for statistics. If you add the standard deviation to the mean (for example, $13 + 12.83 = 25.83$) and subtract it from the mean (for example, $13 - 12.83 = 0.17$), you will find that roughly two thirds of the data in the original set will lie within this range (between 0.17 and 25.83 trials in our memorization experiment).

Knowing the standard deviation is of real value because, in addition to telling you the range within which the majority of the data lie (a large standard deviation indicates that those two thirds of the data are spread widely and a small one tells you that they are all pretty similar), it helps you evaluate the degree to which one datum deviates from the group as a whole. To cite an important example, the mean IQ in the United States is 100, and the standard deviation is 15. This means that approximately two thirds of the people in the United States have IQ's between 85 and 115. Therefore, you can see that someone with an IQ of 130 is pretty bright compared to the rest of the population; in fact, he is *two* standard deviations above the mean, $100 + 2(15) = 130$. In our hypothetical memorization data, the fellow who took 43 trials is roughly two and one-half standard deviations above the mean, which indicates that he is decidedly different from the rest of the group. Indeed, with such a large discrepancy from the mean you would seriously consider whether he should even be considered a member of the group at all. He must have been doing something quite different from everybody else (remember this point because it forms the logical basis for inferential statistics, which we will discuss in a little while).

2. The *middle range* is used to describe "spread outness" when a median is used to describe central tendency. The variance and the standard deviation cannot be used when the median is used because the mean is used in calculating them.

Finding the middle range is quite simple. The median is the center datum in the array of data. If you find the center datum between the median and the lowest datum and the center datum between the median and the highest datum, the range between these two data will include roughly 50 percent of all the data. In our example, the median is 9, the lower center datum is 5, and the higher center datum is 15. Three of the seven data (5, 9, and 11) lie within the range— which is as near to 50 percent of the data as you can get with only seven data. Unlike the standard deviation, this middle range does not have the property of helping you decide whether or not a specific datum is very extreme. It merely tells you the degree of consensus—if the middle range is large, the data are widely spread; if it's small, they are highly similar to one another.

3. There isn't a measure of "spread outness" for use with the mode that is comparable to the standard deviation or the middle range. About the only way you can make a useful statement in cases such as that illustrated in Figure A1.3 is to report the percentage of observations that are at the mode. Thus, we can say that 45 percent of the people we hypothetically interviewed at Disneyland said that blue is their favorite color and 55 percent favor some other color. As you can see, this is not very informative.

Correlation describes the degree to which one set of data for a group is related to another set of data. Recall the experiment in which we wanted to see if feelings of depression were greater the longer people were on a strict diet. The result could be summarized in a *scatter plot*, where each mark represents both the length of time the person has been on the diet and his "depression score" on the personality test.

Figure A1.4 shows what the results of the experiment might look like (remember, these are totally fictitious). To illustrate how the locations of the marks are determined, the star represents a mark for a person who has been on the diet for five days and has a depression score of 8. Looking at this scatter plot, we see clearly that the longer the people are on the diet, the more depressed they feel. The relation illustrated in Figure A1.4 is called a *positive correlation;* high values of one set of data correspond to high values of the other

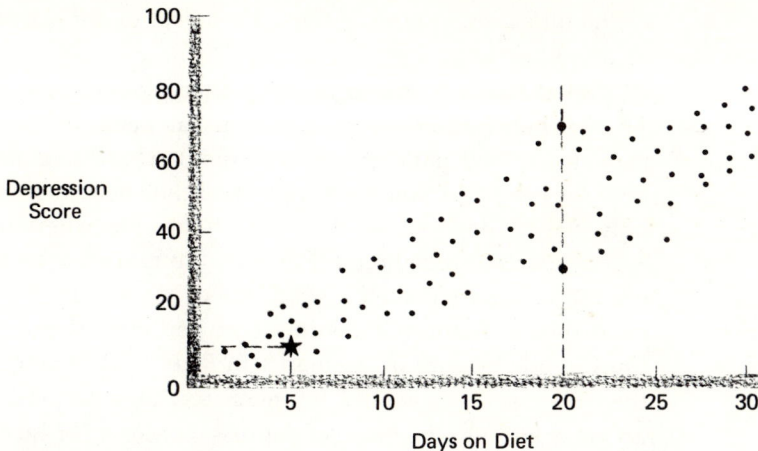

FIG. A1.4 *Hypothetical data for the diet-depression experiment. A scatterplot of the number of days individuals have been on a strict diet and their depression scores. This scatterplot shows a* positive *correlation.*

set, and low values of one set of data correspond to low values of the other set. Of course, it might turn out that excessively heavy people would feel less depressed as they lose their unwanted weight, in which case our experiment might yield results like those in Figure A1.5. The results in Figure A1.5 illustrate a *negative correlation;* high values of one set of data correspond to low values

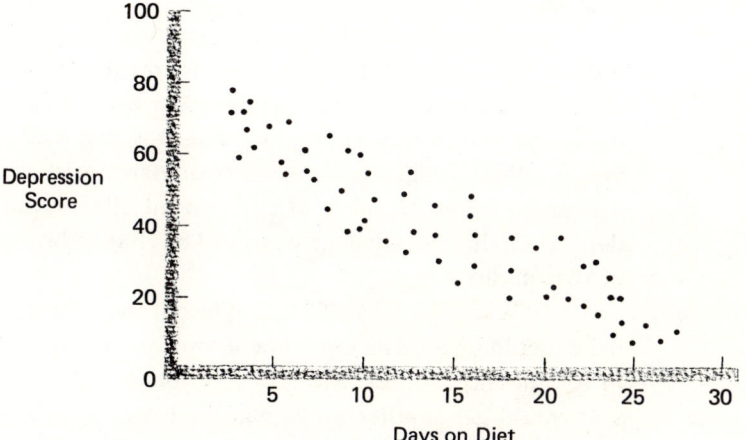

FIG. A1.5 *Hypothetical data for the diet-depression experiment. A scatterplot of the number of days individuals have been on a strict diet and their depression scores. This scatterplot shows a* negative *correlation.*

of the other set, and low values of one set of data correspond to high values of the other set.

Notice that the marks in the scatter plots do not all lie on a single line. That is, knowing how long a person has been on the diet permits you only to make a "ball park" prediction about what his depression score is apt to be. In Figure A1.4, knowing that a man has been dieting for 20 days tells you only that his depression score is apt to be somewhere between 35 and 70, not a very precise prediction. Of course, the more closely the pattern created by the marks approximated a solid line of marks, the better you would be able to predict a person's depression score because the ball park would be smaller. On the other hand, if the marks in Figure A1.4 were even more spread out than they are, you would be much less able to predict with any degree of accuracy because the range of depression scores for each day on the diet would be very broad.

The degree to which a person's datum on the dependent variable is predictable from knowing his location on the independent variable is described by a *correlation coefficient.* The mathematical details and the method of computation of correlation coefficients are too complex for us to go into here, so we'll skip them. The thing for you to know is that values of the correlation coefficient can be anywhere from +1.00 through .00 to −1.00. A coefficient near +1.00 means a high and positive degree of correlation between the two sets of data, and a coefficient near −1.00 means a high and negative degree of correlation. A value near .00 means that there is little or no relation between the two sets of data.

Two warnings about the interpretation of correlation coefficients are in order. First, a correlation of .80 does not mean a relation between two variables is twice as much as is represented by a correlation of .40. The coefficient is not a percentage or anything like that; it is just a general index of relatedness. Second, the correlation between two characteristics does not mean that one causes the other. Number of days on the diet would not *cause* people to feel depressed; the causative factor would be changed body chemistry or something of that nature.

INFERENTIAL STATISTICS Descriptive statistics are used to summarize the data obtained in an experiment, but, as we have seen, these data are seldom in complete consensus. Moreover, if you did the same experiment over again, you would get another set of data that would differ a little from the first set. The problem is to decide whether your manipulation of the independent variable really influenced the dependent variable (thereby telling you something about your hypothesis), or whether the observed changes in the dependent variable were merely the result of chance. The methods used for making such decisions are called inferential statistics.

As with correlation coefficients, the mathematics and methods of inferential statistics are too complex for presentation here, but the logic is fairly simple and the logic is all you really need if you are not actually doing an experiment yourself. Recall the experiment in which we proposed to see if dreaming influenced how well rested people felt. We had two groups, an experimental group that wasn't allowed to dream and a control group that could dream but was awakened throughout the night as frequently as the experimental group was awakened. In the morning the people in both groups rated how well rested they felt on seven-point scales.

The control group was included in this experiment in order to have something with which to compare the experimental group. If both groups felt rested to the same degree in the morning, we would conclude that preventing the experimental group from dreaming had no effect on their rest. If the experimental group felt more rested or less rested than the control group, we would conclude that dream prevention results in either more or less rest.

To compare the two groups, you would compute both the mean ratings of the control group and the experimental group and the standard deviations of their ratings. If the dream prevention had no effect on the people in the experimental group, their mean rating should not differ much from that of the control group. Indeed, you can think of the mean of the experimental group as if it were one person's rating and then see if it is reasonably similar to the ratings given by the people in the control group. You can judge how similar it is by seeing how far it is from the mean of the control group; if it is within the range of one standard deviation above or below the mean of the control group, it is reasonable to consider it as similar to the ratings of the control group.[1] If it is between one and two standard deviations above or below the mean of the control group, it is less reasonable to consider it as similar to the ratings of the control group, but you'd probably be inclined to continue to consider them as similar. However, if the mean of the experimental group is more than two standard deviations above or below the mean of the control group, it is pretty extreme (like the person who took 43 trials in the memorization experiment), and it is improbable that a rating like that would have been obtained by chance alone if the experimental group and control group were

---

[1] This is a bit oversimplified. Actually, the standard deviations from both groups are averaged and then an adjustment is made for the number of data involved, but the logic is the same as that described here.

identical. Therefore, in this case you can conclude that the two groups are *not* the same, and, because dream prevention is the only thing that differed for them, that your hypothesis is likely to be true. In short, the logic is that if the mean for the experimental group is more than two standard deviations above or below the mean for the control group, you reject the idea that the two groups are the same and conclude that the difference between them is a result of your manipulation of the independent variable.

The conclusion you would reach about dreaming and restedness would depend upon whether the mean of the experimental group was larger or smaller than that of the control group. If it was more than two standard deviations below the mean of the control group, you would conclude that dream prevention prevents rest, and therefore that some dreaming is necessary for a person to feel rested the next day. If the mean of the experimental group is more than two standard deviations above that of the control group, you would conclude that dream prevention facilitates rest, and therefore that dreaming interferes with a person's rest.

I have included this discussion of statistics in the discussion of experiments, but these statistical techniques are also used in the other three methods of doing psychological research. We are not going to examine the exact procedure that would be used each time. Merely keep in mind that statistical procedures are at the heart of all of these methods with the possible exception of case histories.

Some drawbacks of experiments   Experiments tend to involve abstract tasks and settings that have little similarity to the participants' daily experiences. People do not ordinarily try to memorize a scrambled poem or go on crash diets, nor are they awakened every time they start dreaming. In some cases, these odd tasks and settings are appropriate and necessary in order to test the hypotheses in which we're interested. In other cases, however, the peculiarity of the situation itself influences the results and makes the test of the hypothesis somewhat suspect.

Because an experiment is not always an appropriate way to test a hypothesis, other psychological research methods have been devised. These methods have less precision than experiments because they do not permit as much control of the task and the setting. However, they compensate for this fault to some degree by being a little closer to reality.

Simulation

Simulation is like an experiment in that the researcher specifies the task and setting, but it differs in that the task and setting are as near as possible to the real situation that the hypothesis is about. For example, before the United

States sent men into space, where there is no gravity, it was hypothesized that astronauts might become disoriented and ill when they were weightless. A simulation was used to test this hypothesis. By flying an airplane in an appropriate arch-shaped course, it is possible to have an upward momentum of the plane counteract the downward pull of gravity, thus providing a few minutes of weightlessness. (It is similar to going over the top of a hill in a car—as you pass over the top, you're lifted slightly off the seat and you have a ticklish sensation in your stomach; in the plane simulation this period of weightlessness can be extended to about three minutes.) The astronauts were required to perform various tasks in the simulated absence of gravity produced by the plane's flight path. The results showed, as you probably realize, that people can get by fairly well when weightless and that elaborate and expensive precautions were unnecessary.

Somewhat less exotic simulations are used when an aircraft company wants to see how well pilots can use some new device for a plane's instrument panel. It is dangerous to install the device in a real plane and send a pilot aloft to see if he can use it; if he can't, the results can be disastrous. Instead, the new device is installed in a fake cockpit (a mock-up) and the pilot tests it by "flying" in various simulated situations. The pilot's ability to use the new device in, say, landing the plane, can be judged by his ability to "fly" and "land" the mock-up—all without endangering anyone's life.

Some of these aircraft simulations are extremely elaborate. For example, some systems have a TV camera that is mounted on a boom that permits the camera to skim over an accurately detailed model of the countryside (like a fancy model train layout). The picture from the camera is projected on a screen that surrounds the cockpit mock-up; the movement of the camera, and thus the movement of the picture, is remotely controlled by the cockpit controls. As a result, the picture corresponds to what the pilot would see if he were actually flying at some specified altitude and speed over the real countryside. Similar devices are used to train astronauts to land their spacecraft on the moon and to rendezvous and dock with another craft in space.

A more psychological example of simulation research is that done to investigate the "bystander phenomenon." A person is ushered into a room on the pretext of participating in an experiment, of filling out a questionnaire, or the like. Then some emergency is simulated and the person's reaction is observed. For example, smoke may start pouring out of the ventilation system, a secretary in the adjoining room may pretend to fall, or a person in the next booth might pretend to have an epileptic seizure. The point is to see under what conditions the "innocent bystander" will take some kind of action by reporting the simulated fire or by helping the person who is in simulated distress. The results are interesting. In general, the more people that are present to witness the incident, the less likely anyone is to take action. Apparently, in a group that has no leader, people hesitate to take the responsibility upon themselves for taking action. The psychologists who do these kinds of simulations are of the opinion that the results explain why a group of people can watch with horror while another person is attacked, robbed, or murdered and refrain from doing anything about it; they hesitate to take the responsibility upon themselves.

Naturalistic Observation

Sometimes even simulation is too contrived to permit a proper test of a hypothesis. In these cases it may be necessary to examine what happens in naturally occurring situations in order to test the hypothesis. For example, suppose your hypothesis were that children use a different vocabulary when talking to other children than when talking to adults. You would be unwilling to trust the situation in which two children were brought into a room where they could play while you wrote down everything that they said to each other in order to compare it with what they say to adults. Your presence, the unfamiliar room, and the general peculiarity of the circumstances would contaminate the results. A much better solution might be to put a microphone in the middle of a preschool playroom. After a few days the children would get used to the presence of the microphone and you could record their conversations as they played with their friends and talked to adults in familiar surroundings. Or you could strap remote-controlled transistorized recorders to each of the children and, after they had worn the recorders long enough to forget about them, you could take samples of their vocabulary as they talked with other children and with adults.

Naturalistic observation is used much more in zoology, anthropology, and sociology than it is in psychology. However, psychologists increasingly are using it, particularly in the study of social behavior. It was through naturalistic observation that zoologists came to understand the dominance hierarchies discussed in Section 4. This was done by observing which animals defer to other animals in the group. A psychologist can do exactly the same sort of thing. Suppose your hypothesis were that in chance encounters with strangers, short men tend to defer to tall men. Then you might go to a crowded downtown street, a zoo, or a park and watch what happens when two men accidentally get in each other's way. You'd keep track of the differences in the men's heights, who got out of whose way, who apologized to whom, and who registered annoyance. Then you would compute the proportion of times that the shorter man was the one who deferred to the taller man. The degree to which you would believe or disbelieve the hypothesis would depend on the magnitude of this proportion: a proportion near 1.00 would support your hypothesis, one near .00 would imply that tall men deferred to short men, and a proportion near .50 would imply that height was not a factor in who defers to whom.

The techniques for naturalistic observation often are extremely ingenious. For example, if you wanted to know what aspect of science interests the most people, you could get a hint from the building maintenance men at the Chicago Museum of Science and Industry or Seattle's Pacific Science Center. You merely have to find out where the floor coverings get the heaviest wear. Excluding the hallways, rest rooms, and restaurants, the floor coverings in front of the most popular exhibits should have to be repaired or replaced most often. Similarly, you could determine which animals in a zoo receive the most attention by painting all of the railings in front of the cages, letting them dry, and then noting where the paint wore away most quickly. This, together with the fact that there would be more candy and chewing gum wrappers and other such litter around the cages of the most popular animals, would give you a pretty clear idea of what interests zoo-goers most.

Case Histories

The fourth psychological research method is adopted from medicine. A substantial part of medical knowledge has come from practicing physicians' published descriptions of diseases they have encountered and treatments they have attempted. Some diseases and syndromes occur so rarely that it would be impractical to try to gather the patients together in one place to study the disease and the treatment. Instead, physicians all over the world publish descriptions of the one or two cases they have treated, and from these diverse observations a clear picture of the disease and its treatment emerges.

In psychology, the case history method is most often used to demonstrate the effects of some treatment technique. For example, one case history (Wolf, Birnbrauer, Williams, and Lawlar, 1965) describes treatment of a retarded child named Laura who vomited in class as many as twenty times a day. The researchers noted that the teacher was inadvertently rewarding Laura by sending her back to her dormitory whenever she vomited. The treatment consisted of making Laura stay in class even though she vomited (thus stopping the reward of getting out of class) and of giving her candy and praise when she went any length of time without vomiting. Over the course of six weeks there was a steady decline in the frequency of Laura's vomiting, and by the end of the six weeks she no longer vomited at all. The following school year, Laura's new teacher again returned her to her dormitory when she happened to vomit, and the whole syndrome began again. The researchers intervened and reinstated the previous year's treatment procedure, and Laura again stopped vomiting.

In a somewhat similar case (Carlson, Arnold, Becker, and Madsen, 1968), an eight-year-old girl named Diane threw tantrums in the classroom. The tantrums consisted of profane screaming, running around wildly, throwing chairs, and attacking other children. This behavior resulted in a wide variety of rewards: As you might well imagine, all of Diane's classmates paid attention to her when she threw a tantrum, she got attention from the teacher, and she was taken out of class to the principal's office where the secretaries and the principal also paid attention to her. Treatment consisted of seating her in the back of the classroom, holding her in her seat when she threw a tantrum, and giving candy to the other children for not looking at her when she threw a tantrum. For each one-half day without a tantrum, the teacher awarded Diane a star; four stars in a row and Diane was permitted to pass out treats at a little class party. After the first few days, Diane stopped throwing tantrums; the negative rewards of being held in her chair, of being ignored by the other children, of not being able to get the attention of the teacher and the staff, and of not being able to get out of class, together with the positive rewards both of getting to earn a party for the class and of getting to be the hostess, made it worthwhile for Diane to stop throwing tantrums. As was true in the case of Laura, Diane reverted to tantrums the following year in school. Unfortunately, Diane's new teacher did not reinstate the treatment procedure. Instead, she did as the previous teacher had done when Diane had first begun to throw tantrums; she interrupted the class and took the girl to the principal's office. As a result, Diane's tantrums became more frequent and even worse than before, and she was finally put into a class for emotionally disturbed children.

Note that while these two case histories differ in many ways, a central theme emerges (and there are many other case histories that support the theme). This simply is that the children's disruptive behavior depended on whether they got rewarded for it or not. When the child's vomiting or tantrums gained attention from classmates and the teacher and permitted the child to leave class, she was likely to do it again. When such rewards were eliminated and non-vomiting and nontantrums were rewarded by candy, praise, and attention, the undesirable behavior stopped. Thus, by examining a collection of such case histories, which are not identical but have underlying similarities, a picture emerges, and a simple statement can be made about what appears in each isolated case to be a very complex psychological problem.

Generalizability

It is appropriate to end this discussion with a word of caution about interpreting the results of psychological research. Each of the four research methods has its individual strengths and weaknesses. However, all four have one weakness in common. This is the fact that the results are very dependent upon who participated in the research and upon the specific setting in which the research was conducted. Most psychological research is done at colleges and universities, and the participants are college students. Thus, there is danger in assuming that the results can be regarded as general, or *generalizable,* to everybody in the world. Most college students are young, bright, and middle class, and they ordinarily want very much to please the researcher. Older and less intelligent people, people from other social classes, or people who are less motivated to comply might not behave in the same way if they were given the opportunity.

Another limitation on the generalizability of research results is the number of people who are included in the study. Certainly, one feels better about conclusions based on an experiment in which one hundred people did roughly the same thing than about conclusions based on only ten people. In experiments, simulation, and naturalistic observation, the number of people who are included in the study is controlled by the researcher. In case histories, there are seldom many people included in one report, so a large number of reports are needed before you can attempt to draw conclusions and generalize them to other people.

The number of people needed in a study in order to safely generalize the results depends on what you're studying. For example, if you're studying a visual phenomenon such as after-images (see Section 2), not many people are needed because most people's eyes are pretty much the same—an odd eye would yield recognizably odd results; such studies normally use only two or three people. On the other hand, if you're studying a social phenomenon such as how people choose where to sit in a waiting room, you'd want to observe many people, because people's idiosyncrasies may obscure the general tendencies that underlie everyone's choices. That is, most people like to have at least one seat between themselves and a stranger, but not all people follow this rule. Unless you observe many people, you might not detect that the rule exists.

The effect of the research setting on the generalizability of the results also depends on what is being studied. If you are examining how quickly adults can learn a poem, any reasonably quiet, nondistracting setting will do. But if you are studying the same task with retarded children, for example, you would want to conduct the research in a setting that is familiar to them and that would help them do the best job possible. Taking them to a laboratory in some strange building would be likely to frighten them so much that they would perform poorly and lead you to the false conclusion that they are less able to learn than they really are.

In short, your willingness to accept research results as generalizable to a broad range of people must be tempered by the kind and number of people who were studied and the possible contaminating effects of the setting in which the research was conducted.

SUMMARY

1   The *scientific method* consists of careful *observation*, formulation of a *hypothesis*, execution of *research*, interpretation of *results*, and communication of the *conclusions* to other scientists and eventually to the public at large.

2   There are four *psychological research methods: experiments, simulation, naturalistic observation,* and *case histories.* Experiments, while being the most precise and tightly controlled of the four methods, are often very artificial. Simulation is more natural, but still falls short of complete reality. Naturalistic observation attempts to interfere as little as possible with that which is being studied. Case histories are descriptions of isolated events; consideration of many similar case histories sometimes reveals commonalities that permit scientific insights into certain problems.

3   Because data from psychological research are seldom unequivocal, it often is difficult to reach a clear-cut decision about a hypothesis without the aid of statistics. *Descriptive statistics* summarize the *central tendency* and the *variability* of the data and, in some cases, the *correlation* between two sets of data. *Inferential statistics* are the methods for deciding whether observed changes in a *dependent variable* are a result of manipulation of an *independent variable* or whether they occurred merely by chance.

Further Reading

AGNEW, N. McK., and S. W. PYKE.   *The Science Game*
Englewood Cliffs, N.J.: Prentice-Hall, 1969, 188 pages (paperback).
Treating science as a game that researchers play, the authors of this book set out to show the reader that it is the same game he plays in his everyday truth-seeking activities. Entertaining supplementary reading about research methods used in the behavioral sciences.

ANDERSON, B. F.   *The Psychology Experiment* (2d ed.)
Belmont, Calif.: Brooks/Cole, 1971, 184 pages (paperback).
An excellent introduction to the scientific method, written specifically for the non-scientist. Covers the designing of experiments, the conducting of experiments, analysis of the results, and the writing of research papers.

DETHIER, V. G.   *To Know a Fly*
San Francisco: Holden Day, 1962, 119 pages (paperback).
Although this book is specifically about obtaining knowledge about the common house fly, it clearly illustrates the basic principles underlying the scientific method in general. The author's informal style, plus the book's humorous cartoonlike illustrations, makes this a pleasure to read, and it really gets its point across.

HUFF, D.   *How to Lie with Statistics*
New York: Norton, 1954, 142 pages (paperback).
A pleasant book on statistics. Emphasis is placed on how statistics is used to deceive rather than to inform. Full of analyses of statistical reports the author has found in popular magazines and newspapers.

McCAIN, G., and E. M. SEGAL.   *The Game of Science*
Belmont, Calif.: Brooks/Cole, 1969, 178 pages (paperback).
A book written to give the reader a broader perspective about scientific attitudes and a more realistic idea of what science is, who scientists are, and what scientists do. Written in a very entertaining and readable style.

Brain Mechanisms
APPENDIX 2

In the discussion of sensation and perception (Section 2), we visualized the human being as a roving information gatherer that had specialized sensing devices mounted on it. These sensing devices relayed messages to a central computer, which in turn interpreted and interrelated the messages in order to derive a coherent, unified evaluation of the things that were being sensed. The discussion that followed focused on the sensing devices and on the resulting evaluations, but not much was said about the intermediate steps of transmission of the information to the computer or about the computer itself. This appendix supplements that earlier discussion by describing how the transmission occurs and how the computer works. Unfortunately, many important questions about the operation of the computer are still unanswered; but the basic picture is becoming clear, and while this description will, by necessity, be abbreviated, you can get at least a general idea of what that picture looks like.

Some Basic Concepts

For the time being let us continue to rely on our analogy between the human being and the hypothetical information gatherer. The gatherer's basic components would be (1) the *sensing devices* that receive and code incoming information, (2) *transmission cables* for the coded incoming information, (3a) the *computer*, (3b) subsections of the computer that receive and interpret *incoming information* from specific sensing devices, (3c) an *integration system* that interrelates subsections of the computer and regulates the flow of incoming information and outgoing messages, (3d) subsections that initiate *outgoing messages* in reply to the incoming information, (4) *transmission cables* for the outgoing messages that cause some parts of the system to act upon either the sensed objects in the environment or upon the sensing devices themselves (for example, to turn them off or to change their focus of attention). This sort of design would permit our hypothetical device to gather information, interpret and integrate it, and initiate actions in light of it.

Let us look at the physiological counterparts of this system in human beings. The sensory devices are your sense organs, which, as you know, react to patterns of light, sound, pressure, temperature, chemistry, gases, gravity, and so on, and they code what they sense into patterns of electrical activity. The transmission cables are your nerves. They react to the sense organs' patterns of electrical activity by themselves becoming electrically active and thereby carrying the coded information to the brain. The computer is the brain, and it has subparts that receive and integrate information from the various sense organs. Roughly speaking, there is a central clearinghouse in the center of the brain which receives the information first; from this clearinghouse visual information goes to the back of the brain, auditory information goes to the sides, touch and muscle information goes to the top, and information about the body's vital functions and about posture and muscle movement goes to the bottom of the brain. In each case, the incoming information is also integrated with other incoming information (you *hear* a man speak and *see* his lips move at the same time) and with information from past experience that already is stored in the brain's memory (you *understand* what the man says because you already have learned the language).

After the incoming information is received and interpreted, it is checked to see if a reply is necessary. If so, an outgoing message is transmitted through the outgoing cables to the appropriate muscles or organs. For example, an outgoing message to your eye muscles may change the direction in which you are looking in order to see some object better. Or if your body temperature were too high or too low, an outgoing message would call for sweating or shivering in an attempt to solve the problem.

This is all very complex—indeed, the brain is more complex than any computer we can imagine. As a result, our analogy only begins to give the flavor of what is actually going on.

Transmission Cables: Nerves and Neurons

Most of the transmission cables are bundles of lines a bit like a telephone cable. These bundles are called *nerves* and the component lines are called *neurons.* Usually a neuron is fairly short and does not extend the full length of the nerve. Rather, neurons pass their electrical activity (called *impulses*) from one to another in a chain, and this chain extends from the sense organ to the brain.

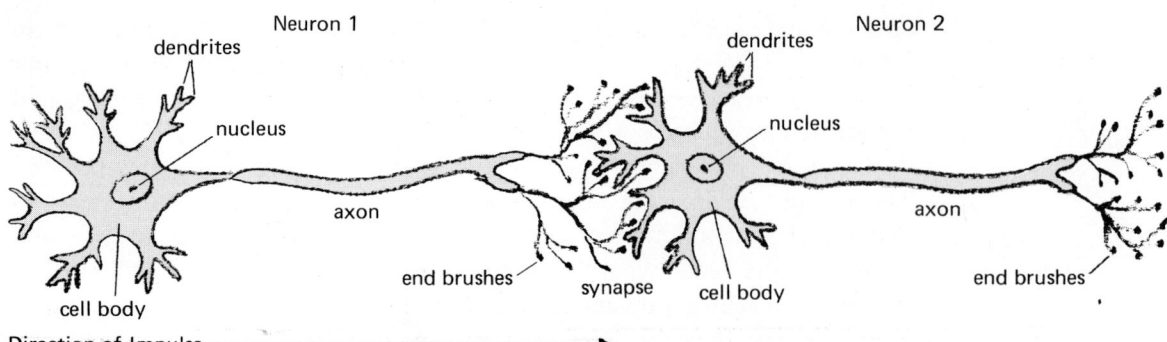

FIG. A2.1   *Typical neurons. Stimulation of the dendrites of neuron 1 causes an electrical impulse to travel down the axon of the neuron to the end brushes. After reaching the end brushes, this electrical impulse initiates chemical changes in the synapse which, in turn, result in the stimulation of the dendrites of neuron 2.*

Neurons look generally like the diagram in Figure A2.1. The *cell body*, as with all cells, supplies the nutrients that keep the cell alive and functioning at its best. The *dendrites* are short arms that extend from the edges of the cell body, and the *axon* is a long tail that has brushlike arms at its end, called *end brushes*.

Electrical transmission of impulses within a neuron always begins at the dendrites and moves down the axon toward the end brushes. Electrical transmission between neurons occurs when the end brushes of the axon of one neuron stimulate the dendrites of the next neuron. The end brushes and dendrites do not actually touch each other; transmission occurs because of chemical activity occurring at the *synapse* (the gap between the end brushes of one neuron and dendrites of another neuron). This chemical activity is initiated by the electrical impulse reaching the end brushes; the chemical activity causes an electrical impulse to be initiated in the second neuron. This impulse travels down the axon of the second neuron to its end brushes where again chemical activity at the synapse causes stimulation of the dendrites of the third neuron, and so on.

Some Limitations on Transmission

The transmission of impulses from one neuron to another is, of course, not as simple as this description might imply. First, a specific amount of chemical activity is required at the dendrites of a neuron in order for its electrical impulse to be triggered. This specific amount is called the neuron's *threshold*, and sometimes more than one neuron acting on the dendrites are needed to exceed this threshold. When the threshold is exceeded, the electrical activity always occurs at full strength (called the *"all-or-none"* principle because electrical activity either occurs or it does not).

Second, after having transmitted its impulse, there is a very short period during which the neuron is fairly insensitive to stimulation of its dendrites. That is, the threshold is high immediately after the neuron has been active. As the neuron recovers its sensitivity, the threshold level decreases to normal. But until full recovery occurs, only strong activity on its dendrites will induce another spasm of activity.

Third, transmission of the impulse from neuron to neuron can be influenced at the synapse by other neurons which meet at the same synapse. Depending upon the circumstances, this influence can result in decreased or increased activity, phenomena known as *inhibition* and *facilitation,* respectively.

These three limitations on a neuron's activity (threshold, recovery times, and inhibition and facilitation) are thought to interact so that a bundle of neurons, a nerve, ends up transmitting complex codes from the sense organs to the brain. All three limitations influence impulse transmission and, therefore, information which eventually reaches the brain can be coded in a variety of ways—in terms of the pace, duration, and patterning of impulses.

The Spinal Cord

Nerves from throughout the trunk and limbs of the body go to the spinal column where they enter between the bones and form a large cable called the *spinal cord* (Fig. A2.2). Some of the nerves in the spinal cord relay incoming information to the brain and some relay outgoing information back to the body. The nerves relaying information about the senses in the head (eyes, ears, taste, smell, scalp, face, and so on) all connect directly to the brain and are not part of the spinal cord.

The Somatic and Autonomic Systems

The nervous system has two components. The first, the *somatic system,* relays messages to and from the muscles and sense organs, permitting movement and sensory functioning. The second, the *autonomic system,* carries messages to and from internal organs such as the heart, lungs, stomach, and so forth. The autonomic system can either arouse the body to action by increasing heart rate, blood pressure, the adrenalin in the blood, sweating, and overall alertness or relax it by decreasing heart rate, blood pressure, and so on. Thus, the autonomic system can arouse you to fight or escape from danger, or it can relax you so you can peacefully digest a meal or doze pleasantly in the sun.

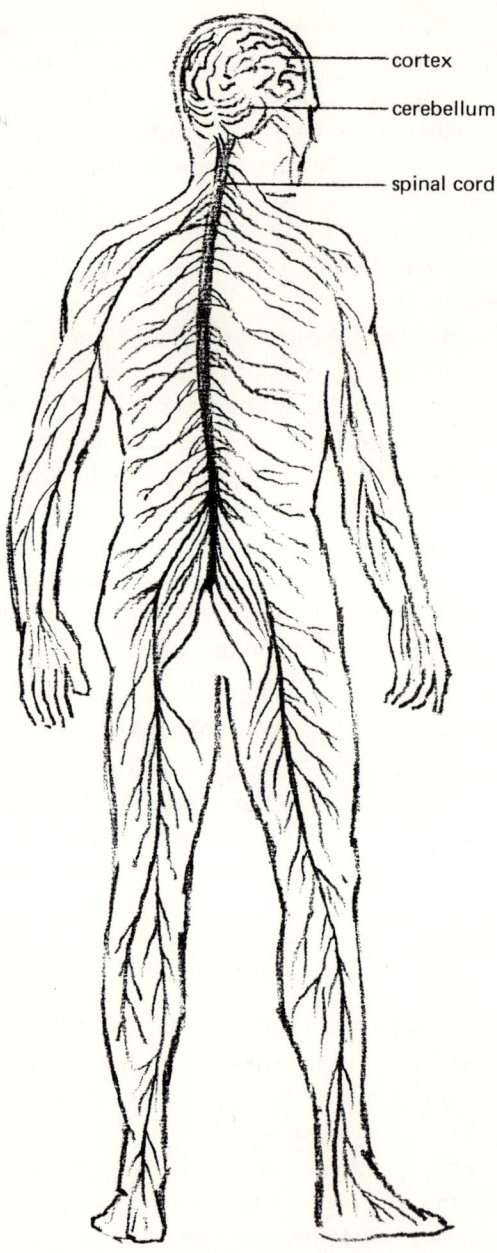

cortex

cerebellum

spinal cord

FIG. A2.2   *Nerves carrying information to and from the trunk and limbs of the body connect to the brain via the spinal cord.*

BOX A2.1

ESB: Electrical Stimulation of the Brain

Because the nervous system is an electrochemical device, it is not surprising to find that it can be influenced by electrical stimulation. This was first demonstrated in 1791 when an Italian physiologist, L. Galvani, noted that if an electrical current was applied to an amputated frog leg, it would cause the leg to kick. While interest in this phenomenon prompted quite a lot of physiological research, it was not until the rather recent development of sophisticated surgical and electronic techniques that its psychological implications could be examined. Among these was the development of electrodes, thin needlelike wires that can be inserted painlessly into the living brain. After insertion it is possible to use the electrodes either to record the brain's own electrical activity or to send very small impulses into the brain, a process known as *electrical stimulation of the brain* (ESB), which, by the way, also is painless.

Through precise placement of the microelectrodes, ESB can be used to trigger behavior. The triggered behavior often is fairly stereotyped and predictable in lower animals, in part, perhaps, because these animals' ordinary behavior is heavily based on reflexes and instincts (see Section 3, Part 2). In human beings, however, ESB-triggered behavior appears to be less predictable. This may be

The Computer: The Brain and Its Parts

It is customary to discuss the structure and function of the brain as though it were composed of many rather independent subparts, but this is done only in order to simplify discussion. From the beginning you should understand that this is only a fiction; the brain is a highly integrated system. Some parts of the brain appear to be more or less specialized, but every job executed by the brain involves many different parts. Moreover, in many cases there are back-up systems, so that if one part of the brain is damaged through disease or accident, other parts eventually take over at least some of the function of the damaged part.

General Structure

Figure A2.3 shows a diagram of the general shape and structure of the human brain. It is slightly bigger than a man's two clenched fists held side by side. It is divided into two halves, left and right, that are connected to one another in the middle by a large cable of neurons called the *corpus callosum*. Were it not for this connection, the two halves would operate essentially as two separate brains. Strangely enough, the two halves control the opposite sides of the body; the left side of the brain controls the right side of the body, and the right side of the brain controls the left side of the body. Thus, if a person has a stroke

because our ordinary behavior is more heavily based on our past experiences rather than upon innate programing. But it also may be that research has failed to find much stereotyped behavior because ESB is done on human beings only as part of medical treatment and, as a result, there understandably is less experimentation and less is known about its effects on human beings than on animals.

Predictable or not, ESB-induced behavior in both animals and human beings is not wholly rigid but usually takes the situation at hand into account. For example, Dr. Jose Delgado, a physiologist at Yale University and one of the best-known investigators of ESB, found that when some of the monkeys in a rhesus monkey colony were made aggressive through ESB, they never attacked a monkey who was higher than they were in the monkey colony's social hierarchy.* Even

*J. M. R. Delgado, *Physical Control of the Mind: Toward a Psychocivilized Society.* New York: Harper & Row, 1969.

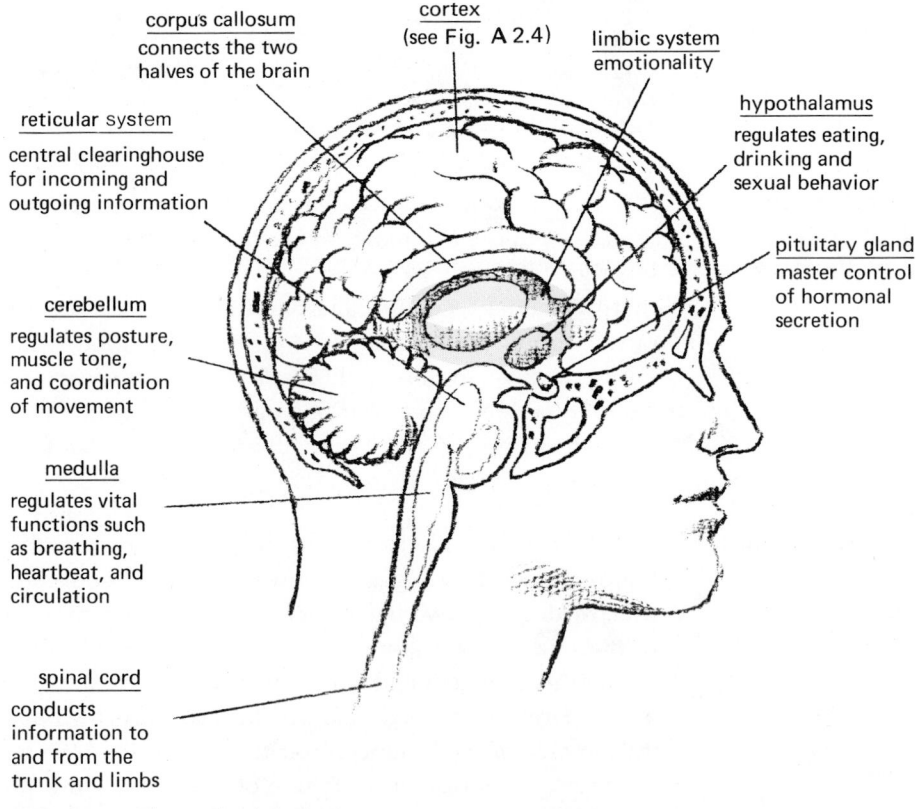

FIG. A2.3 *The inside of the brain.*

corpus callosum
connects the two
halves of the brain

cortex
(see Fig. A 2.4)

limbic system
emotionality

reticular system
central clearinghouse
for incoming and
outgoing information

hypothalamus
regulates eating,
drinking and
sexual behavior

cerebellum
regulates posture,
muscle tone,
and coordination
of movement

pituitary gland
master control
of hormonal
secretion

medulla
regulates vital
functions such
as breathing,
heartbeat, and
circulation

spinal cord
conducts
information to
and from the
trunk and limbs

human beings when made aggressive through ESB express their aggressiveness in socially acceptable ways (for example, tearing up a piece of paper rather than hitting someone). Clearly, ESB does not produce totally mechanical behavior like something out of a science fiction fantasy; it apparently can initiate or inhibit existing behavior, but the actual expression (or inhibition) of the behavior is also dependent upon past experiences and the usual social and moral constraints that normally influence the things we do. In short, ESB cannot make us into robots.

Dr. Delgado has performed some extraordinary experiments using ESB to inhibit behavior. It is possible to connect the electrodes to "stimoceivers" (so called because they can both *stimulate* the brain and *receive* electrical information from the brain) that are fastened to the heads of animals and of human beings. This permits ESB to be done via radio transmission, eliminating the need for wires and allowing the animal or human being to move freely. Using this technique, Dr. Delgado has been able to stop a charging bull in its tracks, which is most

or accident that damages the left side of his brain, his right arm and leg are likely to be paralyzed. In most animals the two halves of the brain are pretty much equal partners, but for human beings one side is *dominant.* For most of us, the left half is dominant, which may account for the fact that most of us are right handed.

Parts of the Brain   **Medulla and cerebellum**   Let us begin our discussion of the various parts of the brain with the parts that lie near the bottom. These parts are located in the area where the spinal cord connects with the brain; they play an important role in routing information in and out of larger parts of the brain and in regulating various body processes and emotional activities. At the top of the spinal cord is the *medulla,* which regulates such vital functions as breathing, heartbeat, circulation, and the like. For example, it receives information through spinal nerves about the carbon dioxide content of the blood and the muscle tension in the muscles that move the chest cavity and expand the lungs. Using this information, the medulla can *excite* the muscles so that you inhale when you need to and then *inhibit* this excitement so that you can exhale when necessary. Of course, it is not simply a mechanical activity because you can inhale or exhale voluntarily. Or you can hold your breath until the carbon dioxide level gets high enough to make you dizzy; when you do this you make other parts of the brain override the medulla's basic mechanism.

Adjacent to the medulla is *cerebellum,* which regulates posture, muscle tone, and coordination of movement in a manner similar to that used by the medulla to regulate breathing.

impressive. He also has shown that when ESB is used to inhibit the aggressiveness of the "boss" monkey in a colony, the monkey soon loses his dominant status. The monkey's aggressiveness and status come back after ESB is discontinued, but if his stimoceiver is controlled by a lever in the cage, other monkeys in the colony soon learn to press the lever to give him a calming dose of ESB whenever he starts to get too aggressive. In yet another experiment, Dr. Delgado demonstrated that ESB could make a monkey stop eating a banana and even spit out the part that remained in his mouth.

The fact that ESB can initiate and, more important, inhibit some kinds of behaviors provides promise for the treatment of certain kinds of medical and psychological problems. For example, treatment of chronically depressed persons with ESB has been successfully demonstrated. In the future, a person who suffers from bouts of extreme depression may elect to have electrodes and a stimoceiver implanted in his brain; when depression sets in, he merely will have to administer ESB to himself and his mood will change. Current research using ESB to treat epilepsy has also been quite successful. The day may come when an epileptic can have a stimoceiver implanted in his brain in order to monitor his brain's activity. The information would be relayed to a computer, which would analyze

Reticular system   The next level beyond the medulla and cerebellum is the *reticular system.* This is a complex system involving many identifiable parts of the brain, but for our purposes it is sufficient to regard it as a single unit. The reticular system acts as the central clearinghouse for most incoming and outgoing information to and from the brain. It directs incoming information to the appropriate parts of the brain where it is interpreted in light of previously stored information. Then, outgoing messages are routed through the reticular system on their way out of the body.

In the course of monitoring the incoming and outgoing information, the reticular system also assigns priorities to what is coming in. By inhibiting activity at both the sense organ and further along the transmission route, the reticular system can give specific priority to one information source over another; in short, the reticular system controls attention. By cutting down the information from your ears, nose, skin senses, and so forth, and giving specific priority to your eyes, your reticular system permits you to concentrate on reading this book. However, the other senses do not close down completely. If you suddenly heard someone shout "Fire!" your attention would immediately shift from the book to the source of the sound.

This matter of attention regulation is very important. If your brain could

it for signs of the beginning of an epileptic seizure. When such signs appeared, the computer would instruct the stimoceiver to administer ESB to stop the seizure before it began. Experiments have been carried out using ESB to treat intractable pain, tremors, schizophrenia, aggressiveness, anxiety, fear, and obsessive and compulsive behaviors.

Most of the ESB research is still in the experimental stages where it is proving valuable in investigating the functions of various parts of the brain. Once these functions are better understood, ESB may well be the key to treating a variety of medical and psychological problems (such as those mentioned above) that currently are difficult to treat. Of course, like any experimental technique, ESB may have its dangers if not used with restraint and with respect for personal rights. Doubtless, few of us would want to see it used as a method of crime control or political pacification. But this is somewhat unlikely, since use of ESB requires a great deal of knowledge and skill in medicine, electronics, and so on. Also, it should be remembered that ESB cannot introduce new behaviors. All it can do is initiate or inhibit behaviors that already exist in the behavior repertory of the animal or human being. Since its potential for good is so great, abandonment of ESB for fear of its misuse might be rash.

not inhibit the incoming flow of irrelevant information, you would be unable to concentrate on the important things long enough to learn much. A number of scientists have suggested that malfunction of the reticular system's attention mechanism may be one underlying reason that some mentally retarded people can't learn quickly. Some retarded people can learn some tasks as quickly as normal people once they focus on the important components of the task—it merely takes them longer to focus. The suspicion is that their reticular systems are not permitting them to exclude the irrelevant; their attention is diverted so easily that they are unable to concentrate on the task long enough to learn it. While this hypothesis is still unproved, it may turn out to be a key to understanding and eventually helping some mentally retarded people.

Another function of the reticular system's control of attention is that it can close down virtually all senses and let you sleep. Indeed, unless there is information to process, the reticular system will not keep you awake. So, when you want to sleep you lie down in a quiet, dark room so that your senses transmit very little information. Most animals sleep whenever the information isn't very interesting, day or night. Human beings are one of the few animals that try to stay awake for long stretches at a time in spite of how dull it may be. We also apparently are the only animals who suffer from insomnia (the inability to go to sleep). This is probably because only human beings have to turn off a flood of complex information from memory, imagination, contemplation, and so forth in order to go to sleep.

Hypothalamus   Working closely with the reticular system is an important regulatory system called the *hypothalamus*. The hypothalamus regulates eating, drinking, and sexual behavior. Apparently, we would continue to eat or drink until we overflowed if it were not for inhibitory control by the hypothalamus. The hypothalamus receives information about the blood-sugar level, the fullness of the stomach, the muscle action of chewing and swallowing, and so forth, and uses it to determine when to inhibit eating. It uses signals concerning the concentration of chemicals in the blood and the blood volume to determine thirst. It can even stop thirst before these adverse signals disappear; it takes a little while for the water to go from the stomach into the blood so that the hypothalamus can detect a change, but the hypothalamus apparently can compensate for this delay and inhibit drinking before too much water has been taken in. It is not clear how sexual behavior is regulated in human beings. In most other animals, sexual behavior is controlled by hormonal changes in the female, regulated in part by the hypothalamus, which controls the *pituitary gland* (the master control of hormonal secretion). The sight and smell of a sexually ready female arouses a male animal (apparently this is also dependent upon hormonal regulation by the hypothalamus).

The hypothalamus is of particular interest to psychologists because it seems to play a role in the reactions of animals to reward and punishment. That is, by means of an electrode that is like a long needle (the brain has no pain receptors, so it doesn't hurt), weak electrical stimulation of specific parts of the hypothalamus and surrounding areas will act as reward or punishment and thus promote learning by rats, monkeys, cats, and other animals. Stimulation of some of these areas apparently is pleasurable; rats, for instance, can be taught to press a switch which will deliver a short burst of electricity to a particular area. Indeed, they will sit and work the switch several thousand times an hour until they drop from exhaustion. Electrical stimulation in other parts of the brain apparently is unpleasant; animals will quickly learn to switch off such stimulation or even to press a switch to prevent it when a warning light is turned on.

No one is quite sure whether the feeling arising from this kind of artificial brain stimulation is similar to the pleasantness we feel when we are elated, sexually aroused, or happy or to the unpleasantness we feel when we are depressed, rejected, unhappy, and so on. However, it seems plausible that the stimulation is mimicking the neural activity that takes place when we feel such emotions. This seems even more reasonable when we consider that the hypothalamus is closely linked to the system which will be discussed next, a system that primarily is involved with emotionality.

Limbic system   The *limbic system* surrounds the reticular system and feeds information into it through the hypothalamus and other centers. Moreover, it sends and receives information to and from the senses as well as to and from other parts of the brain. Research thus far is quite incomplete, but the limbic system clearly plays a role in emotionality. A wild animal that has had damage done to a specific part of his limbic system becomes docile and friendly; a wildcat that couldn't be approached before, for example, can be safely petted. Damage to other parts of the system can do just the opposite; a normally gentle white rat will turn into a vicious, ill-tempered beast who will attack anything and anybody. Damage in yet other areas of the system produces an animal that has difficulty in learning to anticipate and avoid painful experiences. In a normal animal, the fear emotion produced by a dangerous situation is sufficient to motivate it to learn to get out of the situation. While it is not really clear-cut, the research suggests that some kinds of limbic damage prevent the fear emotion and thus interfere with learning to avoid danger. At any rate, these observations demonstrate the involvement of the limbic system with emotion.

Reception, integration, and response-formulation centers   Thus far, we have followed incoming information from the senses through the spinal cord, through or by the medulla and cerebellum to the reticular system from which it goes to the hypothalamus, limbic systems, and to the *cortex*. The cortex consists of the large puffy parts of the brain in Figure A2.3. It is made up of literally millions of neurons that are complexly interconnected. Some parts of the cortex receive information from specific senses while other parts play a role in formulating outgoing messages in response to this information. All of this involves use of information from past experience that is stored in memory, but no one knows how it all works. The best that scientists have been able to do is to discover the parts of the cortex that appear to be specifically involved with information from specific senses and with formulation of response messages to specific parts of the body.

FRONTAL-PARIETAL CORTEX   As you can see in Figure A2.4, there are four general divisions of the cortex that seem to be assigned to specific senses. The *frontal-parietal cortex* is primarily for the body senses. Figure A2.5 shows

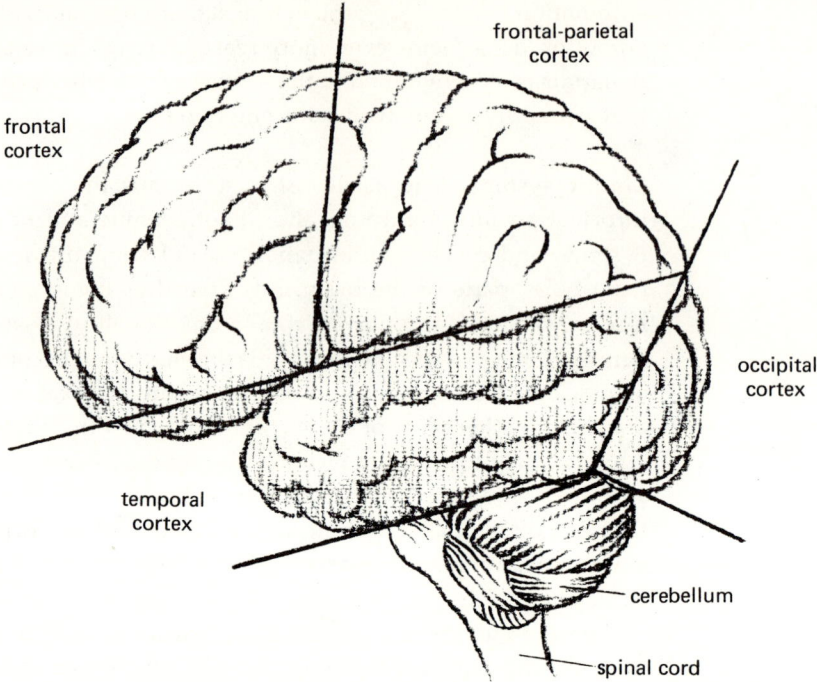

FIG. A2.4 *The outside of the brain.*

how it is schematically arranged. Sensory information from the various parts of the body is received in this area. Movement of the corresponding body parts is controlled by the adjacent areas. Of course, the interpretation of the information and the particular movements that are made in response involve many other parts of the brain.

OCCIPITAL CORTEX The *occipital cortex* is involved in vision. Figure A2.6 shows how the optic nerves come out of the back of the eyeballs, divide, and end in the occipital cortex. The result is that information on the right half of the retina of each eye goes to the right half of the occipital cortex and that on the left half of the retina of each eye goes to the left half of the occipital cortex. If one of the halves of the occipital cortex is damaged (say in an accident or through disease), the person loses the ability to see one half of his visual field.

The occipital cortex is only beginning to be understood. The neural elements in the retina are interrelated in complex ways so that they are sensitive to particular colors, shapes, and directions of movement of light patterns. This information is relayed to the occipital cortex where different areas of the cortex specialize in specific kinds of information from specific parts of the retina. Then, together with information from the other senses and from memory, this information is interpreted and the appropriate response is formulated. Again, no one knows how the integration or response formulation takes place.

TEMPORAL CORTEX The third major sensory area is the *temporal cortex* which receives auditory information. It is organized in a fairly simple manner; different parts are specifically for different sounds. Again this information is

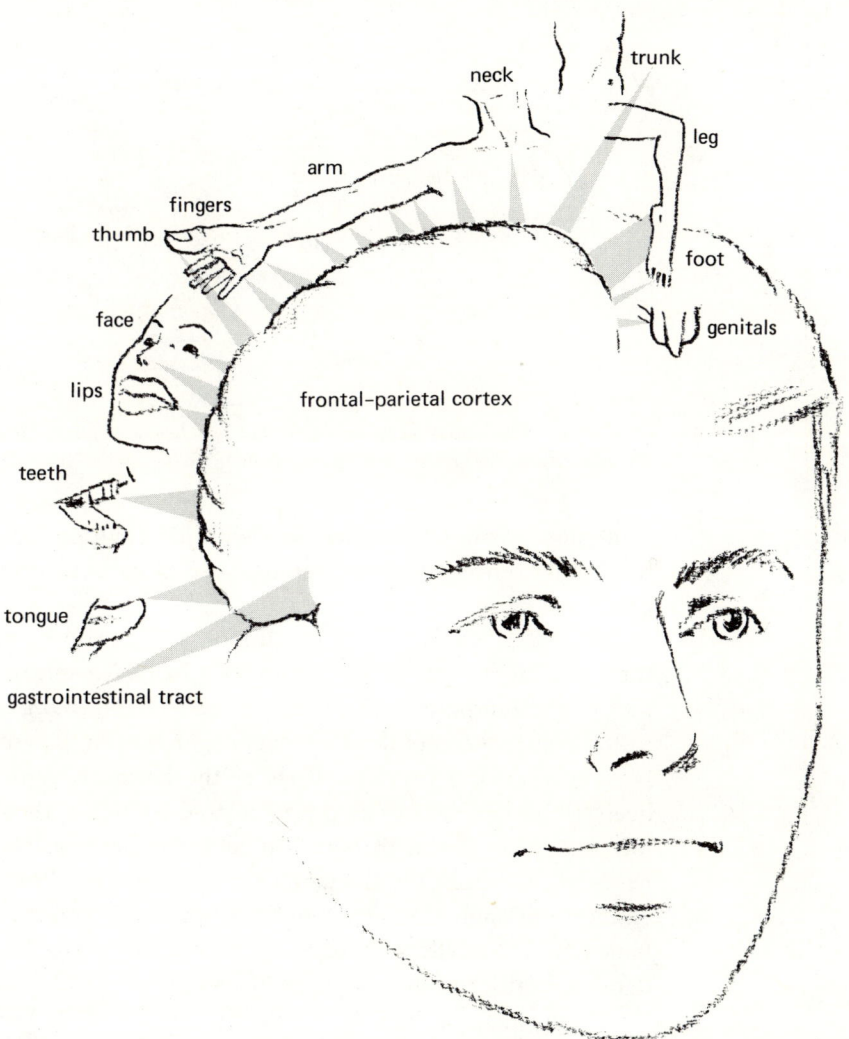

FIG. A2.5 *A schematic arrangement of the specific areas in the frontal-parietal cortex where sensory information from various parts of the body is received.*

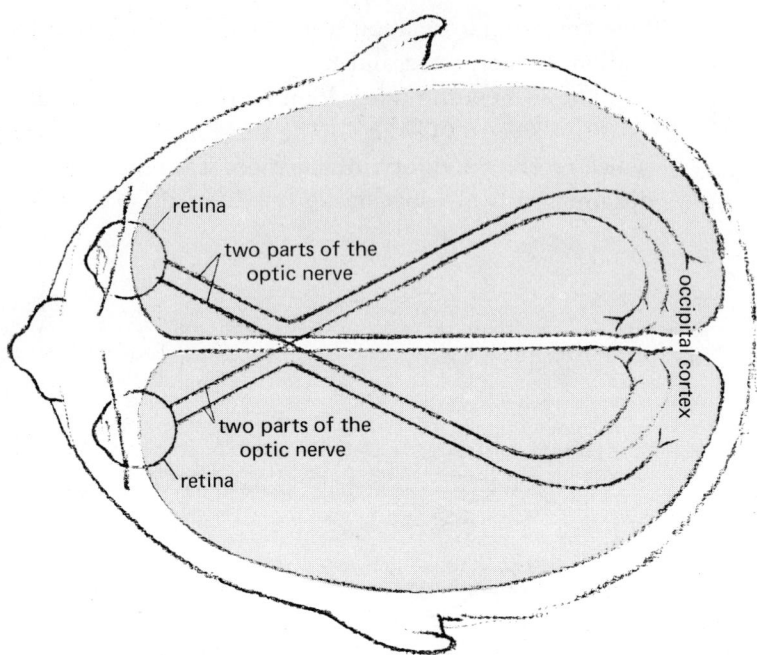

FIG. A2.6   *The neural pathways from the eyes to the occipital cortex. This view is as though you were above the brain, looking downward.*

combined in some unknown way with information from past experience and from other senses to yield meaningful auditory perceptions and prompt appropriate responses to them.

FRONTAL CORTEX   If you'll look at Figure A2.3 again, you will see that there are large parts of the cortex that haven't been discussed. Aside from a part of the temporal area in the left half of the brain which is pretty specific to the comprehension and production of speech, the remainder of the cortex is somewhat of a mystery. Parts of the cortex near the areas that have just been discussed are in some way related to aiding those areas in doing their job, but just how isn't clear. In fact, for medical reasons it is sometimes necessary to surgically damage or remove parts of these auxiliary areas, and, strangely enough, there frequently is little or no obvious effect on the patient's behavior. What effect there is seems related to the amount of cortex that is damaged rather than to the specific locality of the damage.

The *frontal cortex* was at one time thought to be where thinking took place. This idea seemed reasonable because this area of the brain is larger for human beings than for other animals and, therefore, might be expected to reflect the uniquely human characteristic of prolonged and abstract thought. But again, removal or damage of this part of the cortex produces problems only when large areas are affected. Such results have dashed hopes that this area might be the primary storage location of past experience, that is, of memory. Indeed, memories are probably stored all over the brain (for example, the electrical stimulation of some temporal areas will cause the patient to remember things he probably could not voluntarily recall).

A Final Note

It is impossible to appreciate fully how little is actually known about how the brain works unless you ponder the stunning complexity of its organization and the overwhelming amount of information it so skillfully integrates. For example, imagine yourself at a very bad symphonic concert. As you sit there squirming in your seat, twisting your program, listening to the orchestra butcher your favorite overture, and watching the various musicians, you become aware of the fact that you are sleepy, even though you also are rather angry about the performance. Adding to your discomfort, the salt on the food you had for dinner has made you very thirsty.

Now, consider some of the major things that are going on in your brain. Your frontal-parietal cortex is receiving information about the hardness of the seat and at the same time is causing you to squirm to relieve the numbness. It also is regulating your fingers' nervous play with the program. Your temporal cortex is receiving information about the music, which is then compared to your information from past experience about how this music *ought* to sound. Your eyes dart about from one part of the orchestra to another, receiving a bewilderingly complicated sequence of visual impressions that are relayed to the occipital cortex where they are somehow interpreted as violinists, drummers, clarinetists, and so forth. Your limbic system is involved with your disgust about the poor performance. Your hypothalamus is reacting to the effect of the salt on your blood and is screaming for water. Finally, your reticular system is fighting a losing battle to keep you awake and to keep your attention on the music. When you view all of this activity as happening simultaneously and when you realize that this brief description is really giving you only the grossest picture of what is actually going on, maybe you can get a feeling for how truly amazing and complicated the nervous system and brain actually are.

SUMMARY

1   *Neurons* and bundles of neurons, *nerves*, are transmission cables that run from the senses to the brain. They also are the stuff of which the brain is made. Impulses are initiated at the neuron's *dendrites* and proceed along the *axon* to

the *end brushes* where chemical activity at the *synapse* transmits the impulse to the dendrites of the next neuron.

2   The nervous system has two components, the *somatic system* for muscles and the sense organs and the *autonomic system* for internal organs.

3   The brain receives, integrates, and formulates responses to the information received through the nervous system. It is composed of a number of highly integrated parts, primary among which are the *medulla* and the *cerebellum*, which regulate the body's vital functions; the *reticular system*, which is the clearinghouse for incoming and outgoing information; the *hypothalamus*, which controls eating, drinking, and sexual behavior (in animals, at any rate); the *limbic system*, which plays a role in emotionality; and the *cortex*, which receives and integrates information and initiates responses.

Further Reading

Asimov, I.   *The Human Brain: Its Capacities and Functions*
New York: New American Library, 1965 (c. 1963), 357 pages (paperback).
Well known as an excellent writer of science fiction, Asimov is also known for the clarity of his writing on almost any detailed scientific topic. In this particular book, he describes how the brain organizes and controls the total functioning of the individual through its control over the nervous system, the senses, the glands, and the hormones.

Crichton, M.   *The Terminal Man*
New York: Alfred A. Knopf, 1972, 247 pages.
A novel about an attempt to control a violent man by connecting his brain to a computer. Although this book is fiction, it is based on actual research. It also touches on the social implications and moral issues of electrical stimulation of the brain (ESB). Entertaining as well as informative.

Delgado, J. M. R.   *Physical Control of the Mind*
New York: Harper & Row, 1971 (c. 1969), 288 pages (paperback).
A fascinating book about control of behavior through electrical stimulation of the brain (ESB). ESB experiments done with cats, bulls, monkeys, chimpanzees, and human beings are described and possible future uses of ESB are discussed.

Stevens, C. F.   *Neurophysiology: A Primer*
New York: Wiley, 1966, 182 pages.
A well-written description of the structure and properties of neurons and of how neurons interact with each other in the nervous system. The author also discusses how information gets in and out of the nervous system and the various methods for

determining the functions of groups of cells. Although this book is fairly detailed, its clarity and its use of many simple diagrams make it easy to understand.

TART, C. T.   *Altered States of Consciousness*
New York: Wiley, 1969, 575 pages.
Although technical at times, this is a fascinating book of readings about the physiological behavior and thought processes that occur during altered states of consciousness. Covers the topics of sleep and dreams, meditation, hypnosis, and drugs. Some articles are strongly research oriented while others are speculative and thought provoking.

REFERENCES

Section 1:
Background
and Biases

Wertheimer, M. *A Brief History of Psychology.* New York: Holt, Rinehart and Winston, 1970.

Section 2:
Sensation
and Perception

Gibson, J. J. *The Senses Considered as Perceptual Systems.* Boston: Houghton Mifflin, 1966.

Graybiel, A., R. S. Kennedy, E. C. Knoblock, F. E. Guedry, W. Mertz, M. E. McLeod, J. K. Colehour, E. F. Miller, and A. R. Fregly. Effects of exposure to a rotating environment (10 RPM) on four aviators for a period of twelve days. *Aerospace Medicine,* 1965, **36**, 733–754.

Gregory, R. L. *Eye and Brain: The Psychology of Seeing.* New York: McGraw-Hill, 1966.

Held, R. Plasticity in sensory motor systems. In R. C. Atkinson (Ed.). *Contemporary Psychology: Readings from Scientific American.* San Francisco: Freeman, 1971.

Janis, I. *Psychological Stress.* New York: Wiley, 1958.

Kohler, I. Experiments with goggles. *Scientific American,* 1962, **206**, 63–72.

Lipscomb, D. M. High intensity sounds in the recreational environment. *Clinical Pediatrics,* 1969, **8**, 63–68.

Magee, K. R. Congenital indifference to pain. *The Archives of Neurology,* 1963, **9**, 635–640.

Michotte, A. *The Perception of Causality* (translation by T. R. Miles and E. Miles). London: Methuen, 1963.

Miller, G. A. The magic number seven, plus or minus two: Some limits on our capacity for processing information. *Psychological Review,* 1956, **63**, 81–97.

Morgan, C. T. *Physiological Psychology.* New York: McGraw-Hill, 1965.

Neff, W. D. (Ed.). *Contributions to Sensory Physiology,* Vol. 1. New York: Academic, 1965.

Section 3:
Memory and Rules

Anand, B. K., G. S. Chhina, and B. Singh. Some aspects of electroencephalographic studies in Yogis. *Electroencephalology and Clinical Neurophysiology,* 1961, **13**, 452–456. Reprinted in C. T. Tart (Ed.). *Altered States of Consciousness.* New York: Wiley, 1969.

Atkinson, R., and R. Shiffrin. Human memory: A proposed system and its control processes. In K. Spence and J. Spence (Eds.). *The Psychology of Learning and Motivation,* Vol. 2. New York: Academic, 1968.

Bakan, D. Learning and the principle of inverse probability. *Psychological Review,* 1953, **60,** 360–370.

Bandura, A. *Principles of Behavior Modification.* New York: Holt, 1969.

Bartlett, F. C. *Remembering.* Cambridge: Cambridge University Presss, 1932.

Bobrow, S. A. Memory for words in sentences. *Journal of Verbal Learning and Verbal Behavior,* 1970, **9,** 363–372.

Brown, R. W., and D. McNeill. The "tip-of-the-tongue" phenomenon. *Journal of Learning and Verbal Behavior,* 1966, **5,** 325–337.

Gibson, E. J., and R. D. Walk. The "visual cliff." *Scientific American,* 1960, **202,** 64–71.

Hess, E. H. "Imprinting" in animals. *Scientific American,* 1958, **198,** 81–90.

Hunt, E. B., and T. Love. How good can memory be? In A. Melton and E. Martin (Eds.). *Coding Processes in Human Memory.* New York: Halsted, 1972.

Kamiya, J. Operant control of the EEG alpha rhythm and some of its reported effects on consciousness. In C. T. Tart (Ed.). *Altered States of Consciousness.* New York: Wiley, 1969.

Kasamatsu, A., and T. Hirai. An electroencephalographic study on the Zen meditation (Zazen). *Folia Psychiatrica et Neurologica Japonica,* 1966, **20,** 315–336. Reprinted in C. T. Tart, (Ed.). *Altered States of Consciousness.* New York: Wiley, 1969.

Kohlers, P. A. Bilingualism and information processing. *Scientific American,* 1968, **218,** 78–86.

Lawick-Goodall, J. Van. *In the Shadow of Man.* Boston: Houghton Mifflin, 1971.

Lorenz, K. *King Solomon's Ring.* London: Methuen, 1952.

McGaugh, J. L. Time dependent processes in memory storage. *Science,* 1966, **153,** 1351–1358.

Miller, N. E. Learning of visceral and glandular responses. *Science,* 1969, **163,** 434–445.

Milner, B. Memory and the medial temporal regions of the brain. In K. H. Pribram and D. E. Broadbent (Eds.). *Biology of Memory.* New York: Academic, 1970.

Morris, R., and D. Morris. *Men and Apes.* New York: McGraw-Hill, 1966.

Pavlov, I. P. *Conditioned Reflexes.* New York: Oxford, 1927.

Penfield, W., and L. Roberts. *Speech and Brain Mechanisms.* Princeton, N.J.: Princeton University Press, 1959.

Peterson, L. R., and M. J. Peterson. Short-term retention of individual verbal items. *Journal of Experimental Psychology,* 1959, **58,** 193–198.

Piaget, J. *The Origins of Intelligence in Children.* New York: International University Press, 1952.

Skinner, B. F. *The Behavior of Organisms.* New York: Appleton, 1938.

Tolman, E. C. *Purposive Behavior in Animals and Men.* New York: Appleton, 1932.

Tolman, E. C. Principles of purposive behavior. In S. Koch (Ed.). *Psychology: A Study of a Science,* Vol. 2. New York: McGraw-Hill, 1959.

Watson, J. B., and R. Rayner. Conditioned emotional reactions. *Journal of Experimental Psychology,* 1920, **3**, 1–14.

Section 4:
Social Interactions
and Group
Membership

Averill, J. R. Grief: Its nature and significance. *Psychological Bulletin,* 1968, **70**, 721–748.

Asch, S. E. Effects of group pressure upon the modification and distortion of judgments. In E. M. Maccoby, T. M. Newcomb, and E. L. Hartley (Eds.). *Readings in Social Psychology.* New York: Holt, 1958.

Berscheid, E., and E. H. Walster. *Interpersonal Attraction.* Reading, Mass.: Addison-Wesley, 1969.

Biller, H. B. Father absence and the personality development of the male child. *Developmental Psychology,* 1970, **2**, 181–201.

Bowlby, J. Grief and mourning in infancy and early childhood. In *New Perspectives in Psychoanalysis.* New York: Grune & Stratton, 1965.

Byrne, D. Interpersonal attraction and attitude similarity. *Journal of Abnormal and Social Psychology,* 1961, **62**, 713–715.

Emerson, R. M. Exchange theory. Part II: Exchange relations, exchange networks, and groups as exchange systems. In J. Berger, M. Zelditch, and B. Anderson (Eds.). *Sociological Theories in Progress,* Vol. II. Boston: Houghton Mifflin, 1972.

Fiedler, F. E. *Leadership.* New York: General Learning Press, 1971.

Fiedler, F. E. Validation and extension of the contingency model of leadership effectiveness: A review of empirical findings. *Psychological Bulletin,* 1971, **76**, 128–148.

Foa, U. G. Interpersonal and economic resources. *Science,* 1971, **171**, 345–351.

Hall, E. T. *The Silent Language.* New York: Doubleday, 1959.

Hall, E. T. *The Hidden Dimension.* New York: Doubleday, 1966.

Harlow, H. F. The nature of love. *American Psychologist,* 1958, **13**, 673–685.

Harlow, H. F., and M. K. Harlow. Social deprivation in monkeys. *Scientific American,* 1962, **207**, 136–146.

King, J. A. The social behavior of prairie dogs. *Scientific American,* 1959, **201**, 128–140.

Milgram, S. Liberating effects of group pressure. *Journal of Personality and Social Psychology,* 1965, **l**, 127–134.

Morris, D. *The Human Zoo.* New York: McGraw-Hill, 1969.

Newcomb, T. M. Attitude development as a function of reference groups: The Bennington study. In E. M. Maccoby, T. M. Newcomb, and E. L. Hartley (Eds.). *Readings in Social Psychology,* New York: Holt, 1958.

Seay, B., and H. F. Harlow. Maternal separation in the rhesus monkey. *Journal of Nervous and Mental Diseases,* 1965, **140,** 434–441.

Sherif, M. Group influences upon the formation of norms and attitudes. In E. M. Maccoby, T. M. Newcomb, and E. L. Hartley (Eds.). *Readings in Social Psychology.* New York: Holt, 1958.

Sherif, M., O. J. Harvey, B. J. White, W. R. Hood, and C. W. Sherif. Intergroup conflict and cooperation: the Robbers' Cave experiment. Norman, Okla.: Institute of Group Relations, University of Oklahoma, 1961.

Singh, S. D. Urban monkeys, *Scientific American,* 1969, **221,** 108–115.

Skeels, H. M. Adult status of children with contrasting early life experiences. *Monographs of the Society for Research in Child Development,* 1966, **31,** whole no. 3.

Sommer, R. *Personal Space.* Englewood Cliffs, N.J.: Prentice-Hall, 1969.

Suomi, S. J., H. F. Harlow, and C. J. Domek. Effect of repetitive infant-infant separation of young monkeys. *Journal of Abnormal Psychology,* 1970, **76,** 161–172.

Woolpy, J. H. The social organization of wolves. *Natural History,* 1968, **77,** 46–55.

Section 5:
Crisis and Change

Coleman, J. C. *Abnormal Psychology and Modern Life.* Chicago: Scott, Foresman, 1956.

Ellis, A., and R. A. Harper. *A Guide to Rational Living.* North Hollywood, Calif.: Wilshire Book Company, 1961.

Fordyce, W. E. Operant conditioning as a treatment method in management of selected chronic pain problems. *Northwest Medicine,* 1970, **69,** 198–206.

Hall, C. S., and G. Lindzey (Eds.). *Theories of Personality.* New York: Wiley, 1970.

Heath, R. G., A. F. Guschwan, and J. W. Coffey. Relation of taraxein to schizophrenia. *Diseases of the Nervous System,* 1970, **31,** 391–395.

Heath, R. G., S. Martens, B. E. Leach, M. Cohen, and C. Angel. Effect on behavior in humans with the administration of taraxein. *American Journal of Psychiatry,* 1957, **114,** 14–24.

Heath, R. G., S. Martens, B. E. Leach, M. Cohen, and C. A. Feigley. Behavioral changes in non-psychotic volunteers following the administration of taraxein, the substance obtained from serum of schizophrenic patients. *American Journal of Psychiatry,* 1958, **114,** 917–920.

Holmes, T. H., and M. Masuda. Life change and illness susceptibility. Paper presented at meetings of the American Association for the Advancement of Science, Chicago, December 1970.

Holmes, T. H., and R. H. Rahe. The social readjustment rating scale. *Journal of Psychosomatic Research,* 1967, **11,** 213–218.

Kallman, F. J. The genetics of mental illness. In S. Arieti (Ed.). *American Handbook of Psychiatry.* New York: Basic Books, 1959.

Kety, S. S. Biochemical theories of schizophrenia (Part I). *Science,* 1959, **129,** 1528–1532, 1590–1596 (Part II).

Kübler-Ross, E. *On Death and Dying.* New York: Macmillan, 1969.

Lang, P. J. Experimental studies of desensitization psychotherapy. In J. Wolpe, A. Salter, and L. J. Reyna (Eds.). *The Conditioning Therapies.* New York: Holt, 1966.

Mark, J. C. The attitudes of the mothers of male schizophrenics toward child behavior. *Journal of Abnormal and Social Psychology,* 1953, **48,** 185–189.

Perls, F. S. *Gestalt Therapy Verbatim.* Lafayette, Calif.: Real People Press, 1969.

Rogers, C. R. *Carl Rogers on Encounter Groups.* New York: Harper & Row, 1970.

Smith, K., G. F. Thompson, and H. D. Koster. Sweat in schizophrenic patients: Identification of the odorous substance. *Science,* 1969, **166,** 398–399.

Vogel, W., C. G. Lanterbach, M. Livingston, and H. Holloway. Relationships between memories of their parents' behavior and psychodiagnosis in psychiatrically disturbed soldiers. *Journal of Consulting Psychology,* 1964, **28,** 126–132.

White, R. W. *The Abnormal Personality* (3rd ed.). New York: Ronald, 1964.

Wolpe, J. The systematic desensitization treatment of neuroses. *Journal of Nervous and Mental Disease,* 1961, **132,** 198–203.

Yates, A. J. *Behavior Therapy.* New York: Wiley, 1970.

Section 6, Part 1: Language

Berko, J. The child's learning of English morphology. *Word,* 1958, **14,** 150–177.

Chomsky, N. *Aspects of a Theory of Syntax.* Cambridge, Mass.: M.I.T. Press, 1965.

Conversations with a chimp. *Life,* 1972, **72,** 55–60.

Dale, P. S. *Language Development: Structure and Function.* Hinsdale, Ill.: Dryden, 1972.

Ferster, C. B. Arithmetic behavior in chimpanzees. *Scientific American,* 1964, **210,** 98–106.

Ford, B. How they taught a chimp to talk. *Science Digest,* 1970, **67,** 11–17.

Gardner, R. A., and B. T. Gardner. Teaching sign language to a chimpanzee. *Science,* 1969, **165,** 664–672.

Lenneberg, E. H. Understanding language without ability to speak: A case report. *Journal of Abnormal and Social Psychology,* 1962, **65,** 419–425.

Lenneberg, E. H. *Biological Foundations of Language.* New York: Wiley, 1967.

Lieberman, P. Primate vocalizations and human linguistic ability. *Journal of the Acoustical Society of America,* 1968, **44,** 1574–1584.

Premack, D. The education of Sarah. *Psychology Today*, 1970, **4**, 55–58.

Premack, D. Language in chimpanzee? *Science*, 1971, **172**, 808–822.

Section 6, Part 2: Beliefs, Values, and Decisions

Edwards, W., and A. Tversky (Eds.). *Decision Making*. Baltimore, Md.: Penguin, 1967.

Gray, C. A. Factors in students' decisions to attempt academic tasks. Unpublished doctoral dissertation, University of Washington, 1971.

Lee, W. *Decision Theory and Human Behavior*. New York: Wiley, 1971.

Scheibe, K. E. *Beliefs and Values*. New York: Holt, 1970.

Section 6, Part 3: Love, Marriage, and Sex

Cox, F. D. *Youth, Marriage and the Seductive Society*. Dubuque, Iowa: Brown, 1968.

Dymond, R. Interpersonal perception and marital happiness. *Canadian Journal of Psychology*, 1954, **8**, 164–171. Reprinted in H. Toch and H. C. Smith (Eds.). *Social Perception*. Princeton, N.J.: Van Nostrand, 1968.

Ellis, A., and A. Abarbanel (Eds.). *The Encyclopedia of Sexual Behavior*. New York: Hawthorne, 1961.

Fujita, B., N. N. Wagner, and R. J. Pion. Contraceptive use among single college students: A preliminary report. *American Journal of Obstetrics and Gynecology*, 1971, **109**, 787–793.

Kinsey, A. C., W. B. Pomeroy, and C. E. Martin. *Sexual Behavior in the Human Male*. Philadelphia: Saunders, 1948.

Kinsey, A. C., W. B. Pomeroy, C. E. Martin, and P. H. Gebhard. *Sexual Behavior in the Human Female*. Philadelphia: Saunders, 1953.

Masters, W. H., and V. E. Johnson. *Human Sexual Response*. Boston: Little, Brown, 1966.

Masters, W. H., and V. E. Johnson. *Human Sexual Inadequacy*. Boston: Little, Brown, 1970.

McCary, J. L. *Human Sexuality*. Princeton, N.J.: Van Nostrand, 1967.

Reiss, I. L. *Premarital Sexual Standards in America*. Glencoe, Ill.: Free Press, 1960.

Zelnick, M., and J. F. Kanter. Sexuality, contraception and pregnancy among young and unwed females in the United States. Final Report to the Commission on Population Growth and the American Future, 1972.

Section 6, Part 4: Psychological Aspects of Poverty

Bee, H. L., L. F. VanEgeren, A. P. Streissguth, B. A. Nyman, and M. S. Leckie. Social class differences in maternal teaching strategies and speech patterns. *Developmental Psychology*, 1969, **1**, 726–734.

Harrington, M. *The Other America*. Baltimore, Md.: Penguin, 1962.

Hess, R. Maternal teaching styles and the socialization of educability. Committee on Human Development Conference, September 5, 1964.

Hollingshead, A. B., and F. C. Redlich. Social stratification and psychiatric disorders. *American Sociological Review*, 1953, **18**, 163–169.

Karnes, M. B., A. S. Hodgins, R. L. Stoneburner, W. M. Studley, and J. A. Teska. Effects of a highly structured program of language development on intellectual functioning and psycholinguistic development of culturally disadvantaged three-year-olds. *Journal of Special Education*, 1969, **2**, 405–412.

Kershaw, J. A. *Government against Poverty*. Washington, D.C.: Brookings Institution, 1970.

Miller, W. B. Lower class culture as a generating milieu of gang delinquency. *Journal of Social Issues*, 1958, **14**, 5–19.

Section 6, Part 5: Drugs and the Drug Experience

Becker, H. S. History, culture and subjective experience: An exploration of the social bases of drug-induced experiences. *Journal of Health and Social Behavior*, 1967, **8**, 163–176.

Bender, L., and D. V. S. Sankar. Chromosome damage not found in leukocytes of children treated with LSD-25. *Science*, 1968, **159**, 749.

Crancer, A., Jr., J. M. Dille, J. C. Delay, J. E. Wallace, and M. D. Haykin. Comparison of the effects of marihuana and alcohol on simulated driving performance. *Science*, 1969, **164**, 851–854.

Green, J. R., L. M. Halpern, and T. A. Rogers. Pseudoaddiction to heroin. *Bulletin of the King County Medical Society* (King County, Seattle, Wash.) 1968, **47**, 245.

Grinspoon, L. *Marihuana Reconsidered*. Cambridge, Mass.: Harvard University Press, 1971.

Irwin, S., and J. Egozcue. Chromosomal abnormalities in leukocytes from LSD-25 users. *Science*, 1967, **157**, 313–314.

Jacobson, C. B., and V. L. Magyar. Genetic evaluation of LSD. *Clinical Proceedings of the Children's Hospital of the District of Columbia*, 1968, **24**, 151–152.

Manheim, D. I., G. D. Mellinger, and M. B. Balter. Marijuana use among urban adults. *Science*, 1969, **166**, 1544–1545.

Weil, A. T., N. E. Zinberg, and J. M. Nelson. Clinical and psychological effects of marihuana in man. *Science*, 1968, **162**, 1234–1242.

Appendix 1: Tools for Psychological Research

Carlson, C. S., C. R. Arnold, W. C. Becker, and C. H. Madson. The elimination of tantrum behavior of a child in the elementary classroom. *Behavior Research and Therapy*, 1968, **6**, 117–119.

Scott, W. A., and M. Wertheimer. *Introduction to Psychological Research*, New York: Wiley, 1962.

Wolf, M. M., J. S. Birnbrauer, T. Williams, and J. Lawlar. A note on apparent extinction of the vomiting behavior of a retarded child. In L. P. Ullmann and L. Krasner, *Case Studies in Behavior Modification*. New York: Holt, 1965.

Appendix 2: Brain Mechanisms

McCleary, R. A., and R. Y. Moore. *Subcortical Mechanisms of Behavior*. New York: Basic Books, 1965.

Glossary

The following definitions correspond to the usage of the terms in the text rather than to general dictionary definitions. An italicized term in the definition is itself included in the glossary. The terms in parentheses following the definition are in some way related to the term that is being defined and can be found elsewhere in the glossary.

Abstinence: The practice of refraining from a particular behavior (for example, sexual intercourse).

Abstract Thinking: The assumption that the world has continuity and existence apart from one's own immediate experience; also the ability to understand and use abstract concepts such as love, emotions, other people's feelings. (see *Concrete Thinking*)

Accommodation: The process of changing the shape of the *lens* so an image can be focused on the *retina.*

Acquired Status: Status obtained by an individual through his or her own personal efforts or demonstration of ability. (see *Ascribed Status*)

Acrophobia: Irrational fear of heights. (see *Phobias*)

Adaptation: Adjustment (primarily by a sensory system) to some constant level of stimulation.

Adultery: Extramarital sex.

Aerial Perspective: A *monocular* cue for *space perception.* Because of moisture, dust, and so on, in the air, there is a slight change in the color of distant objects toward bluish gray.

Affectional Bonds: The bases of social animals' demonstrated preferences for particular members of their own or other species (for example, love, friendship).

After-images: Visual images that are experienced as an after effect of having looked directly at a brightly lighted object. If the after-image is of the same color as the color of the object, it is called a *positive after-image*. If the after-image is the complement of the color of the object, it is called a *negative after-image*.

Alcoholism: Addiction to alcohol.

All-or-none Principle: The fact that an electrical impulse in a *neuron* either occurs at full strength or does not occur at all. (see *Threshold*)

Alpha State: The relaxed, peaceful, alert experience that accompanies a preponderance of *alpha waves* in the brain.

Alpha Wave: The brainwave recorded on an *electroencephalogram* that is an 8–14 cycle per second wave; of interest because this wave is observed when a person is unusually relaxed and peaceful but still alert. (see *Alpha State*)

Amnesia: When, usually as a result of extreme psychological stress or a physical trauma, a person forgets either who he is and/or all or part of his past life; loss of long-term memory. (see *Dissociative Reactions*)

Amphetamines: Drugs, commonly found in diet pills or pep pills, which excite a person (as opposed to relaxing him). Examples are Benzedrine, Dexedrine, and Methedrine. (see *Speed*)

Anosmia: Lack of the ability to smell.

Antidepressants: Drugs used to treat depression; antidepressants are often used during the initial process of therapy. (see *Drug Therapy*)

Anxiety: The emotional component of a *life crisis* or *psychological conflict*. (see *Stress*)

Anxiety Attack: A short period during which *anxiety* becomes overpowering, physiological reactions dominate, and, for the most part, the person is unable to behave with his normal efficiency and composure.

Armchair Approach: A method of studying psychology which consists of watching people or events around you, examining your own thoughts and feelings, and then sitting down and drawing conclusions from your observations. (see *Research*)

Ascribed Status: Status given to a person by virtue of a specific job that he or she performs. (see *Acquired Status*)

Attached Shadow: A *monocular* cue for *space perception* consisting of those parts of an object that do not receive direct light from the light source and therefore are shadowed. (see *Cast Shadow*)

Attitudes: Opinions about how people ought to behave and how things ought to happen. (see *Norms*)

Audition: The passive reception of sound. (see *Hearing*)

Auditory Nerve: The cable of *neural elements* that carries auditory information from the *cochlea* to the *temporal lobe* of the brain.

Author: An innocent who undertakes the seemingly simple task of writing a book and who is pushed to the edge of madness by such details as having to write a glossary! (see *Anxiety, Ego Defense Mechanisms, Depression, Schizophrenia*)

Autonomic Nervous System: One of two major parts of the nervous system. It carries messages back and forth from the brain to internal organs such as the heart, lungs, and stomach. (see *Somatic Nervous System*)

Aversion Therapy: A *behavior therapy* technique that reduces the attractiveness of a situation which previously has promoted the use of an undesirable rule, thereby helping the person give up the undesirable rule and develop new ways of coping with the situation.

Axon: The long tail of a *neuron;* it transmits electrical activity from the *cell body* of the neuron to the *end brushes.*

Balanced Relation: A social interaction in which both persons give and receive *social resources* and both are happy with the interaction.

Barbiturates: Drugs prescribed by physicians either to help people sleep or as pain killers. Examples are Nembutal, Seconal, and Amytal.

Basilar Membrane: The platform in the *cochlea* that supports the *organ of Corti.*

Behavior Modification: See *Behavior Therapy.*

Behavior Therapist: A psychotherapist who uses *behavior therapy* techniques.

Behavior Therapy: A set of techniques designed to help people deal with problem behavior. Behavior therapy focuses on changing the problem behavior rather than on prolonged investigation of the origins of the behavior. Also called behavior modification. (see *Desensitization Therapy, Aversion Therapy*)

Belief: The degree to which a person thinks something either is true now or may turn out to be true in the future. When quantified, a belief is a *subjective probability.*

Bilingual: The ability to speak two languages fluently.

Binocular: Pertaining to the use of two eyes rather than merely one. (see *Monocular*)

Binocular Disparity: A *binocular* cue for *space perception.* Because the two eyes are about two inches apart, each one receives a slightly different image of the object being viewed. The differences between the two images serve as a cue for the distance of the object.

Bisexuality: Being sexually involved with members of both sexes. (see *Heterosexuality, Homosexuality*)

Bone Conduction: The sensation of sound that results from vibration of the skull.

Brain: The "central computer" of the nervous system. Located in the head and protected by the skull, the brain has many parts, primary among which are the *medulla, cerebellum, reticular system, hypothalamus, limbic system, corpus callosum,* and *cortex.*

Case History: A detailed description of an individual person's behavior. Comparison of a number of case histories sometimes reveals similarities that cast light on some particular hypothesis. (see *Experiment, Simulation, Naturalistic Observation*)

Cast Shadow: A *monocular* cue for *space perception* consisting of the shadow that begins at the base of an object and stretches along the surface upon which the object is resting. (see *Attached Shadow*)

Cell Body: The central part of a *neuron* which supplies the nutrients that keep the neuron alive and functioning.

Central Tendency Measures: Descriptive statistics that are summary statements about the average of a group of data; the *mean,* the *median,* or the *mode.*

Cerebellum: The part of the *brain* that regulates posture, muscle tone, and coordination of movement.

Classical Conditioning: See *Pavlovian Conditioning.*

Claustrophobia: Irrational fear of closed spaces such as an automobile, a closet, or an elevator. (see *Phobias*)

Coalition: When two or more persons join together to alter the balance of power in a social relation. (see *Balanced Relation*)

Cochlea: The coiled cavity in the head that contains those *neural elements* sensitive to sound-induced vibrations within the auditory system. (see *Organ of Corti*)

Color Constancy: The tendency for an object's color to appear unchanged in spite of changes in the color of the surrounding illumination and consequent changes in the color of the object on the observer's *retina.* (see *Object Constancy*)

Compensation: An *ego defense mechanism* which consists of excelling in some area of life as a way of making up for the fact that one is unable to do well in some other area.

Compensatory Education: Enriched preschool educational programs that focus upon developing the skills necessary for success in school. (see *Head Start*)

Complementary Colors: Pairs of colors that when mixed together produce gray; red-green, blue-yellow, black-white.

Compulsive Acts: Behaviors that a person feels he must perform and over which he feels he has little control; for example *kleptomania,* compulsive eating, and compulsive drinking. (see *Ritual Behaviors*)

Concrete Thinking: The assumption that the world consists only of the experiences of the moment; also a lack of the ability to understand and use such abstract concepts as love, emotions, other people's feelings. (see *Abstract Thinking*)

Conditioned Aversion: A *behavior therapy* technique that involves making an attractive situation unattractive through use of *Pavlovian conditioning.* (see *Satiation Therapy*)

Conditioned Reflex: A learned reaction to a specific *environmental* event. (see *Unconditioned Reflex*)

Conditioned Response: See *Conditioned Reflex.*

Conditioned Stimulus: An *environmental* event which, after having been paired with an *unconditioned stimulus* a certain number of times, comes to elicit a *conditioned reflex.*

Condom: A rubber sheath that covers the penis during sexual intercourse; a form of *contraception.*

Cones: The *neural elements* in the *retina* that are sensitive to the *wavelength* of light, which we experience as color. There are three kinds of cones, one yielding primarily a sensation of blue, one of green, and one of red. Any perceived color is the result of a mixture of the activities of these three types of cones. (see *Rods*)

Conform: To behave in accordance with a group's *norms.* (see *Social Pressure*)

Conservation: A concept learned during the third stage of a child's *intellectual development;* the realization that a quantity remains unchanged no matter how it is altered so long as nothing is added or taken away; for example, conservation of mass.

Contraception: Methods and devices used during sexual intercourse in order to prevent pregnancy. (see *Condom*)

Control Group: In an experiment the group that is identical to an *experimental group* but that does not receive the *independent variable.*

Convergence: A *binocular* cue for *space perception;* the turning of the two eyes toward each other in order to keep the image of an object in focus on the *fovea* of each *retina.* The degree to which the eyes must turn inward gives the viewer a cue to the distance of the object.

Cornea: A clear membrane that covers the front of the eyeball, thereby protecting the inner parts of the eye.

Corpus Callosum: The large cable of *neurons* that lies between (and connects) the right and left halves of the *brain.*

Correlational Relation: The degree to which the occurrence of one kind of event can be predicted by the fact that some other event has occurred; there is no necessary causal link between the two events, they merely co-occur.

Correlation Coefficient: A *descriptive statistic* that summarizes the degree to which one set of data is related to another. (see *Positive Correlation, Negative Correlation*)

Cortex: The outer parts of the *brain* made up of millions of complexly interconnected neurons. The cortex receives information from other parts of the brain and plays a role in formulating outgoing messages in response to the information received. (see *Frontal-Parietal Cortex, Occipital Cortex, Temporal Cortex, Frontal Cortex*)

Credibility: The degree to which a *model* is perceived to be a reliable source for an *imitated rule.*

Crista: A brushlike group of cells located in each *semicircular canal;* they monitor rotary movements of the head. (see *Vestibular Kinesthetic System*)

Crossed Images: A *binocular* cue to *space perception* that utilizes *binocular disparity.* All objects that lie between the observer and his *fixation point* produce double images that are crossed; that is, the image seen by the left eye lies to the right of the fixation point, and vice versa; this information serves as a cue to the distance of the object producing the image. (see *Uncrossed Images*)

Cross-sectional Method: Observation of a particular behavior or behaviors among members of several groups of people, each group of people being different in, say, average age or some other characteristic. (see *Longitudinal Method*).

Cross-sex Bonds: Affectional ties between members of the opposite sexes. (see *Affectional Bonds*)

Curare: A drug that paralyzes all skeletal muscles while leaving the internal organs unparalyzed.

Custodial Care: Care of psychologically disturbed people solely through maintenance at home or in a hospital with no attempted treatment.

Dark Adaptation: The increase in one's ability to see at lowered levels of illumination as a result of having been in that lowered level of illumination for some time. (see *Light Adaptation*)

Deep Structure: The underlying meaning of a sentence. (see *Surface Structure, Grammar*)

Defer: When a low-status person or animal allows a higher-status person or animal to take precedence. (see *Dominance Hierarchy*)

Delusions: A form of *psychotic behavior* in which people persistently retain a bizarre opinion that can be demonstrated to be false. (see *Hallucination*)

Dendrites: Short arms that extend from the edges of the *cell body* of a *neuron* and that receive electrical activity from the preceding neuron.

Dependent Variable: Those aspects of a person's behavior that an experimenter observes and measures on the assumption that any change in the behavior is due to manipulations of the *independent variable.*

Depression: An emotional state in which a person may become listless, tearful, dejected, and withdrawn.

Depressive Psychotic Behavior: A form of *psychotic behavior* in which a person becomes so dejected and withdrawn that it is virtually impossible to communicate with him; he may sit and weep, stare into space, and/or have *hallucinations* and *delusions.* Sometimes this behavior occurs in alternation with *manic psychotic behavior.*

Descriptive Statistics: Statistics used to summarize data obtained from an *experiment.* (see *Inferential Statistics*)

Desensitization Therapy: A *behavior therapy* technique that promotes changes in the perception of a threatening situation, thereby reducing the person's emotional reaction to the situation and permitting him to learn a new rule for coping with it.

Detail Perspective: A *monocular* cue for *space perception* consisting of decreasing distinctiveness in surface detail as the distance between a viewed object and the viewer increases. (see *Texture Gradient*)

Determinism: The belief that all events are caused by other events or by an active agent and do not occur solely of themselves. (see *Free Will*)

Deviant Behavior: Behavior that is different from what ordinarily is done by the majority of the people in a particular group.

Dialect: A form of a language that is peculiar to a specific region, community, or social group—the dialects that are derived from the same language often are, to some degree, mutually intelligible to the different groups who speak them.

Displacement: An *ego defense mechanism* in which aggression is redirected from an unassailable target to an inappropriate but assailable target.

Dissociative Reaction: A psychological reaction to an extremely stressful situation; the person forgets either who he is or some aspect of his life, for example, as manifested by *amnesia* and *multiple personality.*

Dominance Hierarchy: The social structure within a group of animals, including human beings, that consists of the relative status among the members of the group.

Double Standard: The social convention that condones premarital and extramarital sex for men but not for women.

Drug Abuse: For socially acceptable drugs (for example, alcohol or diet pills) abuse commonly is used to mean overuse and addiction; for socially unacceptable drugs (for example, LSD or marijuana) it commonly is used to mean virtually any use at all. It is not a very useful term.

Drug Therapy: The use of drugs in the psychotherapeutic treatment of psychologically disturbed people.

Eardrum: A membrane of skin that is stretched across the end of the *external canal* of the ear and that vibrates when struck by sound waves.

ECS: See *Electroconvulsive Shock.*

EEG: See *Electroencephalogram.*

Ego Defense Mechanisms: The behavior patterns one uses in times of *psychological conflict* to defend one's *values* against change. Often people are unaware of the ego defense mechanisms they use.

Ejaculation: The sudden ejection of *seminal fluid* from the male's penis during sexual excitement, ordinarily occurring simultaneously with *orgasm.* (see *Ejaculatory Incompetence*)

Ejaculatory Incompetence: The inability of a male to *ejaculate* and attain sexual *orgasm.*

Electrical Stimulation of the Brain (ESB): A procedure in which minute amounts of electricity are introduced into the *brain,* thereby altering ongoing behavior. (see *Electrode, Stimoceiver*)

Electroencephalogram (EEG): A recording of the electrical activity of the *brain.* (see *Alpha Wave*)

Electroconvulsive Shock (ECS): The passage of an electric current through the *brain* of an animal or human being, thereby producing a convulsion and brief loss of consciousness. (see *Electroconvulsive Shock Therapy*)

Electroconvulsive Shock Therapy: The use of *electroconvulsive shock* to treat severely psychologically disturbed people. (see *Insulin Shock Therapy*).

Electrode: Either a needlelike wire that can be inserted into some portion of the nervous system or a small plate that can be affixed to the skin near some part of the nervous system. Electrodes are used to pick up information about the electrical activity present in the nervous system as well as to electrically stimulate the nervous system. (see *Stimoceiver, Electrical Stimulation of the Brain*)

Emotional Maturity: The ability to weather personal problems without becoming so upset that you cannot function adequately.

Encounter Group: A group of friendly strangers who gather together for the purpose of talking about their problems and getting feedback from one another. (see *Marathon*)

End Brushes: The brushlike arms at the end of the *axon* of a *neuron.*

Environment: A global term that includes all of the objects, persons, and events, both internal and external, that impinge upon one's sensory systems at any given moment.

Epilepsy: An illness, apparently due to short-circuiting within the *brain,* that causes a person to suffer from convulsions.

ESB: See *Electrical Stimulation of the Brain.*

Eustachean Tube: A tube that extends from the *middle ear* to the throat; it serves to equalize the air pressure between the middle ear and the outside world.

Excitement Phase: The first stage of the *sexual response cycle* consisting of the beginning of sexual play. (see *Plateau Phase, Orgasmic Phase, Resolution Phase*)

Expected Value: The end result of having balanced the good *payoffs* and their *probabilities* against the bad payoffs and their probabilities for any given action. (see *Belief*)

Experiment: One of four methods commonly used for psychological research. Experiments are carefully controlled tasks that people perform while the experimenter manipulates the *independent variable* and observes the *dependent variable*. (see *Simulation, Naturalistic Observation, Case History*)

Experimental Group: The group that receives the *independent variable* in an *experiment*. (see *Control Group*)

Explicit Values: Those *values* that we clearly understand and knowingly use in evaluating situations and events. (see *Inexplicit Values*)

External Canal: That part of the ear that lies between the *pinna* and the *eardrum*.

Extinction: Abandonment of a *rule* in light of its failure to produce desired results (*reinforcement*) or its inability to predict events reliably.

Extramarital Sex: Sexual relations with someone other than one's spouse. (see *Premarital Sex, Marital Sex*)

Facilitation: An increase in the electrical activity of a *neuron* as a result of activity in those neurons which converge at its *synapse*. (see *Inhibition*)

Fields of Psychology: The major, and rather arbitrarily defined, subdivisions of the discipline of psychology. In this book they are defined as sensation and perception, behavior acquisition, social behavior, counseling and psychotherapy, and child psychology. (see *Specialty Areas*)

Fixation Point: That point in the *visual field* at which vision and attention are focused. (see *Crossed Images, Uncrossed Images, Convergence*)

Fixed Interval Reinforcement: A form of *partial reinforcement* in which a *rule* is rewarded only after a specified period of time has elapsed since the last rewarded use, the period of time between rewards remaining constant. (see *Variable Interval Reinforcement*)

Fixed Ratio Reinforcement: A form of *partial reinforcement* in which a *rule* is rewarded only after being used a certain number of times, the required number of times remaining constant. (see *Variable Ratio Reinforcement*)

Fovea: The area of the *retina* where the *neural elements* of the eye are most densely packed, where the visual image is focused, and where vision is the most sensitive.

Free Nerve Endings: Small *neural elements* embedded in the skin that are associated with pain sensitivity.

Free Will: The notion that a human being is capable of making choices and determining his own behavior quite independently of any external events or other forms of motivation. (see *Determinism*)

Frequency Evaluation: A source of *beliefs* (that is, *subjective probabilities*) based on the percentage of the time that a given action has worked in the past in achieving desired *payoffs*.

Frontal Cortex: The frontal parts of the *cortex* of the *brain*, the exact function of which is unclear.

Frontal-Parietal Cortex: That part of the *cortex* of the *brain* that is primarily involved with the body senses.

Fugue State: A state that occasionally accompanies *amnesia,* during which a person wanders away and sometimes even begins a new life elsewhere.

Grammar: The set of linguistic rules by which *surface structure* (a sentence) is generated from *deep structure* (meaning).

Greeting Ritual: A series of behaviors that animals engage in when meeting one another. In human beings this commonly consists of such things as shaking hands, smiling, asking about one another's health.

Grief Syndrome: A series of behaviors that characteristically follow an extreme loss or change in one's life. The syndrome has three stages: shock, despair, and recovery.

Grooming: A frequently observed behavior among social animals that consists of cleaning each others' fur, stroking, and so on. It usually denotes trust and affection.

Group Cohesion: The extent to which the individual members of a group cooperate and have a feeling of group unity.

Group Effectiveness: The degree to which a group is successful in attaining the goal it is designed to attain.

Gustation: The sense of taste.

Hallucination: A form of *psychotic behavior* in which people imagine that they hear and/or see things that really don't exist. (see *Delusions*)

Hard Drugs: Dangerous drugs such as *narcotics* and *amphetamines.* (see *Speed*)

Hashish: A concentrate of the resin found in the top leaves of the Indian hemp plant, *Cannabis sativa;* a very powerful form of *marijuana.*

Head Start: A preschool *compensatory education* program sponsored by the federal government.

Hearing: The active, complex process which occurs after the passive reception of sound and which consists of the interpretation of the sounds as words and/or as having been caused by some object or person in the *environment.* (see *Audition*)

Heterosexuality: Sexual relations between members of the opposite sexes. (see *Homosexuality, Bisexuality*)

Hierarchy: A step-by-step plan used by a *behavior therapist* to help a person achieve a change in his or her behavior.

Highlight: A *monocular* cue for *space perception* consisting of the intense reflection of light from the part of an object that is nearest the light source.

Homosexuality: Sexual relations between members of the same sex. (see *Heterosexuality, Bisexuality*)

Hypochondria: An anxious preoccupation with one's own health and a tendency to interpret virtually every minor bodily malfunction as a serious illness.

Hypothalamus: The part of the *brain* that regulates eating, drinking, and sexual behavior.

Hysterical Symptoms: Physical disorders caused by psychological disturbances rather than by physiological malfunctioning.

Identification: The special affection for and resulting *imitation* of one or the other parent or some other person.

Imitated Rules: Rules that are acquired by *observation* of a *model* using them and/or by receiving written or verbal *instruction.*

Imitation: See *Imitated Rules.*

Impotence: The inability of a male to attain an erect penis and therefore an inability to engage in conventional sexual intercourse. (see *Ejaculatory Incompetence*)

Independent Variable: That part of an experimental situation the experimenter manipulates in an attempt to influence the behavior of the people who are in the *experiment.* (see *Dependent Variable*)

Inertia: The tendency of matter to remain at rest or to continue in some fixed direction until affected by some outside force.

Inexplicit Values: Values we don't realize we have that influence our evaluations of the situations and events that occur around us. (see *Explicit Values*)

Inferential Statistics: Statistics used for making decisions about whether observed changes in a *dependent variable* in an *experiment* are merely the result of chance or whether they can reasonably be attributed to changes in the *independent variable.* (see *Descriptive Statistics*)

Inhibition: A decrease in the electrical activity of a *neuron* as a result of activity in those neurons that converge on its synapse. (see *Facilitation*)

Innate: Those characteristics that a person or animal is born with (that is, that are genetically determined) as opposed to those that are acquired through experience. (see *Reflex, Instinct, Predisposition*)

Inner Ear: The *cochlea.*

Instincts: Innate *what-to-do rules* that are more flexible than *reflexes* but less flexible than *predispositions.*

Instrumental Learning: The formation of a *what-to-do rule* as a result of one's behavior leading to a desirable outcome (that is, *reinforcement*) or an undesirable outcome (that is, *punishment*).

Insulin Shock Therapy: A procedure for treating severely disturbed people which consists of injecting insulin into the bloodstream, thereby causing the person to go into a state of shock. (see *Electroconvulsive Shock*)

Intellectual Development: The growth of a child's ability to formulate *intellectual rules.*

Intellectual Rules: Rules that result from a thoughtful, reflective process and an attempt to "figure it out."

Intervening Variable: An unobservable characteristic of a person that presumably can be inferred from his observable behavior; that aspect of a person that is supposedly influenced by the *independent variable* and therefore is reflected in changes in the *dependent variable* (for example, anger, intelligence, love).

Iris: The colored area that surrounds the *pupil* of the eye. It is a muscle that opens and closes in order to regulate the amount of light entering the eye.

Kinesthesis: Sensitivity to movement; the sensory system that monitors movement of the body as well as posture and location of the body parts relative to gravity. (see *Vestibular Kinesthetic System, Touch Kinesthetic System*)

Kleptomania: Compulsive stealing. (see *Compulsive Acts*)

Learned Rules: What-to-do rules and *what-to-expect rules* formed on the basis of experience. (see *Instrumental Learning, Pavlovian Conditioning*)

Lens: A transparent membrane of variable thickness that serves to focus the light entering the eye on the *retina.*

Lesbian: Homosexual relations between females; a female homosexual.

Level of Analysis: A term used to describe the degree to which a *speciality area* of psychology focuses upon basic processes such as physiological correlates of psychological events (*molecular analysis*) or the degree to which it focuses upon more broadly defined phenomena such as social interactions (*molar analysis*). (see *Fields of Psychology*)

Life Crises: Large-scale stress periods in one's life that require severe changes in one's *values,* how one lives, and how one thinks about things.

Light Adaptation: The increase in one's ability to see at heightened levels of illumination as a function of having been in that heightened level of illumination for some period of time. (see *Dark Adaptation*)

Limbic System: The part of the *brain* that feeds information into the *reticular system* through the *hypothalamus* and other centers; it plays a major role in emotionality.

Linear Perspective: A *monocular* cue for *space perception* which relies upon the fact that objects look closer to one another and look smaller as the distance between them and the observer increases.

Linguistics: The science dedicated to the study of language.

Lobotomy: See *Psychosurgery.*

Longitudinal Method: Observation of a particular behavior or behaviors in the same people over a long period of time. (*see Cross-sectional Method*)

Long-term Memory: That part of *memory* which contains permanently stored information. (see *Short-term Memory*)

LSD: (D-lysergic acid diethylamide) A powerful synthetic drug that induces *hallucinations* and an altered state of consciousness.

Manic Psychotic Behavior: A form of *psychotic behavior* that is a caricature of happiness; the manic person smiles too easily and too much, is too exuberant and happy, talks too loudly, and proclaims his joy too strongly. Sometimes this behavior occurs in alternation with *depressive psychotic behavior.*

Marathon: A very long and intense *encounter group* meeting often lasting an entire weekend.

Marijuana: A "*soft drug*" made from the dried stems and leaves of the Indian hemp plant *Cannabis sativa.* (see *Hashish*)

Marital Sex: Sexual relations between persons who are married to one another. (see *Premarital Sex, Extramarital Sex*)

Masturbation: Self-manipulation of one's sex organs, usually until *orgasm* has been reached.

Mean: A measure of *central tendency;* more specifically, the sum of the individual data divided by the number of data. (see *Descriptive Statistics*)

Median: A measure of *central tendency;* more specifically, the datum that lies in the middle of the array of data. (see *Descriptive Statistics*)

Medulla: The part of the *brain* that regulates such vital functions as breathing, heartbeat, and circulation.

Memory: The name given to the repository in which information is stored so that it can be used at some time in the future. (see *Short-term Memory, Long-term Memory*)

Methadone: A drug that can be substituted for heroin which allows the addict to stop using heroin without going through the pain of *withdrawal.*

Michotte Machine: A mechanical device for studying the perception of cause-and-effect relationships.

Middle Ear: The chamber directly behind the *eardrum* which contains three small bones (the *ossicles*) that convey sound-induced vibrations from the eardrum to the *oval window.*

Middle Range: A measure of variability; more specifically, the middle half of an array of data from an experiment. (see *Descriptive Statistics*)

Mnemonic Methods: Procedures designed to improve one's memory by introducing meaningfulness and structure into a memory task, thereby facilitating later *recall.*

Mode: A measure of *central tendency;* more specifically, the datum that occurs most frequently in a group of data. (see *Descriptive Statistics*)

Model: A person who serves as the source of an *imitated rule.*

Modeling: The process of acquiring a rule through *imitation.*

Molar Analysis: The study of broadly defined, complex psychological events such as the development of cooperative behavior patterns within social groups. (see *Level of Analysis, Molecular Analysis*)

Molecular Analysis: The study of narrowly defined basic psychological events such as vision or pain. (see *Level of Analysis, Molar Analysis*)

Monocular: Pertaining to the use of only one eye rather than both eyes. (see *Binocular*)

Monocular Movement Parallax: A *monocular* cue for *space perception* in which differential rates of movement of the images of different objects across the *retina* provide a cue to the relative distances of the objects from the observer.

Motivation: Those conditions that promote the formulation of a *rule* as well as the conditions under which the rule subsequently is used. Motivation is related to one's *values* for the outcomes of rules.

Multiple Personality: A personality that has several selves; a person with a multiple personality will at one time behave as though he were one person and at another time as though he were some other person. (see *Dissociative Reaction*)

Nanometer: A unit for measuring the wavelength of light. One nanometer equals one millimicron.

Narcotics: A class of extremely powerful and addicting *"hard drugs"* consisting of heroin, codeine, and morphine, all of which derive from opium, and meperidine, which is a synthetic

Naturalistic Observation: A research method which consists of watching animals or people in their normal environment and then drawing conclusions from the observations. (see *Experiment, Simulation, Case History*)

Need Complementarity: The degree to which a relation between two people fulfills each individual's private needs; that is, the degree to which one person's strengths complement the other person's weaknesses, and vice versa.

Negative After-image: See *After-image.*

Negative Correlation: A *descriptive statistic* which measures the relation between two sets of data in which high values of the first set of data correspond to low values of the second set, and low values of the first set correspond to high values of the second set. (see *Correlation Coefficient, Positive Correlation*)

Negative Transfer: See *Transfer.*

Nerves: Bundles of *neurons.*

Neural Element: The general term used throughout this book to denote *receptor cells, neurons, nerves,* and all manner of components of the nervous system.

Neuron: The basic unit of the nervous system. It consists of a single cell having a *cell body, dendrites,* an *axon,* and *end brushes.* (see *Nerve*)

Neurotic Behavior: An overdependence on *ego defense mechanisms.* (see *Psychotic Behavior*)

Neurotic Trap: A vicious spiral in which *neurotic behavior* arouses other people's antagonism, which, in turn, leads to more dependence upon neurotic behavior, and so on.

Nicotine: An "acceptable" drug found in tobacco.

Nonpersons: Persons who because of their job or some other function can violate one's *territory* without fear of retribution; for example, delivery men, mail carriers, and meter readers.

Norms: Those *values* and *roles* that are regarded as appropriate by the members of a given group. (see *Conform, Social Pressure*)

Object Constancy: The tendency for an object to seem unchanged even though its image has undergone pronounced transformations on the *retina.* Object constancy consists of *color constancy, size constancy,* and *shape constancy.*

Object Permanence: The concept that objects have permanence and exist even after they have disappeared from sight. According to Piaget, this is one of the *rules* that a child develops during the first stage of *intellectual development.*

Obsessive Thoughts: Recurrent and persistent thoughts that drown out almost all other thoughts. (see *Ritual Behaviors*)

Occipital Cortex: That part of the *cortex* of the *brain* that is involved in vision.

Olfaction: The sense of smell.

Olfactory Bulbs: Neural elements located in the nasal passages that are sensitive to chemical stimulation and that give rise to *olfaction.*

One Hundred Percent Reinforcement: Continuous rewarding of a *rule.* (see *Partial Reinforcement*)

Open Class Words: A set of nounlike words acquired by a child when he begins to learn language. The child begins to pair these words with verblike *pivot words* in order to convey messages to those around him.

Operant Conditioning: See *Instrumental Learning.*

Optic Nerve: The cable of *neural elements* that extends from the *retina* to the *occipital cortex* of the *brain.*

Organ of Corti: The structure within the *cochlea* that contains *neural elements* that are basic to hearing.

Orgasm: The climax or culmination of a sexual act.

Orgasmic Phase: The third stage of the *sexual response cycle* which consists of experiencing *orgasm.* (see *Excitement Phase, Plateau Phase, Resolution Phase*)

Ossicles: Three small bones located in the *middle ear* which mechanically transmit vibrations of the *eardrum* to the *oval window* at the base of the *cochlea.*

Oval Window: A small hole covered by a flexible membrane at the base of the *cochlea* which receives vibrations from the *ossicles,* thereby conveying sound-induced vibrations from the *eardrum* to the cochlea.

Papillae: Small structures located on the tongue that contain chemical-sensitive *taste buds.*

Paranoia: A form of *psychotic behavior* in which a person suffers from *delusions* of persecution.

Parent-Child Bonds: An affectional relation between a parent and a child. (see *Affectional Bonds*)

Partial Overlap: A *monocular* cue for *space perception* in which nearer objects partially conceal those that are farther away from the observer.

Partial Reinforcement: Less than one hundred percent rewarding of a *rule.* (see *One Hundred Percent Reinforcement, Fixed Interval Reinforcement, Variable Interval Reinforcement, Fixed Ratio Reinforcement,* and *Variable Ratio Reinforcement*)

Pavlovian Conditioning: The formation of a *what-to-expect rule* $(S_1 \rightarrow S_2)$ as a result of a neutral event (S_1) being paired with an event (S_2) that automatically elicits a given behavior. After several pairings, the neutral event also elicits the behaviors. Also called *classical conditioning.*

Payoff: The expected or the obtained result of an action. Used interchangeably with the word *reinforcement.*

Peer Group: In the broadest sense one's peer group consists of everyone of the same socioeconomic level, educational background, age, and so on, as oneself. In the narrow sense it merely is one's circle of friends.

Person-oriented Leadership Style: A leadership style that is nondirective, considerate, fairly democratic, and aims primarily at getting the job done while simultaneously keeping the group members happy. (see *Task-oriented Leadership Style*)

Personality: The term used to describe one's internal psychological characteristics and the kinds of *strategies* one uses to cope with *psychological conflict* and *life crises.*

Personal Space: The space that immediately surrounds you wherever you are and that is regarded as inviolable without your permission.

Personal Values: Those *values* which are idiosyncratic to the individual who holds them. (see *Social Values*)

Phobias: Irrational fears of common objects and situations.

Physiological Addiction: When various physiological functions of the body become dependent upon the presence of a specific drug. (see *Psychological Addiction*)

Physiological Nystagmus: Minute, rapid, side-to-side movements of the eyes.

Pig Latin: A "secret language" often used by preadolescent children. Its *rule* consists of taking the first sound in an English word, moving it to the end of the word, and then adding "ay"; for example, "cup" becomes "upcay."

Pinna: That part of one's ear that protrudes from the side of one's head.

Pituitary Gland: The master control gland for hormonal secretion.

Pivot Words: A small set of verblike words that a child acquires when he begins to learn language. The child pairs these words with nounlike *open class words* in order to convey messages to those around him.

Placebo: A harmless "fake" drug (often a sugar solution) given to an individual under the pretense that it is a real drug or medicine.

Plateau Phase: The second stage of the *sexual response cycle,* which consists of manipulation of sex organs, soft stroking, and other sexually stimulating behavior. (see *Excitement Phase, Orgasmic Phase, Resolution Phase*)

Positive After-image: See *After-image.*

Positive Correlation: A *descriptive statistic* which measures the relation between two sets of data in which high values of the first set correspond to high values of the second set and low values of the first set correspond to low values of the second set. (see *Correlation Coefficient, Negative Correlation*)

Positive Transfer: See *Transfer.*

Precipitating Event: A specific event that apparently brings about the beginning of *psychotic behavior.*

Predispositions: Hypothesized *innate* rules which, while similar to stereotyped, automatic instinctual rules, are more flexible than *instincts* and depend on experience in order to develop fully.

Premarital Sex: Having sexual relations before one is married. (see *Marital Sex, Extramarital Sex*)

Projection: An *ego defense mechanism* that is used when one's *values* conflict with one's immediate feelings; *psychological conflict* is avoided by attributing one's immediate feelings to someone else.

Proximity: Closeness, nearness, adjacency.

Psychiatrist: A physician (M.D.) who has additional training in counseling and whose practice tends to be entirely devoted to helping people who have psychological problems.

Psychological Addiction: When a person's psychological well-being depends upon the presence of a specific drug. (see *Physiological Addiction*)

Psychological Conflict: A situation (1) in which conditions in the external world fail to conform to the conditions that would satisfy one's *values* and (2) that results from having inconsistent values that make it impossible for any situation to be satisfactory.

Psychosomatic Illness: Physiological disorders resulting from prolonged psychological stress (for example, peptic ulcers, hypertension, asthma).

Psychosurgery: The most extreme form of medical therapy for severely psychologically disturbed people. It consists of surgically severing neural pathways between the front part of the *brain* and the brain centers that are involved with emotions.

Psychotherapy: A procedure wherein a psychotherapist attempts to help a troubled person gain an understanding of what his troubles are and how to deal with them; the goal is to help the person cease to be a victim of his difficulties.

Psychotic Behavior: The most severe form of reaction to *psychological conflict* and *life crises* consisting of *depressive* and *manic* behaviors, *paranoid* behavior, and *schizophrenic* behavior.

Punishment: The occurrence of some undesirable outcome when a *what-to-do rule* is used; punishment implies that the *rule* has not worked and therefore it should not be relied upon in the future. (see *Reinforcement, Instrumental Learning*)

Pupil: The hole in the front of the eye that admits light into the eye; the size of the pupil is regulated by the *iris.*

Rationalization: An *ego defense mechanism* that consists of making up false excuses for one's failures, unacceptable feelings, and so on.

Reaction Formation: An *ego defense mechanism* in which the person denies he has a high *value* for some socially unacceptable event or object or feels guilty because he has a low value for some socially acceptable event or object; as a result the person behaves in a manner opposite that of his value.

Recall: A retrieval process for searching *memory* for a specific bit of information. (see *Recognition*)

Recognition: A retrieval process of searching *memory* to see if the specific situation, object, person, or event at hand has ever been experienced before. (see *Recall*)

Reference Group: A group of persons whose *values* and modes of behavior one both accepts as being "proper" and attempts to imitate.

Reflexes: Innate what-to-do rules that are genetically determined and over which an animal has no control. They are the least flexible forms of *rules.*

Regression: An *ego defense mechanism* that consists of reverting to childish behavior in order to avoid responsibility for one's own behavior or the problems one faces.

Rehearsal: The process of repeating information over and over to yourself, thereby permitting it to be held in *short-term memory* for long periods of time.

Reinforcement: The occurrence of a desired outcome as the result of using a *what-to-do rule;* its occurrence means that the *rule* has worked and, therefore, that it is reasonable to strengthen (that is, reinforce) reliance upon the rule in the future. (see *Instrumental Learning, Punishment*)

Repression: An *ego defense mechanism* that represents an extreme form of denial; it consists of the person being unable to remember an unpleasant object or event.

Research: An approach to the study of psychology which, like the *armchair approach,* begins with observations, moves on to the formulation of hypotheses, but then goes a crucial step beyond the armchair approach by requiring that the hypotheses be checked against the facts.

Resolution Phase: The final part of the *sexual response cycle* during which sexual excitement decreases. (see *Excitement Phase, Plateau Phase, Orgasmic Phase*)

Response: Used broadly to mean any behavior; used narrowly to mean a specific reaction to a specific *environmental* event.

Response Generalization: Substitution of one behavior in a *rule* for another; that is, there is a variety of similar behaviors that will work for a *what-to-do rule* to bring about roughly the same outcome. (see *Stimulus Generalization*)

Reticular System: A complex system involving many parts of the *brain*; it acts as a clearing house for most information going to and from the brain and plays a vital role in regulating attention.

Retina: The lining at the back of the eyeball on which the *lens* focuses *retinal images* and which contains the *neural elements* that are sensitive to light. (see *Cones, Rods*)

Retinal Image: The "picture" that the *lens* focuses on the back of the eyeball; that is, upon the *retina.*

Retrieval Unit: That part of *memory* which extracts information from storage. (see *Recall, Recognition*)

Ritual Behaviors: Obsessive thoughts and *compulsive acts;* those behaviors over which the person feels he has little or no control and that he must constantly think about or perform.

Rods: The *neural elements* in the *retina* that are sensitive to the brightness of light, but not to its wavelength, that is, not to its color. (see *Cones*)

Role: The function that one is expected to play in any given group, as well as the behaviors associated with that function.

Romantic Love: The Western world's version of when, where, and how one experiences love. From the point of view of many non-Westerners, it seems to be an overly emotional and somewhat irrational approach to finding a mate.

Round Window: A small hole, covered by a flexible membrane, that leads from the *cochlea* to the *middle ear.* It is similar to the *oval window,* but it is not attached to the *ossicles.*

Rules: Strategies for making desired events occur (*what-to-do rules*) and for predicting events (*what-to-expect rules*).

Saccule: That part of the *vestibular kinesthetic system* that contains the *neural elements* which are sensitive to acceleration and deceleration of the head. (see *Utricle, Semicircular Canals*)

Same-sex Bonds: Affectional ties between members of the same sex. (see *Affectional Bonds*)

Satiation Therapy: A *behavior therapy* technique that is one approach to *aversion therapy.*

It consists of having the person overindulge in some attractive situation to the point that the situation no longer is attractive. (see *Conditioned Aversion*)

Scientific Method: The generally accepted method for obtaining evidence that will increase or decrease scientists' belief in the truth of a hypothesis. (see *Research*)

Schizophrenic Behavior: A form of *psychotic behavior* that has profound withdrawal from reality as its primary characteristic.

Semicircular Canals: That part of the *vestibular kinesthetic system* which contains the *neural elements* that are sensitive to rotary motion of the head. (see *Utricle, Saccule*)

Seminal Fluid: The fluid that is *ejaculated* by a male during *orgasm.*

Sexual Response Cycle: See *Excitement Phase, Plateau Phase, Orgasmic Phase, Resolution Phase.*

Shape Constancy: The tendency for an object to appear to retain its shape even though it has undergone a change in spatial orientation relative to the observer. (see *Object Constancy*)

Shaping: The process of changing a *rule* in light of feedback until it is the best rule for that particular situation.

Shock Therapy: A form of medical therapy that uses either electricity or drugs to induce a convulsion and unconsciousness. Usually used in the treatment of extreme forms of *psychotic behavior* or *depression.* (see *Electroconvulsive Shock Therapy, Insulin Shock Therapy*)

Short-term Memory: A part of *memory* that is of limited capacity and that operates only on current incoming information. The information either is forgotten or passed on to *long-term memory* for permanent storage. (see *Transfer Unit*)

Simulation: A *research* method similar to an *experiment,* but in which the task and setting are as similar as possible to the real situation, thus avoiding some of the artificiality inherent in an experiment. (see *Naturalistic Observation, Case History*)

Size Constancy: The tendency for an object's size to appear to remain unchanged when it is moved closer to or further away from the observer even though the image on the observer's *retina* has changed in size. (see *Object Constancy*)

Size-Distance Invariance: A *monocular* cue for *space perception* that consists of the orderly change in the size of the *retinal image* as an object of unchanging physical size gets closer to or further away from the observer. (see *Size Constancy*)

Social Power: The degree to which a person who has a monopoly on a *social resource* can use his monopoly to induce another person to *conform* to his wishes.

Social Pressure: Pressure exerted through threat of the group's disapproval or rejection to induce an individual to *conform* to the group's *norms.*

Social Resources: The things that are given and received in a social interaction. They include love, money, goods, services, status, and information.

Social Support: The backing and aid a group provides for its members.

Social Values: Those values that large groups of people hold communally. (see *Personal Values*)

Soft Drugs: Drugs that apparently are nonaddictive and (rightly or wrongly) are used primarily as recreational drugs; for example, *marijuana.*

Somatic Nervous System: One of two major parts of the nervous system. It relays messages back and forth from the *brain* to the muscles and sense organs. (see *Autonomic Nervous System*)

Space Perception: The fact that we perceive objects as being three-dimensional (that is, having height, breadth, and depth) even though the *retinal images* upon which we base these perceptions are two-dimensional (that is, having only height and breadth).

Specialty Areas: The subdivisions of the five major *fields of psychology.* These areas represent specific and narrowly defined topics such as the study of the development of children's language, the study of the physiological bases of vision, or the study of schizophrenic reactions.

Speed: A slang term for *amphetamines.*

Spinal Cord: The large cable of *nerves* in the core of the spinal column.

Spontaneous Ejaculation: Ejaculation that occurs while a male is asleep, sometimes accompanied by sexual dreams (also called "wet dreams").

Spontaneous Recovery: When a *rule* that has been *extinguished* is used again on the off chance that it may again be appropriate.

Standard Deviation: A measure of variability; the square root of the *variance.* (see *Descriptive Statistics*)

Statistics: A set of techniques designed to help a scientist make a decision about whether or not an experimental hypothesis is or is not supported by the data of an *experiment.* (see *Descriptive* and *Inferrential Statistics*)

Stimoceiver: A small device that can both monitor and record the electrical activity of a living *brain* as well as introduce small amounts of electrical stimulation to the brain via implanted *electrodes.*

Stimulation: In the broadest sense, the impingement of an event upon the nervous system.

Stimulus Discrimination: The ability to differentiate among a variety of similar situations and realize that a *rule* applicable to one of those situations is inapplicable to the others. (see *Stimulus Generalization*)

Stimulus Generalization: The application of a specific *rule* to a variety of situations, each of which is slightly different from the others. (see *Response Generalization, Stimulus Discrimination*)

Strategies: The three basic techniques for dealing with *psychological conflict:* (1) changing the situation, (2) withdrawing, (3) changing one's *values.* In this book these are called Strategy 1, Strategy 2, and Strategy 3, respectively.

Stress: The strain or pressure that one feels in the midst of some *psychological conflict* or *life crisis.* The term often is used interchangeably with *anxiety.*

Structured Task: A task which has specific guidelines that dictate how it should be performed; a task with a defined goal. (see *Unstructured Task*)

Subjective Color: A perceived color that results entirely from the way in which the color-sensitive visual system works rather than from the direct observation of an object's color. (see *After-image*)

Subjective Probability: See *Belief.*

Sublimation: An *ego defense mechanism* in which so-called "nervous energy" resulting from *psychological conflict* is redirected into some other activity.

Surface Structure: The actual sentences that make up a communication. Given an underlying meaning (that is, *deep structure*), the *grammar* of a language can be used to form several different sentences (surface structures), all of which convey that particular meaning.

Synapse: The gap between the *end brushes* of one *neuron* and the *dendrites* of the next neuron in the chain.

Task-oriented Leadership Style: A leadership style that is extremely controlling and aimed primarily at getting the job done. (see *Person-oriented Leadership Style*)

Taste Buds: Tiny chemical-sensitive *neural elements* located in the *papillae* of the tongue.

Tectorial Membrane: The membrane that hangs above the *organ of Corti* in the *cochlea*, which, when moved by sound-induced pressure waves in the cochlea, causes the *neural elements* located in the organ of Corti to react.

Temporal Cortex: That part of the *cortex* of the *brain* that is primarily involved in the perception of sound.

Territoriality: The tendency, found in numerous species of animals, to claim and defend a given geographical area. The area can either be in some way involved with dwelling space or it can be an area immediately surrounding the animal, for example, *personal space.*

Texture Gradient: A *monocular* cue for *space perception* consisting of the decreasing distinctiveness of the texture detail of a surface as the distance between the observer and the observed part of the surface increases. (see *Detail Perspective*)

Threshold: The point at which the activity at the *dendrites* of a *neuron* is great enough to cause the neuron to generate an electrical impulse. (see *All-or-none Principle*)

Tip-of-the-tongue Phenomenon: The feeling that a word or some piece of information is right on the "tip of your tongue" but it will not materialize.

Tolerance: Adaptation to a specific drug. With continued use of most drugs increased amounts are needed to get the same effects that were previously experienced with smaller amounts. An exception is *marijuana,* which produces reverse tolerance; that is, with continued use a smaller amount of marijuana is needed to get the same experiences previously produced with greater amounts.

Touch Kinesthetic System: That part of the *kinesthetic* sensory system that monitors movement and location of body parts. It consists of pressure-sensitive *neural elements* that are located in the joints, skin, and muscles. (see *Vestibular Kinesthetic System*)

Touch System: A nonunitary sensory system consisting of the pressure sensitivity, pain sensitivity, and temperature sensitivity of the skin.

Tranquilizers: Drugs prescribed by physicians that help people get through temporary periods of *stress.* Examples are Miltown, Equinol, Librium, and Valium. (see *Drug Therapy*)

Transfer: The facilitation of (positive transfer) or interference with (negative transfer) the learning of a new *rule* as a result of having previously had a similar rule that has been used successfully in the past.

Transfer Unit: That part of *memory* that is involved with taking information from *short-term memory,* selecting its salient parts and deleting the rest, and then transferring the retained portion to *long-term memory.*

Unconditioned Reflex: An automatic, unlearned reaction to a specific *environmental* event. (see *Conditioned Reflex*)

Unconditioned Response: See *Unconditioned Reflex.*

Unconditioned Stimulus: An *environmental* event that automatically elicits an *unconditioned reflex.* (see *Conditioned Reflex*)

Uncrossed Images: A *binocular* cue for *space perception* that utilizes *binocular disparity.* All objects that lie beyond the observer's *fixation point* produce double images that are uncrossed; that is, an image seen by the left eye lies to the left of the fixation point, and vice versa; this information serves as a cue to the distance of the object that is producing the image. (see *Crossed Images*)

Unstructured Task: A task which does not have specific guidelines to dictate how it should be performed; a task with an undefined goal. (see *Structured Task*)

Utricle: That part of the *vestibular kinesthetic system* that contains the *neural elements* which are sensitive to movement of the head relative to gravity. (see *Saccule, Semicircular Canals*)

Values: The complicated collection of ideas, both *social* and *personal,* that each of us has about what is good and what is not; the standards against which we size up external situations and evaluate our own behaviors. (see *Attitudes, Inexplicit Values, Explicit Values*)

Variability Measures: Descriptive statistics that summarize how much or how little consensus there is within a group of data; that is, *variance, standard deviation, middle range.*

Variable Interval Reinforcement: A form of *partial reinforcement* in which a *rule* is rewarded only after a certain period of use, the required period of use between rewards varying from one time to another. (see *Fixed Interval Reinforcement*)

Variable Ratio Reinforcement: A form of *partial reinforcement* in which a *rule* is rewarded only after being used a certain number of times, the required number of times between rewards varying from one reward to the next. (see *Fixed Ratio Reinforcement*)

Variance: A measure of *variability;* the average of the squared distances between each datum and the group mean. (see *Descriptive Statistics*)

Vestibular Kinesthetic System: That part of the *kinesthetic* sensory system that monitors movements of the head. It consists of the *utricle, saccule,* and *semicircular canals.* (see *Touch Kinesthetic System*)

Visual Cliff: An experimental apparatus used to test for *space perception* in human infants and newborn animals.

Visual Field: That part of the environment which can be seen by the eyes at any given moment. (see *Fixation Point*)

Wavelength: The length of a light wave measured in *nanometers;* the physical property of light that we experience as color. (see *Cones*)

What-to-Do Rules: $S_1 \rightarrow R_1 \rightarrow S_2$ *rules* about what is to be done (R_1) in a specific situation (S_1) in order to achieve some desired end (S_2). (see *Instrumental Learning, What-to-Expect Rules*)

What-to-Expect Rules: $S_1 \rightarrow S_2$ *rules* about what event (S_2) should reasonably follow some previously observed event (S_1). (see *Pavlovian Conditioning, What-to-Do Rules*)

Wishful Thinking: The distortion of one's *subjective probabilities* about the likelihood of getting some *payoff* as a result of one's strong positive or negative *value* for that payoff.

Withdrawal: An *ego defense mechanism* in which a person seemingly avoids *psychological conflict* by completely removing himself from the conflict-arousing situation. A second use of the term has to do with the symptoms that may occur when a person who is *physiologically* and/or *psychologically addicted* to a given drug ceases to use the drug.

Zoophobia: An irrational fear of animals. (see *Phobias*)

AUTHOR INDEX

A

Anand, B. K., 102 *n.*
Ardrey, Robert, 84
Asch, Solomon, 162–164
Averill, James R., 173

B

Bartlett, Frederick, 75
Bee, Helen, 326
Bobrow, S., 251–252, 254–255

C

Chhina, G. S., 102 *n.*
Chomsky, Noam, 243–244
Colehour, J. K., 25 *n.*

D

Davis, Hallowell, 52
Delgado, José, 386–388
Donaldson, Dan, 316

E

Erismann, Theodor, 25

F

Ferster, Charles, 252–253
Fiedler, Fred, 167–171
Fiefel, H., 217 *n.*
Foa, Uriel, 158
Ford, B., 252 *n.*
Fregly, A. R., 25 *n.*

G

Galvani, L., 385
Gardner, Allen, 254
Gardner, Beatrice, 254
Gray, Carol, 273–275
Graybiel, A., 25 *n.*
Gregory, R. L., 49–51
Guedry, F. E., 25 *n.*

H

Harlow, Harry, 126–130
Hartley, E. L., 162 *n.*
Hayes, Keith, 252
Hayes, Mrs. Keith, 252
Held, Richard, 26
Hirai, T., 102 *n.*
Hollingshead, A. B., 333–334
Holmes, T. H., 190–193
Hunt, Earl B., 76–78

J

Johnson, V., 301, 306

K

Kamiya, Joe, 101–102, 103
Karnes, M. B., 324
Kasamatsu, A., 102 *n.*
Kastenbaum, R., 217 *n.*
Kellogg, Winthrop, 251–252
Kellogg, Mrs. Winthrop, 251–252
Kennedy, R. S., 25 *n.*
Knoblock, E. C., 25 *n.*
Kohler, Ivo, 25

SUBJECT INDEX